Abortion in the United States

Recent Titles in the
CONTEMPORARY WORLD ISSUES
Series

Campus Sexual Assault: A Reference Handbook
Alison E. Hatch

Sex and Gender: A Reference Handbook
David E. Newton

The Death Penalty: A Reference Handbook
Joseph A. Melusky and Keith A. Pesto

The American Political Party System: A Reference Handbook
Michael C. LeMay

Steroids and Doping in Sports: A Reference Handbook, second edition
David E. Newton

Religious Freedom in America: A Reference Handbook
Michael C. LeMay

Endangered Species: A Reference Handbook
Jan A. Randall

STDs in the United States: A Reference Handbook
David E. Newton

Women in Sports: A Reference Handbook
Maylon Hanold

Robots: A Reference Handbook
David E. Newton

Homeland Security: A Reference Handbook
Michael C. LeMay

The Opioid Crisis: A Reference Handbook
David E. Newton

Books in the **Contemporary World Issues** series address vital issues in today's society such as genetic engineering, pollution, and biodiversity. Written by professional writers, scholars, and nonacademic experts, these books are authoritative, clearly written, up-to-date, and objective. They provide a good starting point for research by high school and college students, scholars, and general readers as well as by legislators, businesspeople, activists, and others.

Each book, carefully organized and easy to use, contains an overview of the subject, a detailed chronology, biographical sketches, facts and data and/or documents and other primary source material, a forum of authoritative perspective essays, annotated lists of print and nonprint resources, and an index.

Readers of books in the Contemporary World Issues series will find the information they need in order to have a better understanding of the social, political, environmental, and economic issues facing the world today.

Abortion in the United States

A REFERENCE HANDBOOK

SECOND EDITION

Dorothy E. McBride and Jennifer L. Keys

ABC-CLIO ™

An Imprint of ABC-CLIO, LLC
Santa Barbara, California • Denver, Colorado

Library of Congress Cataloging-in-Publication Data

Names: McBride, Dorothy E., author. | Keys, Jennifer L., author.
Title: Abortion in the United States : a reference handbook /
    Dorothy E. McBride and Jennifer L. Keys.
Description: Second edition. | Santa Barbara, California :
    ABC-CLIO, [2018] | Series: Contemporary world issues
Identifiers: LCCN 2018012392 (print) | LCCN 2018013522
    (ebook) | ISBN 9781440853371 (ebook) | ISBN
    9781440853364 (alk. paper)
Subjects: LCSH: Abortion—United States. | Abortion—Law and
    legislation—United States. | Pro-life movement—United States. |
    Pro-choice movement—United States.
Classification: LCC HQ767.5.U5 (ebook) | LCC HQ767.5.U5
    M3727 2018 (print) | DDC 362.1988/80973—dc23
LC record available at https://lccn.loc.gov/2018012392

ISBN: 978-1-4408-5336-4 (print)
       978-1-4408-5337-1 (ebook)

22 21 20 19 18   1 2 3 4 5

This book is also available as an eBook.

ABC-CLIO
An Imprint of ABC-CLIO, LLC

ABC-CLIO, LLC
130 Cremona Drive, P.O. Box 1911
Santa Barbara, California 93116-1911
www.abc-clio.com

This book is printed on acid-free paper ∞

Manufactured in the United States of America

Contents

Preface, xvii
Acknowledgments, xxi

1   BACKGROUND AND HISTORY, 1

Introduction, 1

Criminalization: The 19th-Century Debate, 4

Reform and Repeal: The Road to Decriminalization, 11
    Roe v. Wade and *Doe v. Bolton*, 21

After *Roe*: Pro-Life and Pro-Choice Movements
Face Off, 24
    Pro-Life Movement, 25
    Pro-Choice Movement, 28

Frames and Framing: Tools for Understanding Abortion
Debates, 30

References, 33

2   PROBLEMS, CONTROVERSIES, AND SOLUTIONS, 37

Introduction, 37

Constitutional Legality of Abortion, 41
    Amending the Constitution, 42
    Changing the Court, 44

State Regulation of Abortion, 52

Government Support of Abortion, 58

   Political Polarization, 58

   Hyde Amendment, 60

   Global and Domestic Funding Restrictions, 62

Fighting for the Rights of the Unborn, 65

   Pro-Life Framing, 65

   Partial-Birth Abortion and Infanticide, 68

   Late-Term Abortions, 72

   Prenatal Drug Laws, 74

   Third-Party Fetal Killing, 76

Fighting for the Rights of Women, 78

   Pro-Choice Framing, 78

   The Abortion Pill, 81

   Emergency Contraception, 83

   Accurate Information, 84

   Environmental Safety, 88

   Access, 90

   Stigma, 94

Solutions and Common Ground, 96

   Shifting Pro-Life and Pro-Choice Frames, 96

   Toning Down the Rhetoric, 100

   Polling to Identify Areas of Consensus, 103

References, 105

3   PERSPECTIVES, 119

Introduction, 119

The Roots of *Roe*: Not Liberty, but Privacy *by Trysh Travis*, 120

Normalizing Abortion: An Interview with a
Reproductive Health Care Provider *by Jennifer
Keys*, 125

The Abortion Diary: Uncovering, Sharing, and Listening
to the Archive We Hold within Our Bodies *by Melissa
Madera*, 134

Treating Each Other Like Drunk Girls in the Bathroom:
A Pro-Life Feminist Finds Acceptance at the Women's
March *by Destiny Herndon-De La Rosa*, 141

Why I Work for Planned Parenthood: Debunking
Common Misconceptions about America's Leading
Reproductive Health Care Provider *by Brigid
Leahy*, 146

Pregnancy Help Centers: Offering Women Choice and
Hope in the Midst of Crisis *by Jay Hobbs*, 153

Fathers and Abortion *by Bertha Alvarez
Manninen*, 157

Who Should or Should Not Be Born?: The Collision
between Reproductive Rights and Disability Rights
by Stefanija Giric, 163

4   **PROFILES, 171**

Introduction, 171

People, 172

On the Pro-Choice Side, 172

Bill Baird (1932–), 172

Jennifer Baumgardner (1970–), 173

Mary Steichen Calderone (1904–1998), 173

Gloria Feldt (1942–), 174

Sherri Chessen Finkbine (1930–), 175

Kim Gandy (1954–), 176

Alan Guttmacher (1898–1974), 176

Frances Kissling (1943–), 177

Lawrence Lader (1919–2006), 178

Kate Michelman (1942–), 179

Willie Parker (1963–), 180

Cecile Richards (1957–), 181

Margaret Sanger (1879–1966), 182

Eleanor Smeal (1939–), 183

George Tiller (1941–2009), 184

Sarah Weddington (1945–), 185

On the Pro-Life Side, 185

Philip Benham (1948–), 185

Judie Brown (1944–), 186

Marjorie Dannenfelser (1965–), 187

Serrin Foster (1955–), 188

Wanda Franz (1944–), 189

Paul T. Hill (1954–2003), 190

Henry Hyde (1924–2007), 191

Paul Marx (1920–2010), 192

Norma McCorvey (1947–2017), 192

Bernard Nathanson (1926–2011), 193

Troy Newman (1966–), 194

Joseph M. Scheidler (1927–), 195

Christopher Smith (1953–), 196

Horatio Robinson Storer (1830–1922), 197

Randall Terry (1959–), 198

Charmaine Yoest (1964–), 199

Organizations, 200

    Common Ground, 202

        Common Ground Network for Life
           and Choice, 202

        Exhale, 202

    On the Pro-Life Side, 203

        American Center for Law and
           Justice (ACLJ), 203

        American Coalition of Life Activists
           (ACLA), 203

        American Life League (ALL), 204

        Americans United for Life (AUL), 204

        Army of God (AG), 205

        Center for Bio-Ethical Reform (CBR), 205

        Center for Medical Progress (CMP), 205

        Christian Coalition of America (CCA), 206

        Concerned Women for America (CWFA), 206

        Crisis Pregnancy Centers (CPC), 207

        Democrats for Life of America (DLA), 208

        Elliot Institute (EI), 208

        Family Research Council (FRC), 209

        Feminists for Life of America (FFL), 209

        Focus on the Family (FOF), 210

        Lambs of Christ (LC), 210

        Live Action (LA), 211

        March for Life Education and Defense Fund
           (ML), 211

        Moral Majority Coalition (MMC), 212

        National Right to Life (NRL), 212

New Wave Feminists (NWF), 213

Operation Rescue (OR), 213

Operation Save America (OSA), 214

Pharmacists for Life International (PFLI), 214

Physicians for Life (PL), 215

Priests for Life (PFL), 215

Pro-Life Action League (PLAL), 216

Pro-Life Alliance of Gays and Lesbians (PLA-GAL), 216

#ProtestPP (#PPP), 217

Republican National Coalition for Life (RNCL), 217

Students for Life (SL), 218

Susan B. Anthony List (SBAL), 218

TooManyAborted.com (TMA), 218

Traditional Values Coalition (TVC), 219

United States Conference of Catholic Bishops (USCCB), 219

On the Pro-Choice Side, 220

Abortion Care Network (ACN), 220

Abortion Conversation Project (ACP), 220

The Abortion Diary (TAD), 220

Abortion Rights Mobilization (ARM), 221

Advancing New Standards in Reproductive Health (ANSIRH), 221

American Civil Liberties Union (ACLU) Reproductive Freedom Project, 221

American Law Institute (ALI), 222

Black Women's Health Imperative (BWHI), 222

Catholics for a Free Choice (CFFC), 222

Center for Reproductive Rights (CRR), 223

Center on Reproductive Rights and Justice (CRRJ), 223

Feminist Majority (FM) and Feminist Majority Foundation (FMF), 224

Guttmacher Institute (GI), 224

If/When/How: Lawyering for Reproductive Justice, 225

Medical Students for Choice (MSFC), 225

NARAL Pro-Choice America, 226

National Abortion Federation (NAF), 226

National Advocates for Pregnant Women (NAPW), 226

National Latina Institute for Reproductive Health (NLIRH), 227

National Network of Abortion Funds (NNAF), 227

National Organization for Women (NOW), 228

National Women's Law Center (NWLC), 228

Physicians for Reproductive Choice and Health (PRH), 228

Planned Parenthood Federation of America (PPFA), 229

Religious Coalition for Reproductive Choice (RCRC), 229

Reproductive Health Technologies Project (RHTP), 230

Republican Majority for Choice (RMC), 230

Sex Information and Education Council of
the United States (SIECUS), 230

#ShoutYourAbortion (SYA), 231

Sistersong: Women of Color Reproductive
Justice Collective (SS)/Trust Black Women
(TBW), 231

Relevant Government Agencies, 232

Internationally Focused Organizations, 232

References, 232

5   **DATA AND DOCUMENTS, 237**

Introduction, 237

Current State Laws Regulating Abortion, 237

Regulations of Abortion Practice, 237

Limits on Public Funding, 238

Right of Refusal, 241

Mandatory Counseling, Waiting Periods, and
Medical Accuracy, 241

Parental Involvement, 247

Abortion Services, 247

Prevalence, 247

Characteristics of Women Having
Abortions, 249

Attacks on Abortion Providers, 252

Public Opinion Polling on Abortion Issues, 254

Historical Documents, 257

Comstock Act (1873), 257

American Law Institute Model Penal Code: Abortion (1959), 259

Abortion in Perspective by Robert M. Byrn (1966), 260

Abortion—A Woman's Decision, A Woman's Right (1969), 262

Redstockings Abortion Speakout (March 21, 1969), 266

Roe v. Wade (1973), 270

The Hyde Amendment (1976), 273

Mexico City Policies (1984–2017), 275

Freedom of Access to Clinic Entrances Act (FACE) (1994), 277

Partial-Birth Abortion Ban Act (2003), 279

Whole Woman's Health v. Hellerstedt (2016), 280

6   RESOURCES, 285

Introduction, 285

Books, 286

Understanding the Abortion Controversy in the United States, 286

A Global Comparative Examination, 294

Further Insights into the Pro-Choice Perspective, 296

Further Insights into the Pro-Life Perspective, 303

Nonprint Sources, 307

Documentary, 307

Feature Films, 312

Internet Sources, 314

7   CHRONOLOGY, 317

   Glossary, 341
   Index, 345
   About the Authors, 389

Preface

"Debate," "controversy," "argument," "conflict," "struggle," "clash," "battle," "war"—all of these terms have been used to describe the status of the abortion issue in American society and politics, and it has been this way for a half century. The conflict plays out in our legislatures, political parties, courts, religious institutions, the military, prisons, the health system, and even foreign policy. And there is no other country where the battles over abortion are so intense and pervasive. What is this conflict? What are people fighting about? Where did it come from? Who are the players and where and how do they engage each other? Why is it so hard to settle? Ultimately, what impact has this contentious climate had on the provision of abortion services and providers, women, and our society? This book describes the origins and changes in the conflict over abortion; the major combatants; what they are fighting about; the arenas for the conflicts; and the effects on politics, policy, and social debate. The objective is to provide timely information to readers and resources for further exploration of the topic.

We start with the basics in Chapter 1. That means looking at the public history of abortion since the founding of the American republic, especially the campaign to criminalize the procedure during the 19th century. Then we see how the criminal laws became out of date in the mid-20th century, provoking a new campaign, this time for reform and repeal of these criminal laws. *Roe v. Wade* was the turning point in 1973. This decision legalized abortion but did not end the debate; in fact, it gave birth to the clashes we live with today. The pro-choice and pro-life movements are the big story after 1973. Movements are a combination of ideas called *frames* and members called *activists*. Chapter 1 concludes with a discussion of the frames that reflect the divergent worldviews of each faction.

After an understanding of the basics, we are ready in Chapter 2 to delve into the war itself, battle by battle, showing the continually shifting winners and losers over 45 years. One of these major conflicts pertains to the constitutionality of abortion law and the campaign to overturn *Roe v. Wade*. But there are also skirmishes over funding, administrative regulations, and emergency contraception. Included in the coverage is the all-too-real and still-ongoing firefight over access to abortion services.

Chapter 3, new to this edition, features the compelling voices of those engaged in the front lines of this battle alongside scholars from a range of disciplinary perspectives. It opens with reflections from a cultural historian on the landmark *Roe v. Wade* decision that is at the heart of this controversy and the implications that follow from the Supreme Court's grounding of the decision in the right to privacy. In an effort to capture more of the lived experience of abortion, there are also illuminating accounts from an abortion provider and a collector of women's abortion stories, who are both seeking to destigmatize abortion. The next set of provocative essays is written by activists. A pro-life feminist reflects on her search for acceptance and common ground at the 2017 Women's March on Washington. A pro-choice feminist explores the motivation behind her work at Planned Parenthood and why the organization is the number one target. The third offers us an insider's look at Heartbeat International, a pregnancy help center, and the efforts of compassionate Christians—women and men—seeking to affirm life by providing a community of support. Two additional contributions take us even deeper into the debate: a philosopher considers what role men should play in abortion decision making, and a bioethicist explores the clash of abortion rights and disability rights.

The remaining chapters provide supplemental materials to fill out the story of this conflict: profiles of activists and organizations in Chapter 4, a carefully curated collection of primary documents and accessible tables in Chapter 5, and a fully annotated and vetted collection of resources that will move readers quickly past the deluge of dubious facts and toward a more complex understanding of the issues in Chapter 6. These do not exhaust the available materials by any means, but they are a good place to start. Readers who want a capsule overview of the waxing and waning of abortion politics will find a chronology from 1821 to 2017 at the end of this book.

This reference handbook is distinctive in its use of two disciplinary lenses—first political science and now sociology. I am indebted to its original author Dr. Dorothy E. McBride for entrusting me to build on the rock-solid foundation she laid, which continues to inform our understanding of the contemporary abortion debate. She dedicated over 35 years of her distinctive career to studying and being captivated by abortion politics. Recognizing that it would be a loss for this book to retire along with her, she did what many activists who devoted their adult lives to the pro-life or pro-choice cause are now doing, that is, passing the torch. I share her endless fascination with the abortion controversy and bring my own intersectional understanding of women's abortion experiences and analysis of movement-countermovement dynamics that relies on scientific evidence to weigh competing claims.

Just as the next generation of scholars will continue to advance new research, fresh voices will continue to enter the still very heated conversation about abortion. This book examines the latest explosive flashpoints, including the fatal shooting of George Tiller in 2009; the conviction of Dr. Kermit Gosnell, a disreputable abortion provider, in 2013; Texas senator Wendy Davis's historic filibuster in 2013; the striking down of Texas TRAP Laws in *Whole Woman's Health v. Hellerstedt* (2016); and the battle currently being waged over the federal funding of Planned Parenthood.

This fiercely polarizing debate is intimately tied to personal experiences and to deeply held religious, moral, and political beliefs. The impassioned rhetoric makes it difficult to achieve empathetic understanding, let alone any common ground. This book goes beyond the intractable ideological arguments to provide a cogent scholarly analysis of the most salient aspects of the abortion debate. It is designed to equip readers seeking to become more informed about the abortion controversy with the key information that they will need to develop their own thoughtful and evidence-informed positions. Modeling a balanced, scholarly investigation of a highly charged controversial issue will help novices to become more resistant to sensational media and inflammatory claims and to hone their critical thinking skills so that they can untangle the complexities of each new issue that emerges in the abortion debate.

Acknowledgments

A special thanks to my student research team, Brittany Butz, Chloe Boden, and Cindy Motkya for their perceptive insights and curiosity about the many different facets of the abortion controversy. I also wish to acknowledge the essay contributors who so generously shared their diverse and illuminating perspectives. As always, I feel tremendous gratitude for my colleagues, friends, and family for their unwavering support and willingness to engage in challenging conversations. Finally, I wish to express admiration to all those who have shown tremendous courage and to all those who have been dedicated to peaceful engagement in this historic and ongoing struggle over the most fundamental rights.

Abortion in the United States

Introduction

The practice of abortion is legal in the United States. This seems simple enough, but just like everything about the abortion conflict, there is no easy way to describe abortion law. The law has many sources—constitutions, legislative statutes, administrative regulations, court decisions—and to become an expert on abortion law, one would have to become familiar with all of them. This book contains information about many aspects of abortion policy. But to begin, it is useful to have a clear reference point that can serve as the framework for looking at all the many forms of government actions that compose U.S. abortion policy.

The foundation of abortion law is the U.S. Constitution as interpreted by the Supreme Court. Constitutional law does not directly regulate abortion. Rather, it sets limits on the powers of the states and the federal government to regulate abortion. The authority to regulate abortion has long been reserved to the states by the Constitution because Article I—which covers

---

In deliberate defiance of U.S. Comstock Laws, Margaret Sanger, an obstetric nurse, poses after her arraignment in the Brooklyn Court of Special Sessions in October 2016. She and her staff were arrested just 10 days after opening the first family planning clinic in the United States, established to provide medically accurate information on pregnancy and contraceptive use. Although her repeated attempts to reopen the clinic failed, and she served 30 days in jail, the publicity Sanger garnered helped transform the private matter of birth control into an issue of public debate. (AP Photo)

the legislative branch—does not give Congress explicit authority to regulate medical practice. However, Congress does get involved in abortion policy through its power to spend money and regulate interstate commerce.

The Court has established this constitutional law of abortion through a series of decisions, called *case law*. States do not have constitutional authority to prohibit the medical practice of abortion before the fetus is viable (i.e., the point at which an unborn child is able to live on its own outside the mother); any laws that make abortion criminal before viability would be unconstitutional. After viability, state governments have the authority, but not the obligation, to prohibit abortion, except when medical judgment decides that the abortion is necessary to save the life or health of the mother. In other words, abortion is legal in the United States without condition before the fetus is viable. After viability, abortion is prohibited in some, but not all, states except when the health or life of the mother is at risk.

The logic underlying this constitutional foundation is the assumption that there are important differences in stages of pregnancy, specifically, before and after the fetus is viable. The point at which a fetus is viable is not fixed; it varies from pregnancy to pregnancy, and it has been pushed back with advances in medical technology. Experts disagree about the exact point of viability, but 22 weeks of gestation is the earliest possible time period for survival, and the success rate, even with aggressive treatment, is very low. The legal definition is that a viable fetus is capable of surviving outside the mother's body on its own or with neonatal assistance but does not include a specific week. Abortion law varies based on a division of pregnancy into stages of "pre-viability" and "post-viability."

With this approach, current U.S. law is quite similar to abortion law in the 18th century when the Constitution was drafted and ratified. Then, all the states had adopted English common law, which made abortion a crime only if it was performed after quickening—what was also called animation. The definition of a "quick" fetus was that the mother felt it move inside her uterus. The common law reflected an ancient debate (at least back to the Greeks) about the moral status of a human embryo and when the developing unborn child became possessed of a soul. There was widespread belief that quickening, which takes place in the second trimester of pregnancy, signaled that something substantial had changed in the pregnancy and that the developing fetus may be possessed of a selfhood, a soul, or even an independent life. At the same time, people believed that if they could see the fetus at this stage, it would look more like a baby and less like a bunch of cells. Thus, it seemed to make sense to punish anyone who killed a quick fetus because it was similar to killing a baby.

The problem was that in those days there was no independent way to determine whether a woman was pregnant; the only one who knew was the mother and only when she could feel the quick movement. Therefore, anyone charged with performing an abortion—a very rudimentary and unpredictable procedure in the 18th century—could use the plausible defense that the pregnancy was unknown. Many women sought help when their periods stopped; the accused could claim to be just helping start the blocked "courses." In this era, therefore, people, especially women, considered the process of menstruation and early pregnancy to be very closely linked.

Both the 18th-century common law and the 21st-century constitutional law are periodic forms of abortion law: the law regulates abortion based on stages of pregnancy, either before and after quickening or before and after viability. The other type of abortion law is conditional. Typically, in conditional laws abortion is criminalized except in certain conditions of pregnancy, such as to preserve the health of the mother, if the fetus is deformed, or if the pregnancy is the result of rape or incest. In the United States, the law allows states to enact conditional laws that come into force only after viability. As we see in the next section, a successful campaign in the 19th century changed the rather liberal common law to criminal laws with very limited conditions that remained in place until the *Roe v. Wade* decision in 1973.

Supreme Court abortion case law has also granted state governments the constitutional authority to enact rules and regulations that may have the goal of influencing abortion decisions by the woman or the doctor as long as these are not an undue burden on the woman's right to seek an abortion. In other words, state governments are permitted to enact requirements that may place hurdles in the path toward abortion, such as waiting periods after mandated counseling, as long as they do not impose a major, substantial, or even insurmountable obstacle. The "undue burden test" has been in use since the 1992 *Planned Parenthood v. Casey* decision, which struck down Pennsylvania's spousal notification laws. Of course, like viability, undue burden has no fixed meaning. To illustrate how tremendously contentious this can be, consider Utah's 2016 fetal anesthesia bill. Pro-choice groups are emphatic that this is an undue burden, making abortion more costly for women with no scientific evidence that a 20-week "fetus" has sufficient neurological development to feel pain, whereas Utah's Governor Gary Herbert, who is pro-life, believes that doctors should compassionately err on the side of reducing any potential pain during abortion for the "unborn child."

Criminalization: The 19th-Century Debate

When we talk about criminalization, what we mean is that governments declare that it is a crime to perform abortions or to help someone else perform them. James Mohr's (1978) book *Abortion in America* is the primary resource for those who want to learn about the process of criminalization in the 19th century. Until the mid-1800s, abortion prior to quickening was legal. Women could self-induce abortion or seek assistance from practitioners who had little training but who had learned abortive techniques through folk medicine, midwives, or other wise women. Acquiring the herbs and concoctions that were peddled was another option but one that often had little effect. Mohr argues that in the early days of the republic, these practices were tolerated primarily as "women's business." When the government tried to prosecute an abortionist, juries regularly acquitted because there was no way to prove the defendant knew the woman was pregnant and because there was widespread sympathy for those who found themselves in the predicament of needing to seek an abortion. Many believed they were helping poor and unfortunate girls and women to resolve a difficult situation. (Note that Olasky 1992 disputes this conclusion that abortion was viewed as morally neutral; rather, he contends that it was not prosecuted simply because of the inability to produce evidence that the terminated pregnancy was past the point of quickening.) The first statute regarding abortion appeared in 1821, when Connecticut legislators determined that destroying the fetus after quickening should be punished by fine or imprisonment; other states followed.

The process of criminalization was gradual and followed changes in the economy, society, and, especially, the practice of medicine. The issue of abortion practice and what to do about it became a public problem in roughly the mid-19th century. Before that, there was a slow increase in writings about abortion; doctors especially began to document that abortions were not a sort of rare last resort for the desperate poor. More and more women were getting them, and they were women of the "respectable" white, Protestant, middle class. Abortion had also gradually become a business, and advertisements marked the commercialization of what was apparently a lucrative practice.

Abortion was not a practice dominated by physicians, as it is today. Back then, doctoring was not a "profession" in the sense that there were rules and regulations limiting who could practice. The 1840s were not far removed from the days of barber physicians or patients being bled. Some physicians or "regulars" were trained—although training was quite rudimentary by today's standards. Scientific knowledge was also limited, but these new formally trained physicians claimed expertise, which they hoped would ultimately trounce their competitors. No issue demonstrated the problem of their profession better than abortion. Anybody could and did use all manner of means to end pregnancies; because of the law that reinforced the doctrine that abortions before quickening were not killing a human being but solving a female problem, the regulars could do nothing about it.

The social and economic modernization of the United States brought increasing attention to standards of education and the professions. To promote these ideas, professional organizations appeared, and the regulars formed the American Medical Association (AMA) in 1847. From the beginning many of the members called for change with respect to abortion. In their campaign to medicalize the entirety of gynecological care, physicians invoked fears of midwifery's potential dangers. They claimed that their scientific knowledge completely refuted the idea that there were fundamental differences between quick and not-quick pregnancies; the embryo and fetus were essentially the same throughout the pregnancy. Further, they argued that the reason there were so many abortions was that women were ignorant; they did not have this knowledge of fetal development. They saw it as their duty to persuade the public, and especially women, that even tiny embryos were human lives, not some blockage of menstrual flow, and thus abortion must be prohibited except in cases where the physician deemed it necessary to save the life of a pregnant woman. Ginsburg (1998) observes that medical doctors strategically employed pro-life rhetoric, but they did not push for a total ban on abortion. Instead, they advocated for laws that allowed doctors to become the custodians of abortion, determining when it was and was not warranted. In 1859, the AMA enacted a resolution to that effect:

> Resolved, That while physicians have long been united in condemning the act of producing abortion, at every period of gestation, except as necessary for preserving the

life of either mother or child, it has become the duty of this Association, in view of the prevalence and increasing frequency of the crime, publicly to enter an earnest and solemn protest against such unwarrantable destruction of human life.

Resolved, That in pursuance of the grand and noble calling we profess, the saving of human lives, and of the sacred responsibilities thereby devolving upon us, the Association present this subject to the attention of the several legislative assemblies of the Union, with the prayer that the laws by which the crime of procuring abortion is attempted to be controlled may be revised, and that such other action may be taken in the premises as they in their wisdom may deem necessary.

Resolved, That the Association request the zealous co-operation of the various State Medical Societies in pressing this subject upon the legislatures of their respective states. (reprinted from Dyer 1999, 14–15)

This resolution reflects the official concern with "saving human life" and "sacred responsibilities," but the underlying motive in the physician's campaign against abortion was that criminalization would deny the competition business. Thus, prominent physicians contacted their friends in the state legislatures and urged that they not only prohibit the irregulars from performing abortions but also develop licensing requirements to deny the right to practice any medicine without proper credentials. The AMA resolution and lobbying activities occurred at the end of what Mohr (1978) calls a transitional phase between the 1840s and the 1860s. After the 1860s, states came into line with the AMA plan and prohibited abortion from conception on; threats to the mother's life were the only exception. In the 1870s, doctors got a substantial boost in their campaign from the anti-obscenity movement led by Anthony Comstock of New York. In those days, many leaders considered sex and childbirth to be inseparable and guided by religious moral principles. Thus, growing interest in contraception and the public discussion of abortion led Comstock and his Committee for the Suppression of Vice to include them in their crusade against the moral degradation of society. Comstock successfully lobbied Congress in 1873 to pass the Comstock Act, which made importation, trade, and commerce in "obscene materials" federal crimes. Among the materials defined as obscene were information about and materials for contraception and abortion. Comstock also made it his business to arrest abortionists by masquerading as a poor husband looking for remedies to his "wife's problem." Comstock had the support of evangelical reformers and allied with some feminists in the social purity movement. He brought important resources to the physicians' campaign. In contrast to later abortion politics, the perspectives of the women's movement leaders and the Roman Catholic Church were not part of the debate in the state legislatures. First-wave feminists or suffragettes were focused on securing the right of women to vote, and in the little they said about abortion they tended to condemn it as evidence of the way men and male lust victimize women. Generally, women's rights advocates, such as Elizabeth Cady Stanton and Susan B. Anthony, viewed the women who sought abortions as desperate because their husbands took little heed of the effects of frequent pregnancies on their health or the well-being of the family. In their view, the way to prevent abortion was for men to exercise sexual restraint and to adopt the moral standard of purity they placed on their wives. To the 19th-century feminists, abortionists were another class of men who preyed on women. Later, "voluntary motherhood" would become their cry. It is important to remember that in this period contraception was primitive (abstinence being the most reliable), married women had few legal rights, marital rape was permitted under common law, and both abortion and pregnancy were routinely life threatening. The prevailing conditions led early feminists to conclude that the status of married women would improve if abortion were suppressed.

Similarly, quiet in the debate in the state legislatures were the voices from the Roman Catholic Church. Although today the official view of church history is that the Roman Catholic Church has always condemned abortion, there was no official church doctrine. Catholic theologians had written tracts about abortion, including St. Augustine (354–430 CE) who maintained that the soul enters the body only after it is formed—at 40 days of gestation for males and 80 days of gestation for females. Before that point, presumably, abortion did not kill a human being. Not surprisingly, the pronouncements of theologians and church leaders fit the knowledge of the time. The view that abortion before quickening was acceptable because there was no child formed until then also fits the Augustinian pronouncements. The distinction between the ensouled (animated) and the nonanimated fetus began to lose support among Catholic theologians as early as the 17th century, yet it was not until 1869 that Pope Pius IX made it official, declaring that the embryo was a being with a soul from conception and abortion was a sin leading to excommunication. Another papal decree in 1884 declared that abortion, even to save the mother's life, was prohibited among Catholics. Some of the same social and scientific changes that influenced physicians likely also had an effect on church leaders, but until the early 20th century, the church did not take a position on the public debate about abortion policy in the United States.

By 1900, all states had dropped the quickening distinction, revoked women's common-law immunities from prosecution (both the woman and the abortionist could now be sent to jail), and prohibited advertising of abortion services. What had been legal, private, and available in 1800 was now criminal, public, and penalized. Therefore, what had changed? Just about everything. The framework of abortion policy shifted from the periodic model to an indications or severe conditions model that allowed saving the life of the mother as the only defense for the crime. The terms of debate also changed. Before, when abortion was rarely discussed as a public problem, it was viewed as a symptom of poverty and victimization of the weak. By 1900, abortion was publicly defined as an immoral taking of a human life, an action so serious that it could take place only if the pregnancy threatened to take the life of another human being—the mother. Medical doctors were charged with the lofty responsibility of determining when that decision was warranted.

When the abortion reform movement rose up in the 1960s and 1970s, activists looked back at the history of this criminalization crusade. One of the issues in the 1960s was the dangers of illegal abortions. Activists learned that abortions had once been legal and abortions, like childbirth, constituted a real threat to women's lives. Before the 1860s abortions were legal but not safe. Medical practice in the late 19th century improved dramatically, however. The invention of the speculum and the dilation and curettage procedure, knowledge of the risk of bacterial infection, and new methods of anesthesia allowed for safe abortions for the first time. Yet just as these medical improvements came along, the legislatures and the doctors whose practice benefited moved to criminalize abortion. To many 20th-century activists, it seemed that the abuses women suffered from so-called back alley abortionists were due to the fact that doctors had worked hard to make it so.

One way to compare abortion policies across governments and over time is to classify them in terms of what some call the abortion triad (McBride Stetson 1996). Any abortion policy distributes powers and resources among the three main players: the government, the doctors with expertise to perform safe abortions, and women seeking abortions. The abortion policy from the 18th to the mid-19th centuries in the United States empowered women. The state largely stayed out of the process of delivering abortion. Women not only were free to seek help from a variety of practitioners but also could perform an abortion on themselves with no punishment. Further, they and only they could determine when criminal laws kicked in—at quickening. From the last decades of the 19th century, abortion policy shows an alliance between the government and doctors and the disempowerment of women. The new criminal laws had a loophole for acquiring an abortion—the life of the mother. Only medical doctors could judge when and if an abortion was warranted. Women who sought to end their pregnancies without a doctor's permission could go to jail. The next section of this chapter briefly summarizes how women coped with the new triad and how it broke down under the pressures of social, medical, and economic change in the mid-20th century.

Reform and Repeal: The Road to Decriminalization

The success of the AMA's 19th-century criminalization campaign had placed the medical profession firmly in control of the practice of safe abortion. Apparently, the major legal shift had little impact on women's desire for abortion. Women sought abortions, and many doctors provided them. This became the women's secret (Reagan 1998). The motives of those who promoted the criminal laws may have been to "protest against such unwarrantable destruction of human life," but in practice medical doctors had varying opinions about when abortion was warranted (Dyer 1999, 14). All the laws had the exception for therapeutic reasons—to save the life of the mother—but whether any pregnancy posed such a threat was determined by the doctor alone. He could perform an abortion in his office or the patient's home, and no one would know about it. Women quietly told their friends about those sympathetic doctors; men left the whole business to women to sort out. Kristin Luker (1984) calls this period the "century of silence." However, anti-abortion doctors made some attempts to expose their more liberal colleagues. None of these moved the issue to the public agenda for long.

As in the 1830s, the increase in abortion rates in the 1930s started the process toward new policy debates on the issue. The Great Depression of the 1930s took an enormous toll on families. People faced with extreme poverty became desperate to find ways to avoid bringing more mouths to feed into the world. At the same time, medical advances had greatly reduced the risk that pregnancy would lead to death; women began to seek to end pregnancies for other reasons. By this time, abortion procedures were conducted in hospitals rather than doctors' offices. Some doctors began to stretch the therapeutic exception to include social conditions of the pregnancy, but most would not. Women increasingly sought solutions that were unsafe and ended up in hospitals, where many died. During the 1930s, as many as 17,000 women are estimated to have died each year (out of 800,000 abortions) from botched abortions (Garrow 1994, 272). In the hospitals where they worked, doctors saw firsthand the effects of all these trends.

One response to the situation was that the police and prosecutors began to crack down on doctors and others who appeared to be performing abortions outside the law. Others reacted by thinking of ways to prevent abortion through family planning. Margaret Sanger was at the forefront of the fight for women's access to birth control, but the Comstock Laws that had been enacted in 1873 stood in the way of her goal of helping women determine both the timing and number of their pregnancies. Sanger constructed a test case to challenge the obscenity law; she had a doctor in one of her clinics import a diaphragm from Japan, which was confiscated by customs officials. In 1936 a federal circuit court judge ruled in *U.S. v. One Package of Japanese Pessaries* (86 F.2d) that unless state laws prohibited it, doctors could prescribe contraceptives to their patients, and the AMA was quick to incorporate birth control into medical practice. In the early 1940s, Margaret Sanger's American Birth Control League changed its name to Planned Parenthood Federation of America and intensified its campaign to expand contraceptive information and use to prevent abortion. At the same time, Dr. Alan Guttmacher called for liberalization of the law at a Planned Parenthood meeting in 1942.

During the 1950s, abortions were illegal, dangerous, and heavily stigmatized, but American women continued to find ways to get them. Messer and May's (1994) *Back Rooms: Voices from the Illegal Abortion Era* is filled with harrowing and heartbreaking first-person accounts, including desperate self-induced miscarriages with coat hangers, which would later become a powerful symbol of the pro-choice movement. Rickie Solinger's (2013) *Wake Up Little Susie: Single Pregnancy and Race before Roe v. Wade* reveals the largely hidden history of the deeply racialized societal response to unwed mothers between 1945 and 1960. White girls in "unfortunate circumstances" were sent away from their homes, expelled from their schools and communities, and pressured to ultimately give up their babies for adoption. In contrast, black women faced a restricted adoption market and negative stereotypes about their lack of sexual restraint and drain on the welfare system. In *The Girls Who Went Away: The Hidden History of Women Who Surrendered Children for Adoption in the Decades before Roe v. Wade*, Ann Fessler (2007), whose own mother had given her up for adoption, tells the stories of more than a hundred women, who represent the estimated 1.5 million women in the post–World War II era, who had no choice but to carry pregnancies to term in secrecy. Many were coerced into surrendering their babies; others felt they had no other viable options or that the child would be better off. It was a painful experience that haunted many of the women for their rest of their lives.

Doctors still had the medical authority to privately exercise their own discretion in whether or not to aid female patients who requested that their pregnancies be terminated. To diffuse some of this responsibility and bring more impartial judgment, hospital abortion committees had been assembled to mediate on a case-by-case basis. It was hoped that by maintaining greater oversight, doctors could also deflect criticism and negative publicity. Women of privilege were more likely to be granted these so-called therapeutic abortions. As Rickie Solinger (1998) explains in *Abortion Wars: A Half Century of Struggle*, the list of approved medical indications expanded and contracted after World War II. Psychiatrists became major players; they could determine that a woman was a suicide risk if forced to continue with the pregnancy or psychologically unfit to be a mother. But there were also new medical advances that would make it possible for women with preexisting illnesses like breast cancer or cardiovascular disease to carry pregnancies to term—conditions that would have warranted a routine therapeutic abortion in the 1930s. New imaging technology also contributed to the declining number of therapeutic abortions granted by helping to construct the fetus in the womb as a "little person" that must be protected. Without centralized reporting structures, it is difficult to estimate the number of abortions being performed during this time. According to Alfred Kinsey's (1953) study, *Sexual Behavior in the Human Female*, 90 percent of pregnancies outside marriage were ending in abortion. The pervasive silence surrounding abortion was beginning to crack. The 19th-century abortion laws had always caused some discontent, but most trace the origins of the movement to reform the law to a 1955 Planned Parenthood conference. This organization provided an arena for doctors and lawyers to discuss the abortion issue and express concern about the laws. Doctors and lawyers had been discussing the problems in professional journals for several years. They soon realized that if anything was going to change, it would be necessary to bring the issue to a public agenda—that is, to awaken public opinion to the need for reform. When that time occurred in the 1960s, reformers were already prepared with a model reform statute that would answer all the concerns doctors and lawyers expressed.

In 1959, the American Law Institute (ALI) outlined a model that, in effect, would amend criminal laws to expand conditions for legal abortion. According to the proposal, "A licensed physician is justified in terminating a pregnancy if he believes that there is a substantial risk that continuance of the pregnancy would gravely impair the physical and mental health of the mother or that the child would be born with grave physical or mental defects or that pregnancy resulted from rape, incest, or other felonious intercourse" (quoted in Davis 1985, 260). Abortion reform meant a slight increase in the number of indicators that would permit legal abortion while keeping most abortions criminalized. Many doctors agreed with this approach. Guttmacher and others in New York formed the Association for the Study of Abortion in 1960 to try to drum up support for the reform.

At this time, most people in America had no idea that there were groups working to change abortion laws, that is, until two events brought the issue to public attention and the national agenda from where it has still not receded. In 1962, Sherri Finkbine, a mother of four, discovered that the sleeping pills her husband brought her from England contained thalidomide—a tranquilizer that causes terrible birth defects. (Thalidomide had not yet been approved for use in the United States.) She and her doctor quietly scheduled an abortion in an Arizona hospital on a Monday. On the Sunday before the procedure, Finkbine called an acquaintance in the news business and suggested she might warn others about the dangers of thalidomide. The next day Finkbine's scheduled abortion was headline news. As a result of the publicity, the hospital canceled her abortion, and she had to go to Sweden for the procedure. The national media picked up the story, focusing on the problems faced by women carrying deformed fetuses. Support for those women took on steam in the next year when a rubella epidemic (a form of measles that also causes birth defects) occurred. The spin in the media was that perhaps the 19th-century laws were too strict and out of date given all the social and medical changes in the 20th century. The change in public opinion necessary for the abortion reform advocates to form a viable movement was finally under way in the early 1960s. Most professional organizations of doctors, lawyers, and health workers endorsed the ALI reform.

With the attention to proposals for limited reform, new voices joined the debate. Proposals for repeal of state criminal laws, not simply reform, arose. Some came from the ranks of the reformers in the law and medical communities. Changes in contraceptive laws had an impact on their views. In 1965, the Supreme Court ruled in *Griswold v. Connecticut* (38 U.S. 479, 1965) that states could not criminalize contraceptive use by married people because such laws interfered with their rights to privacy in their decisions and behavior with respect to sex and procreation. It seemed logical to many that laws that made it a crime for a woman to end a pregnancy would also interfere with her privacy. Many from population, family planning, and health organizations who had campaigned for reform now began to propose that states repeal their laws altogether. Some vowed to take the campaign nationally, holding the First National Conference on Abortion Laws in 1969 in Chicago. At that conference, a few prominent leaders formed NARAL (National Association for the Repeal of Abortion Laws).

Activists in California played an important role in developing the argument for repeal. This stemmed from their realization that the conditional ALI reform merely gave doctors a few more legal justifications to perform abortions. But those reasons—mental health, fetal deformity, and pregnancy by rape and incest—were only a very tiny percentage of the reasons women sought abortions. Such a reform would not decrease dangerous illegal abortions. They questioned why a woman should have to prove she is insane (to two psychiatrists) just because, for her own reasons, she does not want to be pregnant and bear a child. These ideas led women to see that the state was forcing them to remain pregnant against their will or face dangerous procedures: what they labeled "compulsory pregnancy."

Patricia Maginnis, who early in the 1960s had formed the Citizens' Committee for Humane Abortion Laws, asserted that abortion was a woman's business and the government should have no control over this decision. Her demand previewed the mobilization, just a few years later, of the new feminist movement to the cause of repeal. At its second national conference in 1967, the newly formed National Organization for Women endorsed repeal. But the real energy for the repeal campaign came from the more informal Women's Liberation Movement groups. One of these was the Chicago Women's Liberation Union; another was the New York City Redstockings, which held a radical Abortion Speakout in 1969. Women shared stories that moved listeners, thrust abortion issue into the public discourse, and cultivated an atmosphere of support for legal abortion. Black feminist groups joined the cause as well. Feminists advocating for repeal based their claims on women's own experiences as revealed in speak-outs and small group meetings, forming an ideology that linked the question of abortion to the lives of all women. This helped raise women's consciousness that the personal is political. Criminal abortion laws were understood as a manifestation of the male medical establishment's control of women and their bodies. Repealing these laws would liberate women to control their own bodies. Slogans such as "My Body Belongs to Me" and "Get Your Laws Off My Body" went straight to the point. Black feminists told their stories, too, of black women who sought abortions being forced to undergo sterilization as a condition. The feminist demands became: "Repeal All Anti-abortion Laws! No Forced Sterilization! No Restrictive Contraceptive Laws!"

Activists in the movement for repeal used a variety of tactics in their efforts to change the laws nationwide. Activists engaged in collective action through established means by petitioning, lobbying state legislatures, and filing lawsuits to have 19th-century state laws declared unconstitutional (Staggenborg 1991). Those frustrated by lack of progress turned to direct action tactics. Consciousness-raising groups—which were an essential feature of the larger women's liberation movement—encouraged women to learn about their bodies and to develop the self-confidence to confront the doctors who had life-or-death authority over their reproductive lives.

Another effective recruitment tool was the speak-out, where women shared stories that moved listeners, which helped to bring the abortion issue to the public's attention and create an atmosphere of support for legal abortion. The feminists, especially, used nonconventional direct action tactics. Some of the groups set up self-help feminist clinics, referral services for abortions, and even learning how to perform early-pregnancy abortions. "Jane" was legendary; it was the Chicago Women's Liberation Union's underground service that provided safe abortions for over 12,000 women (Kaplan 1996). In 1970, tens of thousands marched in Washington, D.C. and San Francisco in huge demonstrations for their goals. Most scholars agree that the mobilization by the feminist movement in the late 1960s and early 1970s turned the reform movement into an abortion rights movement (e.g., Staggenborg 1991). At the same time, the feminist activism for repeal became the foundation for the women's health movement, which sought to revolutionize women's health care (Morgen 2002).

By 1971, a majority of Americans supported legalization; by early 1973, a stunning 57 percent of Americans, including 54 percent of Roman Catholics, agreed that the abortion decision should be left to the woman and her doctor (Gallup poll, quoted in Garrow 1994, 539). At this time there was little organized opposition to the new abortion rights movement. What little there was came from Roman Catholic doctors and other professionals, largely taken off guard by the speed with which the reform and then repeal bandwagon grew. Black nationalists also opposed both liberal birth control and abortion services for black women, claiming it was part of a long-standing effort by the white establishment to reduce the size of the African American population. Still, although the opposition was weak and the repeal movement growing, many state legislators were resistant even to modest reforms of their laws, let alone repeal. As the pressure grew, the anti-abortion forces gained strength in some states where they organized to maintain criminalization.

By far, the most significant accomplishment of the movement for changing abortion laws was their dramatic effect on the terms of the debate. Since the late 19th century and even through the early years of the movement for reform, the focus had been on negotiating the rights of doctors to prescribe abortion for their patients. Groups concerned about family planning defined abortion as something that must be available to serve their larger goals of reducing unsafe illegal abortions, while zero population activists emphasized the importance of allowing parents to reduce the size of their families. Neither of these perspectives was enough to light any fires for change in the population overall. What did get their attention was the unprecedented, but finally obvious, claim that abortion was a women's issue and legal abortion was a women's rights issue. The terms of the debate shifted from a contest between doctors and the government to a rebellion of women against the medical/government establishment that controlled their reproductive capacity and their bodies. These second-wave feminists believed that "abortion on demand" would liberate women from that oppression.

By 1973, the campaign for changes in abortion laws had achieved legislative victories in 15 states. Beginning with California, Colorado, and North Carolina in 1967, 12 states adopted some version of conditional abortion patterned after the ALI model statute (Arkansas, Delaware, Georgia, Kansas, Maryland, New Mexico, Oregon, South Carolina, and Virginia). Four states repealed their laws—Washington by referendum and Alaska, Hawaii, and New York by legislative action. By 1973, however, the opposition to reform was also gaining strength. In Michigan and North Dakota, referendums for abortion without condition up to 20 weeks of pregnancy failed by large margins. Lobbying efforts in state legislatures stalled, especially those promoting repeal. Because of the New York repeal, many women traveled there to obtain abortions through referrals operated by Planned Parenthood and other organizations. Perhaps this alleviated the pressure presented by illegal abortions. Pope Paul VI's 1968 encyclical, *Humanae Vitae* (Human Life), which reiterated the church's absolute opposition to abortion as well as all forms of contraception and sterilization, may also have stimulated the Roman Catholic

Church to support a more organized anti-abortion presence in the various state and local debates.

Although today some claim that the Supreme Court's 1973 decision interrupted a wave of abortion reform that would have solved the abortion conflict, there is little evidence to support that notion. Reform was quick at first, but it was very limited and did not answer demands from the feminist movement to get the government out of the business of regulating the practice of abortion altogether. At the same time, the speed of the early ALI-style reforms mobilized opposition to further reforms. In New York, the anti-abortion forces were successful in getting the legislature to overturn repeal—which was stopped only by Governor Nelson Rockefeller's veto of the bill to recriminalize.

Reform and repeal activists in the legal profession were well aware of the difficulties of changing laws nationally by trying to pass reforms in 50 state legislatures. They opted for a litigation strategy that would at least undermine the 19th-century criminal laws and force the legislators to consider reform and at most extend the guarantees of privacy won in *Griswold v. Connecticut* to a woman's decision to seek an abortion. Thus, in the late 1960s and early 1970s, many cases were brought challenging the constitutionality of state laws. As litigation spread, the debate over the law spread as well and revealed a wide range of disagreement over the respective rights and responsibilities of government, physicians, and women. Opponents of legal abortion spoke for the rights of the unborn to prevail; many equated all abortion with murder.

Finally, the Supreme Court agreed to consider the constitutional issues and issued its decisions on the status of both the 19th-century criminal laws and the more recent ALI-style reform laws in 1973. These cases—*Roe v. Wade* (410 U.S. 113) and *Doe v. Bolton* (410 U.S. 179)—mark the end of the movements for reform and repeal and the beginning of the contemporary abortion conflict in the United States. The impact of these movements has been enormous and will be the subject of Chapter 2. Here we review the cases in terms of how they answered the various demands of the reform and repeal movements and how the opinions in the cases affected the terms of public debate on the abortion issue.

Roe v. Wade and *Doe v. Bolton*

Roe v. Wade was a challenge to the constitutionality of the criminal law that Texas enacted in the 1850s. The law prohibited anyone to "procure" or "attempt" an abortion except, based on medical advice, "for the purpose of saving the life of the mother" (410 U.S. 113, 118). "Jane Roe" was the pseudonym for Norma McCorvey, who had sought an abortion because she could not afford to raise a child. Two feminist attorneys, Sarah Weddington and Linda Coffee, had been developing a plan to challenge the Texas law and recruited Norma McCorvey to be their "Roe."

Doe v. Bolton was a challenge to Georgia's 1968 reform that criminalized abortion except when the pregnancy endangered the life of the mother, there was grave fetal deformity, or the pregnancy was the result of rape. The Georgia reform, like many of the ALI-inspired laws, was very restrictive. In this case the Georgia legislature had added stringent and cumbersome rules, including a requirement that the abortion decision must be approved by a committee and the medical judgment must be confirmed by two doctors in addition to the woman's own physician. "Jane Doe" was the pseudonym for Sandra Bensing, a victim of domestic violence, who, like McCorvey, sought the abortion because she could not take care of another child. She was represented by Margie Hames and other feminist attorneys who were keen to challenge the restrictive law because efforts to convince the Georgia legislature to repeal the law had stalled.

The justices treated the two cases as a single decision, but it is *Roe v. Wade* that has become the most famous, the symbol for what is right and wrong (depending on your point of view) with abortion law in the United States. Justice Harry Blackmun wrote the decision, which was supported by seven of the nine justices. Second-wave feminists got what they wanted from both cases: both the 19th-century criminal laws and the 1960s' ALI-inspired reform laws were declared unconstitutional violations of the right to privacy as outlined in the precedent *Griswold v. Connecticut* eight years earlier. Although the term "privacy" is not mentioned in the Constitution, justices in these and other cases have recognized that the Constitution does guarantee areas or zones of privacy and that personal privacy, especially, is a fundamental right. What the justices did in *Roe* was to rule that "a woman's decision whether or not to terminate her pregnancy" is in one of those zones of privacy where the government cannot interfere. Included in that zone was also the physician's right to practice medicine. Most of the U.S. state laws at the time prohibited abortions and thus invaded, unconstitutionally, that zone.

At the same time, the Court acknowledged that the right to make the abortion decision was not unlimited, because the state (government) has legitimate interests in regulation and in protecting the fetus. These interests—the woman's, the physician's, and the state's protection of the fetus—seemed to be irreconcilable. The difficulty in finding a compromise among these interests had stymied peaceful reform in many state legislatures since the mid-1960s. To reconcile these interests, the Court divided pregnancy into trimesters, marking the changes in the growing fetus and the complexity of abortion techniques. As pregnancies progress through 40 weeks, the fetus gets closer to viability, and abortion procedures become increasingly dangerous to the woman. Based on this framework, the Court issued constitutional guidelines to the states.

- Before the beginning of the third trimester, the state may not prohibit abortions; the woman's decision with her doctor is in the zone of privacy and is paramount.
- After the beginning of the third trimester, the "state in promoting its interest in the potentiality of human life may, if it chooses, regulate, and even proscribe, abortion except

where it is necessary, in appropriate medical judgment, for the preservation of the life or health of the mother."

- In addition, the state may enact regulations after the first trimester in "ways that are reasonably related to maternal health" (410 U.S. 113, 164).
- What this means is that state governments *may* but are not required to prohibit abortions in the late stages of pregnancy.

The immediate effect of these rulings was that most states had to revise their statutes to get them in line with the Supreme Court's guidelines. But most realized these were just the first of many cases that would be necessary to determine the limits of state power in this area, a process of litigation that continues as legislatures test the limits of the case law. The content of the decision had a great impact on the abortion conflict. As we have seen, before the 1960s the abortion issue was a medical issue in official debate, placed in the hands of doctors to decide within limits set by state governments. In the 1960s, many new views came to the fore and competed for attention. In succession, people argued that abortion law was a public problem because of illegal abortion; limits on medical professional judgment; the need for ways to plan families and limit population growth; invasion of personal privacy; women's rights to control their bodies; and threats to the humanity of the fetus, a person due constitutional protection. Not all of these perspectives could become part of the official terms of debate.

The *Roe* opinion set forth the new terms of debate. The abortion issue was to be a question of the rights to privacy of women and their doctors against the government's interest in protecting potential human life—the fetus. No longer a medical issue, abortion became a privacy issue related to a fundamental right to decide whether to bear a child and the reasonable limits on that right to protect both the woman and the unborn child. The Court ruled that abortion pertains only to private morality and that the state could not promote one view over another of, for example, when human life begins. "We need not resolve the difficult question of when life begins. When those trained in the respective disciplines of medicine, philosophy, and theology are unable to arrive at any consensus, the judiciary, at this point in the development of man's knowledge, is not in a position to speculate as to the answer" (410 U.S. 113, 159). As to the question of fetal personhood deserving protection under the Fourteenth Amendment, the Court ruled "the word 'person' used in the Fourteenth Amendment does not include the unborn" (401 U.S. 113, 157).

The new U.S. abortion law shifted the balance of power significantly in the abortion triad—women, physicians, and government. Before, the state had empowered doctors to control the decision making about abortion with restrictions. For the most part, they were largely unfettered by state interference until the early years of the reform movement. After 1973, however, the Constitution, as interpreted by the Supreme Court, empowered women, along with doctors, to make decisions about abortion. The government lost authority to make even the most limited restrictions on the abortion decision for the first six months of pregnancy.

After *Roe*: Pro-Life and Pro-Choice Movements Face Off

According to sociologists, a social movement happens when "ordinary people join forces in contentious confrontation with elites, authorities and opponents" (Tarrow 1994, 1). This refers to collective action—through groups and organizations— bound by common purposes and solidarity through recognition of common interests. Movement thinkers construct collective action frames as a way of defining their common purposes. They use these frames to mobilize support, organize activists, and communicate with the public. The final section of this chapter on "Frames and Framing" describes the origins and collective action frames of the pro-life and pro-choice movements.

It is important to be aware that people use a variety of terms to identify the movements in the abortion conflict. The most familiar descriptors—pro-life and pro-choice—will be used throughout this book because these are typically chosen by the activists themselves to represent and differentiate their positions on the abortion issue. As we begin to discuss framing tactics, we will see how each side vies for competitive advantage by invoking unflattering labels to negatively characterize the opposition—"pro-abortion" or "anti-choice" are two examples (McCaffrey and Keys 2000). Labels also reflect evolving understandings, agendas, and rebranding efforts to attract new supporters.

Pro-Life Movement

In the debates leading up to *Roe v. Wade*, there were individuals and groups that opposed efforts at reform and repeal. But it wasn't until after *Roe* that a pro-life movement mobilized. Before *Roe*, Catholics had taken the lead in testifying against reform and repeal. The Vatican's renewed interest in the issues of contraception and abortion as signified by *Humanae Vitae* encouraged clergy to speak out. After *Roe*, the church hierarchy and organizations on behalf of official doctrine began to take a more active role in leadership in reaction to legalization of abortion. The National Right to Life Committee was formally incorporated in 1973 with the explicit goal of overturning the decision. On the first-year anniversary of *Roe*, the March for Life in Washington, D.C., became an annual event. However, Catholics were by no means in agreement on how to proceed or even if it was appropriate for the church to be active in the political arena. The diversity of beliefs within the Roman Catholic Church was reflected in the founding that same year of Catholics for a Free Choice, an organization that espouses the belief that Catholicism supports a woman in following her own conscience in matters of sexual and reproductive health.

But a movement needs more than leaders and doctrine from on high. It needs "ordinary people." In her study of pro-life activists in California in the late 1970s, Kristin Luker (1984) found that many were "stunned" by the Court's decision to declare an unborn child a nonperson under the Constitution. Many said they had never considered that this was possible. In fact, they had assumed that everybody agreed with them that an embryo was a human being from conception and equal to all other human beings. Ziad Munson's (2010) later book *The Making of Pro-Life Activists* suggests that it may be a bit of historical mythology that the landmark Supreme Court decision was a lightning bolt for mobilization. He interviewed only a handful of activists who cited *Roe* as an important factor, though it is important to note that some had not yet been born when the decision was handed down. Quite surprisingly, some even expressed pro-choice beliefs prior to their mobilization. Munson contends that the pro-life movement did not arise due to a "preexisting contingency of people with deep moral concerns about abortion," but, conversely, their commitment to the pro-life cause developed as they increased their interaction with the movement (Munson 2010, 95).

Luker also discovered some important demographic similarities in the post-*Roe* activists she studied; most were married women with children, who lived in traditional marriages and did not work outside the home. By deciding that women's choices came first, even if that meant that women could decide to get an abortion for convenience, the Court was in their view, undermining the value of mothers putting their children ahead of their own lives. According to the pro-life ethic, "A woman, involuntarily pregnant, has a moral obligation to the now-existing dependent fetus whether she explicitly consented to its existence or not" (Callahan 2001, 171). Luker (1984) contends the steadfast commitment of activists is attributable to the fact that it is actually "the meaning of motherhood" which is at stake. The pro-life women were loyal to the breadwinner-homemaker arrangement and thought children were a blessing from God. They believed deeply that life begins at conception, and thus they abhorred abortion, as it was equivalent in their minds to the murder of an innocent human being. They also saw sex as sacred and feared that easy access to abortion would remove male responsibility. Ginsburg (1996) echoes Luker's observations: "For most right-to-lifers, abortion is not simply the termination of an individual potential life, or even that act multiplied a million-fold. It represents an active denial of the reproductive consequences of sex and a rejection of female nurturance, and thus sets forth the possibility of women structurally becoming men" (436). These scholars contend that abortion has broader cultural significance and that it is these competing worldviews that generate such impassioned debate.

There were other forces that contributed to the rise of the pro-life movement. In the 1970s, some conservatives in the Republican Party saw an opportunity to recruit supporters for their candidates if they could link economic conservatism to social conservatism. This New Right worked closely with leaders of evangelical churches, including Pat Robertson and Jerry Falwell. The fundamentalist and Pentecostal religions strongly opposed abortion; Republican strategists promoted an anti-abortion platform and candidates in the Republican Party to attract the support of these groups that had typically stayed away from politics. Legalization of abortion without condition was a threat to their fundamental values, and the effect was to politicize religious faith. From their perspective, fundamental beliefs were under attack, so evangelical Christians became fully committed to fighting the evil of abortion.

To be successful, movements need effectively crafted frames that identify what is problematic, who is responsible, and what can be done to address the situation. Ideally, movement frames will garner media coverage and both legitimate and spur action. The main goal with framing is to construct reality in a way that will strike a responsive chord with the targets of mobilization or what social movement scholars call "sympathetic bystander publics" (Snow, Rochford, Worden, and Benford 1986). Pro-life movement organizations and individual activists put forth different arguments that they hoped would be persuasive often in the form of a very simplified and condensed slogan or sound bite. It was not a "fetus" or "embryo" but "a new tiny individual with its own genetic code" (Beckwith 1993, 42). The "unborn baby" was isolated from the mother's body, portrayed in ultrasound images as safely floating in "space." Fighting for the "right to life" was a frame that had widespread appeal because it tapped into the frame of "rights," which already had great cultural resonance in the United States.

Pro-Choice Movement

The advocates for liberal abortion laws had already formed a social movement before the decision in *Roe v. Wade*. Originally, the leaders for reform were doctors, lawyers, and professionals associated with population control and family planning. The rise of the women's liberation movement gave these leaders the ordinary people, who mobilized to gain repeal of the old criminal laws. By the early 1970s, many organizations from what was referred to as the "older branch" of the movement joined to support the idea that women should have the right to choose whether or not to have a child.

Immediately after the *Roe* decision, there was some slump in the activity of the pro-choice organizations while, one suspects, they enjoyed the unexpected triumph of their goals and their frame of the issue in the courts. But they soon began to pick up the banner when faced with the immediate pro-life efforts to amend the Constitution to change the Court's decision. They also saw the mobilization of many individuals and organizations throughout the country to overcome the sudden legalization of abortion nationwide. NARAL led the way; its first action was to change its name to reflect the new challenge. It became the National Abortion Rights Action League in 1973, pledging to "develop and sustain a constituency which effectively uses the political process at the state and national level to guarantee every woman in the United States the right to choose and obtain a legal abortion" (quoted in Wilder 1998, 79).

The pro-choice women in Luker's (1984) study tended to be well-educated and well-paid career women. They did not reject motherhood, but they saw it as one of many important roles in their lives. They desired smaller families so that they could devote more emotional and financial resources to their children. They valued sex for pleasure and sought safe, effective contraceptives. Another significant way in which their worldviews contrasted with pro-life women was that they held a gradualist view of personhood—the embryo not viewed as a full human being until the stage at which it was viable or capable of sustaining its own life. Luker writes, "Once they had choices about life roles, they came to feel that they had a right to use abortion in order to control their own lives" (118).

The phrase "a woman's right to choose" reflects the movement's efforts to frame the debate as being about individual autonomy. In this construction, when a woman with an unwanted pregnancy is unable to obtain a safe and legal abortion, she is being forced into a state of compulsory pregnancy. Moreover, the pro-choice movement has asserted that criminalized abortion laws don't eliminate abortions; they never have and they never will. Women will continue to seek abortions—in other countries, in back alleys, from friends, or by trying to induce a miscarriage—and many will end up in hospitals with damaged uteruses and life-threatening infections.

In this battle to gain the upper hand in the debate, each side attempts to debunk the opposing frames. For example, the pro-choice movement calls out the "false equivalence" between abortion and murder and counterpunches that a woman should not be forced to incubate an "embryo" or a "fetus"—their preferred terminology. Both sides also use vilification techniques that contribute to further polarization (McCaffrey and Keys 2000). Abortion is frequently referred to as a "holocaust" by pro-life activists. Pro-choice groups have branded "pro-lifers" as "extremists" and "religious zealots" seeking to impose their morality into the law. The pro-choice movement has attempted to marginalize the pro-life movement by asserting that theirs is a minority view; a majority of Americans want to keep abortions legal, and most religions, even the Catholics, have pro-choice traditions (Maguire 2001). Trusting in women's ability to make complex decisions about their pregnancies is the bottom line for the pro-choice movement; because it is their bodies and their lives at stake, women must have the choice.

Although much of the pro-choice movement's political activism has focused on abortion laws and practices, there is a broader platform of "reproductive freedom," which includes contraception and the right to say no to sex. It also includes safety from forced sterilization but also access to surgical sterilization if desired. It means the right to have children and raise them with sufficient child care, health care, education, and income so they won't suffer in poverty. African American women were at the forefront of broadening the frame to an even more transformative vision of "reproductive justice," which recognizes that a woman's reproductive decisions are profoundly influenced by the conditions in her community. This intersectional understanding calls attention to persistent inequalities by age, class, race, and place of residence. Loretta Ross of SisterSong, founded in 1997, describes this as paradigm shift: "Instead of focusing on the means—a divisive debate on abortion and birth control that neglects the real—life experiences of women and girls—the reproductive justice analysis focuses on the ends—better lives for women, healthier families, and sustainable communities" (Ross n.d.).

Frames and Framing: Tools for Understanding Abortion Debates

The next chapter describes the range and depth of the abortion conflict in the United States by tracing several policy debates from the early 1970s to the present. A policy debate is a structured discussion that takes place in public arenas for the benefit of policy makers in government. Usually these debates focus on a particular proposal for a law; at other times the debates may pertain to the general approaches to public problems. On the agenda of U.S. federal and state governments are several issues that provoke debates that don't go away. Even though from time to time some government entity—a legislature or a court—makes a formal decision, the debate is not out of the picture and comes back. As long as there are substantial disagreements among groups with sufficient resources to make their views known, such debate will continue over new proposals as well as old proposals that are revisited. The abortion conflict is just this type of conflict. The question is firmly on the government's agenda; powerful activists who are interested in the issue disagree on what the issue is about and how to solve it, and the government has thus far not found a solution that will send the parties home.

Policy debates occur in arenas. Most policy arenas are attached to government institutions at the federal and state levels, such as legislatures, bureaucratic agencies, the courts, or the executive leaders. The arenas are large enough to encompass the expression of views by media, formal organizations, and mass publics. But individuals and organizations, as well as policy makers, are the major participants in these arenas when issues they are interested in or have responsibility for come up. Think of them as "policy actors." They could be spokespersons for social movement organizations like NARAL and the National Right to Life Committee; they could also be legislators and public intellectuals, for example. Their give-and-take on a topic reveals several things of interest in trying to understand what is going on. We can make sense of what they say by using the idea of "frames." We have already discussed collective action frames of social movements in which they present their comprehensive view of the problems and their solutions. Two other kinds of frames are important: strategic frames and issue frames.

Strategic frames show the way policy actors present their claims and goals for the policy debate. They usually consist of two types of statements. One is a definition of the problem showing there is something wrong and why government should act to fix it. This is sometimes referred to as the "diagnosis" part of the frame. The other part is the solution offered to the problem: what should be done, sometimes called the "prognosis." For social movements such as pro-choice and pro-life, strategic frames are excerpts from the more comprehensive collective action frames. However, the movement leaders adjust their frames to fit a particular policy debate and specific proposal. At times, for example, the pro-choice movement may choose not to emphasize a woman's right to control her body and instead talk about the dangers of criminalizing abortion. The latter frame may be more effective in winning support.

Issue frames show how the policy actors who are regular participants on the issue see the problem and solution. Often the issue frame is in the form of a confrontation. For example, we have seen that *Roe* established an issue frame that defined abortion as a question of women's privacy against the state's legitimate interest in protecting fetal life. So *Roe* not only settled, for a time, the policy outcome of the abortion repeal/reform campaign but also officially stated what the terms of debate about abortion would be: a matter between a woman and her doctor except for the period after viability. After that, the goal of the pro-life movement was to change that issue frame by presenting its own strategic frame about abortion. Before too long, the dominant issue frame changed, and the issue was defined as a conflict between women's right to privacy and the right of the unborn child to life.

The goal of many activists is to have their diagnosis and prognosis of the matter, that is, their strategic frame, be adopted as the official frame by the policy makers. A lot is at stake in these frames. Probably most evident is that the decision that results from a policy debate stems directly from the way the issue is defined by the policy makers. If a prognosis is ignored, there is little chance activists will get what they want. Equally important, however, is that the issue frame has a profound effect on who gets access to the policy arenas. By defining abortion as a medical matter in the 19th century, for example, women had no claim to be consulted or have a voice on the question of legal abortion because it was not "about them." However, when the repeal movement successfully claimed that abortion was a woman's issue and pertained to her rights and privacy, women were now part of the debate and guaranteed a place at the table. In the next chapter, we will follow the developing issue frames in various abortion debates stopping to note the official actions (cases, statutes, orders) along the way.

References

Beckwith, Francis J. *Politically Correct Death: Answering the Arguments for Abortion Rights*. Grand Rapids, MI: Baker Books, 1993.

Callahan, Sidney. "Abortion and the Sexual Agenda." In *The Ethics of Abortion: Pro-Life vs. Pro-Choice*, 3rd ed., edited by R. M. Baird and S. E. Rosenbaum, 167–178. Amherst, NY: Prometheus Books, 2001.

Davis, Nanette J. *From Crime to Choice: The Transformation of Abortion in America*. Westport, CT: Greenwood Press, 1985.

Dyer, Frederick. "Horatio Robinson Storer M.D. and the Physicians' Crusade against Abortion." *Life and Learning IX*, 1999. www.uffl.org/vol%209/dyer9.pdf (accessed February 5, 2018).

Fessler, Ann. *The Girls Who Went Away: The Hidden History of Women Who Surrendered Children for Adoption in the Decades before Roe V. Wade*. New York: Penguin, 2007.

Garrow, David J. *Liberty and Sexuality: The Right to Privacy and the Making of* Roe v. Wade. Berkeley: University of California Press, 1994.

Ginsburg, Faye D. *Contested lives: The Abortion Debate in an American Community*. Berkeley: University of California Press, 1998.

Ginsburg, Faye D. "Procreation Stories: Reproduction, Nurturance, and Procreation in the Life Narratives of

Abortion Activists." In *Gender in Cross Cultural Perspective*, 2nd ed., edited by Caroline B. Brettell and Carolyn F. Sargent, 426–440. Upper Saddle River, NJ: Prentice Hall, 1996.

Kaplan, Laura. *The Story of Jane: The Legendary Underground Feminist Abortion Service*. New York: Pantheon Books, 1996.

Kinsey, Alfred. *Sexual Behavior in the Human Female*. Bloomington: Indiana University Press, 1953.

Luker, Kristin. *Abortion and the Politics of Motherhood*. Berkeley: University of California Press, 1984.

Maguire, Daniel C. *Sacred Choices: The Right to Contraception and Abortion in the World's Religions*. Minneapolis, MN: Fortress Press, 2001.

McBride Stetson, Dorothy. "Abortion Policy Triads and Women's Rights in Russia, the United States and France." In *Abortion Politics*, edited by Marianne Githens and Dorothy McBride Stetson, 97–117. New York: Routledge, 1996.

McCaffrey, Dawn, and Jennifer Keys. "Competitive Framing Processes in the Abortion Debate: Polarization-Vilification, Frame Saving, and Frame Debunking." *The Sociological Quarterly* 41(1): 41–61, 2000.

Messer, Ellen, and E. Kathryn May. *Back Rooms: Voices from the Illegal Abortion Era*. New York: St. Martin's Press, 1994.

Mohr, James C. *Abortion in America: The Origins and Evolution of National Policy*. Oxford: Oxford University Press, 1978.

Morgen, Sandra. *Into Our Own Hands: The Women's Health Movement in the United States, 1969–1990*. New Brunswick, NJ: Rutgers University Press, 2002.

Munson, Ziad W. *The Making of Pro-Life Activists: How Social Movement Mobilization Works*. Chicago: University of Chicago Press, 2010.

Olasky, Marvin. *Abortion Rites: A Social History*. Wheaton, IL: Crossway Books, 1992.

Reagan, Leslie J. *When Abortion Was a Crime: Women, Medicine, and Law in the United States, 1867–73*. Berkeley: University of California Press, 1998.

Ross, Loretta. "What Is Reproductive Justice?" The Pro-Choice Public Education Project. http://www.protect choice.org/section.php?id=28 (accessed August 23, 2017).

Snow, David A., E. Burke Rochford Jr., Steven K. Worden, and Robert D. Benford. "Frame Alignment Processes, Micromobilization, and Movement Participation." *American Sociological Review* 51(4): 464–481, 1986.

Solinger, Rickie, ed. *Abortion Wars: A Half Century of Struggle, 1950–2000*. Berkeley: University of California Press, 1998.

Solinger, Rickie. *Wake Up Little Susie: Single Pregnancy and Race before Roe v. Wade*. New York: Routledge, 2013.

Staggenborg, Suzanne. *The Pro-Choice Movement. Organization and Activism in the Abortion Conflict*. New York: Oxford University Press, 1991.

Tarrow, Sidney. *Power in Movement: Social Movements, Collective Action and Politics*. Cambridge, England: Cambridge University Press, 1994.

Wilder, Marcy J. "The Rule of Law, the Rise of Violence, and the Role of Morality: Reframing America's Abortion Debate." In *Abortion Wars: A Half Century of Struggle, 1959–2000*, edited by Rickie Solinger, 73–94. Berkeley: University of California Press, 1998.

2   Problems, Controversies, and Solutions

Introduction

The abortion war in the United States wages on many fronts. It is not simply a showdown between pro-life and pro-choice forces over the constitutional legality of abortion, though that is one of the major clashes. At the core of the conflict are fundamentally different worldviews. This chapter covers a range of disputes and assesses who appears to be winning and losing. Special attention will be given to the "strategic frames," which are the ways that a social movement presents its agenda to the public, including a definition of the problem or the "diagnosis" part of the frame and the solution or the "prognosis" about what should be done. These battles take place in many different arenas—in the courts, federal agencies, Congress, state legislatures, election campaigns, and on the front lines. Arguments erupt in the media, as well as in communities and families.

What else are the combatants fighting about? The list is long. How should abortion be regulated? This chapter explores the

---

Pro-life and pro-choice activists demonstrate outside the Supreme Court on June 20, 2016, in advance of the landmark *Whole Woman's Health v. Hellerstedt* (579 U.S.___2016) decision, which struck down restrictive regulations on abortion providers in Texas. Their signs illustrate the competing frames crafted by social movement organizations in the abortion debate. Some make demands like NARAL's slogan "Keep Clinics Open," while others profess identity like Students for Life's slogan, "I Am the Pro-Life Generation." Resonant frames promote movement solidarity. (AP Photo/ Alex Brandon)

labyrinth of rules about spousal notification, parental consent, informed consent, waiting periods, facilities, and licensing. What role should the government play in funding and supporting abortion? We will see how increased political polarization fuels ongoing debates over the Hyde Amendment and the funding of family planning programs both globally and domestically. Ultimately, whose rights should be paramount? Fighting for fetal rights, the pro-life movement has sought to criminalize "partial-birth abortion" and infanticide, late-term abortions, prenatal drug use, and third-party fetal killing. Pro-life advocates see these measures as protections for society's most vulnerable, but from a pro-choice perspective, these encroachments represent a dangerous slippery slope of policing and controlling women's bodies. Fighting for women's rights, the pro-choice movement has pursued medical advances like the abortion pill and emergency contraception. It has also had to devote resources to debunking inaccurate medical information and to stemming violence against abortion providers. Reproductive justice advocates call attention to the importance of safeguarding abortion access and a broader vision of reproductive rights for all women, regardless of their age, socioeconomic status, or geographic region and for women in the military, prisons, and immigration detention facilities. We must not lose sight of the lived and stigmatized experience of these women who are caught in this political crossfire.

The chapter concludes with the critical question: why is it so difficult to find any common ground? Reducing the number of abortions and teen pregnancies seems like it could be a unifying goal, but the oppositional worldviews dictate divergent approaches to both sex education and birth control. In her book *When Sex Goes to School*, Luker (2006) shows how the two sides disagree on basic questions about human nature and the kind of society in which they want to live. According to sexual conservatives, American culture is saturated with sexually explicit messages that encourage adolescents to prematurely engage in sexual activity, leading to higher rates of promiscuity, disease, pregnancies, and abortions. The solution or prognosis in the pro-life frame to teen pregnancy is abstinence-only education to promote personal responsibility and commitment to marriage. In contrast, sexual liberals champion "safe sex" as a means for promoting sexual health and autonomy. Accordingly, the pro-choice strategic frame diagnoses the problem as the expansion of programs that disregard the realities of premarital sexual activity and have been proven to be ineffective. Their solution is shame-free comprehensive sex education in the schools.

Who is winning? The rate of teen pregnancy has dropped dramatically—67 percent since 1991 to a record low in 2016 of 20.3 births per 1,000 women aged 15–19, according to the Centers for Disease Control and Prevention (CDC). Pro-life claims some credit for more young people abstaining and pro-choice for comprehensive sex education, long-acting reversible contraceptives, and emergency contraception, though there are other factors that have contributed to the reduction like the struggling economy (Patten and Livingston 2016) and even the MTV show *16 and Pregnant* (Kearney and Levine 2014). In terms of which is the more effective curriculum, many studies have found that abstinence-only-until-marriage or sexual risk avoidance programs are scientifically unsound, are ineffective in delaying onset of sexual intercourse, and proffer medically inaccurate and stigmatizing information (Santelli et al. 2017). In terms of funding, however, the pro-life camp now has the upper hand. The Office of Adolescent Health Teen Pregnancy Prevention Program (TPP) was established in 2010 under the Obama administration to implement evidence-based TPP programs. In September 2017, Trump administration unilaterally cut TPP's budget by over $213 million (Lander and Smith-Lin 2017).

Access to birth control was celebrated as a key part of women's liberation from the tyranny of perpetual childbearing, making it possible for women to carefully plan for motherhood, while advancing their own educational and career goals.

In sharp contrast, the pro-life diagnostic frame views the widespread use of contraception as both cause and consequence of a general moral decline; when sex is detached from reproduction, it leads to the devaluation of its sacred purpose of creating life. In the words of GOP presidential candidate, Rick Santorum, who spoke out in 2012 as a Catholic on the dangers of contraception: "It's not okay. It's a license to do things in a sexual realm that is counter to how things are supposed to be" (Scherer 2012). Since the 1980s, the official Catholic doctrine on birth control has found a more central place in the pro-life movement and on the agenda of social conservatives.

In 2010, at the midpoint of President Obama's first term, Republicans took control of the House and expanded their influence in the Senate, and socially conservative Republicans began to go after contraception more openly. They proposed legislation to grant legal personhood to fertilized human eggs, which could outlaw hormonal birth control or devices that prevent implantation, along with bills that would allow employers to refuse health insurance coverage for birth control on religious grounds. The Population Institute (2017) compiled a report titled "Senseless: The War on Birth Control" to call attention to these attacks and to underscore the many positive benefits of birth control. At first the pro-choice movement expressed a mixture of disbelief and alarm, as Cecile Richards, president of Planned Parenthood, put it in her 2012 speech to the Democratic National Convention, "It's like we woke up in a bad episode of Mad Men." But then there was a big win for defenders of religious freedom with the 2014 U.S. Supreme Court ruling, *Burwell v. Hobby Lobby Stores, Inc.* (573 U.S.), which allowed private companies to refuse to provide health insurance coverage for birth control that conflicted with their stated religious principles. In a predictable play to his conservative base, President Trump eliminated President Obama's Affordable Care Act's contraceptive mandate in 2017. This is part of his broader pledge to "not allow people of faith to be targeted, bullied or silenced anymore" (Vitali 2017). It is estimated that hundreds of thousands of women could lose benefits. Each issue we examine in this chapter has its own story of conflicting perceptions and victories and defeats, which illustrates the fascinating complexity of movement-countermovement dynamics.

Constitutional Legality of Abortion

The Supreme Court's landmark decision that the Constitution includes a right to seek abortion was a triumph to some and a tremendous shock to others. The pro-life movement quickly mobilized; leaders sought to restore the world as they knew it before January 23, 1973. When the Supreme Court, the highest court in the land, rules on the meaning of the Constitution, those who oppose its ruling have only two options. Neither is quick or easy. The first is to work to pass an amendment to the Constitution itself. The founders who drafted the document made it very difficult to change. It takes two-thirds approval of both the House of Representatives and the Senate and ratification by three-fourths of the states—38 state legislatures. There is another method—never used successfully—whereby two-thirds of the states would call for a convention to amend the Constitution.

The second option is a litigation strategy to convince the Court to change its ruling. This too is difficult because of the importance of precedent, or stare decisis, in U.S. law. This means official interpretations of laws by the Supreme Court are the law of the land—all courts, including the Supreme Court itself, decide other cases that come before it with respect to the way the courts did before. Of course, the Supreme Court does occasionally overturn a precedent, but that is often many years after the initial decision. The justices accept that conditions and times change and that their rulings must also change. A major condition for overturning precedent is that the members of the Court have changed. The newer justices may feel less bound by the decisions of their predecessors. Each side carefully monitors and does all that it can to influence the balance of the Court.

Amending the Constitution

In an immediate response to *Roe v. Wade*, members of Congress submitted 18 proposals to amend the Constitution to supersede the ruling and a couple of regular bills to prohibit abortion (Packwood 1992). Some form of the Human Life Amendment has been introduced in every Congress to this day. These proposals have taken three forms:

1. To outlaw abortion directly except to save the life of the mother
2. To extend the constitutional definition of person to all human beings from conception
3. To give the states the power to criminalize abortion, the so-called states' rights amendments

Most of the congressional consideration of these amendments took place in the 1970s and early 1980s. Congress heard presentations from pro-life and pro-choice advocates but was reluctant to act. Pro-life activists campaigned at the state level for a constitutional convention and kept pressure on Congress. Beginning in 1974, they staged what would become an annual "March for Life," where they would distribute roses to all members to symbolize the babies murdered by legal abortion. The 1998 march featured Dr. Bernard Nathanson, founder of NARAL, and Norma McCorvey, the plaintiff in *Roe v. Wade*, who had, over time, come to see the horrors of abortion. In 2018, for the first time ever, a sitting president addressed the March for Life participants. In a speech delivered via satellite, President Donald J. Trump described it as a "movement born out of love."

Another opportunity for congressional consideration of a constitutional anti-abortion amendment opened when Republicans took the Senate and the presidency in 1981, and pro-life supporters held key positions in both the administration and the Senate committees. Senator Jesse Helms's bill got the first attention: "The paramount right to life is vested in each human being from the moment of fertilization without regard to age, health, or condition of dependency" (97th Cong., 1st Sess. [1981]). This was followed by Senator Orrin Hatch's constitutional amendment proposal: "A right to abortion is not secured by this Constitution. The Congress and the several States all have the concurrent power to restrict and prohibit abortions" (97th Cong., 1st Sess. [1981]). The extensive hearings on the Helms bill gave leaders of both the pro-choice and pro-life movements a platform to present their views on whether abortion should remain legal. But the most important effect was to focus the debate on the status of the fetus. To address the eternal question of when does human life begin, the pro-life strategy was to claim that it is a scientific rather than a moral question. They wanted that answer to be codified into law.

According to the pro-life frame, modern biology had discovered that every human life begins at fertilization; this is the stage at which the conceptus formed by the sperm and egg cells has the complete genetic information necessary to make it a member of the human species. Ultrasound technology enabled scientists and parents to observe this wondrous development. French geneticist Jérôme Lejeune, who is credited with discovering the chromosomal abnormality behind Down syndrome, testified before the U.S. Senate Judiciary Committee in 1981:

The baby plays, so to speak, on a trampoline! He bends his knees, pushes on the wall, soars up and falls down again. Because his body has the same buoyancy as the amniotic fluid, he does not feel gravity and performs his dance in a very slow, graceful, and elegant way, impossible in any other place on the Earth. . . . We now know what he feels, we have listened to what he hears, smelled what he tastes and we have really seen him dancing full of grace and youth. Science has turned the fairy tale of Tom Thumb into a true story, the one each of us has lived in the womb of his mother. ("When Does Human Life Begin?" Available at https://www.principlesandchoices.com/students/quick-code-library/pcs344/)

Lejeune also chaired the French anti-abortion movement called "Let Them Live." For those who are pro-life, it is no longer a matter of opinion—actual human life begins at conception, and the unborn baby is equal to all other human beings.

Since the pro-life strategic frame ventured into the terrain of science, the pro-choice advocates countered their claim by calling on experts such as Leon E. Rosenberg, a professor of genetics at Yale. He did not quibble with Lejeune's observations but rather pointed out that the phrase "actual human life" is not a scientific term. It is true that the fertilized egg is a potential human life, but when it becomes "actual" is not determined by science. Some say it is conception, others say when there is brain function, and still others say when the fetus moves and looks like a baby or when it can live outside the uterus. The embryo development process is continuous; no definite break exists where one can say it is actual human life after and not before. As Rosenberg argued, "I maintain that the concepts such as humanness are beyond the purview of science because no idea about them can be tested experimentally" (Rosenberg's testimony, reprinted in *The Miami Herald*, May 3, 1981, 1).

Although the Judiciary Committee had recommended both pieces of legislation to the full Senate, neither the Helms bill nor the Hatch amendment passed. A Republican senator from Oregon, Robert Packwood, filibustered by reading a book on the history of abortion until both were withdrawn. The Human Life Amendment would become the standard term for hundreds of proposals in the following years, which would have the effect of overturning *Roe v. Wade*. The "Hatch-Eagleton" version of the amendment did get a full floor debate in 1983, but it was defeated 49–50, falling 18 short of the 67 required for passage. The pro-life forces could, nonetheless, claim a victory. They successfully reframed the abortion debate as a matter of the personhood and thus life of the fetus versus the privacy of women.

Changing the Court

The pro-life movement agrees on the diagnosis that abortion is wrong, but they have not always agreed on the prognosis. While some activists focused on the solution of promoting a constitutional amendment, others took a more political approach. They mobilized their followers in the Republican Party to adopt a pro-life platform and to support Ronald Reagan for president. When Reagan took office in 1981, he was indebted to the pro-life movement and responsive to their demands to appoint pro-life justices. At the same time, pro-life activists worked in various states, lobbying legislatures to restrict access to abortion services. Pro-choice organizations challenged, and from 1973 through 1989, the Court struck down most of these restrictions and reiterated its ruling that states could not interfere in any way with women's right to privacy in securing abortions. However, after 1981, the majorities on the Court supporting *Roe* got smaller and smaller, and each case provided an opportunity to whittle away at *Roe*.

In 1981, President Reagan fulfilled his campaign promise with his first nomination to the Supreme Court—Sandra Day O'Connor—who became the first woman to serve. Her answers about abortion cases in the hearings were vague, but most assumed she would support the pro-life position. And indeed, in the first abortion case after her appointment, she joined the minority opposing the *Roe* position. In *City of Akron v. Akron Center for Reproductive Health* (462 U.S. 416, 1983), the Court struck down five sections of a city ordinance, including requiring parental consent and a 24-hour waiting period, because they restricted a woman's right to obtain an abortion. In her dissent, O'Connor said that given the changes in technology and improvements in neonatal care, *Roe*'s trimester approach was "on a collision course with itself." The anti-abortion tally on the Court was now three.

In 1986, Reagan nominated Antonin Scalia to the Supreme Court to replace William Rehnquist, who had been chief justice. Although Scalia had a well-known anti-abortion record as an attorney and as an appeals court judge, his nomination provoked little controversy. But his influence was soon felt. In *Thornburgh v. American College of Obstetricians & Gynecologists* (476 U.S. 747, 1986), the Reagan administration, for the first time, presented a brief asking the Court to reverse its position in *Roe v. Wade*. They made the point that they were not opposed to a constitutional right of privacy as put forth in *Griswold v. Connecticut* but that abortion was a special case because it involved the killing of an unborn child and was not a matter of privacy. The *Thornburgh* decision invalidated several regulations, including Pennsylvania's "informed consent" requirements, which were determined to "wholly subordinate constitutional privacy interests and concerns with maternal health." But this time the majority was 5–4, showing that the Court was one heartbeat away from reversing the *Roe* decision.

The pro-choice movement raised the stakes for the next candidate in 1987. Reagan nominated Robert Bork, someone who not only was anti-abortion but had written extensively against the rulings in *Griswold* and *Roe*, and against the entire idea of a constitutional right to privacy. The battle during the confirmation hearings was intense and widely publicized (Gitenstein 1992). Bork would replace a "swing" justice, Lewis Powell, who had supplied the crucial fifth vote to protect the right of abortion. The Senate refused to confirm Bork by a vote of 52–48. President Reagan then nominated Anthony Kennedy, who won confirmation with little trouble in 1988. Kennedy, like Scalia, is a Roman Catholic; thus, the pro-choice forces feared that the pro-life forces had finally achieved the majority that would undo *Roe*. Attention turned to the next challenge to state abortion restrictions to make its way to the Court for review: *Webster v. Reproductive Health Services* (492 U.S. 490, 1989). At issue was another set of hurdles women in Missouri would have to face to obtain services. In addition, that state had decreed that life begins at conception and that "unborn children have protectable interests in life, health, and well-being."

Once again, the Department of Justice, which was now under the leadership of President George H. W. Bush, urged the Court to overturn *Roe v. Wade*. Unlike *Thornburgh*, however, this time there was also a majority of justices in favor of sustaining the restrictions in the Missouri statute: Rehnquist, Scalia, Kennedy, and O'Connor as well as Justice Byron White.

Yet they did not speak with one voice about the status of the parent decision, *Roe v. Wade*. Scalia clearly asserted that he wanted to overturn the previous ruling and invited direct challenges from the states. O'Connor continued to question the trimester framework but said there would be time to reconsider *Roe* in the future. But the dissenting justices, especially Justice Harry Blackmun, who had written the *Roe* decision, sent out the warning that "a plurality of this Court implicitly invites every state legislature to enact more and more restrictive abortion regulations to provoke more and more test cases, in the hope that sometime down the line the Court will return the law of procreative freedom to the severe limitations that generally prevailed in this country before January 22, 1973." He went on: "I fear for the future. I fear for the liberty and equality of millions of women who have lived and come of age in the 16 years since *Roe* was decided" (492 U.S. 490, 539).

The *Webster* opinions spurred both pro-choice and pro-life groups into action. Pro-choice groups sent out the word that the Supreme Court now had the dreaded pro-life majority and that the next case could easily rob women of the rights they had been granted. Their leaders claimed that abortion would soon become a crime. Pro-life groups persuaded sympathetic state legislators to enact laws that would violate the *Roe* ruling to give the Court a chance to do what some justices promised—overturn *Roe v. Wade*. This was more successful in some states than others. Utah, for example, passed a very strict conditional law—abortion only for health of woman or fetal deformity. In Florida, Montana, Alaska, and California, on the other hand, pro-life proposals ran counter to guarantees of privacy in the state constitutions. Governors in Louisiana and Idaho vetoed new restrictions as probably unconstitutional. However, Pennsylvania's governor, Robert Casey, signed that state's new law, which put in place five new hurdles for women seeking abortions: special informed consent of woman seeking abortion, parental consent for minors with judicial bypass, notification of husband, compulsory anti-abortion lecture by a doctor

24 hours in advance of the procedure, and stringent reporting requirements for facilities providing abortions. A challenge to this Pennsylvania law by Planned Parenthood made its way to the Supreme Court. And it was this case—*Planned Parenthood v. Casey*—that many thought would be the crucial test for *Roe*, especially when Clarence Thomas replaced Justice Thurgood Marshall—one of the *Roe* majority in 1991. Thomas was questioned during his confirmation hearings about his views on the abortion case, but he had no written record and claimed he had never discussed *Roe* with anyone. Nevertheless, because he was a conservative attorney appointed by the pro-life George H. W. Bush administration, pro-choice activists counted the votes on the Court to add up to an anti-*Roe* majority for the first time.

Facing the inevitable, the attorneys for Planned Parenthood formally asked the Court to take the opportunity in this Pennsylvania case to either affirm the right to abortion as a fundamental constitutional right or overturn the *Roe* decision altogether. They wanted to confront what they feared might be a gradual erosion of abortion rights. The Bush administration lawyers were not as keen to make this case the final test of *Roe* before the 1992 presidential elections, where President Bush would be challenged by Governor Bill Clinton—a pro-choice politician. As a backup strategy, pro-choice movement leaders had joined with allies in Congress to promote the Freedom of Choice Act (FOCA) to codify the ruling in *Roe:* "A State may not restrict the right of a woman to choose to terminate a pregnancy (1) before fetal viability; or (2) at any time, if such termination is necessary to protect the life or health of the woman." If the Court overturned *Roe*, then they would push this act through Congress, figuring there would be sufficient support once people realized that otherwise abortion would become criminalized again. They also planned to make this a major issue in the presidential campaign, especially if President Bush vetoed the FOCA.

Both sides looked to the Court's decision in the Pennsylvania case with anticipation and some dread. When the Court announced the outcome, neither side could claim a victory. The pro-choice camp was disappointed that the Court upheld all but one—the requirement of husband's notification—of the administrative hurdles and invited the states to enact more. The pro-life camp was unhappy that the Court did not overturn the *Roe* ruling; even more frustrating was that the plurality uphold-ing it included Justice O'Connor, one of Reagan's appointees, and Justice David Souter, appointed by President George H. W. Bush in 1990. Both pro-life and pro-choice organizations publicly criticized the ruling. Perhaps that meant the Court had struck a compromise between the women's rights and lib-erty and the fetus's right to life. The ruling and the opinions were complicated. No opinion was signed by a majority of the justices, but there was an outcome:

1. A majority of the justices confirmed the Court's central ruling in *Roe v. Wade*: "A recognition of the right of the woman to choose to have an abortion before viability and to obtain it without undue interference from the state" (505 U.S. 833, 846).

2. A plurality of the justices agreed that the trimester frame-work was no longer in force. The place to draw the line with respect to states' power to prohibit abortion would be viability.

3. Justices agreed that prior to viability the state could put administrative hurdles in place as long as these did not con-stitute an "undue burden" on a woman's liberty. "A finding of an undue burden is a shorthand for the conclusion that a state regulation has the purpose or effect of placing a sub-stantial obstacle in the path of a woman seeking an abor-tion of a nonviable fetus" (505 U.S. 833, 877).

The *Planned Parenthood v. Casey* decision cooled the turmoil over *Roe v. Wade* for more than a decade. Pro-choice leaders pursued the FOCA, but many members of Congress did not want to go on record for a woman's right to choose. At the same time President Bill Clinton appointed two pro-*Roe* justices to the Court: justices Ruth Bader Ginsburg in 1993 and Stephen Breyer in 1994. The movements turned their attention to other debates until another pro-life president, President George W. Bush, took office in 2001. Activists calculated the ages of the justices, thinking about who would be likely to retire during the second Bush administration.

In 2000, the Supreme Court heard the case of *Stenberg v. Carhart* (530 U.S. 914), which examined a Nebraska law that made it a felony for a doctor to "partially deliver vaginally a living unborn child before killing the . . . child." The complicated 5–4 ruling struck down state bans on partial-birth abortions on the grounds that these were unconstitutionally vague and violated the liberty protected by due process of the Fourteenth Amendment. Justice Scalia's impassioned dissent was notable:

> The method of killing a human child—one cannot even accurately say an entirely unborn human child—proscribed by this statute is so horrible that the most clinical description of it evokes a shudder of revulsion. . . . It is a value judgment, dependent upon how much one respects (or believes society ought to respect) the life of a partially delivered fetus, and how much one respects (or believes society ought to respect) the freedom of the woman who gave it life to kill it. Evidently, the five Justices in today's majority value the former less, or the latter more, (or both), than the four of us in dissent. Case closed.

Justice Rehnquist who had joined Justice Scalia in the dissent and Justice O'Connor who had been part of the majority both retired from the Court in 2005.

The Senate Judiciary Committee held public hearings on President George W. Bush's replacements, John Roberts in 2005 and Samuel Alito in 2006, which drew wide attention because the nominees once again had the potential to shift the Court to an anti-*Roe* majority. Even before the new justices were confirmed, state governments were preparing to pass laws that would violate the *Roe* guidelines. The first to do so was South Dakota. The governor signed the Women's Health and Human Life Protection Act in late 2005 criminalizing all abortions except when the pregnancy is a direct threat to the mother's life. The statute also declares that life begins at conception and that the "guarantee of due process of law under the Constitution of South Dakota applies equally to born and unborn human beings, and that under the Constitution of South Dakota, a pregnant mother and her unborn child, each possess a natural and inalienable right to life" (South Dakota 2006, sec. 1). Throughout the act the fetus is referred to as an "unborn human being." Persons who perform abortions may be prosecuted, but the woman seeking the abortion may not. Most observers expected that pro-choice organizations, such as Planned Parenthood and the Center for Reproductive Rights, would immediately challenge the constitutionality of the statute; instead, they first organized a campaign for repeal, which was successful. In 2006 elections, the restrictive criminal abortion law was rescinded by a voter referendum, which stole from pro-life activists the opportunity to appear before the new Court.

For the first time in 2007, the Supreme Court, in a 5–4 decision, approved abortion restrictions that did not include an exception for women's health. The case, *Gonzales v. Carhart* (550 U.S. 124), determined the federal Partial Birth Abortion Ban Act to be constitutional. President William J. Clinton had vetoed this bill twice, but President George W. Bush signed it in 2003, outlawing the intact dilation and extraction procedure even in cases where the woman's life was in danger. In the dissent, Justice Ginsburg wrote, "The notion that the Partial-Birth Abortion Ban Act furthers any legitimate governmental interest is, quite simply, irrational . . . the Court's defense of it, cannot be understood as anything other than an effort to chip away at a right declared again and again by this Court—and with increasing comprehension of its centrality to women's lives."

The balance of the Court shifted again when President Barack Obama appointed justices Sonia Sotomayor in 2009 and Elena Kagan in 2010. In 2016, they would join justices Anthony Kennedy, Ruth Bader Ginsburg, and Stephen Breyer in the 5–3 ruling in *Whole Woman's Health v. Hellerstedt*, which struck down provisions of Texas's House Bill 2. The Court ruled that the supposed medical benefits of hospital admitting privileges for abortion providers and ambulatory surgical center standards for clinics did not outweigh the burdens placed on women exercising their constitutional right to an abortion. Time will tell, but the expectation is that the most recently appointed Justice, Neil Gorsuch, appointed in 2017 to replace Scalia, will align with the conservative leaning on the Court—Clarence Thomas (1991), Chief Justice John Roberts (2005), and Samuel Alito (2006) to deliver on President Donald J. Trump's campaign pledge to overturn *Roe v. Wade*.

State Regulation of Abortion

After states were prohibited from criminalizing abortion in 1973, a central strategy of the pro-life movement became lobbying states to enact laws that would limit the practice of abortion and women's access to the procedure. Early on, the Court tended to see most of these requirements as unconstitutionally designed to interfere with women's privacy. But as time passed and the membership in the Court changed to reflect the pro-life perspectives of the administration and Congress, the hurdles passed judicial scrutiny. As noted in the discussion of *Planned Parenthood v. Casey* decision, the Court has ruled such regulations to be constitutional unless they place an undue burden on women's liberty in seeking abortions. This section reviews efforts to erect and dismantle administrative hurdles including spousal notification, parental consent, informed consent, waiting periods, facilities, and licensing.

In the 1970s, pro-life activists lobbied for regulations that required a woman, if married, to receive her husband's consent to obtain an abortion. They argued that the father has an interest in the life of his unborn child. The pro-choice response was that because pregnancy had a major impact on women's lives and health, a woman should not have to inform or gain the consent of anyone and the Supreme Court has agreed. In the 1970s, the justices ruled that because the only time the husband's consent would be significant would be to deny a woman the right to choose abortion, and because even the state did not have that authority, it could not grant such an authority to a husband. Another strategy was to promote spousal notification. Pro-life groups aligned with fathers' rights groups that encouraged men to file restraining orders when they believed a woman was trying to terminate a pregnancy that they had fathered. None of these efforts was successful. In *Planned Parenthood v. Casey*, the justices rejected only one of the five administrative hurdles in the Pennsylvania statute: the requirement that a wife notify her husband before obtaining an abortion. The justices noted: "It is an inescapable biological fact that state regulation with respect to the child a woman is carrying will have a far greater impact on the mother's liberty than on the father's. . . . The court has held that, when the wife and the husband disagree on this decision, the view of only one of the two marriage partners can prevail. In as much as it is the woman who physically bears the child and who is the more directly and immediately affected by the pregnancy, as between the two, the balance weighs in her favor" (505 U.S. 833, 896). Although this particular issue has been quiet, one can find new stories like this one: in February 2017, Arkansas governor Asa Hutchinson signed the Unborn Child Protection from Dismemberment Abortion Act, directed at second-trimester abortions and with no exception in cases of rape, which includes a clause that allows a husband to sue the doctor to stop his wife's abortion if he is the father of the child.

Pro-life activists were successful with parental consent laws because they could frame the issue as a matter of parental rights and responsibility—if doctors cannot prescribe an antibiotic without a parent's permission, why should they be allowed to perform an abortion on a girl without her parent at least knowing about it? Taking this a step further—the Child Custody Protection Act would make it a federal crime for anyone who is not the parent to transport a minor across state lines to obtain an abortion. This legislation was first proposed in 2000 and most recently reintroduced in 2017 (S.1173). Pro-life proponents have argued that it is primarily adult men who impregnate and then transport the minors to circumvent the parental notification laws. The most effective pro-choice counterargument has proved to be the warning that under this law grandmothers would be arrested for helping their granddaughters. More broadly, the pro-choice framing of parental consent laws has been that these deprive young women of their constitutional rights to privacy and equality. They are also a hardship for girls from dysfunctional homes. What if her legal guardian is incarcerated or she is a victim of abuse or incest? Or what if she is too afraid to disclose the pregnancy and seeks an illegal abortion or self-induces one instead? The pro-choice movement cited examples of individual girls who suffered fatal consequences like Becky Bell who was too ashamed to tell her parents about her pregnancy and botched abortion; she died of infection in 1988. Her parents blamed Indiana's parental consent laws and began a crusade to raise awareness about the law's harmful effects.

The Supreme Court has determined that parental consent and notification laws are constitutionally permitted if there is a "judicial bypass" procedure for hardship cases. As the 1979 case, *Bellotti v. Baird*, stated: "We therefore conclude that if a State decides to require a pregnant minor to obtain one or both parents' consent to an abortion, it also must provide an alternative procedure whereby authorization for the abortion can be obtained" (443 U.S. 622, 643). Today 37 states require some parental involvement for minors to get an abortion, and 36 of these follow the Court's requirement to have a judicial bypass procedure (to learn more, see Guttmacher Institute 2018, "Parental Involvement in Minors' Abortions"). Silverstein's

(2007) *Girls on the Stand: How Courts Fail Pregnant Minors* documents flaws in this system—many courts are ignorant of their responsibilities, callers have been referred to anti-abortion crisis pregnancy centers, and some judges unilaterally deny petitions. The American Civil Liberties Union (n.d.) contends that these laws will not "convert abusive, dysfunctional families into stable and supportive ones. The laws simply give pregnant adolescents from unhappy homes difficult options at a difficult time in their lives." These laws are especially onerous and confusing to teens in the foster care system, whose parents are incarcerated or undocumented, and for whom English is a second language. Texas's Jane's Due Process and the Louisiana Judicial Bypass Project provide step-by-step guides for navigating these intimidating requirements.

Another type of regulation promoted by the pro-life movement is to require women, now in 35 states, to receive counseling to ensure that the decision to have an abortion is voluntary and based on complete information. Much like the American Medical Association in the 1800s, the pro-life movement is operating on the premise that women who seek abortions are unaware of fetal development and what the abortion procedure entails, including its effects on themselves and the fetus. Informed consent is a fundamental principle in medicine; however, some of the messages that must be conveyed to women are highly contested: as part of compulsory pre-abortion counseling, 6 states mandate that women be told that personhood begins at conception, and 13 states require that women be told that their fetuses may or will feel pain. A waiting period after the counseling is imposed in 27 states, ostensibly to allow the woman to carefully consider what she has learned but also to add another barrier that might ultimately deter her from proceeding. Typically, the wait time is 24 hours, but five states have extended the waiting period to 72 hours—South Dakota does not allow weekends and holidays to be included in the count (to learn more, see Guttmacher Institute 2018, "Counseling and Waiting Periods for Abortions").

The pro-choice movement has framed these requirements as harassment of women who are facing the difficult decision to end their pregnancies and has argued that imposed delays is unfair to women who must adjust work schedules, arrange child care, or travel long distances. In addition, they have sought to expose the distribution of scientifically unsubstantiated information. In the 1992 *Casey* decision, the Supreme Court ruled that pre-abortion counseling and waiting periods are not undue burdens and are thus constitutional, and it has upheld laws that require specific information provided it is "truthful and nonmisleading."

Compulsory ultrasounds have been even more controversial. Eleven states mandate this procedure and three states—Louisiana, Texas, and Wisconsin—have taken this a step further by requiring the doctor to show and describe the image to the woman seeking an abortion (to learn more, see Guttmacher Institute 2018, "Requirements for Ultrasound"). The assumption is that this image will deter women, but does it? In a study by Gatter, Kimport, Foster, Weitz, and Upadhyay (2014), 98.4 percent of women who viewed an ultrasound continued with their plan to terminate. Only among the 7.4 percent of women who reported medium- or low-decision certainty about having an abortion was ultrasound viewing significantly associated with continuing the pregnancy. Given that two-thirds of pregnancies are terminated at eight weeks or earlier, a transvaginal ultrasound probe may be necessary—some have described this a forced intrusion tantamount to state rape. Weitz (2013) cautions against vilifying the probe, because the procedure makes it possible to detect pregnancies as early as four weeks, which can both give women more time to decide and still have the option of a medical abortion. Moreover, priming women to view the medical probe in a negative light could exacerbate distress. Weitz is similarly data driven in her response to the pro-life side; her research with the University of California San Francisco, Advancing New Standards in Reproductive Health, demonstrates that many women who voluntarily viewed the ultrasound image found it helpful in confirming their decision to terminate. She asserts that this hyperbolic rhetoric distracts from the real reasons why mandated ultrasounds are wrong, which is that these increase the costs, diminish patient autonomy, make it harder to provide abortion care, and most critically do not improve women's health outcomes.

The pro-life strategy of quietly increasing licensing requirements for abortion providers, which began in the mid-1990s, accelerated after 2010. Targeted Regulation of Abortion Providers (TRAP) laws is the label invoked by reproductive health advocates to call attention to this imposing of what they view as cumbersome and inappropriately stringent standards onto abortion clinics. Pro-choice advocates assert that these misapplied measures far exceed what is medically necessary to ensure patient safety and contend that these are nothing more than politically motivated attempts to shut down abortion clinics. An often-cited example is that clinics have had to make costly renovations to widen the width of the corridors to allow two medical gurneys to pass in a highly unlikely emergency scenario. A study by Upadhyay et al. (2015) demonstrated that only 1 of 5,491 cases (0.03 percent, n = 15) required ambulance transfers to emergency rooms on the day of the abortion. Despite Senator Wendy Davis's 11-hour filibuster to stop Texas House Bill 2, the omnibus TRAP law passed, which led to the closing of 22 of the 41 abortion clinics in the state. In 2016, the Supreme Court struck it down in a 5–3 decision. It determined that ambulatory surgical center requirements and hospital admitting privileges for abortion providers were unnecessary to ensure patient safety; an excerpt from the *Whole Woman's Health v. Hellerstedt* (579 U.S.) decision is included in Chapter 5. In response, acting president and senior counsel of Americans United for Life (AUL), Clarke Forsythe, lamented that "in striking down these commonsense requirements, the Supreme Court has essentially accepted the abortion industry's argument that it should be allowed to keep its profits high and patient care standards low" (AUL 2016). Twenty-three states still unduly regulate abortion providers; 16 states maintain onerous licensing standards; and 19 specify the sizes of procedure rooms and corridors and mandate that abortion providers be near and have relationships with hospitals. In Mississippi, the clinician must be either a board-certified obstetrician-gynecologist or eligible for certification (to learn more, see Guttmacher Institute 2018, "Targeted Regulation of Abortion Providers").

Government Support of Abortion

Political Polarization

Before 1973, differences between Democrats and Republicans in their views about abortion were not distinct. That is, in both parties, there were those opposed to legalization of abortion and those in favor of reform and repeal. That changed in the 1970s when Republicans became the "pro-life party" and the Democrats became the "pro-choice party." Economic conservatives formed an alliance with the Christian Right to rebuild the Republican Party, starting in southern and western states where they stood a good chance of making inroads. Candidates began to appeal to these new voters for their support, and the Republican strategists used the abortion debate as a wedge issue in state and national elections. Passing a Human Life Amendment to overcome the *Roe v. Wade* ruling and electing Ronald Reagan to the presidency in 1980 where he could push their agenda forward were top priorities. To be acceptable to Reagan as a vice president candidate, George H. W. Bush became a staunch opponent of legal abortion. Pro-choice Republicans started to lose elections, even those who were incumbents of long standing (Packwood 1992).

At the same time, pro-choice movement activists, many of them feminists, became increasingly active in the Democratic Party. They were not happy that President Jimmy Carter, a born-again Christian, had been able to win the presidency in

1976; he consistently opposed pro-choice proposals, including the use of Medicaid funding for abortion. After that the Democratic Party adopted a pro-choice plank in its platform and nominated only pro-choice candidates for president. These candidates were not successful in gaining the White House, however, until 1992 when Bill Clinton defeated the incumbent George H. W. Bush, partly on the abortion issue. This election took place in the wake of the debate over the unsuccessful 1987 Supreme Court nomination of Robert Bork and the 1989 *Webster* decision that mobilized millions of pro-choice voters.

Early in the 2008 election campaign, the candidates tried to steer clear of the culture wars and wedge issues. That changed when the Republican candidate, John McCain selected his running mate, Sarah Palin, an evangelical Christian and a mother of a child with special needs who believes that abortion should be illegal even in cases of rape and incest. To rally their conservative base, Palin portrayed the Democratic candidate, Barack Obama, as a pro-abortion radical. At a Pennsylvania campaign stop, she claimed, "As a state senator, Barack Obama wouldn't even stand up for the rights of infants born alive during an abortion. These infants, often babies with special needs, are simply left to die" (Scherer 2008). Palin appeared to be referring to no votes to that Obama cast against a Born-Alive Infants Protection Acts that would have in his judgment undermined abortion rights.

Fast-forwarding to the 2016 election: the parties remain officially divided on the abortion issue. In the third debate, the candidates finally squared off on the topic of abortion. Donald Trump appealed to pro-life voters by characterizing Hillary Clinton's views on late-term abortions as extreme: "With what Hillary is saying, in the ninth month, you can take the baby and rip the baby out of the womb of the mother just prior to the birth of the baby. Now, you can say that that's okay, and Hillary can say that that's okay, but that's not okay with me" (Tinker 2016). His ghastly characterization was reminiscent of the fiery rhetoric over partial-birth abortion, and such explosive language is difficult to counter. Clinton took a different tone by saying, "I have met with women who toward the end of their pregnancy get the worst news one could get, that their health is in jeopardy if they continue to carry to term or that something terrible has happened or just been discovered about the pregnancy" (Tinker 2016). Her framing of this difficult situation as women's health issue resonated with her pro-choice supporters.

It is important to keep in mind that the platforms do not bind legislators to vote in a particular way; nor do they reflect the views of all party activists, as the existence of organizations like the Republican Majority for Choice and Democrats for Life of America attests. Research has shown a close relationship among party identification, voting, and opinion on the abortion issue (Jelen and Wilcox 2003). However, it is not clear whether people vote Democratic and Republican because of their views on the abortion issue or whether their views on the abortion issue are shaped by their identity with the Republican or Democratic Party. In the 2016 presidential election, fewer than half of voters reported that abortion would be a "very important" in their vote; the economy and terrorism topped the list of important issues according to the Pew Research Center (2016).

Hyde Amendment

As part of their strategy to prevent as many abortions as possible, pro-life leaders have worked with Republican administrations and their allies in Congress and in state legislatures to eliminate any government support to women seeking abortions. This has had an impact on poor women, as well as federal prison inmates, Native Americans covered by the Indian Health Service (IHS), Peace Corps volunteers, military personnel, federal employees, and low-income women living in the District of Columbia. The Hyde Amendment was introduced for the first time in 1974; it was part of the pro-life campaign to reverse the effects of legal abortion. It was named after Congress member Republican Henry Hyde of Illinois, who came up with the strategy of prohibiting government funding of abortion by attaching a rider to the annual appropriations bill for Medicaid, the federal-state health insurance program for low-income and needy people. Hyde expressed his true desire in the debate: "I certainly would like to prevent, if I could legally, anybody having an abortion, a rich woman, a middle-class woman, or a poor woman. Unfortunately, the only vehicle available is the . . . Medicaid bill" (Boonstra 2007). Henry Hyde retired from Congress at the end of 2006, but his legacy lives on.

The general pro-life argument is that many people who oppose abortion do not want their tax dollars to pay for or facilitate the killing of unborn human beings. The debates brought the place of the fetus as a human being to the fore, making it part of the issue frame. This challenged the frame that abortion is a matter of women's privacy to decide, as put forth in *Roe v. Wade*. This pro-life frame has limits because the government funds many things some taxpayers dislike and could hardly justify not funding all of them. In opposing the Hyde Amendment, the pro-choice movement places poor women at the center of the strategic frame, arguing that the denial of Medicaid funding is discriminatory, and government has a responsibility to ensure the equal rights of all citizens. Further, poor women will resort to desperate measures to end their pregnancies subjecting them to risks of infection and death or be forced to bring children into the world that would sink their family further into deep poverty. The Supreme Court has rejected their claims, ruling the Hyde Amendment a constitutional use of government spending power and ruling that there is no constitutional responsibility to pay for health care. Further, poor women have no constitutional right to have an abortion—only to seek abortion. Denying them Medicaid funding does not interfere with this right to seek abortion. Finally, the Constitution does not prohibit governments from passing laws that affect the poor differently (*Beal v. Doe* 432 U.S. 438, 1977;

Maher v. Roe 432 U.S. 464, 1977, reviewed federal powers; *Harris v. McRae* 448 U.S. 297, 1980, addressed states' powers).

The Hyde Amendment typically has exceptions for cases when a woman's life is threatened or when the pregnancy is the result of rape and incest. In 11 states, women must produce documentation of sexual assault to qualify, which is problematic because so many sexual assaults are not reported. It also reflects suspicion that women will lie. In an extreme version of that sentiment, Missouri congressman and Senate candidate Todd Akin ignited a Twitter storm of controversy for his remark in 2012: "It seems to be, first of all, from what I understand from doctors, it's really rare. If it's a legitimate rape, the female body has ways to try to shut the whole thing down" (he lost). Thirty-two states comply with the federal standard and provide Medicaid abortions only in these extreme cases. Hawaii, Massachusetts, New York, and West Virginia voluntarily fund all or most medically necessary abortions, and 13 other states do so by court order. South Dakota is currently violating the federal standard by providing Medicaid funding for abortions only in cases of life endangerment (to learn more, see Guttmacher Institute 2018, "State Funding of Abortion under Medicaid"). In the 2016 presidential race, in line with their party's platforms, Democratic candidate Hillary Clinton called for the repeal of the Hyde Amendment and Republican candidate Donald J. Trump promised to make the annual provision a permanent law. In January 2017, just days after the Women's March on Washington, Representative Christopher Smith (R-NJ) introduced HR7, which would make the Hyde Amendment's restrictions on any federal assistance for abortion a permanent ban. This is the fourth time that a bill like this has passed the House; it has yet to pass in the Senate.

Global and Domestic Funding Restrictions

Since the 1970s, the federal government has funded private and public agencies that provide family planning information and services to the poor both globally and domestically.

The law forbids these funds to be used to perform abortions. President Reagan used his executive authority to issue a rule that agencies receiving federal funds for family planning could not discuss abortion at all, even to give neutral information about options. They were only to discuss adoption or abstinence. Pro-choice activists challenged the constitutionality of the rule, but the Supreme Court upheld it as a constitutional use of executive power to set guidelines on the expenditure of public funds (*Rust v. Sullivan* 500 U.S. 173, 1991).

President Reagan also ordered a rule pertaining to foreign aid, what pro-life activists call the Mexico City policy after the Population Conference where it was announced in 1984. It banned U.S. aid to American and foreign family planning organizations that provided abortions or abortion counseling or that advocated for legal abortion access anywhere in the world outside the United States. Reagan's rationale was that even if an agency involved in both family planning and abortion were given funding only for its family planning functions, it would release funds within the organization for its abortion activities resulting in taxpayer funding of abortion in foreign countries. The pro-choice movement refers to this policy as the "Global Gag Rule," which frames it as impinging on free speech by penalizing groups for the counseling and information they provide. They also argue that it as a terrible blow to efforts of nongovernmental organizations seeking to improve the health and status of women around the world by attempting to decrease the number of unintended pregnancies and unsafe abortions and stop the spread of HIV/AIDS. The prognosis in the pro-choice frame is for the government to simply remove the rule and commit U.S. resources and energies to advancing health and development through family planning.

These rules are at the discretion of the president. Chapter 5 traces the now-ritualistic back-and-forth of Democratic presidents rescinding and Republican presidents reinstating the Mexico City policy/Global Gag Rule. In 2017, President Trump extended the restrictions to an estimated $8.8 billion in

U.S. global health assistance. Pro-choice organizations predict that this move will have deadly and profound consequences, beyond just restricted access to contraception, unsafe abortion, and maternal deaths. The loss of funding may result in cuts to child vaccinations, prevention and treatment of HIV/AIDS, malaria, and tuberculosis, and nutrition programs. Trump's adviser Marjorie Dannenfelser, who is also the president of the pro-life Susan B. Anthony List, celebrated the victory by saying, "Votes in America have international consequences . . . we have officially ceased exporting abortion to foreign nations. . . . This executive order does not cut a single penny from U.S. aid, rather it simply ensures our hard-earned tax dollars are used by other health care entities that act consistently to save lives, rather than promoting and performing abortion. Abortion is not health care" (Quigley 2017).

On the home front, Planned Parenthood has been in the pro-life and Republican crosshairs. Although mostly women's health services organization, some Planned Parenthood clinics do perform abortions. The acrimonious debate concerns Title X, a federally funded program that has since the 1970s provided grants to family planning organizations. (In 2014, Planned Parenthood affiliates received approximately $553 million in government funding, which is about 40 percent of their total revenue, coming from such grants, but mostly in the form of Medicaid reimbursements for health services like cervical cancer screenings and sexually transmitted infections testing.) In 2015, The Center for Medical Progress, which is part of the more militant wing of the pro-life movement, released a now-discredited video, purporting to show that Planned Parenthood was selling fetal tissue. This inspired Senate Republicans to advance bills to federally defund the organization, even though the organization was already prohibited from using the money for abortion. Democrats were incensed by the attacks; Senator Elizabeth Warren described the legislation as "just one more piece of a deliberate, methodical, orchestrated, right-wing attack on women's rights," adding

"And I'm sick and tired of it" (Schwiegershausen 2015). The Republican leadership launched a series of probes, and Planned Parenthood president and CEO Cecile Richards was called to testify before the House Oversight and Government Reform Committee. Representative Jason Chaffetz (R-UT) confronted her with a chart that showed Planned Parenthood's breast cancer screenings were declining, while abortions were increasing. The heated exchange ended, with Richards admonishing the fake data produced by the pro-life group AUL. The battle has also waged in social media, with pro-choice supporters proclaiming #IStandWithPP facing off against #ProtestPP, which represents 40 pro-life organizations seeking to bring down the nation's largest abortion provider. In 2016, before leaving office, President Obama issued a rule that states cannot deny Title X funding to clinics solely on the basis that they also provide abortions. In a demonstration of just how quickly things change, in March of 2017, Vice President Mike Pence, a born-again evangelical Catholic whose faith informs his strong anti-abortion stance, cast the tie-breaking vote in the Senate, allowing states to withhold federal funds from Planned Parenthood and other reproductive health care providers that provide abortion.

Fighting for the Rights of the Unborn

Pro-Life Framing

Today, 45 years after the decriminalization of abortion, the pro-life strategic frame focuses on the tragic number of abortions that have occurred and the babies that continue to die because of this grisly practice. From the moment the *Roe v. Wade* ruling was known—that the fetus was potential human life but not a person in the meaning of the Fourteenth Amendment—pro-life activists have sought to overcome this denial of legal personhood. Technological advances since the 1970s have helped their cause, including a new branch of medicine called perinatology that enables doctors treat fetuses in utero. Ultrasound pictures, now available in four dimension, have also bolstered the pro-life movement's assertions that we are marveling at a "pre-born human being." Public displays of these high-resolution images—ethereally floating in space or bloodied and dismembered—have been a powerful weapon in the pro-life arsenal. The holocaust metaphor has also been invoked to further amplify their message that innocent lives are being destroyed by abortion. In *Defenders of the Unborn: The Pro-Life Movement before Roe v. Wade*, Williams traces the long and enduring history of this connection back to 1951 when Pope Pius XII declared that "every human being, even a child in the mother's womb, has a right to life directly from God" and that destroying "life without value" mirrors Nazi genocidal thinking (2015, 38).

Debates over proposals to codify the personhood of the fetus separately from the personhood of the woman who carries the fetus began in the 1980s and have continued to the present. Pro-life advocates assert that there is no difference between an embryo, a fetus, and a newborn baby other than the stage of development. Therefore, a woman has no right to disregard its status as a person. Instead, as a mother, she has the responsibility to protect and ensure that her child is born in good health. The pro-life movement seeks changes to the law that recognize the equal rights of the unborn child. Pro-choice advocates counter that the fetus is not a separate being; it exists in the pregnant body of a woman, and therefore, the woman must make decisions for both. Even though it has the potential to become a child, the embryo is merely a collection of cells. Pro-choice leaders discredit the pro-life campaign for fetal personhood as just another means of taking away women's rights to abortion.

On the prognosis part of the strategic frame—what can and should be done to address the situation—there is not complete consensus among pro-life activists. As we have seen, since 1973, a primary goal of the pro-life movement has been to overturn *Roe v. Wade* either by overriding it with a constitutional amendment or by making favorable changes in the

Court. An alternative strategy has been to push for laws that make access to abortion services more difficult through administrative hurdles for patients and regulations on clinics. Some activists flow toward this political stream, while others flow toward direct action, individual outreach, or public outreach. Munson elaborates on this structure in *The Making of Pro-Life Activists*. He defines streams as mutually exclusive "collections of organizations and activists that share an understanding of the best means to achieve the goal of ending abortion" (2010, 99). His research illuminates how pro-life activists are "together but not one." To illustrate, the Pro-Life Action League (PLAL) is dedicated to "saving unborn children through non-violent direct action," which may involve individual outreach in the form of sidewalk counseling or direct action in the form of prayer vigils and protests at clinics (www.prolifeaction.org). National Right to Life has an even broader tactical repertoire. It is driven by the mission of defending "the most fundamental right of humankind, the right to life of every innocent human being from the beginning of life to natural death," and it utilizes a three-pronged strategy of education, legislation, and political action, especially to elect "public officials who defend life" (www.nrlc.org).

The outcome of a presidential election can usher in new prognoses about what can and must be done. The inauguration of Republican president Donald Trump has sounded the alarm bells for progressives. According to Nash and colleagues (2017) in the first quarter of 2017, 1,053 provisions related to reproductive health were introduced. There was an increase in pro-active measures, up from 221 in 2015 to 405. While legislation to limit abortion access remained steady with 431 measures introduced, five states passed new pro-life laws, including Arkansas's ban on sex-selective abortion, Utah's counseling mandate to offer women a drug that has not been scientifically proven to stop a medication abortion, and Wyoming's law to give women the opportunity to listen to the fetal heartbeat prior to obtaining an abortion. In anticipation of conservative appointments to the Supreme Court, the pro-life movement will likely step up these efforts to ban abortions. This section discusses efforts to criminalize partial-birth abortion and infanticide, late-term abortions, prenatal drug use, and third-party fetal killing, which are all part of the more general pro-life strategy to establish the independent personhood of the fetus.

Partial-Birth Abortion and Infanticide

Rather than launching a full-frontal attack on all legal abortions, the pro-life movement developed a strategy in the early 1990s to ban abortion procedure by procedure. With the aid of a Republican-controlled Congress, they defined the "partial-birth abortion" procedure as a form of infanticide performed by doctors. This gave pro-life advocates a chance to talk about late-term abortion procedures in vivid detail—poisoning in utero, dismemberment, crushing the fetal skull, and killing a baby outside the womb, who would have otherwise been born alive. Their new strategic frame separated the fetus from the woman's body. Pro-life activists felt confident that the public would see from the graphic drawings that the horrible procedure kills a child just "three inches" away from full citizenship and personhood. They warned their supporters not to be fooled by "pro-abortionists'" use of the term "dilation and extraction," which is, they say, "pseudo-medical jargon." For them, the "facts" about the situation are that generally doctors oppose the practice, but still this brutal killing takes place thousands of times each year in the United States, with most of the procedures performed on healthy mothers and healthy babies who would live if allowed to be born.

Pro-choice activists successfully reinserted women into the issue frame by focusing on the need for this procedure to preserve women's health (McBride Stetson 2001). They received support from President Clinton, who vetoed all partial-birth bans passed by Congress in the 1990s. Regarding terminology, pro-choice activists insisted that "partial-birth abortion" was not actually a medical term; it was manufactured by pro-life strategists as a smoke screen to hide their true motive, which is to criminalize all abortions. In 2000, the Supreme Court gave pro-choice forces a policy victory by ruling (5–4) that state laws banning partial-birth abortion without an exception for the woman's health were unconstitutional (*Stenberg v. Carhart* 530 U.S. 914). Yet in 2003, Congress instituted a national ban without a health exception based on the pro-life movement's deluge of legislative findings that health exceptions are never necessary and are too broadly defined. Pro-choice proponents charged that the "reengaged Congress" had shown a complete disregard for women's health and the judgments of medical professionals.

In 2007, the Supreme Court upheld this congressional ban on the "intact dilation and evacuation" (intact D&E) procedure by a 5–4 decision (*Gonzales v. Carhart* No. 05-380). It justified departing from the precedent in *Stenberg v. Carhart* by arguing that the federal law had remedied the vagueness found in the state laws that the Court had declared unconstitutional in 2000. The two new justices, Chief Justice Roberts and Justice Alito, who were appointed by President George W. Bush, had also tipped the scales. What was most striking was that the justices adopted pro-life strategic frames in their rhetoric, referring to "abortion doctors" rather than obstetricians, the "unborn child" and "baby" rather than the fetus, and the D&E as "ripping" the fetus apart. There were two other startling claims. One was that Congress was acting within its constitutional authority to ban the procedure with no exception for a woman's health because medical opinion was divided on the question of medical necessity. The other was that banning the procedure was not an undue burden on women; instead, it was framed as protecting women from the emotional effects of the procedure. Justice Ruth Bader Ginsburg called the majority opinion "irrational." Her dissent focused on the Court's shift away from promoting women's reproductive rights and liberty. Pro-choice leaders were appalled at what they claimed was a stinging rebuke of women's rights and autonomy. The pro-life leaders rightly hailed the decision as a victory. The immediate effects of the ruling on medical practice were minimal, given the small percentage of second-trimester abortions and the loopholes in the decision.

Another pro-life concern and tactic has been to expose the barbarity of infanticide. In 2002, congressional committees heard testimonies from health care workers that in some late-term abortions, babies survived and that they were instructed not to treat these infants. Jill Stanek, a nurse, recounted disturbing cases, including rocking an aborted Down syndrome baby who was born alive, whose parents did not want to hold him, until the child died. Stanek is now a well-known, pro-life blogger with Live Action News, which is dedicated to exposing what it calls the truth of the abortion industry. She claimed that in 2003 77 viable fetuses had been "born alive" following an abortion and then killed by doctors. However, according to CDC data there are only an average of 37 deaths each year with the cause of death coded as "termination of pregnancy," and this figure primarily represents tragic losses of wanted children (Coutts 2013). Congress responded to the harrowing accounts by granting any infant born alive, regardless of the stage of development, the full protection of the law. The Born Alive Infants Protection Act, signed by President George W. Bush in 2002, stipulated that doctors and hospitals must do what they can to save their lives. Pro-choice organizations tended not to take a position on this law, and many congressional abortion rights advocates voted for it because it did not change the legal status of the fetus as it applied only to infants who had left the womb and were still alive.

The crimes committed by Dr. Kermit Gosnell were proof to some that this federal law had not gone far enough. In 2010, the FBI and the Pennsylvania Department of Health raided Gosnell's clinic exposing the filthy conditions. The now-infamous abortion provider was charged with killing seven infants and killing one woman with an overdose of sedatives; her name was Karnamaya Mongar and she was a desperate Nepalese refugee. The Grand Jury Report noted: "When you perform late-term 'abortions' by inducing labor, you get babies. Live, breathing, squirming babies . . . Gosnell had a simple solution for the unwanted babies he delivered: he killed them . . . by sticking scissors into the back of the baby's neck and cutting the spinal cord" (Friedersdorf 2013). Gosnell received a life sentence in 2013. Leading pro-choice organizations like NARAL Pro-Choice America (PCA), Planned Parenthood, and the National Abortion Federation were quick to distance themselves from Gosnell's "back-alley" criminal enterprise, which they viewed as an affront to properly regulated reproductive health care and a tragic consequence of vulnerable women feeling as though they had no other options in the state of Pennsylvania where 24 weeks was the cutoff for legal abortions. Pro-life groups extended their condemnation, viewing Gosnell's "house of horrors" as emblematic of the atrocities of the abortion industry. The Born-Alive Abortion Survivors Protection Act, which passed the House in 2015, amended the federal criminal code by requiring health care workers to provide care when a child is born alive following an abortion (as indicated by breathing, heartbeat, or movement) or face a fine and up to five years in prison.

The scope of fetal protection over the rights of women who carry them appears to be expanding. In 2011, Bei Bei Shuai, a Chinese immigrant who was pregnant, despairing and alone, attempted suicide by eating rat poison and was charged with attempted feticide. Because she was near the end of her pregnancy, Shuai was said to have knowingly killed a viable fetus. In a plea agreement, Shuai pled guilty to criminal recklessness. Fetal-harm statutes have been invoked in situations where a pregnant woman has fallen down the stairs or driven with blood-alcohol levels over the legal limit. Women with wanted pregnancies have been forced on bedrest or to undergo caesarean sections. Marlise Muñoz was kept on life support for two months (despite her family's objections) to save her fetus. Lynn Paltrow, a lawyer, activist, and executive director of National

Advocates for Pregnant Women, has catalogued more than 700 instances since 1973 of pregnant women being arrested, detained, or subjected to forced medical interventions.

Late-Term Abortions

The *Roe v. Wade* decision stipulated that the right to abortion was not absolute; states could impose restrictions or ban abortions after fetal viability provided exceptions are made for the woman's life or health (both conditions as determined by a physician). Abortion is now prohibited after a certain point in the pregnancy in 43 states. Several states have instituted unconstitutional bans on abortion after 20 weeks' postfertilization when the fetus may not yet be viable, based on the highly contested claim the fetus can feel pain. Eighteen states have unconstitutionally narrowed exceptions to abortions performed to preserve the life or physical health of the woman. In a "born-alive" situation, 13 states require that a second physician treat the fetus (to learn more, see Guttmacher Institute 2018, "State Policies on Later Term Abortions").

In 2006, pro-life members of Congress introduced the Unborn Child Pain Awareness Act. Some physicians testified that a fetus feels pain at 20 weeks. Dr. Kanwaljeet "Sunny" Anand, a professor of pediatrics, anesthesiology, and neurobiology at Stanford University, is the most outspoken proponent of that view. He argues that fetuses respond to stress or other stimuli at 20 weeks, and thus, abortion would cause "severe and excruciating pain." His conclusions are at odds with the larger body of medical literature, which suggests that although the biological pathways for pain sensation may be present at 20 weeks, the brain connections required to feel pain are not formed until at least 24 weeks, which is the earliest possible point of fetal viability outside the womb. Although a majority voted in favor, the act failed to receive the two-thirds support necessary for passage. It would have required doctors to read a statement to a woman undergoing an abortion at 20 weeks after fertilization or more that Congress has determined that there is substantial evidence that the procedure will cause the unborn child pain. A woman would also be given a brochure to reinforce this message unless she waived receipt, and a decision form to indicate her explicit request for or against the administration of anesthesia to the child.

Pro-life activists have continued to push for these laws at both the federal and state levels, propelled by the belief that society's understanding and concern for unborn children is advancing with science. They have found success in framing the issue as a simple matter of providing information to women, so they can make an informed decision—women would be less likely to have abortions if they were not kept in the dark about the suffering it causes. Pro-choice advocates criticized this bill and the subsequent ones as political maneuvers based on speculation rather than scientific fact. This bill says nothing about the pain fetuses suffer in ordinary childbirth and in neonatal treatments, which supports their charge this rhetoric is part of a campaign to undermine abortion services and limit the number of abortions. Moreover, many doctors have opposed the idea of letting Congress determine what doctors must say to patients, and the requirement to offer anesthesia to a fetus overlooks the difficulty in administering such drugs and the dangers to women in doing so. To illustrate, Utah passed a law in 2016 that fetuses beyond 20 weeks must be given anesthesia, but it came with absolutely no guidance for the small number of physicians who perform late-term abortions about how to implement the proscribed procedures.

The latest iteration to pass the House is the 2017 Pain-Capable Unborn Child Protection Act, which would ban abortions after 20 weeks, except in cases of rape, incest, or a threat to the life of the mother. Physicians for Reproductive Health has argued that there is no medical or scientific support; thus, the 20 weeks is just an arbitrary limit set by pro-life politicians. The American College of Obstetricians and Gynecologists has also not concurred that scientific research proves this is the gestational stage at which the fetus can begin to feel pain. Those parents who learn of a fetal diagnosis by ultrasound or amniocentesis would have limited options. Planned Parenthood lambasted this as "unconstitutional" and "dangerous, out-of-touch legislation," and it shared personal stories that capture how the ban would harm women's health (Planned Parenthood Action Fund n.d.-c). Although President Donald Trump had promised to sign the bill, it failed to pass the Senate in early 2018.

Prenatal Drug Laws

In the 1980s, "crack" cocaine had become an epidemic. Reporters told stories about the strength of these drugs and how addicts would do anything to get more crack. The media also brought to light the alarming increase in drug-exposed infants or "crack babies." To many, the women themselves were responsible for this; they were depicted as recklessly endangering their own children. State legislators filed bills to make such behavior a crime and put the mothers in jail. These proposals did not get very far because there was overwhelming evidence that the threat of incarceration would deter the women from seeking help and getting prenatal care. States began to enact other laws, such as requiring drug tests and treatment for pregnant women receiving state assistance like welfare, and declaring drug addiction to be a form of child abuse. Others opted for more service-oriented approaches such as expanding public education and drug treatment programs for addicts.

Considered an exemplar of punitive approaches, the first case of homicide by child abuse was brought before a jury in 1999 in South Carolina. Regina McNight, a young African American woman, who was homeless and possibly mentally impaired, was convicted after delivering a stillborn baby, on grounds that she had used cocaine during her pregnancy. The prosecutor Greg Hembree said he wanted to show "particularly those women who were addicted who may get pregnant" that "there's some consequences for your actions" (Herbert 2001). After a 15-minute jury deliberation, McNight was sentenced to 12 years in prison. Her conviction was finally overturned by the South Carolina Supreme Court in 2008 because she had received inadequate counsel and because other factors might have led to the stillbirth.

Today, substance use during pregnancy is treated as child abuse in 24 states and the District of Columbia, and in 3 of these it is grounds for civil commitment. Health care workers must report suspected prenatal drug use in 23 states and the District of Columbia, and 7 of these mandate drug testing. Taking a less punitive and more public health approach, 19 states have set up drug treatment programs for pregnant women (to learn more, see Guttmacher Institute 2018, "Substance Use during Pregnancy"). Of course, not all women experience the same level of surveillance; race, class, and sexuality factor into decisions. In *Our Bodies, Our Crimes: The Policing of Women's Reproduction in America*, Flavin (2008) documents how the state seeks to determine what a "good woman" and "fit mother" should look like. A consistent theme in Flavin's work is that the fetal protectionist responses of the criminal justice system that emphasize arrests and prosecutions of drug addicted pregnant women draw attention away from the real systemic problems like lack of health care and social supports necessary to care for children (Paltrow and Flavin 2013).

Prenatal drug laws ascribe to the pro-life frame that a woman's main responsibility is to protect her unborn offspring and in the process lose her own rights. While reproductive justice advocates agree that drug addiction needs to be addressed, they have urged state authorities to take women's lives into account. Studies show that addicts are typically also victims of child abuse and domestic battery; they take drugs to avoid the pain these experiences have caused. To put them in jail or charge them with child abuse without considering the mitigating circumstances adds even more pain to their lives. Moreover, with such laws a pregnant woman is no longer carrying her own child in private. Instead, others think they have the right to intervene to criticize a woman for smoking, drinking a glass of wine, or riding on a motorcycle while pregnant. A dystopian future in which women are captive uteri has been chillingly portrayed in the acclaimed 2017 Hulu series, *The Handmaid's Tale*, based on Margaret Atwood's 1985 novel of the same name. It portrays the theocratic Republic of Gilead, which has responded to an infertility epidemic by taking terrifying and oppressive control of women's reproductive capacities. "Blessed be the fruit" is their ominous greeting. This has inspired pro-choice protesters around the country to dress in the signature red capes and white bonnets to confront lawmakers, sometimes with chilling silence and other times carrying signs with foreboding messages about the loss of women's autonomy (see, e.g., #OHHandmaids).

Third-Party Fetal Killing

Although the pro-life movement was one of the leaders in promoting prenatal drug laws, it was less involved initially in bringing the problem of third-party fetal killing to the public agenda. The media also did not make much of the statistics that showed an increase in fetal injury and death due to violence against pregnant women in the 1980s and 1990s. In 1998, Ruth Schroedel (2000) conducted a study of 32 pro-life organizations and found only one, AUL, which considered the issue of fetal death worth promoting. AUL focuses on legislation and offers model statutes to states and Congress for bills they advocate. This lack of interest changed soon after Schroedel's survey, when the National Right to Life Committee (NRLC) launched a campaign for fetal homicide laws. At that time, about half the states had already criminalized third-party killing of a fetus. What was different with the new campaign was that NRLC and AUL promoted laws that explicitly defined when the fetus was a person—from fertilization—and the crime as involving two separate victims—the pregnant woman and the embryo/fetus. Thus, someone who attacks a woman who does not know she is pregnant could be charged with murder.

Pro-choice activists opposed the establishment of a "two-victims" approach, which they claimed was part of the pro-life strategy to dismantle the guarantees for women's choice in abortion in *Roe v. Wade* by legally defining the fertilized egg as a human being. The pro-choice prognosis for the problem of fetal homicide is for states to define the crime as injuries inflicted on a pregnant woman—one victim—and increase the penalties to take into account that injury to the fetus has also occurred. Pro-life frames reject the idea of stiffer penalties for crimes against pregnant women, claiming that an assailant will get a longer prison term for a crime with two victims rather than one. Pro-life activists also insisted that women's rights would not be affected because the proposals explicitly exclude abortion. Others admit, however, that once the fetus is considered a separate human being, it will be harder and harder to justify laws that allow doctors and pregnant women to kill it.

This campaign got a boost in the early 2000s when the murder of Laci Peterson, who was seven months pregnant, was followed closely in the news. When her body was discovered in San Francisco Bay separate from her fetus, whom she had planned to name Connor, the issue of fetal homicide was thrust onto the national agenda. California already had a fetal homicide law dating from the 1970s, so Laci's husband, Scott Peterson, was tried and convicted for two murders—those of Laci and Connor. The pro-life activists convinced Laci's family to let them name their bill, the Unborn Victims of Violence Act (UVVA), "Laci and Connor's Law." All this publicity sealed the fate of the UVVA, and it was passed and signed by President George W. Bush in 2004. Although as a federal criminal law it has limited application, the national debate spurred the passage of identical laws in several states. According to the National Conference of State Legislatures, 38 states currently have fetal homicide laws; 23 of them apply to the earliest stages of pregnancy, defining the fetus as a person or human being at any stage of "gestation," "conception," or "postfertilization"; and only 12 states clearly specify that the act does not apply to abortion (http://www.ncsl.org/research/health/fetal-homicide-state-laws.aspx). Reproductive health care providers are carefully monitoring the pro-life movement's "backdoor" efforts to establish that the fetus is a legal person equal to the woman, which would make it impossible to sustain support for legal abortion.

Fighting for the Rights of Women

Pro-Choice Framing

Another contentious strategic frame in debate over *Roe v. Wade* is the question of whether the Constitution guarantees privacy to women and doctors in making decisions about abortion and how these rights can be balanced with the government's interest in protecting fetal life (McBride and Parry 2016). In cases before the Court, the frame has focused on whether specific abortion regulations constitute an undue burden on women's liberty, especially with respect to their lives and health, and deliberations have been limited to this rather narrow question. Thus, the frame favors the pro-choice position because it keeps the legalization of abortion itself off the table. As demonstrated in the previous section, the pro-life movement has tried to dismantle *Roe* by shifting the frame to define the issue in terms of the equal personhood of an unborn child.

While the pro-choice movement remains committed to defending women's privacy and liberty, it is women's health that is being held up as the key concern in the debate today. Framing abortion restrictions as part of an attack on women's health is proving to be a resonant diagnostic frame, as illustrated by Democratic senator Wendy Davis's dramatic filibuster in the Texas legislature to stop House Bill 2. This widely publicized showdown on TRAP laws took place in 2013. Davis stood and spoke for 11 hours to halt new restrictions on abortion clinics and a ban on abortions after 20 weeks. She chastised her fellow lawmakers to "either get out of the vagina business, or go to medical school" (Lee 2013). In an article she later wrote for CNN, Davis keeps the focus on women's health by saying, "Real Texans don't want any woman to die of cancer because she can't get decent healthcare or medical advice" (Davis 2013).

In a subsequent *Washington Post* op-ed, she explained, "I stood to oppose the bill because it rolled back constitutional rights and would reduce the number of women's health clinics from 42 to 5, thereby threatening the health and safety of thousands of Texas women" (Davis 2013).

The women's health frame has been fully embraced by many pro-choice organizations, including the Planned Parenthood Federation of America. The goal of the Planned Parenthood Action Fund (PPAF) is "to advance access to sexual health care and defend reproductive rights" (Planned Parenthood Action Fund n.d.-a). To fight the latest Republican attacks on birth control, it is mobilizing its supporters to share their stories, to raise money, and to show solidarity by proclaiming: "I stand with Planned Parenthood." To counterframe the debate for its members, PPAF's website uses the rhetorical strategies of frame debunking, frame saving, and polarization-vilification (McCaffrey and Keys 2000). It calls out its enemies by name: "Reproductive health and rights are under attack like never before. Mitch McConnell, Paul Ryan, and their allies in the Trump administration are seizing every opportunity to roll back reproductive rights and cut Planned Parenthood patients off from care. But we're committed to rising up against their extreme agenda—and we're not backing down." Its slogan, "Still fighting. No matter what," expresses bold defiance in spite of a century of struggle (Planned Parenthood Action Fund n.d.-b).

The other important frames to call attention to are reproductive rights and reproductive justice, which have been on the ascendance in the pro-choice movement. The evolution of organizational names for NARAL reflects the broadening agenda. First, it was the National Association for the Repeal of Abortion Laws (1969–1973), and then it became the National Abortion Rights Action League (1973–2003). In 1993 it extended to the National Abortion and Reproductive Rights Action League, and from 2003 to the present it has been NARAL Pro-Choice America (PCA). As president Kate Michelman told *The New York Times*, "Through our name change we are underscoring that our country is pro-choice" (Lee 2003). The countermovement, of course, tried to debunk PCA's new frame. Ken Connor, president of the Family Research Council, deftly maneuvers back to fetal personhood by retorting, "They want to isolate the rhetoric from the reality. They want to talk about pro-choice, but it's not choosing between chocolate and vanilla. We are talking about the right to choose to kill an unborn child" (Lee 2003).

PCA seeks to "elect candidates who will be champions for reproductive freedom" and pledges "to fight to keep abortion safe and legal for all women, regardless of ZIP code or income" (NARAL Pro-Choice America n.d.). This phrasing invokes ideas of intersectional feminism, which recognizes the diversity of identity categories that women occupy as significant in shaping the way they experience the world as potentially privileged in some ways and disadvantaged in others. Nelson's (2003) historical study traces how women of color transformed the paradigm; their experiences and voices defined a new and more inclusive collective action frame—reproductive freedom and justice for all. It is about recognizing the interconnectedness of oppressions and building power in communities to create systemic change, taking us beyond the right to abortion to the creation of a socially just world that safeguards human rights and allows true freedom of choice. (To learn more, read Ross and Solinger's 2017 essential primer *Reproductive Justice*.)

This section highlights additional dimensions of the fight to keep abortion not only legal but also safe and accessible. First, we consider safety in a medical sense by looking at the role the pro-choice movement played in the development and dispersal of the abortion pill and emergency contraception and its debunking of inaccurate medical information. Second, we also address the lack of environmental safety for abortion providers and patients and acknowledge the pro-choice movement's successes in curtailing the harassment and violence that has been perpetrated by anti-abortion protestors and extremists. An intersectional analysis demonstrates how women have differential access to abortion depending on their socioeconomic status and place of residence, and whether their lives are governed by institutions like the military, prisons, and immigration detention facilities. Finally, we discuss the lingering stigma of abortion and social change efforts to normalize the experience.

The Abortion Pill

The French government was the first to accept RU-486—the drug mifepristone—as an abortion procedure in the 1980s. This breakthrough made it possible to induce abortion in the first seven weeks of pregnancy by pills rather than the surgical removal of a fetus. Roussel-Uclaf, the Swiss manufacturer, was nervous about anti-abortion activism from the start. Pro-life groups did indeed threaten a boycott. The company withdrew RU-486 from the French market until the French government ordered it returned. Pro-choice Americans were very interested in the medication, but Roussel-Uclaf had no plans to offer the drug in the United States. It took a long campaign led by the Feminist Majority Foundation and the Population Council (PC) to persuade the Swiss company to donate its patents to the PC, which it finally agreed to do in 1994. The PC sought approval from the U.S. Food and Drug Administration (FDA), which is necessary before any medication can be prescribed and sold. Lawrence Lader and his group, Abortion Rights Mobilization, also contributed by sponsoring their own clinical trials. Because the FDA is a government agency, it is subject to control by Congress and influenced by the president, which is why the timing was favorable with the Clinton administration.

As expected, the debate over RU-486 was contentious. Pro-choice advocates framed the issue as a major advancement in technology that would benefit women's health and their privacy. French women who had had abortions using RU-486 reported that it was much more natural and less traumatic than a surgical abortion. All a woman had to do was take two pills and then wait for a miscarriage that was described as very similar to the menstrual periods. Pro-choice activists also welcomed this pharmaceutical procedure because it could take place between a woman and her doctor, in a regular medical office, bypassing the need to go to a clinic that might be besieged by protesters or subject to violent attacks. Pro-life activists challenged the idea that the pill was simply a way of starting up menstruation as trivializing the poisoning a human baby by likening RU-486 to chemical warfare on the unborn. They also expressed concerns that the FDA was rushing the pill to market and that "medication abortion" would foster reckless attitudes as it was "too convenient" and "too easy."

The FDA approved RU-486 for use in the United States in 2000. It took some time for doctors to be trained in its use and for women to learn about the option. Little information about the pill was in the public arena until 2006, when it was reported that four women had died of infections after taking RU-486. Although health officials pointed out that similar infections occurred during miscarriage and childbirth, pro-life forces seized the opportunity. In 2006, the United States Conference of Catholic Bishops, the American Association of Pro-Life Obstetricians and Gynecologists, and other pro-life groups advocated for "Holly's Law," named after 18-year-old Holly Patterson who died in 2003 of toxic shock after a medical abortion. Congressman Chris Smith, cochairman of the Pro-Life Caucus, in the House of Representatives claimed: "The approval of RU-486 by the Clinton Administration was expedited for political gain at the expense of patient health. Every few weeks a new warning or tragic investigation reminds us that not only is RU-486 used to kill babies, it is a poison that harms and kills women" (Smith 2016). If passed, this bill would have suspended the approval of RU-486.

Today, clinicians can prescribe either mifepristone or methotrexate to women who wish to terminate an early pregnancy. Then, taken a few days later, misoprostol tablets stimulate contractions, which cause the uterus to empty. States have the power to regulate medication abortion. In 34 states, only licensed physicians can prescribe the drugs, even though the World Health Organization and the National Abortion Federation have determined that physician assistants and advanced practice nurses can safely enact the protocol. With the closing of clinics nationwide, one hopeful prospect for reducing the travel time of rural women is telemedicine. Researchers have found video counseling is a safe alternative and does not increase complications, as women receive the same evaluation that they would in an in-person visit; the ultrasound can be viewed remotely by the physician (Grossman and Grindlay 2017). However, 19 states require that the clinician providing a medication abortion be physically present during the procedure (to learn more, see Guttmacher Institute 2018, "Emergency Contraception").

Emergency Contraception

In the pro-choice collective action frames, unintended pregnancies represent serious harm to the health of women and their children. (It is important to note that for many years, the pro-choice activists used the term "unwanted pregnancy," which pro-life activists challenged by arguing that with adoption, no baby is unwanted.) The prognosis or solution to the problem is to expand access to emergency contraception (EC), also known as the "morning after pill," making it readily available in hospitals for rape victims and in drug stores for women who have had unprotected sex or contraceptive failure.

The FDA approved Plan B in 1999. The drug company that makes EC, many doctors, and pro-choice activists demanded that the FDA allow it to be sold over the counter. This is important because EC is most effective when taken soon after sexual intercourse (it can be taken up to five days after). Science advisory committees to the FDA recommended approval in 2003, but action was deferred; critics charged that the FDA was ideologically siding with pro-life notions about EC. The FDA claimed that the drug company had not presented convincing evidence that the drug could be used safely by girls under age 16 without a doctor's supervision. In 2005 senators Hillary Rodham Clinton (D-NY) and Patty Murray (D-WA) blocked Lester Crawford's nomination as commissioner of the

FDA and released their hold only after Health and Human Services secretary Michael Leavitt promised a ruling on the application by September 1. When this did not happen, Susan Wood, director of the Office of Women's Health at the FDA, resigned, accusing the FDA of being influenced by abortion politics. Crawford also resigned, and President George W. Bush nominated Andrew Von Eschenbach, who was similarly blocked by senators Clinton and Murray. On August 23, 2006, the FDA approved over-the-counter sales of EC to those age 18 and over, and it is now available without an age restriction.

Reproductive health advocates explain that because EC *prevents* rather than *ends* a pregnancy, it presents no moral choice. For pro-life activists, EC is an abortifacient because it works to prevent implantation in the uterus, thereby destroying the embryo, the same as an abortion. Disregarding randomized control studies that have shown no link between EC and increased sexual risk behavior (Raine et al. 2005), pro-life advocates assert that EC promotes promiscuity and unsafe sexual behavior. They fear that with easy access to drugs that quickly abort any pregnancies, people will not exercise restraint. The solution is to restrict availability of and access to EC and, for some activists, to limit access to all birth control pills as well, which similarly make the uterus inhospitable to embryo implantation. Like abortion, use of EC presents a moral dilemma for pro-life policy makers, doctors, and pharmacists. "Right of refusal" laws allow pharmacists to refuse to fill prescriptions for so-called abortifacient drugs, including birth control, if it goes against their religious beliefs. Currently, six states allow pharmacists to refuse to dispense EC and other contraceptives. (To learn, read Haussman's 2013 *Reproductive Rights and the State: Getting Birth Control, RU-486, and Morning-After Polls and the Gardasil Vaccine to the U.S. Market.*)

Accurate Information

In *Abortion Politics, Mass Media, and Social Movements in America*, Rohlinger observes that mainstream pro-life organizations have co-opted the agenda of women's health by linking abortion to negative psychological outcomes and to breast cancer (2014, 157). One of the earliest articulations was from family therapist and pro-life advocate Vincent Rue, who testified before Congress in 1981 about women suffering from "postabortion syndrome." His ally David Reardon, founder of the Elliot Institute, helped advance the argument that abortion harms women. In his 1996 book, *Making Abortion Rare*, Reardon wrote, "We must change the abortion debate so that we are arguing with our opponents on their own turf, on the issue of defending the interests of women" (8). As the sanctity of human life appeared to lose resonance, frame transformation was necessary, and a "Pro-Woman, Pro-Life" contingent of the movement emerged (Trumpy 2014). Pro-life websites disseminate "facts" about the detrimental impact of abortion on women's health, and some do in a way that is almost indistinguishable from credible scientific sources. LifeSiteNews, for example, offers "The Ultimate Guide to Understanding How Abortion and Breast Cancer Are Related," illustrated with a photo of a physician wearing a pink ribbon, a lengthy and complex text, and an extensive bibliography (LifeSiteNews .com n.d.).

Does abortion actually increase the risk of breast cancer? No. The American Cancer Society helps explain the faulty rationale and the research design challenges. This concern has been raised because the normal hormonal cycle of pregnancy is interrupted by abortion. For obvious reasons, it is not possible to conduct an experimental study, in which subjects would be randomized to receive abortion. One of the best observational studies was conducted in Denmark in the 1990s, where detailed medical records are kept on all citizens, making it possible to gather complete and accurate information about both abortions and breast cancer and no connection was found. While there have indeed been studies that have shown a small increased risk, The American College of Obstetricians and Gynecologists Committee on Gynecologic Practice concluded that the totality of the evidence suggests: "Early studies of the relationship between prior induced abortion and breast cancer risk were methodologically flawed. More rigorous recent studies demonstrate no causal relationship between induced abortion and a subsequent increase in breast cancer risk" (American College of Obstetricians and Gynecologists 2009, Reaffirmed 2018). If the preponderance of evidence shifts, women should absolutely be informed, but using scare tactics only deepens the divide.

What about the oft-cited, pro-life claim that women suffer from postabortion syndrome? Coleman, Coyle, Shuping, and Rue (2009) published results in the *Journal of Psychiatric Research* that abortion can lead to a whole host of psychiatric problems like post-traumatic stress disorder, panic disorders, depression, substance abuse, and suicide. The research has been widely criticized for failing to screen subjects to determine whether these disorders were present before their abortions. This bad data has been used as a justification for requiring that women be warned about these psychological risks prior to an abortion, even though high-quality research shows that abortion does not lead to negative psychiatric outcomes. The American Psychological Association advises against making universal claims about how women feel after terminating a pregnancy (Major, Appelbaum, Beckman, Dutton, Russo, and West 2009). A woman's ideology, for example, can influence her emotional response to abortion. If she is pro-life, the "feeling rules" suggest that guilt and grief are warranted after what she believes to be killing her unborn child, but if she is pro-choice, the emotional script normalizes feeling a sense of relief (Keys 2010).

The discredited links to breast cancer and postabortion syndrome are still being disseminated by crisis pregnancy centers (CPCs), with the goal of dissuading women from choosing abortion. Their proliferation is a growing concern for the pro-choice movement; there are estimated to be over 4,000 currently operating in this country. Self-described as pregnancy help centers, CPCs offer free pregnancy tests and even ultrasounds; some also provide baby care items and offer classes on childbirth, life skills, and financial management. Many are affiliated with Catholic and evangelical churches and are part of three major nonprofit networks: Care Net, Heartbeat International, and Birthright International. This has become the most active stream of the pro-life movement (Munson 2010). Questions have been raised about the deceptive practices of CPCs—false advertising, evasiveness, intimidation, propaganda, and misinformation about the health risks of abortion (NARAL 2016). The documentary *12th and Delaware* shows the use of manipulative strategies, including graphic descriptions of abortion practices and personifying the fetus by writing "Hi, mommy" on the ultrasound image.

George Delgado, a physician for the CPC Culture of Life Family Services in San Diego, claims to have developed a method for reversing medical abortion for women who experience regret after taking the first abortion pill. Based on anecdotal evidence of its success, in 2015 Arizona became the first state to require physicians to tell their patients about the abortion reversal procedure, thereby legitimating the pro-life frame that women regret their abortions. Researchers who tracked 667 women for three years after their abortions found that regret is rare; approximately 95 percent of women consistently felt that the abortion had been the right decision for them. Women who had more difficulty deciding to terminate the pregnancy, higher perceived community abortion stigma, and lower social support reported experiencing more negative emotions; the intensity of these feelings decreased over time (Rocca, Kimport, Roberts, Gould, Neuhaus, and Foster 2015). In 2017, the Supreme Court agreed to hear the California case, *National Institute of Family and Life Advocates v. Becerra* (No. 16-1140), which concerns a state law that requires CPCs to provide women will the full range of information about their options, including abortion, which pro-life activists say violates their right to free speech.

Environmental Safety

"This Clinic Stays Open" is a slogan often seen on the front lines, which reflects the determination of pro-choice activists to protect access to abortion even in the face of intimidation and violent attacks. After *Roe v. Wade*, most hospitals surrendered to pressures from the pro-life movement and stopped performing first-trimester abortions. Abortion services were relegated to free-standing clinics, which were visible, public spaces. Some leaders in the pro-life movement, such as Joseph Scheidler who in 1980 formed the PLAL, advocated a direct approach to shutting down abortion clinics. This inspired Randall Terry to form Operation Rescue (OR), which took the tactics to new levels. While Scheidler was a former Roman Catholic priest, Terry mobilized his troops among the Christian fundamentalists forming a new wave of "Christian soldiers." OR proclaimed a holy war against the "child-killing industry." Its mission was to rescue America from moral decline by preventing women from aborting their children. Adhering to a "higher law" of "Bible disobedience," its tactics included conducting "sidewalk counseling" with clients, blocking access to facilities, verbal and physical confrontations, theatrical stunts with fake blood and funerals for aborted fetuses, and more menacingly tracing license numbers and making threatening phone calls.

Clinics fought back by forming alliances with pro-choice organizations to protect their facilities and their clients and by fortifying their facilities and seeking injunctions. But the protesters were relentless in inviting arrest and challenging the injunctions as violations of their First Amendment rights. Pro-choice activists won an important victory in 1994 when Congress passed the Freedom of Access to Clinic Entrances Act, which makes it a federal offense to use force or threats of force against an organization that provides reproductive services and counseling. However, despite National Organization for Women's contention that the increasingly violent tactics of PLAL qualified as racketeering and extortion, a trilogy of

Supreme Court cases against Joseph Scheidler—1994, 2003, and 2006—ultimately ruled in Scheidler's favor.

OR faded from the scene, but the militancy it inspired did not. During the 1990s, a new wave of "pro-life terrorism" arose. Direct action took a deadly turn with anthrax attacks, fire bombings, and murders and attempted murders of abortion providers (Baird-Windle and Bader 2001). According to the National Abortion Federation (2016), which has been tallying violence and disruption statistics since 1977, by 2016 there have been 252,470 pickets, 1,643 acts of vandalism, 2,925 trespassings, 411 reported invasions, 69,191 hate e-mails, 583 cases of stalking, and 11 murders. Those who advocated and defended the violence called out the evil of abortion, which they believed was bringing down the wrath of God on America. Pat Robertson even blamed the terrorist attacks of September 11, 2001, on feminists and abortionists. Violent extremists claimed they were an Army of God waging war with the devil and fighting as Lambs of Christ (Mason 2002). The Army of God celebrated Paul Hill—who was executed for the murders of Dr. John Britton and his bodyguard James Barrett—as a martyr for Jesus. In 2009, Scott Roeder killed Dr. George Tiller, who was one of the few remaining doctors who provided abortions late in pregnancy, which had made him a target for relentless protesters. The latest deadly attack took place in 2015 in Colorado Springs, Colorado, when a police officer and two people in a Planned Parenthood clinic were shot and killed.

Pro-choice organizations have attributed the recent surge in hate speech, threats, and violence against abortion providers to the deceptively edited videos released by the Center for Medical Progress in 2013 (Planned Parenthood 2015). This self-described group of citizen journalists posted edited footage from a hidden camera that they claimed showed a criminal conspiracy with doctors at Planned Parenthood to sell aborted fetuses. Republican House Speaker John Boehner expressed disgust and quickly called for an investigation of

Planned Parenthood's abortion practices. In a letter to lawmakers, Planned Parenthood vehemently denied the accusations. Planned Parenthood insisted that it is the most trusted women's health care provider in the country and that it complies with all federal regulations, including those stipulating that clinics can be reimbursed only for costs of processing fetal tissue donations. It also fired back by characterizing the videos as attacks perpetrated by extremists who have for years sought to intimidate women and doctors. An independent analysis later exposed the videos as fraudulent; their creators were charged with felony invasion of privacy. Nevertheless, Father Frank Pavone, the director of Priests for Life, has pledged to grow an army of "intelligence operatives" to infiltrate Planned Parenthood. Pavone warns, "Be on your toes, because we are in your midst" (Resnek 2016). Ominous threats like these and the lack of environmental safety have severely reduced the number of doctors trained to perform abortions and have kept others from staying in the practice. As of 2017, there is just one remaining abortion provider in each of five states—Kentucky, Mississippi, North Dakota, South Dakota, and West Virginia. Women living in rural areas often must travel long distances for care, as there are no abortion providers in 87 percent of counties in the United States or in 97 percent of all rural counties, where 35 percent of women aged 15–44 live (Jones and Kooistra 2011).

Access

Reproductive justice advocates call attention to the fact that a woman's ability to access abortion services is shaped and constrained by the social identity categories that she occupies. For many poor women, the cost of abortion becomes an insurmountable obstacle. Recall that the Hyde Amendment prohibits federal funds from being used to cover abortions. As Justice Thurgood Marshall had predicted this in his dissent in *Harris v. McRae* (448 U.S. 297), the case which determined that states were not obligated to fund medically necessary abortions under the Medicaid program: "The consequence is a devastating impact on the lives and health of poor women." He added, "I do not believe that a Constitution committed to the equal protection of the laws can tolerate this result."

Ely, Hales, Jackson, Maguin, and Hamilton (2017) focus on the disproportionate impact that restricted funding has had on women of color. The study examined close to 4,000 cases helped by the George Tiller Memorial Fund, which prioritizes support for women seeking second-trimester procedures and is affiliated with the National Network of Abortion Funds. Roughly half the women seeking financial assistance were black, which is noteworthy because African Americans represent only 13 percent of the U.S. population and just 36 percent of all women who have abortions. The closing of clinics increased the travel times of Tiller Fund recipients dramatically from 97 to nearly 200 miles between 2010 and 2015, and that figure was double for women in their second trimester. The average cost was $2,248, and poor women are unlikely to have credit cards or social support networks that they can rely on to raise the money. This puts them in a race against the clock, which is why 20-week abortion bans are so troubling to activists sensitized to the constraints women are facing. Race also factors into access to EC. Only 80 percent of IHS pharmacies carry Plan B—according to a 2014 survey conducted by The Native American Women's Health Education Resource Center—9 percent do not offer Plan B at all, 11 percent require a prescription, and 72 percent still impose the age restrictions that should have been removed in 2013. The pro-choice organization If/When/How: Lawyering for Social Justice has created a series of informative issue briefs that use an intersectional reproductive justice lens to examine the disparate impact of laws and policies on marginalized individuals and communities—women of color, women with disabilities, and women in the prison system.

The military is another institution that regulates women's access to abortion. In January 2013, President Barack Obama signed the Shaheen Amendment to provide servicewomen coverage for abortions if they are victims of sexual assault, but women in the armed forces still face barriers. Their health insurance, TRICARE, cannot be used to cover the cost of abortion, and even if the woman has private insurance she cannot receive abortion care in military medical facilities. If a woman is deployed in Iraq, Afghanistan, or another country where abortion is outlawed and unsafe, going off-base for the procedure is not an option (https://www.ifwhenhow.org/support-resources/academic-support/). Immigrant detention centers have come under the spotlight recently as well. In October 2017, the Trump administration aggressively blocked a 17-year-old undocumented immigrant from leaving the facility where she was being held in Texas despite the fact that she had obtained a judge's permission to have an abortion without parental consent. "Jane Doe" finally underwent the procedure thanks to the assistance of the American Civil Liberties Union but only after weeks of delay.

What happens when women are denied access to abortion? Although it is difficult to estimate the number of attempted self-induced or "DIY" abortions, Google searches provide some insight into underground phenomenon. According to economist Stephens-Davidowitz (2016), there were more than 700,000 Google searches for methods to self-induce abortions in 2015. "Buy abortion pills online" and "free abortion pills" were common search terms. There were also thousands of inquiries about herbal remedies like parsley or vitamin C. There were over 4,000 searches on performing an abortion with a coat hanger and a few hundred on bleaching one's uterus and punching one's stomach. Mississippi, where there is only one remaining abortion clinic, had the highest rate of google searches. Another indicator of this trend is that the Dutch pro-choice group Women on Web, which sends abortion pills to women in countries where abortion is banned, reported receiving more than 600 e-mail requests for help in terminating pregnancies from women in the United States in 2015. Excerpts from letters they received and shared with *The Guardian* speak of desperation: a woman trapped in an abusive relationship, a homeless woman who could not afford the $650 fee for abortion services, a teenager whose parents refused to consent to the abortion (Redden 2016). Women have been prosecuted for ordering abortion pills online. Jennifer Whalen, a 39-year-old mother living in a rural area in Pennsylvania, was given a 9- to 18-month sentence in 2014 for trying to help her 16-year-old daughter terminate an unintended pregnancy.

The voices of women who must continue with an unwanted pregnancy are rarely heard in the debate. Advancing New Standards in Reproductive Health conducted a study to learn more about the experiences of women who are turned away from abortion clinics because they are past the gestational limit. Foster's (2014) findings dovetail with the concerns women themselves expressed about future outcomes; they found lower scores on child development for the children of women denied abortions compared to the children whose mothers received an abortion. It is often overlooked that the majority of women who have abortions are already mothers, and these women frequently cite the desire to provide better care to existing children and the inability to afford another child as factors in their decision to terminate. In an illuminating qualitative study by Jones, Frohwirth, and Moore (2008), women express love for the children they are raising but also recognize that motherhood can be emotionally, physically, and financially taxing, especially when caring for children with special needs or when managing one's own health problems. Women desire the "ideal" conditions for their children, which embodies ideas of financial stability, as well as the ability to provide high levels of care and attention. Being able to parent children with adequate social support in safe and healthy environments is another fundamental human right in the reproductive justice framework.

Stigma

> But amidst the fog of abortion wars, something has gotten lost. This is the possibility of conversation at a lower decibel by women concerning their own decisions and experiences. We understand why most women don't talk about abortion at the level of individual experience. Yet this form of silence takes a toll on women's well-being; it turns out there is something literal about being "weighed down by a secret."
>
> (Sanger 2017, xiii)

American culture still "slut shames" women for their sexual agency. Abortion compounds the stigma, particularly if the woman's reasons are deemed "frivolous" or her "transgression" is repeated. Scholars have theorized about the reasons that abortion is so heavily stigmatized—it is perceived as a violation of "feminine ideals" of womanhood, the fetus has been increasingly personified with technological advances, excessive legal regulations evoke criminality or morally wrongdoing, abortion practice is thought to be dirty or unhealthy, and shame has been rained down on women by those opposed to abortion (Norris, Bessett, Steinberg, Kavanaugh, De Zordo, and Becker 2011). Consider, for example, The Radiance Foundation's confrontational billboards targeting African American women with messages like: "The most dangerous place for an African-American is in the womb." These play on the worst stereotypes about African American women's inability to protect their children and cast them as not just baby killers but pawns in racial genocide. In July 2016, following the brutal deaths of Alton Sterling and Philando Castile, who joined the long list of black lives tragically lost to police violence, activity on #UnbornLivesMatter surged. Critics have called out their hijacking of the Black Lives Matter Movement's message. Ryan Bomberger (2016) defended the pro-life movement's use of the frame: "Just to put things into perspective, Planned Parenthood kills more unarmed black lives in one day than police are accused of killing in one entire year." It has been reported by clinic escorts that anti-abortion protesters have even shouted "hands up, don't abort" to black women entering abortion clinics. Loretta Ross (2008), cofounder of SisterSong Women of Color Reproductive Justice Collective, scoffs at their insincere nod to social justice and the inherent victim blaming: "We are now accused of 'lynching' our children in our wombs and practicing white supremacy on ourselves. Black women are again blamed for the social conditions in our communities and demonized by those who claim they only want to save our souls (and the souls of our unborn children). This is what lies on steroids look like."

In light of these many controversial firestorms, it is perhaps not surprising that the practice of abortion remains hidden behind a veil of secrecy and shame even though it is a very common medical procedure. As Cockrill and Nack (2013) explain, abortion is associated with negative stereotypes of "bad girls" who were promiscuous and careless, which women may internalize. The women they interviewed expressed that they felt stigma as they imagined judgmental reactions if they were to disclose the unintended pregnancy or abortion. Some experienced stigma from pro-life medical practitioners who attempted to dissuade them, friends who withdrew, and partners who harshly rebuked. To manage the feelings of shame on an individual level, women used a variety of techniques, including excuses, justifications, stigma transference, cover stories, passing, and appealing to higher loyalties like responsibilities to care for existing children.

Since the 1960s, the pro-choice movement has tried to destigmatize abortion on a societal level with "speak-outs," and it continues to do so with online activism. In 2003, Patricia Beninato created imnotsorrydotnet.wordpress.com/ to debunk the frame that everyone who has an abortion is ashamed or has a negative experience. In 2015, #ShoutYourAbortion went viral. It was created by Amelia Bonow and Lindy West in response to the campaign to defund Planned Parenthood. The two were suddenly struck with the realization that even as pro-choice feminists they had been whispering about their abortions and only to their closest friends, thereby ceding the contested territory. In West's words, the pro-life movement then gets to "define it however suits them best. They can cast those of us who have had abortions as callous monstrosities, and seed fear in anyone who might need one by insisting that the procedure is always traumatic, always painful, always an impossible decision. Well, we're not, and it's not" (West 2015).

Solutions and Common Ground

This chapter has described the impassioned disputes over the legality of abortion, state regulation, government funding, fetal rights, and women's health. Even this lengthy examination does not exhaust the list of contested matters. Looking at these heated arguments, it is easy to understand why some fear that abortion is an unresolvable issue. Nevertheless, scholars and writers have proposed solutions that might bridge the chasm between the pro-life and pro-choice movements. This section gives a summary of a few intriguing proposals that address the way we frame our arguments about abortion, how we talk about abortion, and where we actually seem to agree on abortion. Based on what you have read about the conflict, what is the likelihood that any of these ideas could gain traction or move us closer to a ceasefire in abortion wars?

Shifting Pro-Life and Pro-Choice Frames

Amidst the furor over *Webster v. Reproductive Services*, Laurence Tribe (1990), a Harvard professor of constitutional law, labeled the abortion conflict as "the clash of absolutes" between the absolute right of the fetus to life and the absolute right of a pregnant woman to liberty. He also noted that each side ignores the worth, if not the very existence, of the other side in their frames. Pro-life activists show photos of fetuses at anti-abortion rallies with no acknowledgment of where these fetuses actually live. In turn, pro-choice activists rarely acknowledge injury to the fetus—the images of wire coat hangers, for example, focus our attention only on the injury inflicted on women. "Giving voice to the human reality on each side . . . may be the only way to avoid the no-win battle that mercilessly pits women against their unborn children and leaves us all impoverished" (Tribe 1990, 6). Tribe asserts that there is common ground between the sides, and that is to reduce the number of unintended pregnancies and abortions. The tagline "safe, legal, and rare," which was popularized by President Bill Clinton in 1996, captures this idea and debunks the framing of the pro-choice movement as "pro-abortion." Public policies that could advance this goal include the pro-life movement's promotion of abstinence and the pro-choice movement's call for better sex education and access to contraception, and both sides working together on affordable health and child care to help families raise children.

As the collective action frames and the strategic frames derived from them seem to permit no compromise, some have called on their own side to shift position to permit to meet more in the middle. Anne Hendershott (2006), a sociologist with sympathies for the pro-life perspective, believes that more attention can now be given to providing public services to pregnant women and less to changing abortion laws, now that the fetal personhood frame has been successfully established. In her view, pro-life activists could move away from the philosophic absolutism of the past debates and move toward some real dialogue with pro-choice counterparts who also want peace.

Naomi Wolf (2001), writing as a pro-choice feminist, agrees that pro-choice has lost out to the pro-life movement in the debate. In focusing on women's privacy and rights, pro-choice rhetoric completely ignores the fetus, as if it means nothing. "We need to contextualize the fight to defend abortion rights within a moral framework that admits that the death of a fetus is a real death; that there are degrees of culpability, judgment, and responsibility involved in the decision to abort a pregnancy; that the best understanding of feminism involves holding women as well as men to the responsibilities that are inseparable from this country's high rate of abortion" (Wolf 2001, 180). Wolf asks the pro-choice movement to concede that abortion is an immoral thing, while maintaining that it is sometimes necessary and that it is up to women to make the judgment. In 2005, Senator Hillary Rodham Clinton expressed a similar sentiment by saying "abortion in many ways represents a sad, even tragic choice to many, many women." Clinton called on "people of good faith" to find "common ground" in abortion prevention: "We should be able to agree that we want every child born in this country to be wanted, cherished and loved" (Healy 2005).

According to William Saletan (2003), a political correspondent for *Slate*, pro-choice activists have been most successful when they find common ground with conservatives in a privacy framework. Saletan credits the pollster Harrison Hickman for the recasting of the abortion rights argument during the late 1980s to reach 60 percent of voters who defined themselves as neither pro-choice nor pro-life. Hickman advised, "We must not stress the individual's right to abortion, but rather, that the government does not have the right to say that abortion is never acceptable" (Saletan 2003, 24). NARAL's president, Kate Michelman heeded his advice. She understood that "sexual freedom" and "a woman's right to choose" would be unwelcome in the Bible belt, and so the organization advanced a new resistance to government intrusion frame—"Who Decides?"—that gave NARAL the upper hand in the debate in the early 1990s.

There are other frames that have gained little traction but are worth considering because they destabilize our routine thought patterns. Eileen McDonagh (1996), a professor of political science, has proposed a rethinking of the entire basis for legal abortion. McDonagh advocates accepting the pro-life view that the fetus is a human being with equal rights to all other humans. If the fetus has the same rights, it must also have the same responsibilities. The fetus is the result of a fertilized egg that implants itself in a woman's body—with or without her consent. With her consent, it is welcomed and loved and without her consent, there is no obligation for the woman to provide protection. Just like with rape, a woman's body is violated against her will. Having a baby will change her life, and it may harm her health or even kill her. No human being has the right to impose that on another human being. A pregnant woman has a right to destroy the fetus to stop the danger, and the state has the obligation to keep her from being hurt by other persons. "It is how we think about pregnancy, therefore, not merely how we think about the fetus, that justifies abortion" (McDonagh 1996, 17).

Alexander Sanger (2004), grandson of Margaret Sanger and chair of the International Planned Parenthood Council, also offers a new collective action frame for those who favor legal abortion. Using the science of evolutionary biology as a foundation, Sanger argues that reproductive freedom, which includes legal birth control and abortion, is essential to humanity as it allows each generation to reproduce in the best possible way. Women who can control their childbearing have a better chance of surviving and ensuring that if they have children they will be raised to be healthy and well equipped to start the reproductive cycle over again. The pro-life argument that every fertilized egg should be protected goes against the scientific laws of natural selection. Reproductive freedom is not granted by government—humans have it naturally—but government can try to take that freedom away. Sanger posits, "If a moral rule helps community survival, the rule will last. If it does not, it will wither away" (2004, 85). Efforts to deny this control will be ignored, or they will work to the detriment of the health of the human community. Human beings must have some control over the reproductive process to advance the overall well-being of humanity.

"Could there *really* be anything else left to say?" This is the question that Charles Camosy, a Catholic ethicist, poses in the introduction to his book, *Beyond the Abortion Wars: A Way Forward for a New Generation* (2015, 1). He eschews the labels of pro-choice and pro-life as a crude binary that masks areas of overlap. It is not the case that pro-choice people have no regard for the fetus and it is also not the case pro-life people are unequivocally against choice. The Republican and Democratic parties have a vested interest in stoking the flames of division on abortion to turn out voters to the polls, as do the news media in driving up ratings and website hits. Pro-choice supporters will most likely bristle at his suggestion that "prenatal children" be granted equal protection and that abortions be outlawed in most cases, with an eight-week gestational limit, and a stipulation that rape victims produce a signed affidavit. However, it is possible to envision bipartisan support for a Mother and Prenatal Child Protection Act that focuses on the advancement of gender equality by tackling pregnancy discrimination, parental leave, collection of child support, and domestic violence. Both sides can work together on ensuring that women have the resources they need to keep wanted children.

Toning Down the Rhetoric

Now that we have thoughtfully considered the intricate web of beliefs that underlie the abortion debate, we must critically reflect on the ways that those beliefs are being expressed. We hear the loudest voices shouting past one another with a divisive and sometimes even hateful tone intent on winning the argument. Changing how we talk about abortion is not just about empathetically listening and speaking to one another respectfully; it is also about agreeing on standards of evidence and engaging the scholarly community to inform our understanding of the issues. There is such widespread misinformation being circulated; shocking statistics are hurled by both sides, often without proper attribution to the original source. When presented in a tweet, a soundbite, or on a bumper sticker, there is no contextualization or nuance. To stem the rising tide of fake news and "alternative facts," we need to insist on scientifically credible claims, wherever the data may lead us. Of course, the implications of the findings will still have a subjective element, as deeply held ideologies will influence interpretation, but we must work to eradicate falsehoods.

Women amid reproductive decision making need to have the most accurate information to make an informed choice. As discussed in the previous section, the pro-choice movement has tried to debunk grossly misleading pro-life claims, but the idea that abortion is harmful to women has been disseminated so broadly that it has seeped into mainstream consciousness. Kavanaugh, Bessett, Littman, and Norris (2013) conducted a survey to investigate what Americans know about abortion. They began with an extensive review of the literature to identify areas of scientific consensus on various aspects of abortion and other reproductive health matters. A random selection of 639 online survey respondents, men and women between the ages of 18 and 44, were then asked to evaluate a series of statements. On a very basic question about whether abortion in the first trimester was legal, about two-thirds correctly indicated that it was, but 7 percent guessed that it was illegal, and 10 percent were unsure. On five other questions about abortion, fewer than half of the respondents answered correctly. When asked "Which has a GREATER health risk for a woman, abortion or giving birth?" only 30 percent gave the correct answer, which is giving birth. A first-trimester abortion also does not put a woman at a greater risk of having to face future fertility problems, but 36 percent of the sample incorrectly assumed that it did. On the link between first-trimester abortion and breast cancer, 37 percent indicated that is true even though the claim has been discredited by medical researchers. When asked whether a woman who has an abortion in the first trimester is more at risk of a serious mental health problem, 31 percent incorrectly answered "yes."

Are pro-choice politicians and organizations also prone to distortion and exaggeration? What about the pro-choice assertion that *one in three* women will have had an abortion by the age of 45? Pro-choice supporters have grabbed onto this statistic to destigmatize abortion by showing how common the experience is. It is actually based on sound data from the Guttmacher Institute. However, since 2008 when the finding was published, there has been a significant decline in abortion. In 2014, an estimated 926,200 abortions were performed, which was a drop of 12 percent since 2011. The abortion rate fell 14 percent over that period from 16.9 per 1,000 women aged 15–44 in 2011 to 14.6 abortions in 2014, which was an all-time low (Jones and Jerman 2017). The lifetime incidence statistic is currently being analyzed by the Guttmacher Institute. Now that is obviously more information than is possible to convey on a bumper sticker, but it is an important reminder of how much more we can learn by digging deeper into the scholarly literature.

The pro-choice movement has tried to keep alive the fear of the dangers of illegal abortion with harrowing stories of coat hangers and back-alley butchers, though the frame has become less resonant 45 years after the legalization. But would we really go back to that if *Roe v. Wade* were overturned? Rickie Solinger (2013), a prolific scholar on the history reproductive rights, reflects on the trends in the data over time. In 1930, before antibiotics, abortion was listed as the cause of death for almost 2,700 women, but by 1965 fewer than 200 women in the United States were dying from illegal abortion. It is also a misnomer that abortionists were all dangerous extortionists; some were skilled practitioners and compassionate officials who would look the other way to help a woman in distress. Solinger suggests that pro-choice movement's "consumer-protection" argument distracts from the more important matter: "Before legalization, laws against abortion endangered women, keeping them from making fundamental decisions about their lives." This example is instructive in terms of what it teaches about evaluating rhetoric. It asks us to take a critical approach to commonly held beliefs. It challenges us to scrutinize not just the utility of a frame but also its accuracy. It brings to light new aspects of the controversy that have formerly been overlooked or obscured. It falls short in delving deeply into both the data and the lived experiences of the illegal abortion era in citing only one credible expert, but it invites further scholarly investigation. Perhaps cooler heads will prevail with less sensational and more methodological approaches that truly illuminate the complexity of the abortion issue. There are several useful websites for fact checking information like Factcheck.org, a project of the Annenberg Public Policy Center of the University of Pennsylvania, which scrutinizes claims made about major U.S. politicians to "reduce the level of deception and confusion in U.S. politics" (FactCheck.org n.d.).

Polling to Identify Areas of Consensus

In a 2011 Gallup Poll, 47 percent of Americans identified as pro-life and 47 percent as pro-choice. The data suggests that there are eight policies that are favored by only one side in the abortion debate. One of these is whether abortion should be legal when a family cannot afford a child, which was favored by 64 percent of pro-choice Americans compared to only 9 percent of pro-life Americans. About three-quarters of pro-choice Americans were supportive of abortion when the baby is mentally or physically impaired; about the same percentage of pro-life Americans were opposed. The majority of pro-life Americans want to require ultrasounds (73 percent), ban federal funding (58 percent), and allow opt-out provisions for pharmacists and health care providers (61 percent), whereas over 70 percent of pro-choice Americans are opposed to these policies (Tables 2.1 and 2.2).

But what if we were to look at polling data with an eye toward compromise? This is the approach Saad (2011) takes in an article appropriately titled "Plenty of Common Ground found in the Abortion Debate." There is, in fact, some clear policy consensus among Americans. Here are the nine areas where the majority on each side agree. Regarding informed consent, 86 percent of pro-choice Americans and 87 percent

Table 2.1   Areas of Abortion Policy Conflict between Pro-Choice and Pro-Life Arguments

	Pro-Choice	Pro-Life	Difference
Only pro-choice adults favor			
Abortion legal when woman or family can't afford child	64	9	55
Abortion legal in first trimester	89	35	54
Abortion legal when baby may be mentally impaired	76	26	50
Abortion legal when woman's mental health endangered	87	37	50
Abortion legal when baby may be physically impaired	75	27	48
Only pro-life adults favor			
Require ultrasounds at least 24 hours before abortion	29	73	−44
Ban federal funds for abortion providers	23	58	−35
Allow opt-out provisions for pharmacists/health care providers	30	61	−31

Source: Gallup June 9–12; July 15–17, 2011. http://news.gallup.com/poll/148880 /plenty-common-ground-found-abortion-debate.aspx. Used by permission.

Table 2.2   Areas of Abortion Policy Consensus between Pro-Choice and Pro-Life Arguments

	Pro-Choice	Pro-Life	Difference
Abortion legal when woman's life endangered	97	69	28
Abortion legal when woman's physical health endangered	96	68	28
Abortion legal when pregnancy caused by rape or incest	91	59	32
Require informed consent for abortion patients	86	87	−1
Make abortion illegal in third trimester	79	94	−15
Ban partial-birth abortions	63	68	−5
Require parental consent for minors	60	81	−21
Require 24-hour waiting period	60	79	−19
Abortion illegal in the second trimester	52	90	−38

Source: Gallup June 9–12; July 15–17, 2011. http://news.gallup.com/poll/148880 /plenty-common-ground-found-abortion-debate.aspx. Used by permission.

of pro-choice Americans believe this is sound medical practice. There also appears to be discomfort on both sides about the legality of third-trimester procedures—79 percent of pro-choice and 94 percent of pro-life want the practice to be illegal— and partial-birth abortions—63 percent of pro-choice and 68 percent of pro-life want to ban the practice. Saad suggests, "While such positions may not square with those taken by the leading pro-choice and pro-life lobbying groups in Washington, enacting them would greatly narrow the scope of the debate among Americans as a whole."

References

The American Cancer Society. "Abortion and Breast Cancer." 2014. https://www.cancer.org/cancer/cancer-causes /medical-treatments/abortion-and-breast-cancer-risk.html (accessed December 21, 2017).

American Civil Liberties Union. "Minors' Rights to Confidential Health Care." https://www.aclu-nj.org/yourrights/publi cations/confidentialhealthcare/ (accessed April 24, 2018).

American College of Obstetricians and Gynecologists Committee Opinion No. 434. "Induced Abortion and Breast Cancer Risk. *Obstetrics & Gynecology*. 113: 1417–8, 2009 and Reaffirmed 2018. https://www.acog.org /Clinical-Guidance-and-Publications/Committee-Opinions /Committee-on-Gynecologic-Practice/Induced-Abortion- and-Breast-Cancer-Risk (accessed April 25, 2018).

Americans United for Life. "Supreme Court Rejects Texas Health and Safety Standards for Abortion Clinics; AUL Says Fight to Protect Women from Predatory Abortion Industry Continues." June 27, 2016. http://www.aul.org /2016/06/supreme-court-rejects-texas-health-and-safety- standards-for-abortion-clinics-aul-says-fight-to-protect- women-from-predatory-abortion-industry-continues/ (accessed April 24, 2018).

Baird-Windle, Patricia, and Eleanor J. Bader. *Targets of Hatred: Anti-Abortion Terrorism*. New York: Palgrave, 2001.

Bomberger, Ryan Scott. "#Blacklivesmatter, White Guilt and the Marketing of Racism." 2016. https://www.theradiance foundation.org/blacklivesmatter-white-guilt-and-the-marketing-of-racism/ (accessed January 13, 2018).

Boonstra, Heather D. "The Heart of the Matter: Public Funding of Abortion for Poor Women in the United States." *Guttmacher Policy Review* 10(1): 12–16, 2007. https://www.guttmacher.org/sites/default/files/article_files /gpr100112.pdf (accessed April 24, 2018).

Camosy, Charles C. *Beyond the Abortion Wars: A Way Forward for a New Generation*. Grand Rapids, MI: Wm. B. Eerdmans Publishing, 2015.

Cockrill, Kate, and Adina Nack. "'I'm Not That Type of Person': Managing the Stigma of Having an Abortion." *Deviant Behavior* 34(12): 973–990, 2013.

Coleman, Priscilla K., Catherine T. Coyle, Martha Shuping, and Vincent M. Rue. "Induced Abortion and Anxiety, Mood, and Substance Abuse Disorders: Isolating the Effects of Abortion in the National Comorbidity Survey." *Journal of Psychiatric Research* 43(8): 770–776, 2009.

Coutts, Sharon. "'Born Alive' Claims." *Rewire*. October 28, 2013. https://rewire.news/article/2013/10/28/centers-for-disease-control-disputes-anti-choicers-born-alive-claims/ (accessed January 3, 2018).

Davis, Wendy. "Wendy Davis: It's the Real Texans Who Count." CNN. https://www.cnn.com/2013/07/12/opinion/davis-standing-up-for-texas/index.html (accessed April 24, 2018).

Davis, Wendy. "Why I Stood Up for Texas Women." *Washington Post*. July 15, 2013. https://www.washington post.com/opinions/wendy-davis-why-i-stood-up-for-texas-women/2013/07/15/07bc14fa-eb67-11e2-aa9f-c03a72 e2d342_story.html?utm_term=.cc0c4901e3a3 (accessed April 24, 2018).

Ely, Gretchen E., Travis Hales, D. Lynn Jackson, Eugene Maguin, and Greer Hamilton. "The Undue Burden of Paying for Abortion: An Exploration of Abortion Fund Cases." *Social Work in Health Care* 56(2): 99–114, 2017.

FactCheck.org. "Our Mission." n.d. https://www.factcheck .org/about/our-mission/ (May 9, 2018).

Flavin, Jeanne. *Our Bodies, Our Crimes: The Policing of Women's Reproduction in America.* New York: New York University Press, 2008.

Foster, Diana Greene. "Effect of an Unwanted Pregnancy Carried to Term on Existing Children's Health, Development and Care." *Contraception* 90(3): 305–305, 2014.

Friedersdorf, Conor. "Why Dr. Kermit Gosnell's Trial Should Be a Front-Page Story." *The Atlantic.* April 12, 2013. https://www.theatlantic.com/national/archive/2013/04/why-dr-kermit-gosnells-trial-should-be-a-front-page-story/274944/ (accessed April 24, 2018).

Gatter, M., K. Kimport, D. G. Foster, T. A. Weitz, and U. D. Upadhyay. "Relationship between Ultrasound Viewing and Proceeding to Abortion." *Obstetrics & Gynecology* 123(1), 81–87, 2014.

Gitenstein, Mark. *Matters of Principle—An Insider's Account of America's Rejection of Robert Bork's Nomination to the Supreme Court.* New York: Simon & Schuster, 1992.

Grossman, Daniel, and Kate Grindlay. "Safety of Medical Abortion Provided through Telemedicine Compared with in Person." *Obstetrics & Gynecology* 130(4): 778–782, 2017.

Guttmacher Institute. "Counseling and Waiting Periods for Abortions." January 1, 2018. https://www.guttmacher .org/state-policy/explore/counseling-and-waiting-periods-abortion (accessed January 2, 2018).

Guttmacher Institute. "Emergency Contraception." January 1, 2018. https://www.guttmacher.org/state-policy /explore/medication-abortion (accessed January 8, 2018).

Guttmacher Institute. "Parental Involvement in Minors' Abortions." January 1, 2018. https://www.guttmacher.org /state-policy/explore/parental-involvemen t-minors-abortions (accessed January 2, 2018).

Guttmacher Institute. "Requirements for Ultrasound." January 1, 2018. https://www.guttmacher.org/state-policy /explore/requirements-ultrasound (accessed January 1, 2018).

Guttmacher Institute. "State Funding of Abortion under Medicaid." January 1, 2018. https://www.guttmacher.org /state-policy/explore/state-funding-abortion-under-medicaid (accessed January 3, 2018).

Guttmacher Institute. "State Policies on Later Term Abortions." January 1, 2018. https://www.guttmacher.org /state-policy/explore/state-policies-later-abortions (accessed January 4, 2018).

Guttmacher Institute. "Substance Abuse during Pregnancy." January 1, 2018. https://www.guttmacher.org/state-policy /explore/substance-use-during-pregnancy (accessed January 4, 2018).

Guttmacher Institute. "Targeted Regulation of Abortion Providers." January 1, 2018. https://www.guttmacher.org /state-policy/explore/targeted-regulation-abortion-providers (accessed January 3, 2018).

Haussman, Melissa. *Reproductive Rights and the State: Getting the Birth Control, RU-486, and Morning-After Pills and the Gardasil Vaccine to the US Market*. Santa Barbara, CA: ABC-CLIO, 2013.

Healy, Patrick D. "Clinton Seeking Shared Ground over Abortion." *New York Times*. January 25, 2005. http://www .nytimes.com/2005/01/25/nyregion/clinton-seeking-shared-ground-over-abortions.html (accessed January 12, 2018).

Hendershott, Anne. *The Politics of Abortion*. New York: Encounter Books, 2006.

Herbert, Bob. "In America; Stillborn Justice." *The New York Times*. May 24, 2001. https://www.nytimes.com/2001 /05/24/opinion/in-america-stillborn-justice.html (accessed April 24, 2018).

Jelen, Ted G., and Clyde Wilcox. 2003. "Causes and Consequences of Public Attitudes toward Abortion: A Review and Research Agenda." *Political Research Quarterly* 56: 489–500, 2003.

Jones, Rachel K., Lori F. Frohwirth, and Ann M. Moore. " 'I Would Want to Give My Child, Like, Everything in the World': How Issues of Motherhood Influence Women Who Have Abortions." *Journal of Family Issues* 29(1): 79–99, 2008.

Jones, Rachel K., and J. Jerman. "Abortion Incidence and Service Availability in the United States." *Perspectives on Sexual and Reproductive Health* 49(1): 17–27, 2017. https://www.guttmacher.org/sites/default/files/pdfs /journals/psrh.46e0414.pdf (accessed December 21, 2017).

Jones, Rachel K., and Kathryn Kooistra. "Abortion Incidence and Access to Services in the United States, 2008." *Perspectives on Sexual and Reproductive Health* 43(1): 41–50, 2011.

Kavanaugh, M. L., D. Bessett, L. L. Littman, and A. Norris. "Connecting Knowledge about Abortion and Sexual and Reproductive Health to Belief about Abortion Restrictions: Findings from an Online Survey." *Women's Health Issues* 23(4): e239–e247, 2013.

Kearney, Melissa S., and Phillip B. Levine. "Media Influences on Social Outcomes: The Impact of MTV's 16 and Pregnant on Teen Childbearing." The Brookings Institution. 2014. https://www.brookings.edu/research /media-influences-on-social-outcomes-the-impact-of-mtvs- 16-and-pregnant-on-teen-childbearing/ (accessed January 1, 2018).

Keys, J. "Running the Gauntlet: Women's Use of Emotion Management Techniques in the Abortion Experience." *Symbolic Interaction* 33(1): 41–70, 2010.

Lander, Jessica, and Carolyn Smith-Lin. "Trump Administration Cuts Funding for Teen Pregnancy Prevention Programs." *Washington Post.* September 7, 2017. https://www.washingtonpost.com/news/answer-sheet /wp/2017/09/07/trump-administration-cuts-funding-for-teen-pregnancy-prevention-programs-here-are-the-serious-consequences/?utm_term=.110bfa57b25a (accessed January 1, 2018).

Lee, Jennifer S. "Abortion Rights Group Plans a New Focus and a New Name." *New York Times.* 2003. http://www .nytimes.com/2003/01/05/us/abortion-rights-group-plans-a-new-focus-and-a-new-name.html (accessed January 5, 2018).

Lee, Traci G. "Wendy Davis' Epic Effort to Block Rollback of the Right to Choose in Texas." June 25, 2013. *MSNBC.* http://www.msnbc.com/martin-bashir/wendy-davis-epic-effort-block-rollback (accessed April 24, 2018).

LifeSiteNews.com. "The Abortion-Breast Cancer Link. The Ultimate Guide to Understanding How Abortion and Breast Cancer Are Related." n.d. https://www.lifesitenews .com/resources/abortion/the-abortion-breast-cancer-link (May 9, 2018).

Luker, Kristin. *When Sex Goes to School: Warring Views on Sex—and Sex Education—Since the Sixties.* New York: W.W. Norton & Company, 2006.

Major, Brenda, Mark Appelbaum, Linda Beckman, Mary Ann Dutton, Nancy Felipe Russo, and Carolyn West. "Abortion and Mental Health: Evaluating the Evidence." *American Psychologist* 64(9): 863, 2009.

Mason, Carol. *Killing for Life: The Apocalyptic Narrative of Pro-Life Politics.* Ithaca, NY: Cornell University Press, 2002.

McBride, Dorothy E., and Janine A. Parry. *Women's Rights in the USA: Policy Debates and Gender Roles*, 5th ed. New York: Routledge, 2016.

McBride Stetson, Dorothy. "US Abortion Debates 1959–1998: The Women's Movement Holds On." In *Abortion Politics, Women's Movements and the Democratic State: A Comparative Study of State Feminism*, edited by D. McBride Stetson, 247–266. Oxford: Oxford University Press, 2001.

McCaffrey, Dawn, and Jennifer Keys. "Competitive Framing Processes in the Abortion Debate: Polarization-Vilification, Frame Saving, and Frame Debunking." *The Sociological Quarterly* 41(1): 41–61, 2000.

McDonagh, Eileen L. *Breaking the Abortion Deadlock: From Choice to Consent*. New York: Oxford University Press, 1996.

Munson, Ziad W. *The Making of Pro-Life Activists: How Social Movement Mobilization Works*. Chicago: University of Chicago Press, 2010.

NARAL. "The Truth about Crisis Pregnancy Centers." 2016. https://www.prochoiceamerica.org/wp-content/uploads/2016/12/6.-The-Truth-About-Crisis-Pregnancy-Centers.pdf (accessed January 10, 2018).

NARAL Pro-Choice America. "Issues: Abortion Access." n.d. https://www.prochoiceamerica.org/issue/abortion-access/ (accessed May 9, 2018).

Nash, Elizabeth, Rachel Benson Gold, Zora Ansari-Thomas, Olivia Copello, and Lizmarie Mohammmed. "Laws Affecting Reproductive Health and Rights: State Policy Trends in the First Quarter of 2017." 2017. https://www.guttmacher.org/article/2017/04/laws-affecting-reproductive-health-and-rights-state-policy-trends-first-quarter-2017 (accessed December 12, 2017).

National Abortion Federation. "2016 Violence and Disruption Statistics." 2016. https://5aa1b2xfmfh2e2mk03kk8rsxwpengine.netdna-ssl.com/wp-content/uploads/2016-NAF-Violence-and-Disruption-Statistics.pdf (accessed January 10, 2017).

The Native American Women's Health Education Resource Center. "Indian Health Service Survey of Plan B Availability." 2014. http://nativeshop.org/images/pdf/2014-OTC-Survey-Flyer.pdf (accessed January 10, 2018).

Nelson, Jennifer. *Women of Color and the Reproductive Rights Movement.* New York: New York University Press, 2003.

Norris, Alison, Danielle Bessett, Julia R. Steinberg, Megan L. Kavanaugh, Silvia De Zordo, and Davida Becker. "Abortion Stigma: A Reconceptualization of Constituents, Causes, and Consequences." *Women's Health Issues* 21(3): S49–S54, 2011.

Packwood, Senator Bob. "The Rise and Fall of the Right-to-Life Movement in Congress: Response to the *Roe* Decision, 1973–83." In *Abortion, Medicine, and the Law*, 4th ed., edited by J. Douglas Butler and David F. Walbert, 629–647. New York: Facts on File, 1992.

Paltrow, Lynn M., and Jeanne Flavin. "Arrests of and Forced Interventions on Pregnant Women in the United States, 1973–2005: Implications for Women's Legal Status and Public Health." *Journal of Health Politics, Policy and Law* 38(2): 299–343, April 2013.

Patten, E., and G. Livingston. "Why Is the Teen Birth Rate Falling?" Pew Research Center. April 29, 2016. http://www.pewresearch.org/fact-tank/2016/04/29/why-is-the-teen-birth-rate-falling/ (accessed December 22, 2017).

The Pew Research Center. "2016 Campaign: Strong Interest, Widespread Dissatisfaction." July 7, 2016. http://www.people-press.org/2016/07/07/2016-campaign-strong-interest-widespread-dissatisfaction/ (accessed January 3, 2018).

Planned Parenthood. "Planned Parenthood Outlines Pattern of Unlawful Harassment by Extremists behind Video Fraud." July 20, 2015. https://www.plannedparenthood action.org/pressroom/planned-parenthood-outlines-patter n-unlawful-harassment-extremists-behind-video-fraud (accessed December 8, 2017).

Planned Parenthood Action Fund. "About Planned Parenthood Action Fund." n.d.-a. https://www.plannedparenthood action.org/about-us (accessed May 9, 2018).

Planned Parenthood Action Fund. "Still Fighting. No Matter What." n.d.-b. https://secure.ppaction.org/site/Donation2? df_id=23001&23001.donation=form1 (accessed May 9, 2018).

Planned Parenthood Action Fund. "20-Week Bans." n.d.-c. https://www.plannedparenthoodaction.org/issues/abor tion/20-week-bans (accessed May 9, 2018).

The Population Institute. "Senseless: The War on Birth Control." 2017. https://www.populationinstitute.org/exter nal/Senseless_The_War_on_Birth_Control.pdf (accessed December 29, 2017).

Quigley, Mallory. "Trump Administration Expands Efforts to Stop Taxpayer Funding of Abortion Overseas." *Susan B. Anthony List*. May 15, 2017. https://www.sba-list.org/news room/press-releases/trump-administration-expands-efforts- stop-taxpayer-funding-abortion-overseas (accessed April 24, 2018).

Raine, Tina R., Cynthia C. Harper, Corinne H. Rocca, Richard Fischer, Nancy Padian, Jeffrey D. Klausner, and Philip D. Darney. "Direct Access to Emergency Contraception through Pharmacies and Effect on Unintended Pregnancy and STIs: A Randomized Controlled Trial." *JAMA* 293(1): 54–62, 2005.

Reardon, David C. *Making Abortion Rare: A Healing Strategy for a Divided Nation*. Lakeside, CA: Acorn Books, 1996.

Redden, Molly. "'Please I'm Out of Options': Inside the Murky World of DIY Abortions." *Guardian.* November 21, 2016. https://www.theguardian.com/us-news/2016/nov/21/home-abortions-emails-secret-world (accessed December 29, 2017).

Resnek, Sophia. "Abortion Foes Aim to Grow 'Army' of Planned Parenthood Spies." *Rewire.* January 22, 2016. https://rewire.news/article/2016/01/22/abortion-foes-aim-grow-army-planned-parenthood-spies/ (accessed December 8, 2017).

Rocca, Corinne H., Katrina Kimport, Sarah C. M. Roberts, Heather Gould, John Neuhaus, and Diana G. Foster. "Decision Rightness and Emotional Responses to Abortion in the United States: A Longitudinal Study." *PLOS One* 10(7): e0128832, 2015.

Rohlinger, Deana. *Abortion Politics, Mass Media, and Social Movements in America.* Cambridge, England: Cambridge University Press, 2014.

Ross, Loretta. "Re-Enslaving African American Women." *Rewire.* December 8, 2008. https://rewire.news/article/2008/12/08/reenslaving-african-american-women/ (accessed January 12, 2018).

Ross, Loretta, and Rickie Solinger. *Reproductive Justice: An Introduction.* Berkeley: University of California Press, 2017.

Saad, Lydia. "Plenty of Common Ground Found in Abortion Debate." *Gallup Politics,* 2011. http://news.gallup.com/poll/148880/plenty-common-ground-found-abortion-debate.aspx (accessed April 25, 2018).

Saletan, William. *Bearing Right: How Conservatives Won the Abortion War.* Berkeley: University of California Press, 2003.

Sanger, Alexander. *Beyond Choice: Reproductive Freedom in the 21st Century.* New York: Public Affairs, 2004.

Sanger, Carol. *About Abortion: Terminating Pregnancy in Twenty-First Century America.* Cambridge, MA: Belknap Press, 2017.

Santelli, John S., Leslie M. Kantor, Stephanie A. Grilo, Ilene S. Speizer, Laura D. Lindberg, Jennifer Heitel, Amy T. Schalet, Maureen E. Lyon, Amanda J. Mason-Jones, Terry McGovern, Craig J. Heck, Jennifer Rogers, and Mary A. Ott. "Abstinence-Only-until-Marriage: An Updated Review of US Policies and Programs and Their Impact." *Journal of Adolescent Health* 61(3): 273–280, 2017.

Scherer, Michael. "How Valid Is Palin's Abortion Attack on Obama?" *Time Magazine.* October 13, 2008. http://content.time.com/time/politics/article/0,8599,1849483,00.html (accessed April 24, 2018).

Scherer, Michael. "Rick Santorum Wants to Fight 'The Dangers of Contraception.'" *Time Magazine.* February 14, 2012. http://swampland.time.com/2012/02/14/rick-santorum-wants-to-fight-the-dangers-of-contraception/ (accessed April 24, 2018).

Schroedel, Jean Reith. *Is the Fetus a Person? A Comparison of Policies across the Fifty States.* Ithaca, NY: Cornell University Press, 2000.

Schwiegershausen, Erica. "Elizabeth Warren Schools the GOP on Women's Rights." *The Cut.* August 4, 2015. https://www.thecut.com/2015/08/elizabeth-warren-schools-gop-on-womens-rights.html (accessed April 24, 2018).

Silverstein, Helena. *Girls on the Stand: How Courts Fail Pregnant Minors.* New York: New York University Press, 2007.

Smith, Chris. "Smith Joins Colleagues in Urging Passage of Holly's Law." U.S. Congressman Chris Smith. February 1, 2006. https://chrissmith.house.gov/news/documentsingle.aspx?DocumentID=56332 (accessed April 25, 2018).

Solinger, Rickie. "Five Myths about Abortion Rights." *Washington Post*. April 18, 2013. https://www.washington post.com/opinions/five-myths-about-abortion-rights /2013/04/18/bd53c884-a5e5-11e2-b029-8fb7e977ef71_ story.html?utm_term=.9a80773b3c03 (accessed December 21, 2017).

Stephens-Davidowitz, Seth. 2016. "The Return of the D.I.Y. Abortion." *New York Times*. https://www.nytimes.com /2016/03/06/opinion/sunday/the-return-of-the-diy-abortion.html (accessed December 29, 2017).

Tinker, Ben. "Reality Check: Trump on Clinton Allowing Abortions 'in the 9th Month, on the Final Day.'" October 20, 2016. https://www.cnn.com/2016/10/20 /politics/donald-trump-hillary-clinton-abortion-fact-check/index.html (accessed April 24, 2018).

Tribe, Laurence H. *Abortion: The Clash of Absolutes*. New York: W.W. Norton & Company, 1990.

Trumpy, Alexa J. "Woman vs. Fetus: Frame Transformation and Intramovement Dynamics in the Pro-Life Movement." *Sociological Spectrum* 34(2): 163–184, 2014.

Upadhyay, Ushma D., Sheila Desai, Vera Zlidar, Tracy A. Weitz, Daniel Grossman, Patricia Anderson, and Diana Taylor. "Incidence of Emergency Department Visits and Complications after Abortion." *Obstetrics & Gynecology* 125(1): 175–183, 2015.

Vitali, Ali. "Trump Signs 'Religious Liberty' Executive Order Allowing for Broad Exemptions." *NBC News*. May 4, 2017. https://www.nbcnews.com/news/us-news/trump-signs-religi ous-liberty-executive-order-allowing-broad-exemption s-n754786?cid=sm_npd_nn_fb_ma (accessed April 24, 2018).

Weitz, Tracy. "What We Are Missing in the Trans-Vaginal Ultrasound Debate." *Rewire*. March 1, 2013. https://rewire .news/article/2013/03/01/challenges-in-the-trans-vaginal-ultrasound-debate/ (accessed December 8, 2017).

West, Lindy. "I Set up #ShoutYourAbortion Because I Am Not Sorry, and I Will Not Whisper." *Guardian*. 2015. https://www.theguardian.com/commentisfree/2015/sep /22/i-set-up-shoutyourabortion-because-i-am-not-sorr y-and-i-will-not-whisper (accessed January 10, 2018).

Williams, Daniel K. 2015. *Defenders of the Unborn: The Pro-Life Movement before Roe v. Wade*. New York: Oxford University Press.

Wolf, Naomi. "Our Bodies, Our Souls." In *The Ethics of Abortion: Pro-Life vs. Pro-Choice*, 3rd ed., edited by Robert M. Baird and Stuart E. Rosenbaum, 179–192. Amherst, NY: Prometheus Books, 2001.

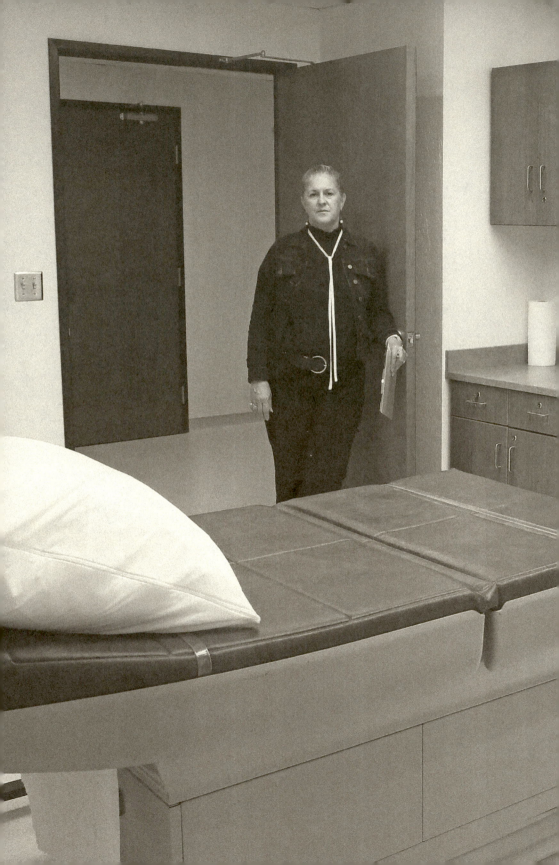

Introduction

Abortion continues to ignite fiery clashes in the public sphere. The inflamed rhetoric in the heavily polarized debate is so off-putting that many people completely avoid talking about this controversial subject in their private spheres. Internally, we may have at one time wrestled or may still wrestle with the fundamental questions—Does abortion end a human life? Should women have the right to choose? Those who gravitate to opposite sides are likely to find discussion of these core issues futile. This chapter makes no attempt to resolve these intractable positions. It will, however, challenge the reader to grapple with other intriguing questions—What are the implications of the Supreme Court's grounding *Roe v. Wade* in the right to privacy? Can abortion care be normalized? Could abortion be further destigmatized by the voices of millions speaking out? Is there room for pro-life feminism in the Women's Marches that proliferated after the election of President Trump? Why has

---

Founder and CEO Julie Burkhart enters a procedure room at the Trust Women South Wind Women's Center in Oklahoma City, September 16, 2016. This newly opened health care facility extends care to underserved communities and provides a range of reproductive health services, including abortion and emergency contraception. Pro-life activists hold prayer vigils outside in opposition to the clinic—the first to be opened there in four decades. Burkhart, a seasoned reproductive justice advocate, is accustomed to being a target, having worked alongside Dr. George Tiller, who was assassinated in 2009. (AP Photo/Sue Ogrocki)

Planned Parenthood been so heavily targeted and what would defunding mean? What alternatives are there to abortion for women facing an unplanned pregnancy? Should men have a say in abortion decision making? How do abortion rights and disability rights intersect and shape our views of who should or should not be born? The perspectives of scholars and activists featured here demonstrate the capacity we all have to put forth reasoned arguments. Considering these questions with an open and analytic mind will hone the reader's ability to think critically about controversial issues.

The Roots of *Roe*: Not Liberty, but Privacy
Trysh Travis

Whether you identify as "pro-choice" or "pro-life," it is useful to actually understand the basis of *Roe v. Wade*, the 1973 Supreme Court decision that "legalized" abortion. That decision is not based, as you might think, on some idea of gender equality or a universal right to bodily integrity. Instead, it is rooted in the right to privacy—a belief that there is a zone of life, and of decision making, into which the state cannot intervene. Asserting such a right carried the day in *Roe*, but it was hotly contested then and remains so today. Whatever your personal feelings about abortion, you should be aware of how this essential Supreme Court decision was crafted and understand the implications of its focus on privacy. A clear understanding of what *Roe* says, and why it says those things rather than the other things it could have said, might even change your mind about preserving or overturning it.

The Supreme Court had been thinking about privacy for several years when the *Roe* case came up for consideration. In *Griswold v. Connecticut*, 1965, the Court overturned as unconstitutional a Connecticut ban on the sale of "immoral material," which included information about and devices for contraception. The state's late 19th-century law, the Court found, impinged on a married couple's right to plan their families—a subject for private deliberation and decision making. The right to privacy was nowhere enumerated in the Constitution, but Justice William O. Douglas argued that it was implicit in "various guarantees" that did appear there. These included the First Amendment right to free association among persons and the Fourth Amendment "right of the people to be secure in their persons [and] houses . . . against unreasonable searches and seizures." "Penumbras" of privacy, argued Douglas, emanated from these explicit rights, creating "zones of privacy" beyond the scrutiny of the state. Marital decisions about contraception took place in such a zone, and the Court ordered that the Connecticut statutes be overturned in *Griswold v. Connecticut* (381 U.S. 479, 1965).

In *Eisenstadt v. Baird* (405 U.S. 438, 1972), the Court took this logic further, striking down a Massachusetts law prohibiting "crimes against chastity" that prohibited the dissemination of contraceptive information or devices to unmarried people. The zones of privacy enshrined in the Griswold decision were reaffirmed—married couples were not the only ones to enjoy them: "If the right of privacy means anything," Justice William Brennan argued in the decision, "it is the right of the individual, married or single, to be free from unwarranted governmental intrusion into matters so fundamentally affecting a person as the decision whether to bear or beget a child."

The stage was set to move beyond the question of contraception to that of abortion, and in the *Roe* decision, Justice Harry Blackmun referred specifically to the precedents put in place by *Griswold* and *Eisenstadt*. Acknowledging that "the Court has recognized the right of personal privacy, or a guarantee of certain areas or zones of privacy, does exist under the Constitution," he affirmed that "this right . . . is broad enough to encompass a woman's decision whether or not to terminate her pregnancy." This right to privacy was the essential holding in *Roe v. Wade* (410 U.S. 113, 1973); it laid the foundation for pregnancy termination as a woman's choice, to be made in consultation with whatever authorities she, and only she, deemed appropriate.

However, a woman's right to choose was not absolute. What of the unborn fetus? Unsurprisingly, the Constitution has nothing to say about fetal rights. In a time of widespread infant mortality, both religious and medical doctrines were unclear and inconsistent about the point at which infants became "persons." The idea that infants might have rights—or, even more counterintuitively, that infants not yet born might have rights—simply was not part of the Founding Fathers' worldview. Thus, the Court was in murky territory.

The *Roe* decision ultimately balanced a woman's right to privacy again the state's "important and legitimate interest in protecting the potentiality of human life," for example, the fetus. Without granting rights to the fetus, Blackmun acknowledged that within pregnancy two sets of interests coexist—that of the mother and that of the "potential life." "These interests are separate and distinct," he noted. "Each grows in substantiality as the woman approaches term, and at a point during pregnancy, each becomes 'compelling.'"

To determine what interests are "compelling" at what point, Blackmun framed pregnancy as a play in three acts or trimesters. In the first trimester, when abortion procedures were safe and an embryo could not exist outside the womb, the mother's interest was compelling. As a result, in consultation with her doctor she was "free to determine, without regulation by the state," whether to terminate her pregnancy. In the second trimester, things became more complicated. The mother's right to privacy was still compelling, but abortion itself was riskier, and the state had a duty to guard her health. Saying nothing about the fetus, Blackmun argued that states could "regulate the abortion procedure" in the second trimester "in ways that are reasonably related to maternal health." In the third trimester, when fetal viability outside the womb became a possibility, the state's interest shifted. When the "potentiality of life" was so much greater, the state could "regulate, and even proscribe, abortion" except when medically necessary to protect the mother's life.

The *Roe* framework, then, made a constitutional argument for unfettered access to first-trimester abortion by strongly affirming the right to privacy established in *Griswold* and *Eisenstadt*. In doing so, it helped to lay the groundwork for cases like *Lawrence v. Texas* (539 U.S. 558, 2003). In 2003, that case struck down a state law criminalizing homosexuality by arguing that "it is a premise of the Constitution that there is a realm of personal liberty which the government may not enter." Moving beyond the realm of reproductive health and sexuality, we can see other benefits to a body of law that acknowledges and protects a "realm of personal liberty." As corporations mine online data for information about consumers, and the government increasingly monitors individuals' movements through physical and cyberspace, demarcating some zones of life as "protected by law—do not enter" may become increasingly important.

Whether or not privacy was the best grounds for securing women's access to safe, legal abortion is another matter. Significantly, Sarah Weddington, who argued the *Roe* case before the Supreme Court, acknowledged the importance of privacy as laid out in *Griswold* but believed the more compelling constitutional argument lay in the Fourteenth Amendment's promise that no state could "deprive any person of life, liberty, or property, without due process of law; nor deny to any person within its jurisdiction the equal protection of the laws." At the time, pregnant women could be forced out of school, out of jobs, off the welfare rolls, and out of their apartments simply because they were pregnant. Thus, Weddington argued, while "one of the purposes of the Constitution was to guarantee to the individual the right to determine the course of their own lives," an unplanned pregnancy in effect disrupted that right, turning women into second-class citizens. The ability to terminate a pregnancy would restore it—and secure for women the same prospects for self-determination as men, as promised by the due process and equal protection clauses in the Fourteenth Amendment (U.S. Const. amend. XIV. Sec. 1).

The *Roe* decision acknowledged Weddington's argument that access to legal abortion was a matter of women's "right[s] in the concept of personal 'liberty.'" But it brushed past the concepts of rights and liberty in order to talk about privacy and the balance of "compelling interests" across the trimesters. The result, many commentators both conservative and liberal agree, was an absolute mess of lawmaking.

Roe's privacy argument secured a woman's right to terminate a pregnancy prior to fetal viability but at a high cost. The decision instantly opened a battle between pro-choice activists determined to preserve the access *Roe* had created and pro-life activists equally determined to chip away at it. More important, *Roe*'s decision-making framework allowed the Court to dodge two key questions: first, whether women's rights to self-determination are guaranteed within the Constitution and, second, whether fetuses are persons with rights of their own. These questions of liberty, unlike that of privacy, remain to be resolved by future generations—although the struggle between pro-life and pro-choice zealots has generated so much heat and so little light that it is difficult to know whether such complex constitutional matters can actually be entertained in a dispassionate fashion today. In the meantime, as reproductive justice advocate Kimberley Mutcherson argues so powerfully, "Perhaps the best way for a state to show respect for fetal life is to consider the needs of the pregnant woman who carries that fetus" (Mutcherson 1973).

Reference

Mutcherson, Kimberley. "*Roe v. Wade*, 410 US 113 (1973)," 160. In *Feminist Judgements: Rewritten Opinions of the United States Supreme Court*, edited by Kathryn M. Stanchi, Linda L. Berger, and Bridget J. Crawford, 146–167. New York: Cambridge University Press, 2016.

For Further Exploration

It is interesting to note that the *Roe* case was argued twice. At the first argument, in December 1971, there were only seven justices on the Court, due to the sudden mid-term retirements of Justices Hugo Black and John Marshall Harlan II. Given the complexity and gravity of the issues at stake in the case, Justice Blackmun suggested that the case be reargued in front of a full panel, and it was heard again in October 1972, after Justices William Rehnquist and Lewis Powell joined the bench.

A transcript and audio file of the December 13, 1971, *Roe v. Wade* argument, which includes more discussion of the Fourteenth Amendment, is available at https://apps.oyez .org/player/#/burger3/oral_argument_audio/16147.

The 1972 reargument, which includes a very pointed back-and-forth about fetal personhood between Weddington and Justice Potter Stewart, is available at https://apps.oyez .org/player/#/burger3/oral_argument_audio/16650.

Trysh Travis teaches in the Center for Gender, Sexualities, and Women's Studies Research at the University of Florida, where she specializes in the history of medicine and feminist media studies. Her work on gender and self-help in the United States has appeared in diverse outlets like American Quarterly, Raritan: A Quarterly Review, *and* Bitch: Feminist Responses to Popular Culture.

Normalizing Abortion: An Interview with a Reproductive Health Care Provider
Jennifer Keys

According to the National Abortion Federation, which has maintained a comprehensive database of attacks on abortion providers since 1977, there have been countless blockades and hundreds of letters threatening anthrax poisoning, as well as more extreme methods for disrupting abortion services including butyric acid attacks, arsons, and bombings. Abortion providers have been harassed and stalked, and 11 people have been murdered in the war against abortion. These are the dark and terrifying images that flash in our minds when we imagine the daily life of an abortion doctor. This interview was conducted in the summer of 2017 with a reproductive health care provider in New York State, who does not go to work in a bullet proof vest. In fact, his upbringing in a nonreligious, liberal household, his involvement as the president of Medical Students for Choice, his current family medical practice, and even his work as the medical director of Planned Parenthood have by and large been conflict free. Readers seeking gory war stories may find him "boring," which is the word he uses to describe himself. His experience is anything but boring. However, it illuminates a straightforward way of approaching abortion as a normal and necessary part of providing comprehensive reproductive health care.

Interviewer: Let's begin by talking a little bit about your experiences growing up. When did you first become aware of the abortion issue?

Doctor: I grew up in a very liberal household in New York City. I didn't grow up in any religious tradition, you know; sort of atheist from the get go. My mother is very politically involved and always led by example of speaking up for people who can't advocate for themselves. So, I wonder if my work as an abortion care provider grew out of her example—my interests really coincided. Then, I went to Vassar College, which is a very liberal college.

Interviewer: Tell me more about your medical background and your areas of specialization?

Doctor: I went to medical school in the Deep South and I was the head of Medical Students for Choice. During that time, another student created sort of a countergroup I guess, which he called Do No Harm. And we never really had any events, no debates, or confrontation. He's a very friendly guy on a personal level but made it clear that he wanted to make sure there's a counterpoint to the Medical Students for Choice activists trying to encourage people to go on to abortion care or at least learn about it.

Interviewer: Was there a professor who helped spark your interest in abortion care?

Doctor: I had several professors that were active in the pre-*Roe v. Wade* movement. One, in particular, had written a lot about contraceptive care and abortion care. He was actually a pediatrician, and he was from the Deep South and originally was anti-choice. As he took care of presumably girls (not women) since he was a pediatrician in the hospital who were suffering from the consequences of poorly performed abortions, that's what changed his mind. From hearing their stories he became pro-choice in a time and place when it was a very—you know, it wasn't encouraged at all. So, I had a one-month elective with him in reproductive health that included didactic sessions with him, which was really inspiring. Then spending time in a sort of contraceptive-focused clinic at the school, shadowing the providers there, and then also doing surgical abortions with the providers there.

Interviewer: Can you talk about the differences between your current family care practice setting and working as the medical director of Planned Parenthood?

Doctor: So, I'm a family physician. You know, I'm not an OB-GYN. I certainly find the abortion care I provide in the family medicine office much more satisfying because I feel like it's part of the entire care that I provide for the woman and her family. I think the patients appreciate it tremendously because they don't have to go to a place where they might feel stigma. You know, in my office, when they're waiting to be called for their appointment, they're sitting next to people who have colds or bring their children in for a visit or whatever. Not just a lineup of women just waiting for their abortions. So, I think patients find it much more private and little less scary. Plus, it's just with a doctor they know. At Planned Parenthood, it's with a complete stranger.

Interviewer: Can you describe the difference between medical abortion and surgical abortion?

Doctor: Medical abortion is a pill that stops the action of progesterone, which sort of keeps the pregnancy from progressing, and the uterus can't support the fetus anymore, followed a day later by medications that induce cramping, which are contractions of the uterus which bring out the pregnancy and the fetus. That can be done up to 10 weeks.

Every provider is a little different, but for me generally after about 7 weeks up to 15 weeks and 6 days I can provide a surgical abortion. In the family medicine office, we have manual aspirators, which allows you to do it up to 11 or 12 weeks or so. At Planned Parenthood, we have electric vacuums, which allows you to do the procedure much later in the pregnancy. The cervix is dilated open with some instruments that kind of just very gently force it open and then a very small vacuum is introduced into the uterus to suck everything out. So, that is the fetus, the placenta, all the supporting tissue. At Planned Parenthood, we do it with conscious sedation if the patient wants, which is IV medicine to help relax the patient and then local anesthesia, so numbing medicine around the cervix to minimize, but not eliminate cramping from the procedure.

Interviewer: What about the demographic profile of women you see?

Doctor: So, at our family medicine office, we don't take patients without insurance. So, right there, there is a branch point in the type of patients you will see. At Planned Parenthood, they can immediately get emergency Medicaid, which is really easy to get for pregnant women in New York State. So, a lot more uninsured women at Planned Parenthood. I mean, all types of people go in. I think a lot more undergraduate students used Planned Parenthood for their reproductive health care.

Interviewer: After the procedure is complete, what kinds of reactions are you typically seeing? Are there moments that remind you of the importance of the work or that feel career rewarding?

Doctor: Often there's gratitude. You know, periodically like "I'm really glad you're here. Thank you for doing this. I'm glad that this is available." I didn't realize that people are so thankful about this. I didn't realize how easy it is to integrate this into primary care.

One example I can think of for that is a patient of mine who is a protestant minister. I delivered two of her babies and did her pregnancy care and just always wondered if she found out that

I provide abortions how she would feel about it? Apparently she had heard from my schedule once that I was working at Planned Parenthood that day. I said, "Oh, I didn't know she told you that." She replied, "Yup. And I just want to say thank you, you know, that you're doing that. I think it's wonderful that you deliver babies and do that." You know, surprises like that are very encouraging.

Interviewer: As you know there is an abortion provider shortage. As someone who is training the next generation of doctors, are you doing anything to try to increase the ranks?

Doctor: I teach residents. You know, I try to show by example, showing that I really believe abortion care is perhaps best done within the context of primary care rather than having stand-alone clinics, which in many parts of the country are necessary, but showing that this is part of taking care of people. You know, I don't feel someone should be forced to provide care that they don't feel comfortable providing. But what I try to do is normalize it. Every year I do a lecture on pelvic exams for the medical students between their second and third year as part of a clinical boot camp. I just kind of use abortions as an example. You know, different techniques I might use, different pieces of equipment. You know, I use this for a Pap smear or an abortion. I just try to normalize it. That's one of the things I talk about with the medical students when we learn how to do pelvic exams. Like, "Okay, let's talk about all the social taboos we're about to break right here and why it's okay, but it's also okay to be disturbed by it at first."

I don't try to hide that it's care I provide or try to hide that I think it is important care to provide to people. You know, I do encourage people to become politically active, to call the representatives, things like that. You know? But again, I would never force anyone to do something they're not comfortable with.

Interviewer: Do students ever talk to you about whether they feel any internal conflict about maybe delivering babies one day and then doing a later-term abortion on another day?

Doctor: Generally not. I haven't had any students break down. It's something that I will try to bring up just to kind of let them know it's okay to talk about that stuff. I may ask, "How do you feel doing this?" And usually, the response I get is it's actually pretty similar to my feeling. I mean, you know, especially with the early second-trimester stuff we do, it's not my favorite of the day, but it's a necessary part of providing this care. It is nice that a lot of the students and residents who are contemplating providing abortion care find it to be a normal part of medical care. I always try to make sure the resident or the student goes in with me to make sure that all the products of conception are there and try to engage in that discussion.

Interviewer: Can you say a little bit more about your terminology, the "products of the conception"? Do you use term "fetus"? Are you mindful of the language?

Doctor: So, I talk very differently with patients and model that for the students depending on what their intentions are and I try to talk about when the patient comes in, maybe not so much at Planned

Parenthood, but in the primary care office when the patient comes in because she's pregnant, not assuming. I always talk before so I know sort of what her feelings are about the pregnancy. "How do you feel about this?" "Is this a surprise? Were you expecting this?" Yeah. If the patient is not gonna continue, you know, I try to talk to the students about choosing your words carefully and the pregnancy and make sure "Okay, I'm gonna do an ultrasound. Do you want me to turn the screen away from you? What's your preference?"

Interviewer: Have you ever felt threatened by anti-abortion protesters?

Doctor: At the Planned Parenthood affiliates here, we actually stopped the escort program because there's no need for it. There were never any protestors. They're in big multi-office buildings. No one knows where you're going. You know, I do recommend to people not to carry things that identify them as medical students or residents, but with the caveat that I never see a protestor. See? I'm boring.

Interviewer: Did providing abortions feel riskier to you after you got married and had a family?

Doctor: I certainly think about how it impacts my family more now that I have children. And again, I feel very fortunate to live in a place where it doesn't seem to impact my family. Again, this is something I did from the time I was a medical student. I guess the settings where I was, I always felt like even though people might have different opinions than me about it, it was never threatening to me to provide that care. So, I didn't have to make decisions like that that many doctors are faced with. You know, if I had lived in a place—You know, if I lived in Mississippi, you know, I think, yes, it would change the calculation quite a lot.

Interviewer: How do you talk to your children about your work?

Doctor: My daughters are 8 and 10. So, we talk about how someone for various reasons can't continue being pregnant. And so, you know, I'm able to help them with that as a doctor. They've never really asked about details of that and I have to think carefully about how I will talk about that. You know, with the medical abortion, I think, you know, that's my cop out. You know, I go say, "Well, there's pills that can help a woman not be pregnant." And I imagine when they ask, which I'm sure they will at some point, that's how we'll start the conversation.

Interviewer: Do you see any common ground in the abortion debate?

Doctor: I mean, obviously, contraception is not going to be a common ground, but is that something that you think a lot of people could agree on, but no. People are using abortion politics as sort of a populist message when the real goal is to just keep women subjugated. It might have nothing to do with being pro-child or wanting children to have healthy lives, but really it's just about controlling women. I am fighting that in my own little way both through teaching medical students and residents and the care I provide patients. Nobody's proabortion is the common ground and reducing the need for abortion.

Interviewer: What other final thoughts would you like to share?

Doctor: I feel like I'm cheating. You know, my family is very liberal. My wife's family is very liberal.

Providing women with comprehensive reproductive health care just feels like a normal thing
to me, you know. Like my experience is so easy
and normalized compared to the experience that
many other providers have. I wish that can be
the experience that everyone has. I guess I would
just have people know that there's a range of experiences that providing abortions does not necessarily have to be a scary thing depending on
where you live.

*Notes: The full interview (14,423 words) was fully transcribed
and coded to extract the key themes with the assistance of my
undergraduate research assistant Cindy Motyka. To enhance read-
ability, there was some reordering of the topics and editing of the
mostly verbatim responses.*

The Abortion Diary: Uncovering, Sharing, and Listening to the Archive We Hold within Our Bodies
Melissa Madera

Abortion happens every day. The Guttmacher Institute (2016)
estimates that over 50 million people worldwide will have an
abortion each year. Yet how many times have you heard someone share their abortion story? Have you ever? The majority
of people will never talk about their abortion experiences, and
very few people will ever hear their stories. I started The Abortion Diary in 2013 in order to provide a space to share and
listen to our stories.

Before delving further, it is important to take a moment to
reflect on terminology. Abortion is often framed as a wom-
en's issue and, although the majority of research and language
about abortion uses the term "women," I have made an effort
to use gender-neutral language in order to include people who
have abortions who do not identify as women, are transgender,

or are gender nonconforming, and men who choose to share their stories. The reader will also note that I do not use the terms "pro-choice" and "pro-life" because I am not focusing on the political battle or debates about abortion. Abortion is not a political act; it's a personal experience.

The Abortion Diary asks: What if millions of people broke their silence and told the truth about their lives and choices? What if people could access and listen to those truths? Initially, I began this project in order to create a community around an experience that can be extremely isolating and overly politicized, and provide an intimate space for sharing, listening, and, most important, feeling listened to by others. When I asked Nikki why she wanted to share her story for the podcast, she said, "I feel like nobody should have to experience anything in life without sharing it. I feel like through our experiences it teaches us a lesson and I feel like we owe it to the world to share it." Nikki's words reflect the core purpose of this project. I seek to provide people with a safe and supportive environment to share stories that are rarely told. The Abortion Diary offers people the opportunity to openly and candidly talk about a full spectrum of experiences in their reproductive lives. They share their unmediated, nuanced, and complicated experiences without feeling that they need to follow a script or adhere to the expectations of political movements that can be disconnected from the reality of people's lived experiences.

Through this podcast I was also able to break my own silence. I didn't talk about my abortion for 13 years. And, honestly, I began The Abortion Diary to fill my own need. I wanted to share my own abortion story and connect with other people who had their own stories to tell. But, like many of the other people who have shared their abortion story with me, I didn't feel like I had a community and yearned to hear people's voices. I found that digital media in the form of podcasts was the perfect platform to create the community I longed for.

Within the academic discourse, political debate, and activism around abortion storytelling, this podcast is unique, something that anyone can access and listen to anywhere and at anytime. People can listen at home, in a car, on the bus, on a plane or train, on a run, while walking: in short, anywhere. The public gets to listen to our personal experiences and to history. With very little media coverage and outreach, The Abortion Diary has garnered listeners in every state in the United States and in over 40 other countries.

Since beginning the project in July 2013, I have traveled to over 20 states across the United States, over 10 European cities, Canada, the Dominican Republic, and Thailand with the podcast. I have listened to and recorded over 280 people share their reproductive experiences. I've slept on countless couches, floors, and guest rooms. I've been hosted by friends and strangers. The experiences that have been shared are quite diverse across socioeconomic background, ethnicity, race, religion, and gender, and span from the mid-1950s to 2016. The ages of the storytellers have ranged from 18 to 85, and the geographic locations include 33 U.S. states and 21 countries.

This podcast connects, through shared experience, people across generations, socioeconomic status, and ethnicity and promotes personal introspection and cultural inspection. While it is a space for sharing, listening, and healing, The Abortion Diary has also become an archive: providing historical context and creating a public record for future generations. As an oral history project, it elucidates people's real experiences with abortion and challenges the common notions and dominant discourses about abortion. This archive also provides us with a unique opportunity to learn about the social and cultural history of abortion through personal story.

The more I listened to people's stories, the more questions I had about the history of abortion. I realized that people weren't always silent about their abortion experiences. I wondered when and why that had changed. Why was I hearing about postabortion rituals all of a sudden? Why are we so afraid to talk about sadness, mourning, and loss when it comes to abortion? And why do so many people who share their stories with me use those words? Why would people tell me, a total stranger, about such a deeply personal experience when they wouldn't tell their family, friends (even their best friends), partners, or doctors? And then allow me to put it on a podcast anyone can hear. Listening to these stories continues to bring up questions. It also helps me answer them.

I've learned from people like Judith Arcana, a Jane in The Abortion Counseling Service of the Chicago Women's Liberation Union, and Barbara, who helped establish an underground abortion service in Tulsa, Oklahoma, about what it was like to help people gain access to safe and affordable, although illegal, abortion services before *Roe v. Wade*, the historic Supreme Court ruling guaranteeing the right to safe and legal abortions in the United States. Devra, Sondar, Paul, Judi, and many other people have shared their pre-*Roe* abortion experiences. In sharing her story Jean wants us to remember that "abortions were illegal, and that women were dying." Indeed, while some people were privileged enough to access a relatively safe abortion with a private physician through connections made by family or friends, or by traveling to another country, such as Puerto Rico, others, particularly poor people or people of color, were more likely to face unsafe and dangerous conditions or attempt to self-induce an abortion. Some people, like Abby, were able to get approval for an abortion at a hospital because she lived in a state where it was possible if it was deemed necessary to protect her physical or mental health.

I've listened to people talk about the difficulty of obtaining an abortion and the often dangerous and unsafe conditions. Devra was picked up at a bus stop by a stranger and taken to an unknown location. Cathy endured sexual harassment from her abortionist while lying on a dinette table in a seedy motel room. Sue talked about the high cost and desperate need to borrow money. Judy had to travel across state lines, while Jean and Emily traveled to other countries. It was illegal and risky but necessary.

Through my listening I realized the importance of capturing those experiences. After all, I am a historian and I crave story, and those experiences so desperately need capturing. As Linda Kerber notes, there is a scarcity of research and knowledge about what the 1973 *Roe v. Wade* Supreme Court decision has meant for people and our local communities over the past 45 years. Moreover, she warns of the "rapidly fading memories" of those who struggled for reproductive rights and obtained illegal abortions before the *Roe* decision and highlights the "opportunity to capture a history that still shapes American lives and politics" (Kerber 2012). This project has, inadvertently, responded to Kerber's call for action and activism.

But the stories shared on this podcast go beyond that call by furthering our understanding of what getting an abortion has been like over the past 45 years. These interviews reveal the accessibility and inaccessibility of abortion around the country. While abortion is now legal and easily accessible to some people in many parts of the country, a short drive or subway ride to a nearby clinic, for many abortion is unaffordable and inaccessible. They talk about how they have experienced the closing of clinics in their communities, clinic violence, and the rise of anti-abortion rhetoric and legislation, such as parental notification laws, state-directed mandatory counseling, medication abortion restrictions, mandatory ultrasounds, the lack of public funding for abortion, and state-funded crisis pregnancy centers. For example, Kristie and Hunt were given false information and shamed at Crisis Pregnancy Centers in two very different parts of the country. Meg, Kate, and Katie traveled long distances. Bess fought for a judicial bypass in Michigan. Another story-sharer had to navigate accessing an abortion as an undocumented high school student. And some, like Luz, Kristina, and Toya, have self-induced their own abortions because of long wait times or because they were financially strapped. One story-sharer in Louisiana traveled out of state for an abortion, although there was an abortion clinic just two miles from her home, because she lacked information about resources in her city.

These stories illuminate how laws, identities, race, structural inequalities, religion, societal and cultural norms, and a variety of barriers affect people's experiences with and access to basic reproductive health care. These story-sharers talk about all aspects and realities surrounding their abortion experience, something that happens every day around the world. Many talk about their experiences with silence, stigma, isolation, and misconceptions surrounding abortion. They talk about their experience at abortion clinics and hospitals, the medical professionals they encountered, their physical and emotional experience, the cost, and who they told and didn't tell. They also break stereotypes that people have about community beliefs around abortion and the personal choices that they make. They are myth breaking as they are risk taking, breaking the myths that abortion is to be difficult or easy, traumatic or simple, life-altering or uneventful, disempowering or empowering. Every experience is different, and its meaning is different for every person. Through this podcast we are truly learning from a community of voices.

As oral historians have argued, "The interviewing of eye-witness participants in the events of the past for the purposes of historical reconstruction" allows us to include within the historical record the experiences and perspectives of groups of people who might otherwise have been hidden from history (Perks and Thomson 1998). Certainly that is the case around abortion narratives. Very few people ever find the space to tell this personal story. This oral history project is rooted in the belief that all of our full, complex stories should be shared, listened to, and honored. Unfortunately, our stories are so often reduced to one-dimensional, two-minute soundbites that are told for us rather than by us. Through The Abortion Diary I have been able to capture the real voices of people as they share their own stories in their own words. These stories reimagine and redefine what we view as the archive, where history and our stories are held. Our body is an archive; it holds our stories. These narratives provide us with a unique opportunity to hear the real stories of real people about marginalized, silenced experiences and uncover the archive within our own bodies.

References

Guttmacher Institute. "Induced Abortion Worldwide." Fact Sheet. March 2018. https://www.guttmacher.org/fact-sheet/induced-abortion-worldwide (accessed May 10, 2018).

Kerber, Linda K. "The 40th Anniversary of Roe v. Wade: A Teachable Moment." *Perspectives on History: The Newsmagazine of the American Historical Association.* October 2012.

Perks, Robert, and Alistair Thomson. *The Oral History Reader.* London and New York: Routledge, 1998.

Originally from Washington Heights, New York, Dr. Melissa Madera (aka. the abortion diarist) is a first-generation Dominican American and founder of the Abortion Diary. She travels the world with her podcast and is a story-sharer and dedicated story-listener, public speaker, recovering academic, multimedia historian, full-spectrum doula, and a bilingual reproductive justice educator and advocate. Dr. Madera is also the curator of "ar·ti·facts: abortion stories and histories," a traveling multimedia exhibit that gives voice to untold and silenced experiences through audio stories, images, and objects, artifacts gathered by Melissa over the past four years for the Abortion Diary. She has been featured on the front page of The Washington Post, *on NPR's Weekend Edition, a Q&A with* Cosmopolitan *magazine, Latina.com, Rewire, ThePool.com, Univision, and MSNBC. She holds a BA in history from Baruch College (CUNY), a master of science in social studies education from Pace University, and a master of arts and a PhD in*

Latin American and Caribbean history from the State University
of New York at Binghamton.

Treating Each Other Like Drunk Girls in the Bathroom: A Pro-Life Feminist Finds Acceptance at the Women's March
Destiny Herndon-De La Rosa

"If we all treated each other like drunk girls do in the bathroom, the world would be a much better place."

A friend of mine posted a picture of a worn wooden plaque that read this on my Facebook wall back in January. I'm sure it was copied off a Pinterest board, linking to an Etsy shop. I smiled but really didn't give it much thought until two weeks later when my feminist group was removed as a sponsor from the 2017 Women's March on Washington (WMoW) simply for being pro-life.

Well, actually, let me clarify; they knew we were pro-life when they accepted our sponsorship application, but we were removed when the entirety of feminist twitter lost its ever-loving mind and posted a deluge of tweets demanding our immediate removal. The organizers caved in to the pressure and took our name off the WMoW website.

I got it. There were no hard feelings. Because, trust me, when you are a pro-life feminist, you're used to getting hated on from all sides. Still, it stung. It hurt to know that feminists far and wide saw my group, New Wave Feminists (NWF), as a threat.

Truth be told, if pro-lifers have to exist, we're the kind you want. Founded over a decade ago with just a handful of members, NWF's mission has always been to add a life-affirming contingent to the feminist movement, while also calling on the pro-life movement to understand the many causes leading women to feel pressured into abortion in the first place. We saw that abortion was often viewed even by the pro-choice side as a "necessary evil." So we wanted to work to find nonviolent alternatives instead.

Feminism does an amazing job focusing on the needs of women, while the pro-life movement is wonderful about providing support for unborn children. However, both movements often times only see one person, either the woman or the child. Pro-life feminists work to support and protect both through social change. We believe laws follow culture, not the other way around. While many pro-life groups look to overturn *Roe v. Wade*, that's simply not our focus. We'd rather our energy and resources go toward creating a world where women are supported so well they never have to abort their own child in order to live a happy and successful life. And because of that vision, our membership has grown to over 27,000 strong.

Plus, bottom line, it's exhausting always being against everything, and so negative. We wanted to be *for* alternatives. It's one thing to be anti-abortion, but what does it mean to be truly pro-life? For us it meant not just focusing on life in the womb. That was a starting point, but we wanted our activism to go far beyond that. When I heard Senator Eddie Lucio of Texas, who's a pro-life Democrat, refer to himself as "pro-lifetime," a lightbulb went off. That's what NWF had been doing all along. That's why we subscribe to the Consistent Life Ethic, which is a belief that human beings should be free from violence for the duration of their lifetime. We're against unjust war, the death penalty, torture, and abortion (when we believe all human beings are at their most weak and vulnerable). Basically, we're *pro*-human dignity.

And once you start looking at life through that lens, you start seeing the humanity of every member in the human family regardless of race, religion, gender, sexual orientation, or nationality. You see people as these uniquely beautiful and wonderful creations, and you truly want what's best for them.

To put it in a less poignant way, you kind of become a drunk girl in the bathroom. In case you don't know this, drunk girls in the bathroom love eeeeeeeeeeeeeeeeeeeveryone! Walk into a bar bathroom on a Saturday night and suddenly your self-esteem is wrapped in a nice warm hug. You'll hear squeals of

"Girl, you look amazing in that top!" and "OMG, your hair is fabulous!" and "Woman, I will trade you my first born for those heels!" There's just something so magical about drunk chicks in a communal restroom. There is a kind of sisterhood there that allows a woman to borrow a tampon from a total stranger, an ethic of care when someone holds your hair back as you are leaning over the toilet because you have had too much to drink, and an unwritten code of looking out for one another. Need to fend off creepers? I am happy to pretend to be your lesbian girlfriend. It's like all of our differences fade away and we can't stop ourselves from supporting one another.

After we were removed as sponsors from the WMoW I was literally doing phone, newspaper, and TV interviews for seven straight days, from the moment I woke up until I went to bed each night.

At first a majority of the coverage was coming from right-wing media outlets. But the more I talked about the Consistent Life Ethic, the more a broader audience started listening. While others might disagree with us on the abortion issue, when we got beyond abortion there was so much common ground to stand on. We all want to see an end to war, violence, and innocent lives being lost. We all want to live in a nation built on respecting other's inherent rights and human dignity. There is a growing recognition that Trump's presidency might be threatening that. We needed more voices speaking out, not fewer.

That's when NPR, VICE News, and *The New York Times* started calling. Reporter after reporter would tell me that they understood where I was coming from. Even if the reporters disagreed, almost all of them were at least listening to why some people might be opposed to an act which they truly believe ends a human life. We were not just "bumper sticker" believers; we were investing our time, talents, and resources into helping women find nonviolent alternatives.

Bottom line, no one ever *wants* an abortion. It is not a fun procedure. So, how do we focus on removing the necessity? *That* is our common ground.

Therefore, when the day finally came and my group went to the WMoW, I won't lie, I was nervous. I spoke with my husband that morning, and he reminded me that I have children so I needed to be careful and have a plan for not ending up in jail or in the hospital because of an altercation. We were hoping for the best but prepared for the worst. I knew I was going to have to take out my "I AM A PRO-LIFE FEMINIST" sign eventually so that everyone would be able to find us through the throngs of women. But I was scared. What if this whole sea of sisters had the same mindset as the organizers and those exclusionary feminists on Twitter?

Slowly I brought it out from my bag and set it on the ground, leaning it against my shin. Nothing happened. No one got in my face or even gave me a dirty look. I brought it a little higher. Still, nothing. Finally, I mustered the courage to raise to my shoulders so that our friends would be able to see it, and that's when it happened.

A woman in her seventies dressed head to toe in pink, with a Planned Parenthood scarf wrapped around her neck and a giant Planned Parenthood sign in her other hand came rushing up to me. She got about six inches from my face and said, "I'm glad you're here!" I was shocked. She continued, "Obviously I disagree with you ladies, but I think it was wrong for them to remove you. Your voice matters too." In that moment my apprehensions dissipated, and I felt safe because these unlike-minded women were letting us know they had our backs.

That conversation happened again and again and again throughout the entire march. These women knew that we had a shared common goal—to help those facing crisis pregnancies by offering support and options like free medical care, housing, child care, and any other resources they might need.

At one point I had to get to the steps of the Smithsonian because a camera crew was meeting me there for an interview. The only problem was the steps were about 50-yards away, and at this point we were all packed in like sardines. I knew I was going to have to be that jerk who shimmied my way through hundreds of people, all the while holding my pro-life feminist sign.

I took a deep breath and began making my way to the steps. All of a sudden something truly magical happened. As I walked through this immense crowd of women, they cleared a pathway for me. I heard, "GIRL! I LOOOOOOVE YOUR HAIR! OH. MY GOSH!" I turned around to thank the woman who said it when someone shouted out, "And that jacket! You are *owning* that jacket!" Suddenly all eyes were on me, and before I knew it, every woman within a 10-foot radius started complimenting everything from my hair to my sunglasses to my jewelry. Finally I said, "Can I just stay here forever and ever and ever? Y'all are my new best friends!"

It might seem silly, but that to me was a small sliver of the sisterhood—an ethic of care, looking out for one another, and an acceptance of differences. We didn't agree on everything and we didn't have to. We just had to understand that each and every one of us was working to support women in our own way.

The irony here is that my group accidently started a national conversation about who is allowed to sit at the feminist table. And while some people might say that pro-life feminists are not welcome, that's okay because I guess I'd rather hang out with the rad chicks building each other up in the proverbial feminist bathroom anyway.

For Further Exploration of Pro-Life Feminism

Brennan, William. *Dehumanizing the Vulnerable: When Word Games Take Lives.* Toronto: Life Cycle Books, 2000.

Browden, Sue Ellen. *Subverted: How I Helped the Sexual Revolution Hijack the Women's Movement.* San Francisco, CA: Ignatius Press, 2015.

Derr, Mary Krane, Rachel MacNair, and Linda Naranjo-Huebl. *ProLife Feminism: Yesterday and Today.* Kansas City: Sulzberger & Graham Publishing, 1995.

Levy, Ariel. *Female Chauvinist Pigs: Women and the Rise of Raunch Culture.* New York: Free Press, 2006.

Sweet, Gail-Grenier. *Pro-Life Feminism: Different Voices.* Toronto: Life Cycle Books, 1985.

Destiny Herndon-De La Rosa is the founder of New Wave Feminists, a feminist pro-life group that aims to reshape the divisive rhetoric surrounding the abortion debate. Inspired by her own experience as a young mother, Destiny founded the group to provide women with enough support to make motherhood a viable option. She lives in Dallas, Texas, with her husband and children. She loves wine and queso and hates writing in third person.

Why I Work for Planned Parenthood: Debunking Common Misconceptions about America's Leading Reproductive Health Care Provider
Brigid Leahy

"It's starting to feel like when I first started at Planned Parenthood," I said. It was October 2015. I was sitting across the desk from my boss, Pam Sutherland, the vice president for public policy education for Planned Parenthood, who has now retired after 35 years of fighting for reproductive rights, equality, and sexual education.

Over the summer, anti-abortion extremists had released deceptively edited videos that made false claims about Planned Parenthood. Eventually, the fake videos were completely debunked, but anti-abortion members of Congress, state legislators, and presidential candidates continued to use them to push their anti-Planned Parenthood and anti-abortion agenda.

I began working as a lobbyist at Planned Parenthood in March 1993 around the time of the first murder of an abortion provider, Dr. David Gunn. During the preceding decade, anti-abortion politicians passed numerous state-level bills designed to chip away at the rights guaranteed by *Roe v. Wade*. At the same time, extremists staged massive protests at women's health centers across the nation. Their rhetoric and tactics had become increasingly more hateful and aggressive, and deadly.

The violence of the 1980s and early 1990s led to the enactment of the Freedom of Access to Clinic Entrances Act, which resulted in a precipitous decrease in the most extreme forms of violence against women's health centers.

Planned Parenthood moved forward, continuing our focus on our mission. For me, that meant going beyond fighting against anti-abortion legislation and advocating for public policies aimed at protecting and ensuring reproductive self-determination. In Illinois, we successfully pushed for laws that improve the health and well-being of women. We passed legislation ensuring access to emergency contraception for rape victims, requiring insurance coverage of contraception, making sure that pharmacies filled prescriptions for birth control, improving sex education in public schools, and guaranteeing that patients have complete and accurate information even when a health provider refuses care because of a religious objection.

The laws I have worked to enact have one thing in common. Each one empowers individuals to make well-informed health decisions based on what is best for them given their personal circumstances.

Why Is This So Controversial?

One hundred years ago, Margaret Sanger opened the first birth control clinic in the United States. Planned Parenthood, as it came to be known, was founded on the revolutionary idea that women should have the information and care they need to live strong, healthy lives and fulfill their dreams. In 1916, this was controversial. This was a time when sharing information about anatomy and sex could land you in jail. Birth control was classified as "obscene" under the Comstock Laws, and state governments had forced sterilization programs.

Planned Parenthood pushed back on the social and legal mores of the early 20th century. Its vision is generally accepted by the American public today—every individual should have access to quality health care, education, and information. And, because Planned Parenthood doesn't just engage in advocacy but directly provides services to people, we fight for common-sense policies that promote reproductive health.

An estimated one in five women in the United States has visited a Planned Parenthood health center at least once in her life. Planned Parenthood has 56 independent local affiliates that operate more than 600 health centers throughout the United States, providing high-quality services to 2.4 million women, men, and teens.

I work in one of those health centers. I share a lunchroom with staff dedicated to making sure that our patients receive high-quality health care, no matter what, no matter their income, insurance coverage, sex, gender, identity, race, or ethnicity.

Our staff members are amazing people. They come to work every day to provide care with compassion and respect. They have seen and heard it all. It is through them that I learn how the policies I support directly impact people. I'll never forget one of our social workers explaining how a patient who was ending a pregnancy that resulted from rape said she was so relieved to see the news of the law requiring emergency rooms to tell sexual assault patients about emergency contraception because other women wouldn't have to go through what she had. Stories like these keep me grounded in my work. They help me understand that I'm not just advocating for lofty ideals but for real women.

I repeatedly tell the health center staff that I don't think I could work directly with patients. You see, I take all of this personally.

In 1902, one of my maternal great-grandmothers gave birth at home in a snowstorm to her 13th child, Henry, my grandfather. He was an unexpected midlife baby. I wonder if my grandmother had mixed feelings on realizing that she was pregnant again. In 1904, my other maternal great-grandmother died after giving birth to my grandmother. Eva was named "Mary" at her baptism by a priest who expected her to die.

Eva married Henry in 1939. One year and a day later she gave birth to my mother who had bilateral club foot. Eva was afraid to have another child because she knew that club foot was an inherited condition. But Henry told her that he thought having Mary Lee was one of the best things to happen to them. My aunt was born when Eva was 41.

Mary Lee married my father, in 1964. After the wedding, Eva and Mary Lee stood in front of the ladies room mirror checking their makeup before heading out to the reception. Looking into the mirror, Eva asked, "Do you know what's going to happen tonight?" Mary Lee replied, "Yes. Andy bought me a book." Eva said, "Okay." That was their first and only conversation about sex.

Mary Lee likely became pregnant on the honeymoon, and she hid her pregnancy for fear of being kicked out of law school. My sister was born before my parents' first anniversary in 1965. Mary Lee asked her doctor what giving birth would be like. This was before Lamaze and fathers in the delivery room. Her obstetrician said, "Don't worry. I'm going to give you gas." My mom was pregnant again within a year but miscarried. In 1967, I was born after months of anxiety because my mom repeatedly went into preterm labor.

These women had fairly privileged lives. They were able to pursue education and live middle-class lifestyles. But they had one thing in common with all American women of their time. They did not have the ability to control their own fertility. Before the 1960s, women commonly did not have sex education, became pregnant within the first year of marriage, had large families, and risked dying in childbirth.

This changed with my generation. Estelle Griswold of the Planned Parenthood League of Connecticut opened a clinic in 1961 to test the state's ban on birth control. In 1965, *Griswold v. Connecticut* legalized contraception for married couples. In 1972, the right was extended to unmarried people. The next year, *Roe v. Wade* recognized that a woman has a right to privacy when it comes to decisions about her pregnancy.

Growing up, both of my parents talked to me about sex. In fact, when I was little it was my dad who explained how babies were made. He didn't squirm or say, "Ask your mother." My dad thought nothing of taking me to watch one of his trials in which his client was denied treatment that would have led to a diagnosis of syphilis. My mom provided legal representation to Equal Rights Amendment protestors. When I was in high school, mom told me, "If you get really serious about somebody, come to me. I'll take you to Planned Parenthood."

My sister tells people that I went into the family business because, like my parents, I chose a career of political activism and advocacy for people's fundamental rights. I've spent the past 24 years fighting for access to reproductive health care and abortion rights with Planned Parenthood, an advocate of high-quality, affordable health care for women, men, and young people. We've made a lot of progress.

Even so, anti-abortion politicians continue their long-standing crusade against Planned Parenthood. The anti-abortion movement has focused on Planned Parenthood because it is the nation's leading provider. If your goal is to interfere in people's personal, private medical life by cutting off access to health care and accurate sexual health information, it is far more effective to focus on just one entity than to target the many organizations across the country that engage in the same work.

In 2007, Mike Pence introduced the first Planned Parenthood defunding bill in Congress. Women's health advocates spoke out, lobbied U.S. representatives, and stopped it. But the attacks haven't stopped. In order to further their anti-abortion agenda, politicians are willing to block patients from turning to Planned Parenthood health centers for preventive care such as birth control, Pap smears, STD tests, and breast and cervical cancer screenings.

Let's be clear, these politicians target Planned Parenthood because they want to outlaw abortion. And they're trying to do it by chipping away at access to health care, bill by bill. After the 2010 elections, anti-abortion politicians pursued a nation-wide strategy of restricting access to abortion. Thirty percent of the state laws restricting abortion since *Roe* were enacted in the past six years (Nash, Gold, Mohammed, Cappello, and Ansari-Thomas 2017).

As part of its strategy, the anti-abortion movement developed messaging expressing concern for women's well-being. For example, Texas passed a law mandating numerous regulations on abortion providers, claiming it would improve the health and safety of women. As a result clinics were forced to close and thousands of women lost access to not just abortion but also other reproductive health services. While the number of abortions performed in Texas decreased after the law went into effect, the number of women who had abortions out of state increased and the number of second-trimester abortions increased. In addition, women lost access to health care providers, who also provided basic reproductive health care services like birth control and pelvic exams. The law ended up harming women's health. The U.S. Supreme Court would eventually overturn it in 2016 in *Woman's Health v. Hellerstedt* because of its imposition of an undue burden on women. Despite all of the evidence, the anti-abortion movement continues to argue that women's health can be protected by passing similar restrictions in other states.

In 2012, we reached a new low when none of the Republican candidates for president supported access to birth control. At a campaign event, Mitt Romney said, "Planned Parenthood, we're going to get rid of that." I watched the debates with my mom, who was undergoing treatment for terminal pancreatic cancer. She commented, "I never thought we'd still be fighting for all of this."

Anti-abortion extremists stepped up their game by releasing the fake videos in 2015. In the September Republican presidential debate, Ted Cruz stated that Planned Parenthood was a "criminal enterprise." In an October debate, he said "When millions of Americans rose up against Planned Parenthood, I was proud to lead that fight." Jeb Bush claimed that Planned Parenthood was "not actually doing women's health issues."

The summer of 2015 marked a noticeable return to the past in tone. I knew something was changing. I had no idea how right I was.

A few weeks after the conversation in my boss's office, I headed to Las Vegas to celebrate Thanksgiving with my family. The day after, there was a mass shooting at a Planned Parenthood health center in Colorado. Iraq war veteran Ke'Arre M. Stewart, Jennifer Markovsky, and police officer Garrett Swasey were murdered. Nine others were shot, including five police officers. The shooter held anti-abortion beliefs and made statements similar to those of activists and politicians.

As Trump's political aspirations grew, he reversed previous pro-choice position. In a 2015 CNN interview, Trump, who was once pro-choice, said that Planned Parenthood is "like an abortion factory," and he fully supports defunding our organization. A year later, I watched news coverage as Donald Trump was elected president. I called my aunt who said, "All I can say is I'm glad your mom isn't alive to see this."

We face an uncertain future. But I know one thing for sure. I am not backing down. I believe in access to health care, reproductive services, and abortion. I know the majority of Americans share my values. We do not want to go back to a time when a woman did not have personal autonomy, when she could not make the most fundamental of decisions about her future.

I have seen what the anti-abortion movement is capable of, and the consequences are inconceivable. If they were to have their way, we would lose the protections of *Roe v. Wade* and possibly even the right to birth control as provided in *Griswold*. A woman's ability to access reproductive health care, including abortion, would depend on where she lived and how much money she made. In vast areas of the United States, women would be denied the personal autonomy to make fundamental health care decisions, just like my great-grandmothers were.

I choose to stand up and fight back. Planned Parenthood will never stop providing the care patients need. This is just what we do.

Reference

Nash, Elizabeth, Rachel Benson Gold, Lizmarrie Mohammad, Olivia Capello, and Zohra Ansari-Thomas. "Laws Affecting Reproductive Health and Rights: State Policy Trends at Midyear, 2017." The Guttmacher Institute. https://www.guttmacher.org/article/2017/07/laws-affecting-reproductive-health-and-rights-state-policy-trends-midyear-2017 (accessed August 21, 2017).

Brigid Leahy is a graduate of Knox College and studied American studies at the University of Minnesota. She has worked for Planned Parenthood in Illinois since 1993. As director of public policy, she has successfully lobbied for the enactment of numerous laws improving access to health care and sex education.

Pregnancy Help Centers: Offering Women Choice and Hope in the Midst of Crisis
Jay Hobbs

Midway through her final year as a premed student at Virginia Tech, Lauren was at a crossroads. On the one hand, she was just a few months away from going to medical school to pursue her dream of entering the medical field to help others. On the other, she was staring at a positive pregnancy test.

With so much life in front of her, Lauren felt paralyzed. All at once, the future she had for so long envisioned seemed in danger of slipping out of her grasp. As much as she desperately wished she weren't pregnant, there was no denying that she was in fact carrying a baby.

Lauren knew she had a choice to make. Given her medical training, Lauren could have recited all the relevant facts about fetal development, reproductive health, and the like in a classroom setting, but this was different. This was happening to her, and all of a sudden, she was at a loss as to how to move forward.

In the midst of what we in the pro-life pregnancy help community refer to as "the valley of decision," Lauren remembered a radio advertisement for her hometown pregnancy help center. It had been a rather forgettable ad, really, with a voice teetering on the brink of believability, and posing a familiar set of questions and promises: "Are you pregnant? Do you feel scared and alone? Come to our center and we will help you think through your options. You matter. You don't have to do this alone."

Back when she first heard that ad, Lauren remembered thinking how desperate she would feel if she ever faced an unexpected pregnancy. She didn't envy anyone who would have to walk that road, and yet here she was, in that very situation she never imagined she'd be facing.

Therefore, Lauren reached out to a local pregnancy help center for help. As she remembers it, she was crying hysterically just minutes after she first walked into the center and met with a volunteer. This was real, and there was no going back.

Something changed for Lauren even in that first meeting, however. For the first time since she first realized she might be pregnant, Lauren was able to share her feelings with someone who took the time to listen. No agenda, no judgment, just listening. Even as she told her story, Lauren felt the burden of her crisis pregnancy lightened just enough to think clearly and reevaluate her options. The women at the pregnancy help center then walked with Lauren as she told her family and boyfriend that she was expecting, empowering her to see she was not alone.

Every pregnancy carries with it three legal options in the United States. An expectant mother can choose to carry to term and either raise her child or place the child into the arms of an adoptive family. Alternatively, a mother can choose to end her child's life through abortion.

Like most women seeking abortion, Lauren was religiously affiliated. She had grown up in a Christian church, which holds to the Bible's teaching that persons are made in the image of God and thus intrinsically valuable from the moment of conception. According to ongoing research from the Guttmacher Institute, 24 percent of women who have abortions are Catholic, 17 percent are mainline Protestant, 13 percent are evangelical Protestant and 8 percent espouse another religion (Jerman, Jones, and Onda 2008). Finding a faith-based pregnancy help center helped Lauren think through her pregnancy from the moral and ethical framework she had grown up believing, but that through shame had suddenly felt inaccessible in her crisis.

In time, Lauren decided to give birth to her daughter, Adrianna Grace, who is now the oldest of three children that Lauren and her husband—who is also Adrianna's father—are raising together. The crisis of Lauren's unexpected pregnancy passed, and Lauren is now a physician assistant in North Carolina.

There is no such thing as "typical" when it comes to unexpected pregnancies, but Lauren's positive experience at a pregnancy help center is actually quite typical. Out of 70,000 respondents over a two-year period, 9 out of 10 clients report the highest level of satisfaction from their visit, compared to just 80 total clients who reported a negative interaction (Godsey 2017). Lauren's gratitude for the support she received sparked her passion for helping others in crisis. She volunteers during her lunch breaks at a pregnancy help center next door to her office.

According to the Worldwide Directory of Pregnancy Help, there are 2,600 pregnancy help centers and ultrasound-equipped medical clinics in the United States. Local communities across the nation understand their value, and they generously support local efforts with local dollars. In fact, 90 percent of all pregnancy centers' funding comes from local donors, saving communities and taxpayers an estimated $56 million every year (Hobbs 2016).

Every year, pregnancy centers in the United States serve well over 600,000 women, who, like Lauren, need help in an unexpected pregnancy. Like Lauren, each of these women deserve to have all the information and support necessary to make the healthiest decisions for everyone involved in her pregnancy.

Pregnancy centers exist to provide women with real choice, tangible support, and ongoing help so that no woman ever feels so afraid, alone, or coerced that she ends her child's life through abortion.

References

Godsey, Jor-El. "Pregnancy Help Centers Achieving Highest Customer Satisfaction Rating." Pregnancy Help News. 2017. https://pregnancyhelpnews.com/pregnancy-help-centers-achieving-highest-customer-satisfaction-rating (accessed September 1, 2017).

Hobbs, Jay. "Care Net Report Delivers Valuable Snapshot of Pregnancy Centers." Pregnancy Help News. 2016. https://pregnancyhelpnews.com/care-net-report-delivers-valuable-snapshot-of-pregnancy-centers (accessed September 1, 2017).

Jerman, Jenna, Rachel K. Jones, and Tsuyoshi Onda. *Characteristics of U.S. Abortion Patients in 2014 and Changes since 2008*. New York: Guttmacher Institute, 2016.

"Worldwide Directory of Pregnancy Help." Heartbeat International. https://www.heartbeatinternational.org/worldwide-directory (accessed September 1, 2017).

For Further Exploration of the Pregnancy Help Movement

Ensor, John. *Answering the Call: Saving Innocent Lives, One Woman at a Time*. Colorado Springs, CO: Focus on the Family, 2003.

Ensor, John, and Scott Klusendorf. *Stand for Life: A Student's Guide for Making the Case and Saving Lives.* Peabody, MA: Hendrickson Publishers, 2012.

Hartshorn, Margaret H. *Foot Soldiers Armed with Love: Heartbeat International's First Forty Years.* Columbus, OH: Heartbeat International, 2011.

Koop, C. Everett, and Francis A. Schaeffer. *Whatever Happened to the Human Race?* Westchester, IL: Crossway Books, 1979.

Jay Hobbs is director of marketing and communications for Heartbeat International, a global network of 2,100 locally operated pregnancy centers, ultrasound-equipped medical clinics, maternity homes, and nonprofit adoption agencies on every inhabited continent. A pastor, husband, and father of three, Jay's writing appears regularly at conservative outlets, including The Federalist *and* The Christian Post.

Fathers and Abortion
Bertha Alvarez Manninen

Many years ago, when I was teaching applied ethics at a community college, a young man who was in my class entrusted me with one of his most painful life stories. The year prior, he and his girlfriend had discovered that they were pregnant and although unexpected, they had decided to keep and raise the child together. Not long afterward, they also discovered that the fetus had Down syndrome, and despite his pleas to her and his promise that he was still committed to caring for the child, my student's girlfriend obtained an abortion. He told me his story while in tears, repeatedly claiming that he had failed the child, that he missed being a father, and that every day he thought about how old the child would be had he been born. His pain opened up a new ethical dilemma for me—although I am pro-choice, I believe there is a moral imperative to take into account voices like his in the wider conversation about abortion ethics.

Our society has a cultural expectation that a man is supposed to sever any emotional ties toward his fetus if his partner chooses abortion and that his grief is not as relevant as the woman's, if at all. Yet men can, and often times do, suffer emotionally as a result of a partner's abortion. While waiting for his partner to finish the abortion procedure, one man notes: "I didn't talk to anyone. The other guys, like myself, were all there because they cared. They were all equally nervous. Consequently, everyone was in their own troubled world of guilt, relief, and, the hardest to swallow, giving up a child that was part of yourself" (Shostak and McLouth 1984, 23). A 21-year-old man tells the following story following his and his partner's decision to obtain an abortion:

> I guess I sort of slipped into a trance or something because I went many stops past my own before I realized what was happening . . . across the aisle a guy was sitting holding an infant, and the guy was about my age, and I just couldn't stop staring at the baby thinking, "Damn, that baby could be my son!" So I just stayed on the trolley, staring and smiling, until the two of them suddenly got off . . . and the spell was broken. (Shostak 1979, 572)

After conducting in-depth studies on the effects of abortion on men, sociologist Arthur Shostak concludes that "much more could and should be offered as optional mental health services for all males involved in abortion experiences. A distinct minority of those men studied have found the abortion experience to be bewildering and painful beyond their coping abilities" (Shostak 1979, 574).

While many may agree that there should be more counseling options for men who have experienced an abortion, there are still thornier ethical issues to contemplate. First, let us consider why men should not be given any *legal* recourse over a woman's pregnancy decisions. Pregnancy is physically precarious and can even be life threatening. Possible health complications include, but are not limited to, anemia, constipation, mental health conditions, hypertension, gestational diabetes, hyperemesis gravidarum, hypertension, placental abruption, and the birthing process itself that may entail either vaginal tearing or major abdominal surgery if a caesarean section is required. A woman does not "rent out" her womb as a landlord rents to a tenant; pregnancy can bring with it potentially dangerous, and sometimes permanent, consequences to a woman's health.

Philosopher Judith Jarvis Thomson writes that, even if we assume (controversially) that fetuses are persons with a full right to life from conception onward, this does not entail that abortion is impermissible. No human being is under any obligation to use their body against their will to sustain the life of another human being; just as I cannot be compelled to submit to unwanted bodily intrusion in the form of a blood or bone marrow donation to save the life of someone who may be in desperate need of these fluids, a woman cannot be compelled to undergo bodily intrusion in the form of pregnancy (which is far more invasive) to save the life of the fetus. It isn't that the fetus lacks a right to life, Thomson argues; rather, it is that the fetus's right to life, like everyone's right to life, has limits as to what can be demanded of others in order to sustain that life (1971, 47–66). If we cannot force bodily intrusion on others to save the life of a needy third party, we cannot, likewise, force a woman to gestate in order to sustain fetal life.

While it is controversial to assume that fathers have rights over fetuses, since giving them rights effectively also gives them rights over the pregnant woman, to argue that men have rights to interfere in a woman's pregnancy decision would mean that he would have the right to force her either to abort when he does not want the baby (even if she does) or to gestate against her will——a much more invasive state of bodily intrusion (if he wants the baby and she does not), with all of the potentially dangerous physical consequences mentioned earlier.

Nevertheless, there is an ethical dimension to this issue that extends beyond what we can legally compel women to do; morality is not always exhausted by legal considerations. Therefore, let us briefly consider two complicated situations where men and women may disagree over the outcome of a pregnancy. Suppose it is the man who wants the abortion, but the woman chooses to continue the pregnancy and raise the baby—should men have the option to simply walk away and not be held financially responsible for the resulting child? In 2004, Matthew Dubay made this case against his ex-girlfriend, Lauren Wells, who became pregnant after repeatedly assuring him that she was infertile and, in addition, using contraception as well for good measure. Dubay argued that he told Wells several times that he did not wish to be a father and that if women were able to "opt out" of parenthood via abortion, men should be equally able to opt out of the financial responsibility for a child they did not want. Dubay's argument was foreshadowed by philosopher Steven Hales, who calls this the "right of refusal":

> There are a variety of reasons some women no longer want to be pregnant: They cannot afford another child, they are not psychologically prepared to be a parent, a child would hinder the lifestyle they wish to pursue. . . . Now consider the case of the father. He, too, is facing future duties; in fact (aside from pregnancy itself) the same ones as the mother. . . . However, the father, having participated, cannot escape the future duties he will have toward the child. A man has the moral right to decide not to become a father (in the social, nonbiological sense) during the time that the woman he has impregnated may permissibly abort. (Hales 1996, 7–12)

Hales's argument, and by extension Dubay's, warrants serious consideration. *If* the right to an abortion is interpreted as a woman's right to opt out of unwanted parenthood, then it would indeed appear that women have a reproductive right that men (perhaps unjustly) lack. Admittedly, there does seem to be good reason to think that this is how the right to an abortion is often interpreted; indeed, the justices who decided *Roe v. Wade* seemed to interpret the right to an abortion in this manner. However, if the abortion right is interpreted in a Thomsonian manner (as I think is preferable), as noted earlier, then Hales's argument collapses, for then there is no unique right women possess that men do not, since men also cannot be compelled to use their bodies to sustain the lives of other human beings.

The second possible case of dissent, the one experienced by my student, is the one that seems most difficult to navigate. While men cannot be given the right to force women to gestate, it still appears that a conversation must be had on the ethical dimensions of obtaining an abortion against the will of a man who desperately wishes to keep the child. In these cases, his pain and loss are real and legitimate, and therefore, his welfare in this regard matters. As I have written extensively about this issue in other venues, it would seem that, in certain situations, considerations of virtue suggest that women voluntarily bring men into the abortion decision-making process and that they take serious account of the man's wishes in situations where he would suffer from the loss of the fetus's life. If women truly want to move toward a society where men are equally involved in parenting outside the womb, then we need to also consider that a man's wishes may have a legitimate role to play in the woman's decision-making process when it comes to abortion. Feminist Kathleen McDonnell puts it thusly:

> We have to acknowledge that there is a grave inconsistency between our eagerness to involve men in all other aspects of reproduction and our unwillingness to allow them a similar role in abortion. This means we must acknowledge and validate men's role in procreation. It really does take two . . . if we are serious in our efforts to, in a sense, right nature's imbalance and make reproduction a truly joint

effort, it behooves us to make more room for men in the abortion process, to allow them a meaningful role that acknowledges their part in procreation. (McDonnell 1984, 62)

In other words, women hold all the cards when it comes to issues concerning pregnancy, gestation, and abortion. Given considerations of bodily autonomy, bodily integrity, and the potentially precarious state of pregnancy, this is the way it ought to be. However, women should be conscientious about how we "play" these cards, and, in certain situations, we should choose to share these cards with the men who desire a more active parenting role in their children's lives. And there may even be some circumstances (which I have detailed in my other writings), where it would be virtuous for a woman to choose to gestate a fetus for the sake of a loving, caring, and sincere man who is already engrossed in his role as a potential father.

References

Hales, Steven. "Abortion and Father's Rights." In *Biomedical Ethics Reviews: Reproduction, Technology, and Rights*, edited by James Humber and Robert Almeder, 101–119. Totowa, NJ: Humana Press, 1996.

Jarvis Thomson, Judith. "A Defense of Abortion." *Philosophy and Public Affairs* 1(1): 47–66, 1971.

Manninen, Bertha Alvarez, and Jack Mulder, Jr. *Civil Dialogue on Abortion*. New York: Routledge, 2018.

McDonnell, Kathleen. *Not An Easy Choice: A Feminist Re-Examines Abortion*. Toronto: The Women's Press, 1984.

Shostak, Arthur B. "Abortions as Fatherhood Lost." *The Family Coordinator* 28(4): 569–574, at p. 573, 1979.

Shostak, Arthur B., and Gary McLouth. *Men and Abortion: Lessons, Losses, and Love*. New York: Praeger Publishers, 1984.

Bertha Alvarez Manninen is associate professor of philosophy in Arizona State University's New College of Interdisciplinary Arts and Sciences. She is the coauthor of Civil Dialogue on Abortion *(2018) and the author of* Pro-Life, Pro-Choice: Shared Values in the Abortion Debate *(2014) and "Pleading Men and Virtuous Women: Considering the Role of the Father in the Abortion Debate" published in* The International Journal of Applied Philosophy *(2007).*

Who Should or Should Not Be Born?: The Collision between Reproductive Rights and Disability Rights
Stefanija Giric

The issues of abortion and disability rights have become deeply intertwined in recent years, as advancements in technology have brought the question of "who should or should not be born?" out of the shadows and into the forefront of mainstream population health discussions. In order to grapple with this question, we must delve into the discipline of disability studies and the complexities it adds to the greater reproductive rights movement's rhetoric on abortion. Though the modern-day battle over women's reproductive rights is typically placed in the context of preserving women's right to access birth control and abortion, the term itself is much broader in scope and refers to the right of all people to enjoy sexual and reproductive autonomy, including having full control over the number, timing, and spacing of children, as well as the right to be free from sexual violence and coercion (United Nations Population Fund 2007).

The question "what *kind* of child we wish to be born" is neither a new nor an irrelevant one. It is, however, an increasingly more urgent one, as advances in prenatal genetic testing technology have made it possible to detect abnormalities in a fetus as early as nine weeks into a pregnancy (American College of Obstetricians and Gynecologists-Society for Maternal-Fetal Medicine 2015). As Marsha Saxton writes in *The Disability*

Studies Reader: "There is a key difference between the goals of the reproductive rights movement and the disability rights movement regarding reproductive freedom: the reproductive rights movement emphasizes the right to have an abortion; the disability rights movement, the right *not to have to have* an abortion" (2006, 105).

Erik Parens and Adrienne Asch, editors of *Prenatal Testing and Disability Rights*, expound on this idea in their seminal work by explaining that the majority of problems for individuals with disabilities are *not* caused by their disabling conditions or impairments but by a society that discriminates against them and is ill-equipped to meet their needs. This viewpoint is consistent with the social model of disability, which considers the way that society is organized to be hostile to individuals with disabilities their main limitation. Conversely, the medical model of disability views a disabled individual's impairments as problems that can (and should) be fixed by medical technology thus: "In this [medical] framework, the proper approach to disability is to 'treat' the condition and the person with the condition rather than 'treating' the processes and policies that constrict disabled people's lives" (Kafer 2013, 5).

While the medical model of disability focuses mostly on disabled individuals' limitations and inability to lead "normal" lives, the social model of disability allows for the possibility that disabled individuals are able to lead rich and fulfilling lives, *not despite* their disabilities, "but because along with their disabilities come other characteristics of personality, talent, and humanity that render people with disabilities full members of the human and moral community" (Asch 1999, 1653). It follows then that a key aspect of disability advocacy within the social model of disability is the call to change the features of a society which cause the exclusion of individuals with disabling impairments.

"Prenatal genetic testing" is defined as a cluster of technologies that allows for the ability to detect abnormalities in a fetus, such as Down syndrome or neural tube defects, while in utero.

Though advocates of prenatal genetic testing assert that this technology facilitates a woman's right to freely choose whether or not she wishes to give birth to a disabled child, critics argue that the process itself is inherently biased, because it is predicated on the idea that if a woman knew the child she is carrying were to be disabled, *she would then not want that child*. As Nancy Anne Press and Carole H. Browner write, the offer of prenatal genetic testing "places in the path of every pregnant woman the possibility of facing a decision about the continuation of her pregnancy based on the presence of a birth anomaly" (1994, 201). Even so, testing is typically offered to every pregnant woman by her medical professional and is seen as a vital public health initiative that gives her access to the information necessary to make the best reproductive choice for herself. Though screening technology has advanced fairly quickly, cures for the conditions that it uncovers have not kept pace (Davis 2001, 15). Therefore, once an abnormality is detected, typically the only "choice" to be made is whether to have an abortion or continue the pregnancy.

Technology that enables detections of fetal abnormalities during pregnancy will continue to advance and, consequently, push the boundaries of what it means to be "normal." Concerns over the normalization of children with selectively modified genetic traits chosen for them by their parents, or "designer babies," seem timelier than ever before as CRISPR-Cas9, a technology that allows scientists to edit genetic code, is currently being tested on human embryos for the first time (Ledford 2017, 13). Now that it seems likely that future generations will have more reproductive choices available to them than we currently do, many wonder what an increased ability to make these choices will mean for our perception of normality, especially the question of who deserves to be born. To illustrate the complexities of how disability rights complicate this choice rhetoric, consider the case of a deaf lesbian couple who deliberately chose a sperm donor with five generations of deaf people in his family in order to increase the likelihood of their giving birth to a deaf child (Davis 2001, 71). Their decision incited intense controversy, with many vehemently decrying it as a selfish one that would deliberately cause harm to their child; however, many members of the Deaf cultural community (as contrasted with "deaf" with a small "d" when used to describe individuals with the auditory condition) consider having a deaf child as an expression of pride for their culture and the desire to protect it from extinction.

The disability rights critiques of prenatal genetic testing and selective abortion add a complex layer to the fight for reproductive rights and especially abortion. Disability has the curious position as an identity that some see as having a responsibility to eradicate and some to protect: Though many people would deny the assertion that the world be a "better" place if no disabled people were born, society's actions may imply otherwise, as it is the hope that gene editing technologies such as CRISPR will eventually "cure" disease and ostensibly prevent disability. Conversely, disability rights advocates have found themselves unlikely counterparts in some conservative politicians who have sought to criminalize abortion on the basis of disability; however, paradoxically, these same politicians tend to oppose increasing spending on social services such as the state disability programs that provide the necessary supports in order to make raising a child with a disability possible. As Alison Piepmeier writes, "[Social context] plays a large role in dictating the value of the fetus, the rational decision, the right thing to do. It generates stigma and stereotypes that have effects not only on individual beliefs but on educational and financial support" (2013, 178). Both unidimensional attitudes toward disability illuminate the need for our social context to support a plurality of voices, so that we take care not to impress onto women standards of choice in the form of legislation, medical technology, stigma, and a lack of social support that leave them with decisions that are anything but autonomous.

References

American College of Obstetricians and Gynecologists-Society for Maternal-Fetal Medicine. *Committee Opinion-Cell-free fetal DNA Screening for Fetal Aneuploidy.* Last modified September 2015. http://www.acog.org/Resour ces-And-Publications/Committee-Opinions/Commit tee-on-Genetics/Cell-free-DNA-Screening-for-Fetal-Aneuploidy.

Asch, Adrienne. "Prenatal Diagnosis and Selective Abortion: A Challenge to Practice and Policy." *American Journal of Public Health* 89(11): 1649–1657, 1999.

Davis, Dena S. *Genetic Dilemmas: Reproductive Technology, Parental Choices, and Children's Futures*, 9–44, 60–90. New York: Routledge, 2001.

Kafer, Alison. *Feminist, Queer, Crip*, 1–46. Indianapolis: Indiana University Press, 2013.

Ledford, Heidi. "CRISPR Fixes Disease Gene in Viable Human Embryos." *Nature News* 548(7665), 2017, 13. https://www.ncbi.nlm.nih.gov/pubmed/28770860.

Parens, Erik, and Adrienne Asch. "The Disability Rights Critique of Prenatal Genetic Testing: Reflections and Recommendations." In *Prenatal Testing and Disability Rights*, edited by Erik Parens and Adrienne Asch, 3–38. Washington, DC: Georgetown University Press, 2000.

Piepmeier, Alison. "The Inadequacy of 'Choice': Disability and What's Wrong with Feminist Framings of Reproduction." *Feminist Studies* 39(1): 159–186, 2013. https://www.law.berkeley.edu/php-programs/centers/crrj /zotero/loadfile.php?entity_key=VISRVWQD.

Press, Nancy Anne, and Carole H. Browner. "Collective Silences, Collective Fictions: How Prenatal Diagnostic Testing Became a Routine Part of Prenatal Care." In *Women and Prenatal Testing: Facing the Challenges of Genetic*

Technology, edited by Karen H. Rothenberg, 201–217. Columbus: Ohio State University Press, 1994.

Saxton, Marsha. "Disability Rights and Selective Abortion." In *The Disability Studies Reader*, edited by Lennard J. Davis, 105–116. New York: Routledge, 2006.

United Nations Population Fund. "Supporting the Constellation of Reproductive Rights." 2007. http://www .unfpa.org/resources/supporting-constellation-reproductive-rights (accessed April 25, 2018)

Stefanija Giric is a bioethicist and researcher residing in Durham, North Carolina. She holds an MA in bioethics and science policy and a BA in public policy, both from Duke University. Her research interests include genome ethics, reproductive rights, and social justice (and come together somewhere in the intersection of all three).

STAND UP FOR
WOMEN'S
HEALTH

STAND UP FOR
WOMEN'S
HEALTH

Introduction

This chapter presents brief biographies of some of the major players in the American abortion debate sorted by ideology and listed alphabetically. The dates after each name show that some of the pioneers in the pro-choice and pro-life movements have retired or are aging. Others have passed away, including Norma McCorvey, the anonymous "Jane Roe" in the landmark Supreme Court case. Her death in 2017 was 44 years after that ruling, and she died lamenting the over 50 million legal abortions—or in her view babies killed—since 1973. A new generation will have to carry on the crusades; for most of them the *Roe v. Wade* decision will not be a personal memory but a historical fact. It remains to be seen how abortion politics will change as a result. The biographies are followed by descriptions of prominent U.S.-based pro-choice and pro-life groups, which are an important part of the abortion debate story. Although a few of these are no longer in existence or have reorganized, they are included because they are an essential part of understanding

---

Cecile Richards, president of the Planned Parenthood Federation of America, speaks to thousands of pro-choice supporters who descended on Capitol Hill for the Stand Up for Women's Health Rally on April 7, 2011, in Washington, D.C. Richards called out members of Congress for playing politics with women's health. Her call to "stop the war on women" and to stand up for women's rights to life saving health care like breast exams and cervical cancer screenings was met with cheers from the crowd. (Leigh Vogel/FilmMagic/Getty Images)

the historical trajectory of activism and policy debates. Featured at the end of this chapter are lists of relevant government agencies and international organizations for those seeking a more global understanding of the abortion issue.

People

On the Pro-Choice Side

Bill Baird (1932–)

Bill Baird has left an indelible mark on the history of reproductive law in the United States. While some in the pro-choice movement have expressed embarrassment about his shock tactics, he defends his role and contribution through his business, the Pro-Choice League, and website (prochoiceleague.org). He was born in Brooklyn to a family of limited means. As a young man he worked for a company that manufactured contraceptive foam in the 1950s. A woman dying in his arms at Harlem Hospital in 1963 with a coat hanger protruding from her uterus was his defining moment. Although he had dropped out of medical school to support his family, he remained committed to women's reproductive freedom. Going rogue, he converted an old truck into a "Plan Van"—a mobile unit to disseminate condoms and foam to poor neighborhoods in New York City. In 1964 he opened the first "aboveground" abortion counseling and referral service. In 1967, after the Supreme Court decision legalizing contraceptives for married couples, students at Boston University invited Baird to give a talk on birth control in direct challenge to the law; his subsequent arrest was all part of his plan. It took five years for his case—*Eisenstadt v. Baird*—to reach the Supreme Court. In 1972 the justices ruled that states could not deny equal protection to unmarried people in getting contraceptives, declaring the right to "bear and beget" a child as a fundamental right. Baird continued his feisty stance toward restrictions, including challenging parental consent laws in *Bellotti v. Baird* in 1979. Over the course of decades of advocacy, Baird has been shouted and shot at, and his clinic has been firebombed. As he told an audience at one of his speeches, "I have no money. I have no political power. But, I will never surrender" (The Associated Press 2009).

Jennifer Baumgardner (1970–)

A central theme in Jennifer Baumgardner's work has been demystifying "common-but-silenced" subjects like abortion. Her book *Manifesta: Young Women, Feminism, and the Future* coauthored with Amy Richards (2000) helped define a new generation of "third-wave" feminists. On her website (jenniferbaumgardner.net), Baumgardner describes growing up in a liberal household where she would engage in imaginative play with Barbie dolls who had abortions and read *Ms. Magazine* where she would later serve as editor from 1993 to 1997. Her award-winning 2005 documentary *Speak Out: I Had an Abortion* destigmatizes and humanizes abortion through candid accounts from 10 women from diverse backgrounds about their personal experiences with abortion. In Baumgardner's 2008 book, *Abortion and Life*, moving abortion narratives from women, including Ani DiFranco and Gloria Steinem, are complimented by beautiful portraits created by photographer Tara Todras-Whitehill—their words and images rise above the political fury.

Mary Steichen Calderone (1904–1998)

Dr. Mary Calderone was to the study of human sexuality what Margaret Sanger was to birth control—the one who nearly single-handedly changed the nation's approach to the topic. Her early life didn't suggest that she would have such an influence one day. The daughter of the noted photographer Edward Steichen, Mary frittered away her days at Vassar and eventually left in the early 1920s to become an actress. Fifteen years later, much had changed in her life. She had graduated from medical school and she was a divorced mother facing challenges in a male-dominated field. She married again in 1941 and spent her career in school and public health positions. In 1953 Calderone became the medical director at Planned Parenthood. From that position, she sponsored a 1955 conference that was the first to publicly discuss the reforming of criminal abortion laws. Although she supported legal abortion and had a role in the reform movement, she preferred to focus on preventing pregnancy. Calderone left Planned Parenthood at the age of 60 to form a new organization: Sexuality Information and Education Council of the United States (SIECUS). There she promoted sex education that was frank, nonjudgmental, and comprehensive. SIECUS has had a role in developing the idea that sexuality is a positive force and that sex education should not enforce any particular standard. With these views, both Calderone and SIECUS provoked strenuous opposition from pro-life activists.

Gloria Feldt (1942–)

Gloria Feldt served as president and CEO of Planned Parenthood Federation of America (PPFA) for nine years. Feldt brought a strong feminist perspective to her leadership as well as a commitment to engaging pro-life adversaries in political and policy arenas. A native of Texas, Feldt had gotten pregnant and married at the age of 15, and by the age of 20 she had three children. She connects her situation in those days directly to the lack of education and access to effective contraception. Availability of the birth control pill in 1962 made it possible for her to start college. It took her 12 years to graduate. Feldt started with Planned Parenthood in 1974 as a regional executive director and then moved to Arizona to lead the national organization in 1996. Her ambitious agenda included revitalizing the local affiliates and their services and developing a 25-year plan for PPFA. She is best known for her leadership in promoting family planning as a human right and contraception as a necessity for women, not an option. She also became head of the Planned Parenthood Political Action Committee and worked to support pro-choice candidates. She was an organizing leader of the 2004 March for Women's Lives. Active in international networks, Feldt was part of the U.S. delegation to the Cairo Plus Five meeting in 1999, a follow-up to the United Nations 1994 Population and Development Conference. She is the author of *Behind Every Choice Is a Story* (2003) and *The War on Choice: The Right-Wing Attack on Women's Rights and How to Fight Back* (2004). Today, Feldt is cofounder of Take the Lead, an organization dedicated to "inspiring women to embrace their power and lead without limits."

Sherri Chessen Finkbine (1930–)

In 1962, Sherri Finkbine was 29 years old, married, the mother of four children, hostess of the local children's TV show *Romper Room*, and pregnant with her fifth child. She was devastated to learn that the tranquilizer thalidomide she had taken during her pregnancy had been linked to fetal deformity. She and her husband Bob were afraid their unborn child would be a victim. Their doctor arranged with the local hospital for a therapeutic abortion based on the threat of the pregnancy to Sherri's mental health. However, hospital officials worried that publicity surrounding the case would invite prosecution and denied the procedure. The Finkbines eventually traveled to Sweden and requested an abortion under its conditional law. Sherri had to see a psychiatrist and receive permission from the Royal Medical Board. Finally approved, the abortion went forward. The Vatican denounced the act as a crime, and Sherri also lost her job at the TV station. The press followed the Finkbines' ordeal closely, and many scholars view this as a pivotal moment in shaping the public's view of abortion. People began to have greater awareness of and empathy for the personal problems that can give rise to the termination of a pregnancy. The tide started to turn against criminal abortion laws and toward the public support that was needed to mobilize the reform movement. The Finkbines had two more children but divorced in

1974. In 1991, Sherri married a physician who had practiced at the Phoenix hospital that had denied her abortion. In 1992, HBO produced a film about the case called *A Private Matter*.

Kim Gandy (1954–)

Kim Gandy served as president of the National Organization for Women (NOW) from 2001 to 2009, and she was at the center of the abortion debates on Capitol Hill for over 20 years. Born and educated in Louisiana, she received her bachelor's degree in mathematics from Louisiana Tech and joined NOW in 1973. Her first successful campaign was to overturn a Louisiana law that gave complete control over a couple's property to the husband. After Loyola University New Orleans School of Law, she soon was working her way up the NOW hierarchy. With expertise in legislation and litigation, Gandy was a key figure in all the pro-choice campaigns of the 1990s, including the battle against the partial-birth abortion ban. She took the lead in NOW's suit against abortion protesters (*NOW v. Scheidler*) and served on the committee that drafted the Freedom of Access to Clinic Entrances Act. She was a lead organizer of the 2004 March for Women's Lives, which rallied over a million supporters committed to access to birth control, reproductive health care, and abortion. As president, she also chaired the NOW Foundation and the NOW Political Action Committee, which publish a list of pro-choice candidates in each election. As chief spokesperson, she articulated a spirited and firm feminist position on a wide range of issues, including access to emergency contraception, appointments to the Supreme Court, and the South Dakota abortion ban. Today, Gandy continues to champion women's rights as the president and CEO of the National Network to End Domestic Violence.

Alan Guttmacher (1898–1974)

After graduating from Johns Hopkins Medical School, Alan Guttmacher had a life-changing experience during his residency where he came face to face with a woman who was dying from an illegal abortion. He embarked on a distinguished career as an obstetrician, including serving as chief of obstetrics at Sinai Hospital in Baltimore, Maryland, but he never stopped working to increase women's information and options for family planning. He became active in the American Birth Control League, the forerunner of Planned Parenthood Federation of America (PPFA). At a PPFA meeting in 1942, he made one of the first calls for the liberalization of abortion laws involving a limited extension of the criminal laws to allow therapeutic abortions when women's health was at risk. As the debate advanced, and more groups got involved, he favored increasing the number of grounds for legal abortions. In his 1959 book, *Babies by Choice or Chance*, Guttmacher called for more liberal and uniform abortion laws across the country. He was present at the 1959 American Law Institute meeting that proposed reform to include health, fetal deformity, and rape and incest conditions and became national president of PPFA in 1962. In 1964, he founded the Association for the Study of Abortion, which began to publicize the issue, and he made it clear that he opposed abortion on demand. Guttmacher lived to see the legalization of both contraception and abortion. In the end, he called the decision in *Roe v. Wade* "wise and courageous." While he was president, PPFA began to develop an institute to do research on family planning and educate the public. As a memorial, it was named The Alan Guttmacher Institute; it continues to be a trusted source of information about sexual and reproduction health issues.

Frances Kissling (1943–)

A noted scholar and activist, Frances Kissling was raised in a Catholic home, attended Catholic schools, and even spent six months in a convent. Nevertheless, she grew up to be one of the most provocative critics of the Roman Catholic Church, committed to provoking a rebellion from the inside. Kissling participated in social activism in the 1960s, which led to working in abortion clinics in the 1970s. She was a cofounder of the

National Abortion Federation and served as its director until 1980. In 1982 she became president of Catholics for a Free Choice (CFFC). In her remarkable 25-year tenure, Kissling campaigned to overturn the Church's staunch pro-life doctrine, which she viewed as an effort to maintain control over women. If they really cared about the unborn, she argued, they would do more to prevent abortions by supporting contraception to prevent unwanted pregnancies. Her activism has won her many allies but has also been extremely controversial. Syndicated columnist Ellen Goodman has called her the thoughtful and eloquent "philosopher of the pro-choice movement," whereas George Neumayr of the *American Spectator* called her a "repulsive heretic." Kissling retired as president of CFFC in 2007 and then became a fellow at the Radcliffe Institute for Advanced Studies at Harvard University. In a 2016 interview, Kissling reflected on finding common ground, "My reputation for being devastating in debate is legendary, and I love a good fight and I love to win. But what I have learned is that . . . you have got to approach differences with this notion that there is good in the other" (Tippit 2011).

Lawrence Lader (1919–2006)

Feminist Betty Friedan quite fittingly named Lawrence Lader the "father of the abortion rights movement." He was born in New York City and graduated from Harvard University. After service in the army in World War II, he began a career as a writer. His book *Abortion (I)* was published in 1966, a time when there was little information on the subject. In his words, which still ring true today, "Abortion is the dread secret of our society" (Martin 2006). In 1969 he published a biography of Margaret Sanger, the pioneer for birth control. In interviews, Sanger told him about the effects of illegal abortions on women's health. Lader became even more convinced that women needed to have control over their childbearing; without it they could not lead independent lives. His investigation produced evidence of the large number of illegal abortions that threatened women's health. Justice Harry Blackmun would later cite Lader's research several times in the *Roe v. Wade* decision. Lader advocated for laws that would extend the right to privacy granted in *Griswold v. Connecticut* to abortion. He joined with Betty Friedan and Bernard Nathanson to start NARAL (National Association for the Repeal of Abortion Laws) to campaign for law repeal, which succeeded in New York with the elimination of abortion restrictions in 1970. *Abortion II: Making the Revolution* (1973) describes Lader's experience with the abortion reform/repeal movement. The book did not foresee the backlash and the rise of the pro-life forces that would stop Lader's "revolution" in its tracks. In 1976, Lader left NARAL to form Abortion Rights Mobilization and concentrated his attacks on the Roman Catholic Church, at one point suing unsuccessfully to remove their tax-exempt status for engaging in pro-life political activities. He also fought for mifepristone, better known as RU-486, and was named "feminist of the year" in 1992 by Feminist Majority for his leadership in getting this "abortion pill" into the United States.

Kate Michelman (1942–)

Kate Michelman served as president of NARAL for 20 years (1985–2004), and her tenure left a major imprint on the abortion debates. *Washingtonian* magazine named her as one of the 100 most powerful women in Washington in 2001, a testament to her acumen as a lobbyist and political strategist. She has been a tireless spokesperson for the pro-choice ideal that women must retain a constitutional right to choose abortion and that the pro-life platform must be defeated. She led through many ups and downs at a time when the pro-choice movement had been forced to assume a defensive posture, struggling to protect the rights that had been won. Michelman led the successful campaign to reject conservative ideologue Robert Bork's Supreme Court nomination in 1987. She campaigned vigorously for Bill Clinton and pushed for him to remove the Mexico City policy and veto the ban on partial-birth abortion. She credits her vigorous stamina in the pro-choice cause to her own life experiences. Her husband had abandoned her in the late 1960s, leaving her pregnant and struggling to care for three young daughters. Nearly driven to suicide, Michelman qualified for a therapeutic abortion under pre-*Roe* policies. Her activism was sparked and sustained by the lasting memory of the humiliation and powerlessness she felt when she had to get approval from an all-male hospital committee and permission from her ex-husband to terminate the pregnancy. Harkening back to that early desperation, Michelman's family was on the brink of bankruptcy in 2009; she was struggling once again against the health care system, this time to cover medical expenses for her second husband and daughter. Her 2005 memoir, *Liberty and Justice for All: A Life Spent Protecting the Right to Choose*, was written to inspire the next generation of activists.

Willie Parker (1963–)

Dr. Willie Parker is an obstetrician-gynecologist, who struggled early in his career to provide comprehensive reproductive health care due to his Christian faith. He recalls reading a passage from the Good Samaritan in a sermon by Rev. Dr. Martin Luther King Jr. and becoming committed to providing abortion services for patients who face gender, economic, and racial inequities, particularly in the South. He believes his decision is consistent with his core spiritual values. Today, Parker is an outspoken and visible reproductive justice advocate, noteworthy for his courage, dignity, and compassion. He appears in the documentaries *The Last Clinic* and *Trapped*. His 2017 book *Life's Work: A Moral Argument for Choice* traces his journey and critiques the pro-life movement's imposition of mandatory waiting periods and onerous requirements for clinics as assaults on the rights of women to control their own bodies and lives. He is spearheading a federal lawsuit to prevent the closure of Mississippi's only abortion clinic, which is currently awaiting a request for hearing by the U.S. Supreme Court. He is the chair of the board of Physicians for Reproductive Health, and he has received many accolades for his work, including a United Nations Office of Human Rights Award, Planned Parenthood's Margaret Sanger Award, and NARAL's Champions of Choice Award. In a 2017 interview with NBC, Parker said, "I was not of the age of accountability during the civil rights movement. I was not born into slavery. I was not born during the labor rebellions of the '20s. In 2017, I'm a women's health provider. This is my time and this is my responsibility" (Rosenblatt 2017).

Cecile Richards (1957–)

With so much recent attention directed at Planned Parenthood Federation of America (PPFA), the presiding president and CEO, Cecile Richards, has become a powerhouse media celebrity. She was closely aligned with the Obama administration and a tireless campaigner for Hillary Clinton. Richards had been prepared for battle by her mother, the trailblazing Texas governor Ann Richards, and by her prior experience as a labor organizer, as the president of America Votes, and as deputy chief of staff for House Democratic leader Nancy Pelosi. Recognizing the need to destigmatize, Richards has talked openly about her own abortion, saying, "When politicians argue and shout about abortion, they're talking about me—and millions of other women around the country" (Richards 2014). Richards took the reins of PPFA in 2006, and she has been a champion for access and health care coverage for reproductive health services. Her $600,000 salary has been criticized by pro-life groups and on Capitol Hill. Richards is a master at seizing the opportunity. When the pro-life organizations Live Action and the Susan B. Anthony List set off on a tour in 2011 to campaign against Planned Parenthood funding, Richards sent out buses painted bright fuchsia to greet them. In 2012, Susan G. Komen Foundation's withdrawal of funding ignited a firestorm, and Richards artfully stoked the flames. Although Komen reversed its decision three days later, the blowback has been calculated to be over $77 million lost in contributions to the foundation. On the undercover videos released by the Center for Medical Progress in 2015 purporting to show that PPFA was selling baby parts, Richards was triumphant in the end: "They spent three years doing everything they could—not to uncover wrongdoing, but rather to create it. They failed." The onslaught of attacks appears to have emboldened Richards and PPFA's supporters, which have tripled in number to more than 10 million. In January 2018, Richards announced her retirement with a promise to continue the fight for women's rights.

Margaret Sanger (1879–1966)

Margaret Sanger is famous today as the founder of the birth control movement in America. Her 1938 autobiography tells the story of her awakening to the plight of desperate poor women who were enslaved by repeated pregnancies. Trained as a nurse, Sanger worked among the immigrant families in New York City slums in the early 20th century, attending more than one woman who was dying from a frantic attempt to self-induce an abortion. She vowed to arm women with knowledge about contraception but soon ran afoul of the federal prohibitions in the Comstock Act of 1873. She had to flee the country at one point and was eventually jailed. Sanger founded the American Birth Control League, which became the Planned Parenthood Federation of America. She also led the campaign to legalize contraception; her most significant victory was the 1936 federal court decision in the *U.S. v. One Package* case 86 F.2d 737 (2d Cir. 1936), which allowed doctors to receive contraception for medical uses. She lived just long enough to see the complete legalization of contraception in 1965. Sanger made conflicting statements on abortion; she focused on birth control to prevent the serious risks of illegal abortion, yet she also understood women's desire for the procedure when contraception failed. Sanger wrote several books, including *What Every Mother Should Know* (1917) and *My Fight for Birth Control* (1931). Sanger remains a symbolic and controversial figure in the abortion debate. Pro-choice feminists are troubled by her association with the eugenics movement but consider Sanger a champion for women's rights to self-determination and a feminist who paved the way for the liberation of women's sexuality.

Eleanor Smeal (1939–)

A graduate of Duke University and the University of Florida, Eleanor Smeal became one of the most important feminist activists in the United States. She served as president of the National Organization for Women (NOW) from 1977 to 1982 and 1985 to 1987. During these years she led the finally unsuccessful campaign for ratification of the equal rights amendment and then turned to the goal of defending *Roe v. Wade* and access to legal abortion for American women. Her 1985 book, *Why and How Women Will Elect the Next President*, explores women's political power and organizing techniques. She organized and led the first National March for Women's Lives in 1986 and developed the legal strategy to counter Operation Rescue and clinic violence that erupted in the late 1980s. Smeal went on to cofound the Feminist Majority Foundation (FMF) in 1987 to empower women to act politically in their own interests, with a major focus on reproductive rights issues. In 1989 she produced two videos—*Abortion for Survival* and *Abortion Denied: Shattering Women's Lives*—to raise awareness of the effects of punitive and restrictive abortion laws. The Clinic Access project has trained over 45,000 volunteers in nonviolent defense techniques. Smeal also led the successful campaign for the Freedom of Access to Clinic Entrances Act, which makes it a federal crime to use physical force to obstruct access to abortion clinics. Undaunted, Smeal waged a 12-year campaign for approval of mifepristone, better known as RU-486 or the "abortion pill." Another part of her strategic vision has been the Choices Campus Leadership Program to recruit young activists. Based on her 30-year tenure as president of FMF, Smeal is frequently called on by the media to weigh in on important topics, and she has testified before Congress on a wide range of women's issues.

George Tiller (1941–2009)

In 2009, Dr. George Tiller was murdered, shot in his church in Wichita, Kansas, by an anti-abortion extremist. For more than three decades, he practiced compassionate reproductive health care and was a proud member of the Abortion Care Network. Tiller was only one of a handful of doctors who were willing to perform late-term abortions, which made him a villain among pro-life groups and a target for extremists. Fox News conservative commentator Bill O'Reilly referred to him repeatedly as "Tiller the Baby Killer." Singular's (2011) book *The Wichita Divide: The Murder of Dr. George Tiller and the Battle over Abortion* autopsies the violent clash. Tiller had been shot before in both arms, and his clinic had been bombed in 1993. His killer, Scott Roeder, a mentally unstable, born-again Christian, said that he acted to save the lives of unborn children in Tiller's "death camp." Roeder received a 25-year sentence for Tiller's murder. The gripping 2013 documentary *After Tiller* explores often tragic circumstances that factor into late-term pregnancy. The interviews with his four remaining colleagues deepen our understanding of why and how Tiller, a deeply religious man, was so committed to this work. The website iamdrtiller.com was created to memorialize the challenging life work of abortion providers everywhere. Kansas now bans abortions after 22 weeks. In Tiller's still-poignant words, "Make no mistake, this battle is about self-determination by women over the direction and course of their lives and their family's lives. Abortion is about women's hopes and dreams. Abortion is a matter of survival for women" (Fetters 2001).

Sarah Weddington (1945–)

Sarah Weddington had been out of the University of Texas law school only six years when she became the youngest person to win a case before the Supreme Court. The opportunity came when a small group of feminist activists involved in the early days of the movement for abortion rights in Austin, Texas, asked her opinion about the legal status of their plan to begin a referral service for women seeking abortions in Mexico. Her research into this question revealed a strategy for challenging the constitutionality of Texas's 19th-century law, which prohibited all abortions except to save the life of the mother. Along with her colleague, Linda Coffee, Weddington located Norma McCorvey, who would become their plaintiff "Roe" in a class-action suit on behalf of all women being denied rights. The *Roe v. Wade* decision, issued January 22, 1973, abolished criminal abortion laws in the United States. Weddington has been a pioneer for women's rights in many other ways. She served in the Texas legislature, 1973–1975, the first woman to be elected from Austin. She then joined the federal government as the first woman to be general counsel in the U.S. Department of Agriculture. In 1981, she became special assistant to President Jimmy Carter for women's issues. Her book describing her experiences in the *Roe v. Wade* case, *A Question of Choice*, was published in 1992. Weddington's distinguished career also includes 28 years as a professor at the University of Texas at Austin where she trained a new generation of leaders in courses on "Gender-Based Discrimination" and "Leadership in America." She now uses The Weddington Center to carry on her work (weddingtoncenter.com).

On the Pro-Life Side

Philip Benham (1948–)

Rev. Philip "Flip" Benham had a long tenure as the director of Operation Save America, formerly known as Operation Rescue National, serving from 1994 to 2014. A reformed bar owner, he received his master of divinity in 1980 from Asbury

Theological Seminary. He is a married father of five. Benham helped facilitate the highly touted pro-life conversion of Norma McCorvey, better known as "Jane Roe," and he baptized her in 1995. Often called on as a spokesperson for the pro-life movement, Benham has condemned the murders perpetrated by anti-abortion extremists; in his view, James Kopp, who assassinated Dr. Barnett Slepian in 1998, "betrayed the pro-life movement" (*Los Angeles Times* 2018). In 2010 Benham was found guilty of stalking an abortion provider in Charlotte, North Carolina, and for taking and distributing photos captioned with "Wanted . . . By Christ, to Stop Killing Babies." In an interview, Benham defended his actions by saying: "We still live in America, and we do have First Amendment rights and, as we call them, responsibilities to speak for those who cannot speak for themselves" (Lohr 2010). Saving "little baby boys and girls who are being led away to slaughter at abortion mills" is still at the organizational core (Rosenfeld 1998). But, Benham has expanded the frame to include other cultural issues that he deeply believes are indicative of moral decline, such as pornography sold in Barnes & Noble bookstores and LGBT-friendly Disney World. In 2017, Benham made headlines when he defended Alabama Senate candidate Roy Moore against charges of sexual molestation by observing, "There is something about a purity of a young woman, there is something that is good, that's true, that's straight and he looked for that" (Winter 2017).

Judie Brown (1944–)

Judie Brown has extraordinary endurance; she has devoted nearly five decades to the pro-life movement. In 1969, with her husband, Paul Brown, she passed out literature opposing a liberal abortion law up for referendum in Washington. In 1976, as a member of Ohio's Right to Life Committee, she participated in the 1976 March for Life and later joined the staff of the National Right to Life Committee (NRLC). While there, she used direct mail to increase the membership but parted with the NRLC leadership after she discovered that developing grassroots organizing was not a high priority for them. In 1979 she formed a new organization—the American Life League (ALL)—which "stands up for every innocent human being whose life is threatened by what Pope Saint John Paul II called 'the culture of death.'" It is now the oldest and largest grassroots Catholic pro-life education organization in the United States. Brown describes contraception as "anti-baby" and advocates a complete ban on abortions—no exceptions. The ALL website is deep with information, and it is also a forum for commentary on timely issues of interest. A recent post by Brown addresses the controversy in Alabama over Roy Moore's bid for the Senate with a spin different from the one used by Benham of Operation Save America. If we were not so enraptured with unproven allegations, Brown concludes, "we would be fighting to save the real victims of our time—the innocent babies whose lives came into being because of sexual activity and whose lives are ended because of our denial of the truth" (Brown 2018). Brown is a prolific author, with 12 books, including her autobiography *Not My Will but Thine* (2002).

Marjorie Dannenfelser (1965–)

Since 1992, Marjorie Dannenfelser has led the Susan B. Anthony List (SBAL), a powerhouse advocacy organization, that seeks to elevate more pro-life women to federal and statewide office. In 2010 *Newsweek* identified her as one of the top 10 "Leaders of the Christian Right," and Donald Trump tapped her to spearhead his pro-life coalition during the 2016 election. Trump had not been the pro-life community's first choice due to his inconsistent pro-life stance and his widely condemned and quickly retracted comments that "there has to be some form of punishment" for women who have abortions (Matthews 2016). Characteristically measured in her response, Dannenfelser said in a 2016 interview with NPR:

"I think he's got the zeal of a convert who hasn't thought very deeply about the consequences of how he articulates the position." She herself had once been active as a pro-choice student leader at Duke University, later converting to the pro-life cause and to Catholicism. In an extensive profile in *The New Yorker* magazine (2014), she reflects on the growing intensity of her commitment: "Now I'm going to sleep thinking, Oh, my gosh, thirty-eight hundred children are going to die tomorrow. What am I going to do to actually save some of them?" She is married to Marty Dannenfelser, former chief of staff to Representative Chris Smith (R-NJ), chair of the Bipartisan Pro-Life Congressional Caucus. They have five children, one with special needs, a situation that has strengthened her conviction that unborn children with disabilities deserve protection from abortion. Although SBAL is more narrowly focused on abortion, Dannenfelser adheres to Catholicism's "culture of life" in opposing contraception, euthanasia, and the death penalty. In 2016, under her leadership, SBAL deployed $18 million in fund-raising to defeat Hillary Clinton and to keep a pro-life majority in Congress. Using an impressive skill set that she developed working for members of Congress, Dannenfelser crafts Republican messages that broadly resonate, particularly with women voters.

Serrin Foster (1955–)

Since its beginning in 1994, Serrin Foster has led Feminists for Life of America, a nonsectarian, nonpartisan organization that thoughtfully debunks the notion that being pro-choice is a feminist mandate. Although not as high profile in the news media as other pro-life leaders, Foster has made an impact through her widely delivered speech "The Feminist Case against Abortion," which educates audiences about the hidden history of 18th- and 19th-century feminists who opposed abortion. In Foster's view, true feminism embraces nonviolence, nondiscrimination, and justice for all. Foster testified before the U.S. House Judiciary Committee in support of the Unborn Victims of Violence Act, also known as "Laci and Conner's Law," which was signed into law in 2004. She is also the creator of the compelling Women Deserve Better® campaign, which frames abortion as society's failure to meet women's needs. To that end, she has worked to develop on-campus resources for pregnant and parenting students, to ensure that health insurance covers prenatal care, to enforce child support, and to reduce poverty. Foster is also the editor of *The American Feminist* magazine, which offers timely commentary on issues like the #MeToo groundswell against sexual harassment. Foster issued a statement in 2017 in response to the American Civil Liberties Union's support of an undocumented immigrant teenager's abortion: "We may very well become a magnet for immigrants seeking taxpayer funded abortions that do nothing to address the unmet needs that these women face. . . . She may feel relief now from whatever desperate situation she faced in her home country, but likely at some point, she will need the help of Project Rachel [a pro-life postabortion support ministry] to mourn and recover from this loss" (*Catholic News Service* 2017). These words reflect Foster's consistent message—her beliefs about the harm abortion causes, her compassion for the victims, and her focus on flawed systems.

Wanda Franz (1944–)

Wanda Franz served as the president of the nation's largest pro-life organization, the National Right to Life Committee (NRLC) from 1991 to 2011. She presented the pro-life perspective on topics of the day through the NRLC website and in speeches, and she has been a key spokesperson, called by the news media to weigh in on issues of importance to the pro-life community. On Fox News in 2008, Franz, denounced a Yale art student, Aliza Shvarts, as a "serial killer" with "major mental problems" and on par with Nazi experimenters for artificially inseminating herself and inducing miscarriages. (Even NARAL viewed the project as insensitive, and Yale immediately issued a press release that it was fictitious performance art.) Franz holds a PhD in developmental psychology and spent her career on the faculty of West Virginia University, teaching and writing articles and books on child development. She became active in the early days of the pro-life movement and was president of the West Virginia Right to Life committee from 1975 to 1990—a post that she has now reassumed after retiring as professor emeritus. Other notable highlights of her career include serving in the Reagan and George H. W. Bush administrations as consultant to the Office of Population Affairs from 1983 to 1991 and as expert adviser on adolescent sex education. She wrote the introduction to Ronald Reagan's book *Abortion & the Conscience of the Nation* (1983). After becoming president of NRLC she played a prominent role at the United Nations Cairo Conference on Population and Development in 1994.

Paul T. Hill (1954–2003)

In 2003, the state of Florida executed Paul Hill by lethal injection for the killing of Dr. John Britton and James Barrett outside a Pensacola abortion clinic in 1994. Hill went to his death without remorse as he had long believed and professed that killing those who perform abortions is a just way to defend the unborn. According to his posthumous manifesto, "Mix My Blood with the Blood of the Unborn," Hill expected to receive God's reward in heaven. Hill was born in Miami and found religion after a somewhat misspent youth. He became a Presbyterian minister in South Carolina but left his congregation after getting active on the abortion issue. Some report he was excommunicated for his radical views, while others say he considered the position of his church on the abortion issue to be too meek. He was in touch with the militant Army of God, eventually moved to Pensacola, founded Defensive Action, and became a fixture outside the Ladies Center there. When Michael Griffin shot clinic physician Dr. David Gunn in 1993, Hill defended the killing as justified and appeared on any TV show that would have him to state his case. When Dr. Britton replaced Dr. Gunn at the clinic, Hill purchased a shotgun and waited for him to arrive on July 29, 1994. Hill shot the doctor in the head and also killed his escort, James Barrett, then he put down the gun, and was arrested within minutes. Although there were some court challenges to Hill's death sentence, he seemed to welcome it and to look forward to being a martyr. Only extremist pro-life groups praised his deadly tactic; many pro-life organizations distanced themselves from the growing violence in the 1990s against abortion providers.

Henry Hyde (1924–2007)

Among the pro-life advocates in Congress, Henry J. Hyde, Republican representative from Illinois, will no doubt be the most remembered. Shortly after he was elected in 1974, Hyde sponsored an amendment to an appropriations bill to deny the use of federal Medicaid funds to finance abortions for poor women except when necessary to save their lives. The amendment passed with little debate that first year and has been reauthorized in Congress ever since. Called the Hyde Amendment, it has withstood lobbying, appeals to public opinion, and litigation from pro-choice organizations challenging its constitutionality. Hyde was born in an Irish-Catholic family and attended Catholic schools, including Georgetown and Loyola, where he earned his law degree. He left the Democratic Party in the 1950s because it was too liberal and joined the Republicans. Hyde became a major spokesperson for the pro-life position, and the party made opposition to abortion an integral part of its platform. In 1981, Hyde sponsored the Human Life Bill authored by Senator Jesse Helms (R-SC) in the House of Representatives, which would have, if passed, codified his belief that human life begins at conception. This proposal, in line with Roman Catholic doctrine, demonstrated his views that religious values should be an integral part of policy debates, especially with respect to abortion. Hyde retired from the House of Representatives in 2006 after 32 years, and he became a sought-after speaker by pro-life groups. He was presented with the Presidential Medal of Freedom by George W. Bush, praising him as a "powerful defender of life," a sentiment that would be widely echoed after his death in 2007.

Paul Marx (1920–2010)

Father Paul Marx was one of 17 children born to a strict Catholic family in Minnesota. He found his calling to the priesthood and became a Benedictine monk in 1947. With the rise of debate about population, birth control, and abortion, he began to speak out frankly on the topic guided by Roman Catholic doctrine. He organized pro-life institutes in several states even before the pro-life movement got under way in the 1970s. Seeing his message as important to the world, he formed Human Life International, located near Washington, D.C., in 1980. From this base he embarked on a worldwide mission, visiting over 90 countries, to promote natural family planning and other aspects of Catholic perspective. Marx was embraced as the "Apostle for Life" in the global pro-life movement, and Pope John Paul II granted a papal audience in which he encouraged Marx to spread the pro-life movement all over the world. He was dedicated to spreading the instruction of Pope Paul VI in *Humanae Vitae* and methods of natural family planning to bring families together. For Marx contraception is a gateway to promiscuity, declining marital quality, infidelity, single-parent families, abusive sex, venereal disease, abortion, euthanasia, and the decline of nations. Marx challenged anyone to show him a nation where widespread use of modern contraception and legal abortion had not resulted in a decline in family morality. Other notable career highlights include founding the Population Research Institute in 1989 and writing 13 books, including his 1997 autobiography *Faithful for Life*. Marx retired in 1999 and returned to his abbey in Minnesota where he passed away in 2010.

Norma McCorvey (1947–2017)

In 1969, Norma McCorvey was living in Texas and pregnant with her third child. She was poor and unemployed and had only a 10-grade education; both her children had been adopted by others. She wanted an abortion but could not afford to travel to California where it was legal, so she told the doctor that she had been raped, but her request was rejected. Attorneys Sarah Weddington and Linda Coffee asked her to be their anonymous "Jane Roe" plaintiff in their class-action lawsuit challenging the constitutionality of Texas's restrictive law. After McCorvey gave birth, she put her third child up for adoption. In 1980, McCorvey publicly identified herself as "Roe" and became involved in the pro-choice movement, eventually working for an abortion clinic. Although it had played no part in the case, her confession to a reporter in 1987 that she had lied about the rape to get an abortion infuriated the pro-life side, while evoking empathy on the pro-choice side. Her 1994 book, *I Am Roe*, detailed her version of the legendary Supreme Court case. In 1995 she was attracted to the work of Operation Rescue and became part of the pro-life movement, converting to Catholicism in 1998 facilitated by conversations with Rev. Philip Benham and Rev. Frank Pavone. Her second book, *Won by Love* (1997), is about this surprising twist in her story. That same year McCorvey set up the Roe No More Ministry, and she traveled around the country to speak against abortion. In 2005, she petitioned the Supreme Court to overturn the 1973 ruling, claiming that it was harmful to women and that she had been a pawn for the feminist lawyers and the pro-choice movement. Her petition was denied. She vowed in her 1998 Senate testimony: "I am dedicated to spending the rest of my life undoing the law that bears my name." McCorvey died in 2017 at the age of 69, without having ever reconnected with the third baby she had given up for adoption.

Bernard Nathanson (1926–2011)

Dr. Bernard Nathanson became famous in the abortion debates for his complete conversion from being a highly influential pro-choice leader to becoming an even more high-profile leader for the pro-life movement. As an obstetrics/gynecology physician, he joined Lawrence Lader and Betty Friedan to found NARAL in the late 1960s and served as chair of its medical committee. In 1971, soon after New York legalized abortion, he opened a large clinic, which performed thousands of abortions for women near and far. In the mid-1970s the use of ultrasound technology allowed Nathanson to study what he called "fetology," and he came to believe abortion was a form of infanticide. He told the story of his change of heart in *Aborting America*, which was published in 1979. Nathanson claimed that, as an insider, he knew the pro-choice movement was built on lies, fabricated statistics, and cynical slogans. He confessed his past as a thoughtless abortionist, including aborting his own child. Nathanson came to national prominence in 1984 with his film, *The Silent Scream*, in which he narrated moving ultrasound images of an abortion: "Once again, we see the child's mouth wide open in a silent scream" as the child is "being torn apart, dismembered, disarticulated, crushed and destroyed by the unfeeling steel instruments of the abortionist." His next film, *The Edge of Reason*, contained a similar graphic portrayal of late-term abortion. Planned Parenthood charged that Nathanson's films were based on ideology, not on medical science. Nevertheless, Nathanson continued on the pro-life speaking circuit, telling the tale of his eye-opening conversion to the cause of the unborn. In 1996, he became a Roman Catholic and wrote *Hand of God: A Journey from Death to Life by the Abortion Doctor Who Changed His Mind*.

Troy Newman (1966–)

Current president of Operation Rescue (OR), Troy Newman is the innovator behind the "Truth Truck" campaign—mobile units with graphic images of aborted fetuses that are strategically positioned at rallies and protests. Newman vividly recalls his own moral shock on seeing such photographs in the early 1990s; this experience and his identity as an adoptee were motivators for his pro-life activism. Newman graduated from Maranatha Bible College and worked as an engineer. He joined Operation Rescue West (ORW) in 1997 and became its president two years later—this group had parted ways with the original Operation Rescue that Randall Terry had founded. In 2002, Newman relocated ORW to Wichita, Kansas, with the goal of shutting down Dr. George Tiller's clinic, where Tiller performed late-term abortions. The "West" was later dropped, the other OR became Operation Save America, and Randall Terry sued Newman for trademark infringement. OR's website offers a detailed account of its claim to ownership along with a scathing critique of Terry. The fullest articulation of Newman's Old Testament–based ideology can be found in his book, *Their Blood Cries Out*, published in 2000. It pleads with Christians to take part in the "rescue" movement to atone for the "blood-guilt" of abortion or incur the wrath of God, and it includes a shaming chapter on "Moms Who Murder." Newman has blamed legal abortion for 9/11, AIDS, and droughts. Newman also compared Tiller to Adolf Hitler and believes the government should execute abortion providers for murder. In 2009, Newman's ties to Tiller's killer, Scott Roeder, were heavily scrutinized, but he insisted that Roeder was unaffiliated with Operation Rescue. With increasing regulation by federal, state, and local authorities, Newman recognized the need to shift tactics away from picketing clinics. OR continued to target Tiller's successor Dr. Le Roy Carhart, but with more emphasis on investigating his medical practices than direct action. Newman is a board member of the Center for Medical Progress, which in 2015 released the now-discredited video alleging Planned Parenthood's "selling" of fetal tissue.

Joseph M. Scheidler (1927–)

Joseph Scheidler is the national director of the Pro-Life Action League (PLAL), founded in 1980. Scheidler is a strong conservative Catholic, who has always opposed abortion. After studying for the priesthood for a time, he married and had seven children. Like other Catholics, the decision that the fetus was not a person in *Roe v. Wade* stunned him and pushed him to work full-time to prevent abortions. His goal was to try to save lives by reducing the number of abortions and shutting down what he called "abortion mills." Patrick Buchanan has called him the "green beret of the pro-life movement." Scheidler first published his direct-action tactical playbook, *Closed: 99 Ways to Stop Abortion*, in 1985. To him, abortion is always immoral, never permitted—it's simple. Every woman who can be persuaded through sidewalk counseling not to go ahead with the abortion is another life saved. Blitzes, barricades, and rescues were eventually outlawed by the Freedom of Access to Clinic Entrances Act. NOW (National Organization for Women) claimed that Scheidler's strategies of violence and intimidation were unlawful, and a 12-year court battle ensued. NOW argued that his nationwide campaign against abortion clinics and their clients constituted a violation of the federal anti-racketeering statute. Both sides had temporary victories, but Scheidler won the war in 2003 when the Supreme Court ruled that this racketeering statute applied only to economic racketeering and not to civil action and protest. His aptly titled memoir *Racketeer for Life: Fighting the Culture of Death from the Sidewalk to the Supreme Court* came out in 2016. His oldest son, Eric Scheidler, has been involved in PLAL since the beginning, and he took over the executive director position in 2009. From its base in Aurora, Illinois, Eric has been instrumental in expanding the group's online presence and creating the #ProtestPP. He has also coordinated the PLAL's Face the Truth tours and other public protests.

Christopher Smith (1953–)

Representative Christopher Smith (R-NJ) heads the Bipartisan Pro-life Caucus in the House of Representatives where he has represented New Jersey since 1981. The abortion issue shaped his early political career. In 1976, he ran as a Democrat while serving as executive director of the New Jersey Right to Life Committee. But he soon switched to the Republican Party when the Democrats supported *Roe v. Wade*. Remarkably, he has had a perfect pro-life voting record in the House on the National Right to Life Committee's scorecard. His view on the issue is absolute: to him all abortion is murder; there are no exceptions for health, rape, incest, or fetal deformity. Smith also considers abortion a threat to women whose lives are destroyed by their experiences in what he calls "torture and killing centers." He has led the pro-life legislative agenda against abortions in military hospitals, in favor of the Mexico City gag rules, and to ban partial-birth abortions. He successfully derailed a bipartisan bankruptcy reform bill over language that prohibited clinic protesters from using bankruptcy to avoid paying damages awarded in court judgments (as Randall Terry had done in 1998). Smith is pushing hard to defund Planned Parenthood, which he has dubbed "Child Abuse Incorporated." Smith takes a moral stand on most policy issues and is prominent in promoting human rights issues. Smith has also formed alliances with feminists to curb sex trafficking and pornography.

Horatio Robinson Storer (1830–1922)

Dr. Horatio Storer, a native of Boston, Massachusetts, earned his medical degree at Harvard. He opened a practice in 1855 in the relatively new field of gynecology and only two years later launched a campaign among physicians to criminalize abortion. He worked successfully on two fronts—building a network of physicians in other states and working to gain the support of the Massachusetts medical associations. This convinced the American Medical Association (AMA) to endorse his campaign. The AMA appointed a committee to make a recommendation on the issue, and Storer drafted the report. He noted the rapidly increasing incidence of abortion and linked it to a dangerous demoralization of American society. He blamed the problem on unscrupulous people seeking to benefit from the demand for abortion and on the ignorance—mainly women's—that abortions end human lives. In 1859, the AMA adopted Storer's report and resolved to work to make abortion a crime in every state except to save the life of the mother. Storer saw his goal achieved fully by 1900. In 1865, Storer's widely distributed essay "Why Not? A Book for Every Woman" counseled about the moral and physical dangers of inducing abortion. Storer is a controversial figure in women's health; pro-choice feminists see him as a contributor to the establishment of male-dominated medical treatment of women and have exposed his theory that women's emotional problems were related to their reproductive systems. To cure them, he removed their ovaries, an operation he performed many times in his career. Early pro-life advocates saw Storer as the grandfather of their movement and the man who saved women from exploitation by quack abortionists.

Randall Terry (1959–)

Randall Terry began his aggressive crusade against abortion in the 1980s. He had grown up in New York, graduated from the Elim Bible Institute, married, and become a leader in his evangelical church. Concerned about the moral decay of American society, he and his wife started Project Life to persuade women not to enter abortion clinics. In 1987, Terry founded Operation Rescue (OR), known for its disruptive direct-action tactic of descending en masse to blockade entrances; Terry is proud to have been arrested more than 40 times. Critics charged that Terry's message inspired violence by tapping into the fervent religious feelings and urging extreme action to stop a purported baby-killing operation. James Kopp, who murdered Dr. Barnett Slepian in 1998, was one of Terry's followers. Terry garnered media attention with theatrical stunts like splattering baby dolls with fake blood. His signature fiery rhetoric was on full display on the Phil Donahue Show in 1991; he accused Faye Wattleton, an African American, president of PPFA, of being a race traitor: "Margaret Sanger . . . wanted to eliminate the black community. . . . You have been bought" (Port 2013). Terry became a codefendant in *NOW v. Scheidler* in 1993, eventually settling the case out of court and later declaring bankruptcy to avoid paying any fines or damages. Terry left OR in the mid-1990s; he fell from grace with his religious followers when he left his wife and married another woman. In 2006, Terry campaigned for the Florida State Senate. Terry also railed against same-sex marriage. Though he is no longer at the center of the abortion debate, his fervor has not dissipated. After being arrested for protesting against Obama's speech at Notre Dame in 2009, Terry issued a statement warning, "A dreadful reckoning is coming. The blood of the innocent cries from the ground to God for justice. We will all be judged for our part in allowing this slaughter to continue. We will be held accountable for what we have done, and what we have failed to do" (*Christian Newswire* 2009). His current website news program, Voice of Resistance, offers training for Judeo-Christian political leaders.

Charmaine Yoest (1964–)

In 2017, President Donald Trump appointed Charmaine Yoest as assistant secretary for health and human services. The move was praised by the pro-life community; Marjorie Dannenfelser, president of the Susan B. Anthony List, described Yoest as one of their side's "most articulate and powerful communicators." Yoest had a conservative upbringing—her mother, Janice Shaw Crouse, had been a policy analyst for Concerned Women for America. She attended the religious Wheaton College, graduating in 2006, and went on to earn a doctorate in politics at the University of Virginia in 2004. She is a married mother of five and author of *Mother in the Middle: Searching for Peace in the Mommy Wars* (1996) about women's struggle to find work-life balance. Her career began with her appointment to President Ronald Reagan's Office of Personnel. Yoest also served as a senior fellow at American Values, a conservative nonprofit that supports "traditional family values." From 2008 to 2016, Yoest was CEO of Americans United for Life, which has been actively supplying policy resources to craft pro-life legislation and calling for a congressional investigation of Planned Parenthood. Yoest has been carefully reframing the pro-life position as pro-women's health, a message that Emily Bazelon's 2012 probing profile in *The New York Times* describes as consistently delivered with a cheerful smile. Pro-choice groups characterize her views as frightening. Yoest, who is herself a breast cancer survivor, has repeatedly claimed that abortion increases a woman's risk of breast cancer despite scientific evidence and the prevailing views of the medical experts. Yoest also opposes abortion in all cases, asserting that embryos have legal rights, and she has described birth control methods like the intrauterine device as having "life-ending properties."

Organizations

On both the pro-life and pro-choice sides there are at least 10 different types of organizational structures. Beginning with this foundational understanding helps us better conceptualize how these variously constituted groups might interact or not interact with one another. As the profiles will make clear, the organizations line up in a highly polarized fashion. Each side even has its own preferred sources of news—those on the pro-choice side may turn to Kaiser Daily Global Health Policy Report, RH Reality Check, or Rewire, while those on the pro-life side are trust LifeNews.com, Catholic News Agency, and National Right to Life News Today. Exposure to information that is aligned with one's existing worldviews and the lack of cross-cutting organizational ties create an echo chamber in which existing beliefs become amplified and reinforced through repetition.

The first type of organizational structure is broad-based organizations like Focus on the Family that oppose abortion along with other forces that are thought to undermine "traditional families." Similarly, for the National Organization for Women, abortion is one of the several rights that are viewed as fundamental to ensuring gender equality. A second type is the pro-life and pro-choice organizations that often face off against one another and whose leaders are frequently called on as spokespersons like the National Right to Life Committee and NARAL-Pro-Choice

America. Third, some organizations concentrate on what they regard as a particularly troubling aspect of the abortion issue. In the pro-life community there are pregnancy help centers, like Heartbeat International, that are dedicated to providing alternatives to abortion, and there are postabortion recovery and support services like Project Rachel. Arising from the pro-choice community are campaigns to destigmatize abortion, like the Abortion Diary, and groups like the National Network of Abortion Funds that are committed to securing the funds for economically disadvantaged women to pay for abortions. A fourth category of organizations can be distinguished by the realms in which they operate. While many pro-life organizations are religiously affiliated, there are also some pro-choice organizations that are faith based like the Religious Coalition for Reproductive Choice. Not surprisingly, there are several organizations that operate in the medical field, such as Pharmacists for Life and Medical Students for Choice. Fifth, there are reproductive health organizations, like the Alan Guttmacher Institute, that are more academically research based and are thus excellent sources of high-quality information; these organizations can also have an evidence-informed advocacy component.

A sixth organization type is distinguished by social change strategy it uses. For example, the Susan B. Anthony List recruits pro-life candidates to run for political office, and the Center on Reproductive Rights and Justice focuses on litigation. There are also extremist organizations, like the Army of God, represented here, though it is important to note that the majority of pro-life organizations are law abiding and peaceful. The seventh organizational structure can be defined by its recruitment of members who share an identity. For example, Students for Life draws a younger crowd. Racial/ethnic minorities have established their own groups like Trust Black Women to ensure that their voices are heard. Particularly fascinating are those organizations that help make marginalized views more visible, like Feminists for Life or Catholics for a Free Choice. The eighth type includes relevant government agencies like the Centers for Disease Control and Prevention, and the ninth is international organizations. Finally, the tenth type of organization draws participants who are ideologically diverse but who are committed to finding areas of overlapping interest; this section begins with two—albeit unfortunately rare—examples that demonstrate the possibilities of both sides coming together. Of course, this organizational typology is not exhaustive or mutually exclusive—an organization can be classified as more than one type.

Common Ground

Common Ground Network for Life and Choice

sfcg.org

Between 1993 and 2000—during a time of extreme polarization and violence in the abortion conflict—the Search for Common Ground, an organization that promotes conflict resolution, formed the Common Ground Network for Life and Choice. The intense discussions took place in Buffalo, New York, and Pensacola, Florida. The goal was to shift the divisive debate over legal abortion from confrontation to collaboration. The steering committee, comprised of pro-choice and pro-life activists, set out the steps: first, bring each side into respectful dialogue to debunk stereotypes and to understand the other's points of view; second, find common values and beliefs; and third, look for ways to move together toward common goals. Mary Jacksteit and Dr. Adrienne Kaufmann elaborate in the manual they produced (http://bit.ly/2ksJgCr). Preventing teenage pregnancy, making adoption more accessible, avoiding violence, increasing options for women, and reducing conditions that increase abortion rates were identified as opportunities where both sides could work together.

Exhale

exhaleprovoice.org

Established in 2000 by and for women who have had abortions, Exhale is a community-led organization that embraces "trend-setting, pro-voice strategies" to support and facilitate connections. To learn more about its philosophy, view cofounder Aspen Baker's Ted Talk, "Pro-Voice: How to Keep Listening When the World Wants a Fight." Exhale is most well known for its after-abortion talk line, which was created in 2002 as a space free of stigma and divisive politics. Volunteers have promoted emotional well-being by listening with empathy to over 30,000 calls and by viewing each individual as a "whole person" with a value system that is worthy of respect. Postabortion e-cards were added in 2007 for loved ones who wanted to express love and support to someone they know who has had an abortion.

On the Pro-Life Side

American Center for Law and Justice (ACLJ)

ACLJ was founded in 1990 to safeguard religious and constitutional freedoms using the tools of advocacy, education, and litigation, including representing clients appearing before the U.S. Supreme Court and international tribunals. The organization has defended the partial-birth abortion ban by filing an amicus brief in the *Gonzales v. Carhart* case in 2007. In 2010, ACLJ Films released a documentary titled *Choosing Life*, which tells the story of the pro-life movement's response to legalized abortion, a decade-long tale of victories and defeats. Chief Counsel Jay Sekulow has been committed to protecting the free-speech rights of pro-life demonstrators. He is also an attorney for President Trump. Sekulow has recently come under scrutiny for misappropriation of funds.

American Coalition of Life Activists (ACLA)

ACLA was associated with the spike in pro-life violence in the early 1990s. It authored a series of wanted-style posters that portrayed abortion providers as criminals and offered a $5,000 reward for success in driving them out of the business. The "Nuremburg" files posted on the Internet in 1996 got the group in real trouble. Dossiers about scores of doctors and clinic personnel were offered to show their "crimes against humanity," and some were subsequently victims of assassinations. ACLA would then draw a line through the photos on its website. Planned Parenthood sued the ACLA and won a $100 million judgment, but it was overturned on appeal, based on First Amendment grounds. The group has disbanded and no longer has its website.

American Life League (ALL)

ALL was cofounded in 1979 by Judie Brown and her husband, and she has continued as president to this day. The organization professes strong pro-life views, declaring that the life of every human being is sacred from conception to natural death and must have equal rights. ALL is one of the most absolutist of the pro-life groups, as they say, "without compromise, without exception, without apology." For ALL the pro-life movement is a moral crusade. Its projects include a Charity Watchlist, Prayer and Fasting, and Resources for keeping Planned Parenthood out of schools and communities. Its 2017 Facilities report, available with e-mail sign-up, purports to show that the "Planned Parenthood empire is imploding."

Americans United for Life (AUL)

AUL describes itself as "the legal architect of the pro-life movement." The group was founded in 1971 to focus on lawmaking and litigation to achieve pro-life goals. AUL attorneys call the 1973 ruling in *Roe v. Wade* a "catastrophe" that ushered in a "culture of death," which AUL wants to replace with a "culture of life" through law reform. AUL's goal is to reverse this decision and its effects by joining in litigation. It has offered its legal expertise to propose model legislation to Congress and the states. CEO, Charmaine Yoest, has been particularly effective in framing abortion as destroying two lives—the child who is killed and the woman's whose physical and mental health suffers. AUL's website touts many victories, including the Hyde Amendment, Fetal Homicide Laws, and spurring a congressional investigation of the "abortion giant" Planned Parenthood.

Army of God (AG)

AG takes up where the ACLA activists left off in carrying the militant pro-life banner. The website, which is maintained by Donald Spitz, contains a few disturbing photographs of alleged abortions attributed to "baby-killing abortionists." It is primarily, however, a tribute to the "heroes" who defended the lives of the unborn, with a smattering of biblical verses like, "Who will rise up for me against the evildoers?" Psalm 94:16. There is an invitation to engage in a prison correspondence with Scott Roeder, who was convicted for the murder of Dr. George Tiller. Tiller's photograph is juxtaposed with that of Adolf Hitler, showing blood dripping down. AG has been compared to an underground terrorist organization. In 2000, it was the subject of an HBO documentary, *Soldiers in the Army of God.*

Center for Bio-Ethical Reform (CBR)

Be aware that when arriving on the CBR website, the viewer will be issued a warning that a disturbing video of an abortion is about to play, which is part of its AbortionNO campaign. The California-based group was founded in 1990 to seek "prenatal justice, and the right to life of the unborn, disabled and aged." To accomplish its pro-life agenda, CBR's strategy is to project images of bloody aborted fetuses so that the public will have to come to grips with what they believe is the true nature of the procedure. Its highly controversial Genocide Awareness Campaign places displays of aborted fetuses next to recognizable images of the Holocaust to force a recognition of what it sees as chilling similarities. CBR articulates its foundational principle to explain its "nonviolent" visual tactics: "Abortion represents an evil so inexpressible that words fail us when attempting to describe its horror. Until abortion is seen, it will never be understood."

Center for Medical Progress (CMP)

A newcomer organization, the CMP has garnered tremendous publicity in the past few years. CMP describes itself as "a group of citizen journalists dedicated to monitoring and reporting on medical ethics and advances." Its Human Capital Project involved a 30-month undercover operation to expose what it claimed was Planned Parenthood's sale of aborted babies. Leaders David Daleiden and Sandra Merritt have been charged with felonies, and their videos have been shown to be deceptive. They claim that human dignity is at the heart of their concerns.

Christian Coalition of America (CCA)

Pat Robertson, the famous host of the *700 Club* on his Christian Broadcasting Network, founded the Christian Coalition (CC) in 1989, the year after he ran for president. For Robertson and his colleague, Ralph Reed, the CC was a means by which Christian fundamentalists could "take over" the Republican Party through grassroots organizing. The CC was a national player during the 1990s with its "pro-family, pro-life agenda," but its political activism got it in trouble with the Internal Revenue Service, which revoked its tax-exempt status. Robertson left the organization in 2000, and it reorganized as the CCA under the presidency of Roberta Coombs. Conservative news and commentary and action alerts are sent out through its mobile app, via twitter to about 50k followers, and on Facebook to over 300,000 fans. Although CCA calls itself "one of the largest conservative grassroots political organizations in America," its visibility and influence has diminished.

Concerned Women for America (CWFA)

CWFA was founded in 1979 by fundamentalist Christian activist Beverly LaHaye, who remains the chairman of the board. CWFA describes itself as the largest women's public policy organization in the United States. Its mission is to bring its fundamentalist view of the Bible and Christianity to government, restoring the nation to the founders' traditional values. Sanctity of life is one of CWFA's seven core issues; it opposes not just abortion but also euthanasia and embryonic and fetal tissue research. CWFA also advocates for pregnancy care centers, postabortion counseling services, sexual abstinence, and the natural distinctions between men and women in marriage. It offers brochures that frame abortion as the "ultimate form of discrimination," that explain how "pro-life is pro-woman," and that promote the scientifically discredited claim that abortion is linked to breast cancer. Under the new leadership of Penny Young Nance, CWFA has been active in pursing abortion bans, TRAP laws, appointments of pro-life judges, and, of course, lobbying to defund Planned Parenthood.

Crisis Pregnancy Centers (CPC)

"Pregnant? Scared? . . . " It is a familiar billboard and bumper sticker. CPCs are typically faith-based efforts to provide pregnant women with alternatives to abortion; some prefer the term "Pregnancy Help" or "Care Center" to reflect that goal. The mission of Care Net, for example, is to offer "compassion, hope, and help to anyone considering abortion by presenting them with realistic alternatives and Christ-centered support through our life-affirming network." Heartbeat International's "mission is to Reach and Rescue as many lives as possible, around the world, through an effective network of life-affirming pregnancy help, to Renew communities for LIFE." CPCs offer free pregnancy testing and counseling about adoption and keeping the baby, and some provide ultrasounds. The offices are commonly located near abortion clinics, and there are thought to be around 3,000 across the country. The best ones help women navigate complicated food assistance programs and Medicaid health insurance coverage, and the worst ones use emotionally manipulative ploys. They are not regulated. Pro-choice organizations have tried to expose CPCs unscrupulous practices and require that they tell the truth. A congressional investigation in 2006 revealed that 20 of the 23 CPCs provided information that was unsupported by scientific evidence, including linking abortion to increased risk of breast cancer, future infertility, or psychological harm. In March 2018, the U.S. Supreme Court appears poised to strike down California's Reproductive FACT Act law in the case *National Institute of Family and Life Advocates v. Becerra*, on the grounds that the requiring CPCs to provide information about abortion services intrudes on First Amendment rights.

Democrats for Life of America (DLA)

DLA was formed in 1999 after several prominent pro-life Democrats were denied the chance to speak at the Democratic Party's presidential conventions. The organization seeks to attract those who do not support the party's pro-choice stand. DLA opposes abortion and euthanasia, but it also opposes capital punishment, a position not usually on the pro-life agenda. It is also attentive to poverty and other injustices that threaten human life. While it agrees that abortion should be illegal, overturning *Roe v. Wade* is not its top priority; instead, it focuses on comprehensive programs that would reduce abortion through preventing unplanned pregnancy and helping pregnant women to find alternatives to abortion. DLA lists the Pregnancy Assistance Fund as one of its proudest accomplishments, which was signed into law as part of the Affordable Care Act; 17 states are now receiving money to support pregnant women. DLA calls for the use of inclusive language in the 2020 Democratic platform that welcomes those who oppose abortion.

Elliot Institute (EI)

The EI was founded in 1988 by Dr. David Reardon, a biomedical ethicist, who has conducted research to prove that women are adversely affected by abortion. His first book, *Aborted Women: Silent No More*, was published in 1987. EI bills itself as a mission and ministerial organization, dedicated to postabortion recovery. EI also collects testimonies of women to use in its "UnChoice" campaign. While the website is deep with resources, the "latest news" posted is from 2013, which suggests the group has become inactive. Reardon's theories have been rejected by the medical establishment for being ideologically biased. In an extensive review of the literature, the American Psychological Association cautions against global statements about how women feel after abortion and concludes that the weight of empirical evidence shows that an abortion does not pose a threat to women's mental health, though stigma can have a negative impact (www.apa.org/pi/women/programs/abortion/).

Family Research Council (FRC)

The FRC is a think tank and lobbying organization that promotes policy that will help realize its vision for "a culture in which all human life is valued, families flourish, and religious liberty thrives." FRC was founded in 1983 with the goal of shaping the debate over families and politics in a conservative Christian direction. To uphold "the inherent dignity of every human life from conception," FRC lobbies against legal abortion, for abstinence-only education, and against government-supported family planning. FRC is also well known for its strong opposition to gay rights. Its leaders have been prominent in right-wing circles, especially Gary Bauer, who ran for U.S. president in 2000, and Tony Perkins, the current president of FRC, who is a frequent guest on conservative talk shows and in debates about social issues.

Feminists for Life of America (FFL)

FFL, formed in 1972, has the goal of meeting the needs of women who are pregnant or parenting and helps them find alternatives to abortion. To FFL, abortion represents society's failure and the victimization of women; its goal is to address the underlying causes that drive women to abortion and promote what it calls the core values of feminism: "justice, non-discrimination, and nonviolence." The organization's primary activities involve outreach to college campuses and speeches to show students they can be both pro-life and pro-feminist.

They gain much of their inspiration from the lives and politics of women's rights pioneers Susan B. Anthony and Elizabeth Cady Stanton, who opposed abortion because they considered it a form of violence against women. Regarding contraception, FFL notes that preconception issues are outside the organization's purview and that members have a diversity of opinions on the matter.

Focus on the Family (FOF)

FOF is a global ministry and media organization that upholds a broad range of conservative Christian values. It believes that "every person, from conception to natural death, possesses inherent dignity and immeasurable worth—including pre-born children, elderly individuals, those with special needs and others marginalized by society." In 2013, *The New York Times* reported that FOF employed a staff of 665 and had an annual budget of $98 million. FOF publishes magazines, books, and videos to disseminate its biblical values, which include abstinence until marriage. There are resources to support parents who are fostering, adopting, or caring for children with special needs. Dr. James Dobson, who founded the organization in 1977, served as president until 2003 and afterward as chair of the board until he stepped down in 2010; today he hosts a daily radio broadcast called *Family Talk*. The new President, Jim Daly, is attempting to rebrand by softening the rhetoric, particularly around its anti-LGBT stance.

Lambs of Christ (LC)

Norman Weston died in 2012; he was a Roman Catholic priest, former army paratrooper, and the founder of LC in 1989, which was a "rapid deployment force" to support anti-abortion militancy. Troy Newman, the current leader of Operation Rescue (OR), remembered him as a "great pro-life hero." Weston had been inspired by OR's disruptive tactics, and he became a beacon for those seeking to escalate the conflict as a form of spiritual warfare. He was known to have dealings with James Kopp, Dr. Barnett Slepian's killer. The Lambs roamed about the country targeting abortion providers through harassment, human blockades with kryptonite locks, and invasions. Their tactic was to do what it took to get arrested and then refuse to give their names—calling themselves either Baby John Doe or Baby Jane Doe, which was intended to tie up the resources of local law enforcement.

Live Action (LA)

Though new to the pro-life scene, LA has a big online presence with 2 million social media supporters. It issues daily reports on important stories that, it says, the mainstream media overlooks like exposing what it sees as the brutality of the abortion industry. LA argues that "many Americans do not realize how developed preborn children are when they are aborted, they are kept in the dark about the risks abortion poses to women, and they have no idea what happens to a preborn child during an abortion" (Live Action n.d.). It also claims that the truth is "changing minds, saving lives, and transforming pro-life education." LA was started by Lila Rose when she was just 15 years old, and it was legally formed as a "nonpartisan, nonprofit" organization in 2008.

March for Life Education and Defense Fund (ML)

The first March for Life was held in Washington, D.C., on January 22, 1974, on the one-year anniversary of the Supreme Court's decision in *Roe v. Wade*. The event proved to be effective for mobilizing the pro-life movement. Leaders formed ML as a nonprofit organization to organize the annual event. The group adheres to a set of "Life Principles," which includes the enactment of a Human Life Amendment. "Love Saves Lives" was the theme for the 2018 March, which included "Silent No More" testimonies outside the U.S. Supreme Court, as well as speeches by President Donald J. Trump (via satellite), House

Speaker Paul Ryan, and NFL quarterback Tim Tiebow. The symbols of the march are red roses, which are delivered to each member of Congress along with a pro-life "Red Rose Letter."

Moral Majority Coalition (MMC)

Rev. Jerry Falwell organized the Moral Majority in 1979 as a mechanism to bring evangelical leaders together to "engage the culture" to the pro-life, pro-traditional family message. In the coalitions of the religious right, the Moral Majority was a key component in promoting pro-life politics, especially the successful campaigns of Ronald Reagan for president. Falwell disbanded the Moral Majority in 1989 to devote his attention to establishing Liberty University. He brought the group back in 2004 in the form of the MMC; its main goal was to mobilize voters for candidates of the religious right and to fight against what Falwell called "out-of-control lawmakers and radical judges—working at the whims of society—to alter the moral foundations of America" (Jones 2008). Falwell died in 2007, and there was no successor.

National Right to Life (NRL)

NRL is an influential single-issue, nonreligious, and nonpartisan pro-life organization and one of the earliest to be established in 1968. Congressman Henry Hyde has called NRL the "flagship of the pro-life movement." The national body is composed of 50 state-affiliated state groups, thousands of community chapters, and hundreds of thousands of members, making it the largest pro-life grassroots organization. NRL asserts, "Our Founding Fathers emphasized the preeminence of the right to 'Life' by citing it first among the unalienable rights this nation was established to secure." With the tools of education, legislation, and political action, fighting legal abortion is NRL's primary mission, but it also opposes stem cell research, euthanasia, and infanticide. It does not take a position or even comment on questions of contraception, sex education, or capital punishment. Carol Tobias has served as the director since 1987. She recently applauded President Donald Trump for the great pro-life strides he has already made in restoring the Mexico City policy and confirming Neil Gorsuch to the Supreme Court.

New Wave Feminists (NWF)

"Bad**s. Pro-life. Feminist." That is NWF's slogan. Its website is just as hip in describing the superpowers of its leadership team. The group made big headlines when it was shut out of the 2017 Women's March on Washington. It was started 10 years ago as the self-funded passion project of Destiny Herndon de La Rosa. The group advocates a "consistent life ethic," which is the principle that "human beings should be free from violence for the duration of their lifetime." Perhaps what makes it new wave, other than its social media savvy, is that NWF extends its platform to include being anti-war, anti-death penalty, and anti-torture. It is not working to outlaw abortion but to make it "unthinkable and unnecessary" by supporting women and their children.

Operation Rescue (OR)

The height of OR's notoriety and arrests for civil disobedience to shut down abortion clinics was in the late 1980s and early 1990s before the 1993 FACE act imposed stiffer penalties for obstructing access. OR continues to be among the most active pro-life Christian activist organizations today. OR still adheres to the strategies of direct action "to restore legal personhood to the pre-born and stop abortion in obedience to biblical mandates." OR had relocated its headquarters to Wichita, Kansas, in 2002, where the infamous "Summer of Mercy" had been staged in 1991. The storyline of organizational mergers and splits is complicated: Newman's OR West dropped the "West"—Newman's group holds the trademark to OR—and Terry's OR became Operation Save America. In

2006, OR purchased the building to force the clinic it had besieged to close; it was one of the few remaining places in the country that performed late-term abortions. Troy Newman has served as the president of OR since 1999. He is far more measured than the creator of the original OR, Randall Terry, but like Terry he grasps the significance of tactical innovation to garner media attention. Newman is the man behind OR's fleet of "Truth Trucks," which confront onlookers with graphic displays of dismembered fetuses, sparking questions about the line between free speech and disrupting the peace.

Operation Save America (OSA)

OSA "unashamedly takes up the cause of preborn children in the name of Jesus Christ" (Operation Save America n.d.). It seeks God's repentance through street action for what it terms the abortion holocaust in America. Rev. Rusty Thomas became the director when Rev. Philip "Flip" Benham stepped down in 2014. Benham had led the organization since 1994 when it was called OR National. He had taken it over from Keith Tucci, who had led the 1991 "Summer of Mercy" in Wichita, Kansas, against Dr. George Tiller's late-term abortion clinic. Tucci had replaced Randall Terry, who was the original founder of OR in 1987. Benham extended OSA's frame of issues to include opposition to homosexuality, pornography, and Islam. Emboldened by the election of President Donald Trump, OSA set its sights on the last abortion clinic in Kentucky, and in 2017 its blockade, which was the first coordinated effort in 13 years, led to 11 arrests of protestors, including the director Reverend Thomas.

Pharmacists for Life International (PFLI)

PFLI was founded in Ohio in 1984, but it has a national and even an international mission. Its motto is "Let the Gift of Medicines promote Life, not destroy Life!" Its founding statement elaborates on its pro-life beliefs: "PFLI defends, upholds and protects the sanctity of all human life from conception to natural death, regardless of age, biological stage, handicap or place of residence." PFLI seeks to promote this goal by persuading pharmacists and other medical personnel to resist the use of any medication that is or could be an abortifacient—an agent that causes an abortion—which PFLI defines as preventing a fertilized egg from implanting in the uterus. PFLI urges pharmacists to refuse to fill prescriptions for any of these drugs—including emergency contraception and many hormone birth control pills—and defend their legal rights to do so as part of their rights of conscience.

Physicians for Life (PL)

Although the organization invites pro-life physicians to join, PL is primarily a website with many links to commentary and research papers about issues from a pro-life point of view. The group's goal is to draw attention to the problems of abortion, euthanasia, stem cell research, cloning, infanticide, sexually transmitted diseases, and out-of-wedlock sexual activity. With the resources it provides, organizers hope to build support and community for physicians who have taken a pro-life stand and encourage them to educate others, including their patients, about the "innate value and sanctity of every human life at all stages of development."

Priests for Life (PFL)

Established in 1991, PFL seeks to "instill a sense of urgency in all clergy . . . and to mobilize their people to help stop abortion and euthanasia." This organization is primarily a vehicle for the work and writings of Father Frank Pavone, who travels the country giving talks and seminars as well as networking with major organizations in the pro-life movement. In 2004, Pavone started assembling a community of priests devoted to missionary work on life issues. Two other top projects are Rachel's Vineyard, a ministry to help women heal after abortion by holding retreats for both women and men who have suffered the loss of children to abortion, and the Silent No More Awareness Campaign, which mobilizes those harmed by abortion to share their testimony. In 2015 PFL and Pavone received praise from the Vatican for his life-saving work. In 2016, Pavone laid an aborted fetus that had been entrusted to him for proper burial on the altar and posted a live video on Facebook to compel onlookers to not to vote for Hillary Clinton. His actions were widely criticized, and Pavone is facing a Diocesan Investigation.

Pro-Life Action League (PLAL)

PLAL formed in 1980 and has been led by its founder Joseph M. Scheidler ever since. PLAL has a prominent place in the pro-life movement through its use of direct but nonviolent action to stop abortions. One of its most important techniques is sidewalk counseling. People are trained as missionaries to intercept clients on their way into the clinic and dissuade them from going through with a planned abortion. PLAL members also picket clinics and sponsor "Face the Truth" tours where they show large photos of aborted fetuses. Scheidler and his organization were the object of a decade-long lawsuit by NOW seeking damages under the federal anti-racketeering statutes. The case was finally resolved in 2003 in Scheidler's favor. PLAL is one of the main backers of #PPP, which is inspiring hundreds of protests and counterprotests at PP affiliates around the country.

Pro-Life Alliance of Gays and Lesbians (PLAGAL)

PLAGAL occupies the margins of both the pro-choice and pro-life movements. Most gays and lesbians are thought to be associated with the ideas of pro-choice, that is, privacy, individual rights, and sexual freedom. The pro-life philosophy, on the other hand, often goes hand in hand with a fundamentalist view of sexuality that condemns homosexuality and fights against gay rights. PLAGAL confounds both sides by claiming that legal abortion is just like homophobia. For example, the group asserts, abortion denies fundamental humanity and rids societies of human beings who are considered undesirable. The organization, formed in 1990, was originally called Gays against Abortion, but it expanded to reflect the membership of lesbians. PLAGAL is a small group, but it distributes position pamphlets and participates in activities such as the March for Life. Its last newsletter on its website is dated 2009, but there are more recent posts on its Facebook page.

#ProtestPP (#PPP)

Bringing down Planned Parenthood (PP) has been a tremendously unifying goal. #PPP is sponsored by the PLAL, Citizens for a Pro-Life Society, and Created Equal and cosponsored by 40 other pro-life organizations. PP has been identified as a target according to the website because it is the largest abortion provider, it has engaged in unethical conduct, and it exaggerates its role in providing health care, and the bottom line for #PPP is that it should not receive federal funding. #PPP urges supporters to spread the truth and provides toolkits for organizing successful protest events.

Republican National Coalition for Life (RNCL)

Conservative activist Phyllis Schlafly formed RNCL in 1990 to counter the attempts by Republican pro-choice organizations to change the Republican pro-life platform. Floor fights occurred at the conventions in 1992 and 1996, but the pro-life coalition has prevailed. Between conventions the organization is little more than a blog, with occasional position papers to connect with the faithful. The network remains in place to "protect and defend the Republican Party's principled commitment to legal protection for all innocent human beings, from conception until natural death" and "to hold Republican lawmakers accountable to the pro-life principles in our platform."

Students for Life (SL)

SL does not just want to fight abortion; it seeks cultural transformation so that the practice becomes "unthinkable and obsolete." The organization began in the late 1970s as C.Am.P.U.S.; then it was rebranded as American Collegians for Life in 1988. Until 2006, it was essentially a student volunteer organization with an annual conference and quarterly publication. In 2006, under the new name SL, the organization professionalized; Kristan Hawkins and other staff were hired. Today, SL reports that there are 1,200 high school and college pro-life student groups under its umbrella. SL offers activist toolkits and leadership training.

Susan B. Anthony List (SBAL)

According to President Marjorie Dannenfelser, SBAL was established "to give voice to women who feel very strongly that the pro-life position is the natural place for women." SBAL supports legislation that protects both unborn children and their mothers from abortion and educates voters on candidates' records. Demonstrating its sophisticated messaging, the organization describes itself as "an arsenal designed not to hurt but to heal, not to shame but to shield." Alongside over 60 other pro-life organizations, SBAL put Congress on notice in December 2017 that it will fight any "Obamacare stabilization funding unless amended so such funds cannot be used for plans that include elective abortion."

TooManyAborted.com (TMA)

In 2010 billboards appeared in Atlanta, Georgia, with the disturbing claim, "Black children are an endangered species," which provoked the ire of pro-choice groups and the many in the black community. The TMA website was launched to spread the message that the abortion industry preys on and profits from the black community's willingness to self-exterminate. The designer of the ad Ryan Bomberger insisted that the intention was not to induce shame but to promote life-affirming choices and resources. He is the cofounder of the Radiance Foundation, which helped launch this initiative, an adoptee and an adoptive father, and the author of *Not Equal: Civil Rights Gone Wrong* (2016).

Traditional Values Coalition (TVC)

TVC, founded in 1980 by Rev. Louis P. Sheldon and now led by his daughter, Andrea Lafferty, seeks to restore the values for strong families based on guidance from a literal reading of the Bible. At the top of the list is the right to life from conception to natural death, but TVC also supports the power of government to execute murderers through capital punishment. Other traditional values include fidelity in marriage, abstinence before marriage, and condemnation of all sex outside of heterosexual marriage. Today, its highest priority seems to be the fight against homosexuality, and the Southern Poverty Law Center has identified TVC as a hate group.

United States Conference of Catholic Bishops (USCCB)

The USCCB is the official hierarchy of the Roman Catholic Church in the United States. The Pro-life Secretariat and Committee is one of the most active in assembling educational materials. It has promoted human life and dignity from conception to natural death with special concern for the poor and vulnerable. The Pastoral Plan consists of four "pillars" to guide pro-life activities, which are public information and education, public policy, pastoral care, and prayer. The USCCB was sued in 2013 in a Michigan federal court by a woman who claims that the Catholic hospital where she was forced to go when her water broke at 18 weeks of pregnancy exposed her to a dangerous infection by not providing accurate medical information or comprehensive care. USCCB is being targeted because the hospital was following its ethical and religious directives by not providing abortion referrals.

On the Pro-Choice Side

Abortion Care Network (ACN)

ACN was founded in 2008 to serve as a national network for independent abortion care providers and supporters based on the promise "We are stronger together." The Uniting Our Voices program offers trainings on media and messaging skills and other opportunities to learn and build a community of support. The sliding membership fee is $1 per abortion patient seen in the previous year. Reproductive health, rights, and justice organizations can join and even individual academics, journalists, and advocates are eligible for the Ally Membership.

Abortion Conversation Project (ACP)

ACP began in 2000 as a sister organization to the National Coalition of Abortion Providers, and it continues to work collaboratively with other pro-choice organizations to realize its vision of "a world in which abortion is affirmed as a moral decision without stigma." ACP believes that the pathway forward is to open safe spaces where pro-choice allies from the medical profession, the clergy, academia, and others can come together. It is believed that honest dialogue about abortion will combat polarization and stigma and promote postabortion emotional health. ACP developed informative handouts on how to facilitate difficult conversations, and it offers small seed grants to individuals and grassroots groups projects that are in keeping with its mission.

The Abortion Diary (TAD)

Based on her personal experience, Melissa Madera PhD was inspired to self-fund the creation of TAD in 2013 as a space for breaking the silence about abortion. She describes it as being "the intersection of self-expression, healing, and the art of story-sharing and story-listening." A new story is posted each Tuesday. The podcasts explore a wide range of abortion experiences and emotional responses and are intended to build community, promote collective healing, and be a disruptive force in the polarized abortion debate.

Abortion Rights Mobilization (ARM)

Lawrence Lader, a leading member of the abortion reform/repeal movement of the 1960s, founded ARM in 1975. A tiny group with no staff or members, ARM was a resource for Lader to promote his various goals for abortion policy. It was active especially in the 1980s and 1990s in the campaign to legalize mifepristone, also known as RU-486 or the abortion pill. With support from the John Merck Foundation, among others, ARM produced a version of the drug and with the Food and Drug Administration's permission conducted trials to meet requirements for more general usage. ARM also brought lawsuits to challenge the tax-exempt status of the Roman Catholic Church, claiming that the Church's abortion activism violated the federal law. With Lader's death in 2006, ARM is no longer in existence.

Advancing New Standards in Reproductive Health (ANSIRH)

Housed in the Bixby Center for Global Reproductive Health at the University of California, San Francisco, ANSIRH is a collaborate group of multidisciplinary researchers who seek deeper understanding of the complexity of individuals' sexual and reproductive lives and the structural inequalities that shape and constrain their experiences. They "envision a world in which all people have the resources, support, and freedom to achieve reproductive wellbeing." ANSIRH's studies of abortion are cutting edge on topics like reproductive health in religious organizations, telemedicine, and ultrasound viewing. Its website is an excellent source for scientifically credible reports.

American Civil Liberties Union (ACLU) Reproductive Freedom Project

The ACLU established its Reproductive Freedom Project in 1974, a year after *Roe v. Wade* decriminalized abortion. A pro-choice organization, ACLU strives to protect the individual's right to make informed decisions about whether and when to become a parent by advancing the broad spectrum of reproductive policies. The project is especially concerned that rights not be limited by income, age, race, or where people live. The ACLU has a staff of attorneys, paralegals, and support personnel, and its main activities are lobbying at federal and state legislatures, litigation in state and federal courts, and public education through press releases, conferences, meetings, and publications.

American Law Institute (ALI)

The ALI was founded in 1923 to bring those with the best legal minds together "to clarify, modernize, and otherwise improve the law." The ALI is composed of judges, practicing attorneys, and legal scholars who are asked to join based on their experience and interest in law reform. ALI made a major contribution to the abortion reform movement by including a conditional abortion law in its model penal code, which was drafted in 1959 and adopted in 1962. This served as a model for reform in many state legislatures and remains a part of the debate over abortion law today.

Black Women's Health Imperative (BWHI)

The National Black Women's Health Project was founded in 1983 by Byllye Y. Avery; the name was later changed to BWHI. It is an education, research, and advocacy organization, focusing primarily on reaching and informing black women about their health options and encouraging self-help and responsibility. BWHI promotes the "empowerment of African American women as educated health care consumers" and is "a strong voice for the improved health status of African American women." Highly attuned to the higher levels of unintended pregnancy among black women, BWHI advocates access to a broad range of reproductive health options, including prenatal care, complete and accurate family planning information and services, safe childbirth, fertility services, adoption, safe abortion, and disease prevention.

Catholics for a Free Choice (CFFC)

Frances Kissling founded CFFC in 1973 to challenge the assumption that the Vatican and the bishops speak for all Catholics on the issue of reproductive rights. Since then, CFFC has offered a way for Catholics who support a woman's right to "follow her conscience in the matters of sexuality and reproductive health" and to come together to support pro-choice policies. CFFC advocates full access to contraception, safe and legal abortion, prenatal and postnatal care, and adoption. With these goals, the organization seeks to establish links with the Catholic traditions of social justice, instead of its more patriarchal natural-law tradition. CFFC focuses on dialogue, education, research, and advocacy and builds coalitions with other national and international pro-choice organizations.

Center for Reproductive Rights (CRR)

Founded in 1992, CRR believes that "reproductive freedom lies at the heart of the promise of human dignity, self-determination and equality embodied in both the U.S. Constitution and the Universal Declaration of Human Rights." CRR utilizes strategies of public education, research, policy analysis, legislation, and litigation to promote reproductive rights, including affordable contraception, safe and accessible abortion, and healthy pregnancies. The group pays special attention to the needs of adolescents and low-income women and to countering violence against women's freedom to exercise their rights. CRR has taken the lead in successful constitutional challenges, including *Stenberg v. Carhart* (2000) and *Whole Woman's Health v. Hellerstedt* (2016). With extensive activities abroad, CRR is also proud of its work to strengthen laws in more than 50 countries.

Center on Reproductive Rights and Justice (CRRJ)

CRRJ is housed within the University of California Berkeley's School of Law but raises its budget from external funding sources. It is an intellectual think tank that promotes research and scholarship, supports reproductive rights and justice organizations, and shapes legal and social science discourse. A special focus of CRRJ's work is on leveraging its privileged position to address the needs of the poor, welfare recipients, Medicaid beneficiaries, and women driven to self-inducing abortion like Purvi Patel, whose 20-year sentence for feticide was overturned in 2016—CRRJ had filed an amicus brief in Patel's defense, authored on behalf of 30 reproductive justice organizations.

Feminist Majority (FM) and Feminist Majority Foundation (FMF)

The FM and its sister organization, the FMF, were formed in 1987. The name came in response to a *Newsweek* poll in the 1980s that showed a majority—56 percent—of women self-identified as feminists and that most men supported the women's rights movement. Both organizations are dedicated to women's equality, reproductive health, and nonviolence. FM focuses on mobilization for direct political action and lobbying before state and federal governments. Currently, it is standing strong in opposition to the defunding of Planned Parenthood and laws that inscribe "Fetal Personhood." The FMF funds research, educational programs, and forums on public issues. Its National Clinic Access Project has tracked violence against abortion providers since 1993. Other campaigns include exposing disreputable crisis pregnancy centers and fostering a pro-choice student network (feministcampus.org).

Guttmacher Institute (GI)

GI provides the highest-quality information on sexual and reproductive matters. It was founded in 1968 as an offshoot of PPFA called the Center for Family Planning Program Development, led by PPFA president Alan Guttmacher. The organization was named to honor his work following his death in 1974. Today GI has a staff of over 120, who are committed to rigorous research, timely analysis, scientific objectivity, and the public dissemination of the findings regardless of the policy implications. The institute publishes two peer-reviewed journals: *Perspectives on Sexual and Reproductive Health* and *International Perspectives on Sexual and Reproductive Health*. In its 2016–2020 Strategic Plan, GI identified the following as focus areas: contraception, unintended pregnancy, abortion, adolescent sexual and reproductive health, reproductive justice, men's sexual and reproductive health needs, STIs/HIV, LGBT, and sexual rights. GI recognizes, "Large inequities persist both across state and national borders and by socioeconomic subgroups, with the poorest and most vulnerable often experiencing the widest deficits in access" (Guttmacher Institute 2016).

If/When/How: Lawyering for Reproductive Justice

In 2016, Law Students for Reproductive Justice changed its name to If/When/How: Lawyering for Reproductive Justice and expanded its scope. If/When/How trains, networks, and mobilizes law students and legal professionals to work within and beyond the legal system to champion reproductive justice. It defines reproductive justice as a world in which "all people can decide if, when, and how to create and sustain families with dignity, free from discrimination, coercion, or violence." If/When/How offers myriad trainings through internships and webinars, organizing toolkits, surveys of curricular offerings, a policy-based fellowship in the District of Columbia and several states, and a Sarah Weddington Writing Prize, as well as informative issue briefs on topics like "Reproductive Justice in the Prison System."

Medical Students for Choice (MSFC)

MSFC responds to the recognized shortage in trained abortion providers in the United States and Canada by working to destigmatize abortion, improve reproductive health service curricula, increase training opportunities, and mobilize medical students. MSFC student groups are found at more than 120 medical schools. MSFC runs an internship program to match students with reproductive health clinics where they can develop the necessary skills to contribute to abortion practice. At their annual convention, students have opportunities to take clinical training as well as learn about the place of abortion in the practice of medicine.

NARAL Pro-Choice America

Formed in 1969 as the National Association for Repeal of Abortion Laws, NARAL remains the leading advocacy organization in the pro-choice movement. Reflecting its expanded mission, the name changed to National Abortion and Reproductive Rights Action League in 1996 and then again to NARAL Pro-Choice America in 2003. NARAL has been at the center of pro-choice victories, including the campaign for legal abortion that ended in *Roe v. Wade*, countering the pro-life resurgence in the 1980s, promoting the Freedom of Choice Act in Congress in the early 1990s, and opposing appointments of anti-*Roe* justices to the Supreme Court. As a tireless advocate for women's privacy and right to choose, NARAL mobilizes activists, lobbies Congress and state legislatures, and uses its political action committee funds to endorse pro-choice candidates regardless of political party. Following President Trump's victory in 2016, NARAL received an outpouring of donations "in honor of" Vice President Mike Pence.

National Abortion Federation (NAF)

The NAF, founded in 1977, is a professional association of abortion providers committed to maintaining abortion as a safe, legal, and accessible procedure for all women, regardless of their income level or other social barriers. Its website provides high-quality resources to provide medical education for reproductive health care providers, to raise awareness of clinic violence, to help women make informed decisions, and to debunk misinformation about abortion, including the myths that abortion causes breast cancer and postabortion syndrome. Its Access Initiative Project is designed to increase the pipeline of qualified clinicians by expanding the training they need to provide safe abortions.

National Advocates for Pregnant Women (NAPW)

NAPW is a nonprofit organization that focuses on safeguarding the rights of pregnant women and mothers. It opposes punitive responses of the criminal justice system to pregnant women who use illegal drugs, which have been demonstrated to jeopardize public health. It employs various strategies to bring about positive social change, including providing direct support for women, public education, community organizing, and litigation. NAPW has created a downloadable guide titled *Indivisible: A Practical Guide for Resisting the Trump Agenda*.

National Latina Institute for Reproductive Health (NLIRH)

NLIRH formed in 1994 under the auspices of Catholics for a Free Choice as part of its initiative to bring Latinas into the discussion about reproductive rights. Its vision is "to create a society in which Latinas have the economic means, social capital, and political power to make and exercise decisions about their own health, family, and future." NLIRH seeks reproductive justice by focusing on the "interconnected" issues of abortion access and affordability, sexual and reproductive health equity, and immigrant women's health and rights. Its primary strategies are building power through community organizing, civic engagement, and training and leadership development.

National Network of Abortion Funds (NNAF)

NNAF's t-shirts proclaim: "Everyone loves someone who had an abortion." NNAF is a national umbrella organization for locally based abortion funds. NNAF arose in response to the denial of federal and state Medicaid funds to poor women. Members express compassion and rely on shoestring budgets to raise money for grants and loans for clients with unmet financial needs. NNAF sees itself as "building power" by "centering" and working alongside the woman to navigate financial and logistical barriers to abortion access. NNAF also describes itself as "organizing at the intersections of racial, economic, and reproductive justice." The Women's Reproductive Rights Assistance Project (wrrap.org) is a similar organization; it offers financial assistance to "pre-approved, qualified medical clinics, in order to help poor and disadvantaged women gain access to safe, legal abortion care and emergency contraceptives."

National Organization for Women (NOW)

In 1967, NOW was the first national organization to advocate repeal of criminal abortion laws; Betty Friedan, NOW's president at the time, identified other top priorities at its first annual convention, including publicly supported child care and the equal rights amendment. NOW has been a powerful force within the pro-choice movement, a strong advocate for safe and legal abortion, birth control, emergency contraception, reproductive health services, and education for all women. NOW Political Action Committee focuses on electing candidates at all levels who share its commitment to women's rights. The NOW Foundation has broadened its agenda to include economic and racial justice, women's health and body image, disability and LGBT rights, and global feminist issues.

National Women's Law Center (NWLC)

NWLC describes itself as "passionate champions of policies and laws that help women and girls achieve their potential throughout their lives." One of its first projects was to protect poor women from coercive contraception and sterilization, and health care and reproductive rights remain an important part of the center's activities. NWLC is a reliable source for evidence-informed fact sheets, including a recent one on why the "Hyde Amendment Creates an Unacceptable Barrier to Women Getting Abortions."

Physicians for Reproductive Choice and Health (PRH)

Founded in 1992, PRH represents doctors who rely on evidence, seek specialized training, and advocate for a full range of reproductive choices, including comprehensive sexuality education, contraception, and abortion. PRH has three areas of action: medical education, communication, and public policy and community organization. PRH reports that 284 people have attended its leadership training academy, and they have made 69 visits to congressional offices to fight abortion bans, medical misinformation, and restrictions on health insurance coverage for abortion. PRH finds it troubling that "abortion care is the only area of medicine where the federal government puts politics and ideology before the doctor-patient relationship, with the intent to criminalize doctors and manipulate patients' health care decisions" (Physicians for Reproductive Health n.d.).

Planned Parenthood Federation of America (PPFA)

Planned Parenthood traces its origins to Margaret Sanger's first birth control clinic in Brooklyn in 1916. It self-identifies and is recognized widely as "America's most trusted provider of reproductive health care." Certainly, PPFA has been a central player in the abortion debate since the 1950s, advocating reform of criminal laws in the 1960s and then defending legal abortion since 1973. Much of its advocacy work is done through its affiliates, which have been litigants in major cases challenging restrictive laws, including *Planned Parenthood v. Casey*. In 2016, PPFA celebrated 100 of care, education, and activism, and with social media savvy, it has launched the #istandwithpp to debunk the widely circulating myths and to counter a new wave of political attacks under the Trump presidency.

Religious Coalition for Reproductive Choice (RCRC)

RCRC tagline articulates its identity: "Pro Faith. Pro Family. Pro Choice." It was founded in 1973 as an interfaith network with the mission of using the moral power of religious communities to ensure reproductive health, rights, and justice. It seeks to counter the religious claims of the pro-life movement using four key strategies: education, prophetic witness, pastoral presence, and advocacy. Notable contributions at the judicial level include filing an amicus briefs in the 2016 Supreme Court Case, *Whole Women's Health v. Hellerstedt*, at the federal level acting to assure abortion access for women in the military, at the state level helping to defeat Mississippi's personhood amendment, and at the grassroots level providing hospitality for women traveling to obtain abortion care.

Reproductive Health Technologies Project (RHTP)

The RHTP was founded in the late 1980s to provide information about the French "abortion pill," RU-486, and to pave the
way for its approval. In a 2016 press release, RHTP announced
that it was shutting down after 25 years of working "to advance
the ability of every woman to achieve full reproductive freedom
with access to the safest, most effective, appropriate, and acceptable technologies for ensuring her own health and determining
whether, when, and how to have children." It trusts that its
many reproductive health and rights colleagues will continue
"prioritizing scientific rigor and evidence-based policymak-
ing and work to improve meaningful access to the reproductive technologies . . . vital to reproductive self-determination"
(Reproductive Health Technologies Project 2016).

Republican Majority for Choice (RMC)

The RMC works to protect reproductive rights by challenging
the official pro-life platform of the Republican Party. It contends that pro-life ideas run counter to the Republican goals
of limited government and personal freedoms. In its words,
"There is nothing more fiscally conservative than the proven
cost-savings of preventative health policies and initiatives." Its
RM4C PAC directs funds in support of pro-choice Republican candidates. To get their endorsement, office-seekers must
demonstrate a proven track record of supporting reproductive
health. It is not clear from the website if RM4C PAC replaced
the Republicans for Choice Political Action Committee
(RCPAC), which was formerly a sister organization of RMC
created by Ann E. W. Stone in 1989. A 2010 analysis from
the Center for Public Integrity revealed that only 5 percent of
RCPAC's fund-raising went to candidates; the rest appeared to
go to Stone's companies.

Sex Information and Education Council of
the United States (SIECUS)

SIECUS was founded in 1964 by Dr. Mary S. Calderone. Then
and now its primary mission has been to promote sexuality

education for all, including reproductive health and services. Its main contribution to the abortion conflict occurred in the 1960s when it provided a forum for raising awareness about the limits of criminal abortion laws and promoted law reform. Abortion is no longer at the center of its mission, but related issues are, such as teen pregnancy and sexual and reproductive health. SIECUS uses its website to offer fact-based sexuality information for educators, policy makers, journalists, and religious leaders.

#ShoutYourAbortion (SYA)

SYA's website succinctly states its position: "Abortion is normal. Our stories are ours to tell. This is not a debate." Harkening back to consciousness-raising groups among the younger branch of the 1970s women's movement, SYA describes itself as "a decentralized network of individuals talking about abortion on our own terms and creating space for others to do the same." Provocative quotes like "I had an abortion when I was 19, and then I lived happily ever after" invite the reader into the woman's story. SYA began in 2015 as a disclosure by Amelia Bonow on Facebook that she had had an abortion and a challenge to others to do the same. The "#" was created so that women could talk openly, no longer confined to whispers. This was counter to the pro-life movement, obviously, but also to the apologetic pro-choice sentiment that abortion should be "safe, legal, and rare." Advocates for Youth's 1 in 3 Campaign are very similar in purpose and structure.

Sistersong: Women of Color Reproductive Justice Collective (SS)/Trust Black Women (TBW)

In 1997, 16 women's organizations drawn from Native American, African American, Latina, and Asian American communities came together to form a collective. To paraphrase their eloquent reflection, there was a shared recognition that their chorus of voices needed to be amplified to overcome reproductive oppression, establish institutional policies that uplift marginalized communities, and usher in a new era of reproductive justice. For anyone seeking a better understanding of what is distinct about the reproductive justice paradigm, SS's website is an excellent place to start. In fascinating display of movement-countermovement dynamics, Trust Black Women (TBW) emerged in 2010 in response to the "Black children are an endangered species" billboards; it was a partnership between SS and other organizations that perceived the ads as "accusing Black women who exercise their human and reproductive rights of committing 'Genocide.'" In solidarity with the Black Lives Matter Movement, TBW stands for the "human right of every Black person, regardless of their gender identity or expression, to end a pregnancy, continue a pregnancy, build a family, and raise children with health, dignity, and freedom from violence."

Relevant Government Agencies

Centers for Disease Control and Prevention, Congressional Pro-Choice and Pro-Life Caucuses, Food and Drug Administration, Title X Family Planning, Office of Women's Health, U.S. Agency for International Development.

Internationally Focused Organizations

Human Life International, International Right to Life Federation, International Women's Health Coalition, Ipas, Marie Stopes International, Pathfinder International, Population Council, Society for the Protection of Unborn Children, United Nations Population Division, UN Women, Women's Global Network for Reproductive Rights, Women on Waves, World Population Fund.

References

"Antiabortion Activist Admits Killing Doctor Near Buffalo." *Los Angeles Times.* http://articles.latimes.com/2002/nov/21 /nation/na-abort21 (accessed April 25, 2018).

"Arrested at Notre Dame; Statement by Randall A. Terry."
Christian Newswire. May 5, 2009. https://www.catholic
.org/news/hf/faith/story.php?id=33463 (accessed April 25,
2018).

The Associated Press. "Massachusetts Birth Control Pioneer
Says Fight Had Personal Cost." April 9, 2012. http://www
.masslive.com/news/index.ssf/2012/04/massachusetts_
birth_control_pi.html (accessed April 25, 2018).

Brown, Judie. "Human Respect in a Toxic Climate." *American
Life League*. December 15, 2017. https://www.all.org
/human-respect-in-a-toxic-climate/ (accessed April 25,
2018).

Fetters, Ann Minter. "Anti-Choice Forces Use Same Vitriol,
Fewer Troops." *Women's eNews*. July 23, 2001. https://women
senews.org/2001/07/anti-choice-forces-use-same-vitriol-
fewer-troops/ (assessed April 25, 2018).

Guttmacher Institute. "Institute Strategic Plan: 2016–2020."
March 2018. https://www.guttmacher.org/report/
guttmacher-institute-strategic-plan-2016-2020 (accessed
May 30, 2018).

Jones, Susan. "Reverend Jerry Falwell Planning an 'Evangelical
Revolution.'" July 7, 2008. *CNS News*. https://www
.cnsnews.com/news/article/reverend-jerry-falwell-planning-
evangelical-revolution (accessed April 26, 2018).

Live Action. "Who We Are." n.d. https://www.liveaction.org
/who-we-are/ (accessed May 9, 2018).

Lohr, Kathy. "Anti-Abortion Activist on Trial for 'Wanted'
Posters." National Public Radio. November 8, 2010.
https://www.npr.org/templates/story/story.php?story
Id=131094218 (accessed April 25, 2018).

Martin, Douglas. "Lawrence Lader, Champion of Abortion
Rights, Is Dead at 86." *New York Times*. May 10, 2006.
https://www.nytimes.com/2006/05/10/nyregion/10lader
.html (accessed April 25, 2018).

Matthews, Chris. "Donald Trump Advocates Punishment for Abortion." *MSNBC*. March 30, 2016. https://www.nbcnews.com/meet-the-press/video/trump-s-hazy-stance-on-abortion-punishment-655457859717 (accessed April 25, 2018).

Operation Save America. "Our Purpose, Meet the Director, Partner with Us." n.d. operationsaveamerica.org/misc/misc/aboutUs.html (accessed May 9, 2018).

Physicians for Reproductive Health. "Abortion." n.d. https://prh.org/abortion/ (accessed May 9, 2018).

Port, Rachel. "A Conversation with Faye Wattleton: Part 3, Family Planning and Race." Planned Parenthood Advocates of Arizona. February 18, 2013. (http://advocatesaz.org/2013/02/18/a-conversation-with-faye-wattleton-part-3-family-planning-and-race/ (accessed April 25, 2018).

"Pro-Life Groups Say Teen Immigrant's Abortion Is Regrettable. *Catholic News Service*. October 27, 2017. https://www.americamagazine.org/politics-society/2017/10/27/pro-life-groups-say-teen-immigrants-abortion-regrettable (accessed April 25, 2018).

Reproductive Health Technologies Project. November 7, 2016. http://rhtp.org/wp-content/uploads/2016/11/Important-Update.pdf (accessed May 9, 2018).

Reyes, Emily Alpert and Mary Rourke. "Norma McCorvey, Once-Anonymous Plaintiff in Landmark Roe vs. Wade Abortion Case, Dies at 69." *Los Angeles Times*. February 18, 2017. http://www.latimes.com/local/obituaries/la-me-norma-mccorvey-snap-story.html (accessed April 25, 2018).

Richards, Cecile. "Commentary: Planned Parenthood President: Extremist Videos Are an Attack on Women." *Chicago Tribune*. July 30, 2015. http://www.chicagotribune.com/news/opinion/commentary/ct-planned-parenthood-abortion-videos-20150730-story.html (accessed April 25, 2018).

Richards, Cecile. "Ending the Silence That Fuels Abortion Stigma." *Elle*. October 16, 2014. https://www.elle.com /culture/career-politics/a15060/cecile-richards-abortion- stigma/ (accessed April 25, 2018).

Rosenblatt, Kalhan. "Christian Abortion Doctor Risks Safety to Keep Reproductive Healthcare in the South." *NBC News*. May 4, 2017. https://www.nbcnews.com/news /us-news/christian-abortion-doctor-risks-safety-keep-rep roductive-healthcare-south-n738606 (accessed April 25, 2018).

Rosenfeld, Megan. "Standing By His Conviction." *Washington Post*. March 18, 1998. https://www.washingtonpost.com /archive/lifestyle/1998/03/18/standing-by-his-conviction /6ab88b5a-0bfd-48a3-af52-1b62d2e65f3c/?utm_ term=.6fe32ce27452 (accessed April 25, 2018).

Tippit, Krista. "Frances Kissling: Listening Beyond Life and Choice." *On Being*. August 11, 2011. https://onbeing.org /programs/frances-kissling-listening-beyond-life-and- choice/ (accessed April 25, 2018).

Winter, Jessica. "Roy Moore, Abortion, and the Presumption of Innocence." *The New Yorker*. November 27, 2017. https://www.newyorker.com/news/news-desk/roy-moore- abortion-and-the-presumption-of-innocence (accessed April 25, 2018).

5 Data and Documents

Introduction

The artifacts pertaining to the abortion conflict found in this chapter include select historical documents presented in chronological order to illustrate the continually swinging pendulum. These primary texts, created by professional associations, activists, lawmakers, presidents, and Supreme Court justices, help situate the contemporary debates within a broader historical context. The data selected illustrates the variability in state restrictions, the shifts over time in public opinion, and the sociodemographic differences and disparities among women who have abortions.

Current State Laws Regulating Abortion

Regulations of Abortion Practice

States have no constitutional authority to outlaw abortion prior to viability, with the possible exception of "partial-birth"

Pro-choice activists cloaked in handmaiden red capes and white bonnets stage a protest in the Texas Capitol Rotunda on May 23, 2017, in Austin. Their haunting costumes warned against the dystopian future portrayed in Margaret Atwood's (1985) *The Handmaid's Tale* and chillingly reimagined in the 2017 Hulu television series where fertile women are enslaved by and forced to procreate for the repressive state. The anti-abortion bill they opposed, SB8, passed. It stipulated that all health care facilities, including abortion clinics, must bury or cremate any fetal remains and banned the donation of aborted fetal tissue to medical researchers. (AP Photo/Eric Gay)

procedures. States can, however, regulate abortion practice and do so in an intricate fashion according to research compiled by the Alan Guttmacher Institute, presented in Tables 5.1 and 5.2. According to the 2017 data, 38 states have specified that only licensed physicians could perform abortions, and 19 have stipulated that the procedure must be performed in a hospital after a particular point in the pregnancy. All but seven states have made it illegal to terminate a pregnancy after 20 weeks, except in cases of the woman's life or health endangerment, and 19 states have moved to ban partial-birth abortion.

Limits on Public Funding

Public funding of abortion continues to be a contentious issue. The federal Hyde Amendment prohibits the states from using federal Medicaid funds for abortions for poor women, and 32 states and the District of Columbia limit public funding for abortion to cases in which the women's life is endangered or the pregnancy is the result of rape or incest. Table 5.1 lists the 17 states that use their own funds to cover all or most medically

Table 5.1   State Regulations of Abortion Practice and Funding

State	Must Be Performed by a Licensed Physician	Must Be Performed in a Hospital If at	Prohibited Except in Cases of Life or Health Endangerment If at	Partial-Birth Abortion Banned	Public Funding for All or Most Medically Necessary Abortions	Public Funding Limited to Life Endangerment, Rape, and Incest	Private Insurance Coverage Limited
AL	X		Viability	20 weeks* ▼			X	
AK	X			▼	X		
AZ	X		Viability	Viability	X	X		X
AR	X			20 weeks† X		X	
CA				Viability	X		
CO						X	
CT			Viability	Viability	X		
DE	X			Viabilityᵃ		X	

State	Must Be Performed by a Licensed Physician	Must Be Performed in a Hospital If at	Prohibited Except in Cases of Life or Health Endangerment If at	Partial-Birth Abortion Banned	Public Funding for All or Most Medically Necessary Abortions	Public Funding Limited to Life Endangerment, Rape, and Incest	Private Insurance Coverage Limited
DC						X	
FL	X	Viability	24 weeks	▼		X	
GA	X		20 weeks*	Post-viability		X	
HI	X		Viability		X		
ID	X	Viability	Viability	▼		X	X
IL			Viability	▼	X		
IN	X	20 weeks	20 weeks*	X		X*	X
IA	X		20 weeks*	▼		X	
KS	X		20 weeks*	X		X	X
KY	X	Second trimester	20 weeks*	▼		X	X
LA	X		20 weeks*	X		X	
ME	X		Viability			X	
MD	X		Viability^Ω		X		
MA	X		24 weeks		X		
MI	X		Viability‡	X		X	X
MN	X		Viability		X		
MS	X^Φ		20 weeks*	X		X^Ω	
MO	X	Viability	Viability	▼		X	X
MT			Viability*	Post-viability	X		
NE	X		20 weeks*	▼		X	X
NV	X	24 weeks	24 weeks			X	
NH				X		X	
NJ	X^ξ	14 weeks		▼	X		
NM	X			Post-viability	X		
NY			24 weeks‡		X		

(Continued)

Table 5.1 (Continued)

State	Must Be Performed by a Licensed Physician	Must Be Performed in a Hospital If at	Prohibited Except in Cases of Life or Health Endangerment If at	Partial-Birth Abortion Banned	Public Funding for All or Most Medically Necessary Abortions	Public Funding Limited to Life Endangerment, Rape, and Incest	Private Insurance Coverage Limited
NC	X	20 weeks	20 weeks			X	
ND	X		20 weeks*	X		X	X
OH	X	20 weeks	20 weeks*	X		X	
OK	X	Second trimester	20 weeks*	X		X	X
OR					X		
PA	X	Viability	24 weeks*			X	
RI			24 weeks‡	▼		X	▼
SC	X	Third trimester	20 weeks*	X		X	
SD	X	24 weeks	20 weeks*	X		Life only	
TN	X	Viability	Viability*	X		X	
TX	X		20 weeks*			X	
UT	X		Viability†,Ω	X		X*	X
VT					X		
VA	X	Second trimester	Third trimester	X		XΩ	
WA			Viability		X		
WV			20 weeks*	▼	X		
WI	X	Viability	20 weeks*	▼		X*	
WY	X		Viability			X	
Total	38	19	43	19	17	32 + DC	11

▼ Permanently enjoined; law not in effect.
* Exception in case of threat to the woman's physical health.
† Exception in case of rape or incest.
‡ Exception in case of life endangerment only.
Ω Exception in case of fetal abnormality.
ᶠ Applies only to surgical abortion.
Φ Law limits abortion provision to OB/GYNs.

Source: The Alan Guttmacher Institute. www.guttmacher.org. https://www.guttmacher.org/state-policy/explore/overview-abortion-laws. Used by permission of the Guttmacher Institute.

necessary abortions for their Medicaid recipients. Private insurance coverage for abortion is now limited in 11 states. In 2017, the Republican governor of Texas, Greg Abbott, signed House Bill 214, a law restricting private insurance coverage for abortions so that no pro-life Texan would have to subsidize a procedure believed to end a human life. For democratic opponents, compelling women to purchase a supplemental plan to cover abortion is tantamount to forcing women to buy "rape insurance."

Right of Refusal

The first amendment right of individuals to exercise their religious beliefs has been applied to situations in which health care professionals refuse to provide abortions on the basis of deeply held moral convictions. Like most professional associations, nearly all states—45 as of 2017—respect the rights of individuals to be contentious objectors without legal, financial, or professional repercussions. As shown in Table 5.2, in 16 of these states the refusal clause is limited to those working in private or religious institutions. This issue has been hotly debated by policy makers and the public for decades. Reproductive health advocates have framed this act as a form of discrimination against and shaming of women and yet another avenue for restricting abortion access.

Mandatory Counseling, Waiting Periods, and Medical Accuracy

States have the authority to mandate counseling and waiting periods for women seeking abortions as long as the regulations are not deemed to be undue burdens on women and do not prevent women from obtaining abortions within the law. While informed consent is an important principle in health care, reproductive health advocates have voiced concerns over the proscribed time lags and the medical accuracy of the counseling materials.

Table 5.2 State Mandates

State	Providers May Refuse to Participate	Institution May Refuse to Participate	Mandated Counseling Includes Breast Cancer Link	Mandated Counseling Includes Fetal Pain	Mandated Counseling Includes Negative Psychological Effects	Waiting Periods (in hours) after Counseling	Parental Involvement Required for Minors
AL						48	Consent
AK	X	Private	X				▸
AZ	X	X				24	Consent
AR	X	X		X[Φ]		48	Consent
CA	X	Religious					▸
CO							Notice
CT	X						
DE	X	X					Notice ξ
DC							
FL	X	X				§	Notice
GA	X	X		X		24	Notice
HI	X	X					
ID	X	X				24	Consent
IL	X	Private					Notice
IN	X	Private		X		18	Consent
IA	X	Private				§	Notice

State							
KS	X	X		X	X	24	Consent
KY	X	X	X			24	Consent
LA	X	X		X	X	24	Consent
ME	X	X				▶	Notice
MD	X	X					Consent
MA	X	X				24	Consent
MI	X	X			X	24	Notice[b]
MN	X	Private		X[Φ]		24	Consent[b]
MS	X	X	X			72	Consent
MO	X	X		X[Φ]		▶	▶
MT	X	Private					Consent
NE	X	X			X	24	▶
NV	X	Private				▶	Notice
NH							▶
NJ	X	Private					▶
NM	X	X					
NY	X						
NC	X	X				72	Consent
ND	X	X				24	Consent[b]

(Continued)

Table 5.2 (Continued)

State	Providers May Refuse to Participate	Institution May Refuse to Participate	Mandated Counseling Includes Breast Cancer Link	Mandated Counseling Includes Fetal Pain	Mandated Counseling Includes Negative Psychological Effects	Waiting Periods (in hours) after Counseling	Parental Involvement Required for Minors
OH	X	X				24	Consent
OK	X	Private	X	X[Φ]		72	Both C&N
OR	X	Private					
PA	X	Private				24	Consent
RI	X						Consent
SC	X	Private				24	Consent
SD	X	X		X		72°	Notice
TN	X	X				48	Consent
TX	X	Private	X	X	X	24	Both C&N
UT	X	Private		X[Φ]		72°	Both C&N
VT							
VA	X	X				24	Both C&N
WA	X	X					
WV					X	24	Notice [ξ]

244

State								Consent[ξ] Both C&N
WI	X	X						
WY	X	Private						
Total	45	42	5	12	6	24	27	37

▼ Permanently enjoined; law not in effect.

§ Enforcement temporarily enjoined by court order; policy not in effect.

Φ Fetal pain information is given only to women who are at least 20 weeks gestation; in Missouri at 22 weeks gestation.

þ Both parents must consent to the abortion.

ξ Specified health professionals may waive parental involvement in certain circumstances.

◊ In South Dakota, the waiting period excludes weekends or annual holidays, and in Utah the waiting period is waived in cases of rape, incest, fetal defect, or if the patient is younger than 15.

Source: The Alan Guttmacher Institute. https://www.guttmacher.org/state-policy/explore/overview-abortion-laws. Used by permission of the Guttmacher Institute.

After the required counseling session, women in 27 states must wait—typically for 24 hours—to obtain an abortion. However, as Table 5.2 shows, five states have instituted a 72-hour waiting rule. This can be especially onerous on women who have to adjust work schedules, arrange child care, or travel long distances.

The Supreme Court has upheld laws that require specific information if it is accurate and not misleading. In addition, medical ethics standards prohibit doctors or anyone else from using personal opinion in lieu of scientifically accepted information. States have the constitutional authority to develop their own materials and require abortion providers to use them. As shown in Table 5.2, 16 states mandate that women seeking abortion be told about at least one of the following medically unsubstantiated claims:

1. *Abortion is linked to breast cancer.* In five states patients must be told that abortion increases the risk of breast cancer despite the fact that the National Cancer Institute issued an official denial of this claim as far back as 2003. Given the widespread misinformation, other states have insisted that women be reassured that there is no link.

2. *Fetuses feel pain.* The science of fetal pain is a new frontier, but scientific experts who have weighed in on the issue have concluded that a fetus's neurological wiring would not be sufficiently developed enough until after the time at which most abortions occur. But these dubious assertions appear to be on the rise. Twelve states now insist that women be told that their fetuses may or will feel pain. In 2016 Utah passed a law that fetuses beyond 20 weeks must be given anesthesia, but the handful of doctors who perform late-term abortions have been given no guidance about how to implement the proscribed procedures.

3. *Women experience psychological trauma.* Pro-life activists believe that women who have abortions are plagued by long-lasting psychological consequences, what they have

termed "postabortion traumatic stress syndrome." Six states include this warning in their counseling materials despite the fact that research in psychology and psychiatry has shown that there is no causal relationship.

Parental Involvement

While many would regard parental support in minors' health care decision making as best practice, reproductive health advocates have expressed concern that compulsory parental involvement may diminish access to services. Only two states and the District of Columbia allow all minors to act as independent abortion decision makers. Based on the Supreme Court's *Bellotti v. Baird* (443 U.S. 622, 1979) ruling, states have the constitutional authority to require parental consent or notification for minors' abortions as long as a judicial bypass is available. As shown in Table 5.2, 37 states require some type of parental involvement in a minor's decision; in 12 of these one or both parents must be notified, and in 21 a parent must give consent. Five states require both parental consent and notification; exceptions are often permitted in cases of medical emergency, abuse, assault, incest, or neglect.

Abortion Services

Prevalence

The Centers for Disease Control and Prevention (CDC), an agency in the U.S. Department of Health and Human Services, has conducted its "abortion surveillance" studies since 1969. The incidence of abortion is typically measured in three ways: (1) absolute number of abortions, (2) abortion ratio: number of abortions per 1,000 live births, (3) abortion rate: number of abortions for 1,000 women of childbearing age (15–44 years). Surveillance data is compiled from reports submitted by health agencies in states, the District of Columbia, and New York City. Although there are concerns about underreporting, the

Table 5.3 Number, Rate, and Ratio of Reported Abortions—1970–2013

	1970	1975	1980	1985	1990	1995	2000	2005	2010	2013
Number	193,491	854,853	1,297,606	1,328,570	1,429,247	1,210,883	857,475	807,680	754,780	652,582
Ratio	52	272	359	354	344	311	245	236	227	200*
Rate	5	18	25	24	24	20	16	15.7	14.6	12.5

Note: See original table for states that did not report that year's abortion numbers to CDC. The figures for 2005, 2010, and 2013 were calculated based on the continuously reporting areas.

* Number of abortions per 1,000 women aged 15–44 years.

Sources: Abortion Surveillance—United States. 2003. Lilo T. Strauss, Sonya B. Gamble, Wilda Y. Parker, Douglas A. Cook, Suzanne B. Zane, and Saeed Hamdan. Surveillance Summaries; CDC, November 24, 2006, 55(SS11), 1–32. www.cdc.gov/mmwr/preview/mmwrhtml/ss5511a1.htm; Abortion Surveillance—United States. 2013. Tara C. Jatlaoui, Alexander Ewing, Michele G. Mandel, Katharine B. Simmons, Danielle B. Suchdev, Denise J. Jamieson, and Karen Pazol. MMWR Surveillance Summaries 2016; 65(No. SS-12), 1–44. doi:http://dx.doi.org/10.15585/mmwr.ss6512a1.

data is useful for documenting trends over time. As shown in Table 5.3, the abortion rate has been on the decline since its peak in the 1980s. While pro-life groups credit ultrasound viewing, reproductive health advocates point to the reduction in teen pregnancy resulting from extended access to contraceptives, particularly long-acting ones, and the closing of abortion clinics.

Characteristics of Women Having Abortions

The CDC also requests information from the central health agencies to better understand the characteristics of women having abortions.

According to the most recent breakdowns for 2013 shown in Table 5.4, 91.5 percent of all abortions took place in the first trimester. In terms of age, 56.8 percent of all women who had abortions were in their twenties, 29.6 percent were in their thirties or early forties, and 11.4 percent were in their teens.

Table 5.4   Characteristics of Women Having Abortions in 2013

Characteristic	Percentage
WEEKS OF GESTATION	
<8	66.0
9–13	25.5
14–20	7.2
≥21	1.3
AGE (YEARS)	
<15 years	0.3
15–19	11.4
20–24	32.7
25–29	25.9
30–34	16.8
35–39	9.2
≥40	3.6

(Continued)

Table 5.4   (Continued)

Characteristic	Percentage
RACE	
White	37.3
Black	35.6
Other	8.1
Hispanic	19.0
MARITAL STATUS	
Married	14.8
Unmarried	85.2
NUMBER OF PREVIOUS LIVE BIRTHS	
0	40.2
1	26.0
2	19.6
≥3	14.1
NUMBER OF PREVIOUS ABORTIONS	
0	55.0
1	24.8
2	11.4
≥3	8.8

Source: Abortion Surveillance—United States. 2013. Tara C. Jatlaoui, Alexander Ewing, Michele G. Mandel, Katharine B. Simmons, Danielle B. Suchdev, Denise J. Jamieson, and Karen Pazol. MMWR Surveillance Summaries 2016, 65(No. SS-12), 1–44. doi:http://dx.doi.org/10.15585/mmwr.ss6512a1.

The racial composition was as follows: 37.3 percent were white, 35.6 percent were black, and 19 percent identified as Hispanic. Most were unmarried (85.2 percent), and the majority had previously given birth (59.7 percent). Finally, the majority (55 percent) were terminating a pregnancy for the first time, while 36.2 percent had one or two previous abortions, and 8.8 percent had had three or more. To learn more, watch the Guttmacher Institute's 2011 data-driven video "Abortion in the United States" on YouTube: https://www.youtube.com/watch?v=rY-bQ6UzhNI

Data from the Guttmacher Institute's 2014 Abortion Patient Survey featured in Table 5.5 fills in some of the profile gaps left

Table 5.5 Additional Characteristics of Women Having Abortions in 2014

Characteristic	Percentage
NATIVITY	
U.S. born	83.9
Born elsewhere	16.1
SEXUAL ORIENTATION	
Heterosexual or straight	94.4
Bisexual	4.2
"Something else" (e.g., "pansexual")	1.1
Homosexual, gay or lesbian	0.3
RELIGIOUS AFFILIATION	
Mainline Protestant	17.3
Evangelical Protestant	12.8
Roman Catholic	23.7
Other	8.2
None	38.0
EDUCATIONAL ATTAINMENT	
Less than high school	8.9
High school graduate/GED	27.0
Some college/associate degree	40.9
FAMILY INCOME AS PERCENTAGE OF THE FEDERAL POVERTY LEVEL	
<100	49.3
100–200	25.7
≥200	25.0
ABORTION PAYMENT METHOD	
Self	53.0
Medicaid	23.5
Private insurance	14.6
Financial assistance	14.0
Other	2.0

Source: Jenna Jerman, Rachel K. Jones, and Tsuyoshi Onda. *Characteristics of U.S. Abortion Patients in 2014 and Changes since 2008*. New York: Guttmacher Institute, 2016. https://www.guttmacher.org/report/characteristics-us-abortion-patients-2014. Used by permission of the Guttmacher Institute.

by the CDC. Although this study excludes the small number of abortions that take place in hospital settings, it is regarded as a highly representative national sample. Most abortion patients are U.S. born (83.9 percent), identify as heterosexual or straight (94.4 percent), and are religiously affiliated (62 percent). In terms of the educational attainment of those 20 years or older, 8.9 percent reported less than a high school degree, 27 percent had earned a high school diploma or general equivalency diploma (GED), and 40.9 had attended college. Perhaps not surprisingly, abortion patients are disproportionately poor (49.3 percent) and low income (25.7 percent). The majority (53 percent) paid out of pocket for abortion services—the typical cost for a medical or surgical abortion is around $500— while 23.5 percent used Medicaid, 14.6 percent used private insurance, and 14 percent received financial assistance. The study authors note that "the onslaught of increased abortion restrictions between 2009 and 2014 likely disproportionately affects poor and low-income women, black women and young adults, as these populations are overrepresented among abortion patients" (p. 13).

Attacks on Abortion Providers

The National Clinic Violence Survey has been conducted on a semiannual basis since 1993 by the Feminist Majority Foundation—an organization that brings together research and action to promote gender equality and reproductive health. Enactment of the federal Freedom of Access to Clinic Entrances Act in 1994 was a contributing factor in the overall reduction of attacks on abortion providers since the peak in 1993. However, the fraudulent videos, which purport to show Planned Parenthood "selling baby parts" in 2015, may have inspired the latest upsurge in unlawful anti-abortion activity. After Robert Lewis Dear killed three and wounded nine at a Planned Parenthood clinic in Colorado Springs that same year, he was quoted as saying, "No more baby parts" (Downing 2015). While the vast majority of pro-life organizations

explicitly denounce violence, some extremist groups like the
Army of God advocate what they consider to be "justifiable
homicide."

For the 2016 survey, 740 providers were contacted to participate, and 319 responded that anti-abortion activity is a regular
occurrence—63.2 percent of clinics reported experiencing it
on a daily or weekly basis. Threats and intimidation of staff
have escalated to 46.4 percent in 2016 compared to 26.6 percent in 2010. For example, 29.3 percent of clinics report the
distribution of menacing leaflets with doctors' photographs
and home addresses. Even more disturbingly, as shown in
Table 5.6, 34.2 percent had experienced one or more incidents
of severe violence (e.g., blockades, invasions, arson, bombings,
chemical attacks, stalking, physical violence, gunfire) or threats

Table 5.6   Reported Clinic Violence, 1993–2016

Year	Percentage Experiencing One or More Incidents of Severe Violence and Threats of Violence	Number of Reporting Staff Resignations due to Violence
1993	50.0	23.0
1994	39.0	9.0
1995	52.2	9.0
1996	28.0	4.0
1997	25.0	7.0
1998	22.0	5.0
1999	20.0	10.0
2000	20.0	5.0
2002	23.0	7.0
2005	18.0	4.0
2008	20.0	4.0
2010	23.5	2.2
2014	19.7	5.5
2016	34.2	5.7

Source: Feminist Majority Foundation. 2017. *2016 National Clinic Violence Survey*.
http://feminist.org/anti-abortion-violence/images/2016-national-clinic-violence-
survey.pdf.

of violence (e.g., bomb, arson, death) in the previous year, up from 19.7 percent in 2014. Clinics located near a crisis pregnancy center appear to be subject to higher rates of violence, threats, and harassment (21.7 percent compared to 6.8 percent). The report illustrates this point with the example of Scott Roeder, who premeditated Dr. George Tiller's murder from an adjacent crisis pregnancy center, a crime that he carried out in 2009.

Public Opinion Polling on Abortion Issues

The *Roe v. Wade* decision ushered in a new era of political divisiveness for the United States, but the attitudes of most Americans (61.8 percent on average) fall somewhere in the middle of the two ideological extremes. These data comes from the General Social Survey, which is a cross-sectional survey of a nationally representative sample of English- and Spanish-speaking households. The repetition of questions makes it possible to take a long-range view of trends over time. The researchers took the combined scores for all seven questionnaire items asked over the period 1977–2012 about abortion and found that only 7.2 percent were absolutely pro-life—rejecting abortions no matter the circumstance, while 31 percent were unequivocally pro-choice in their support of legal abortion for any reason.

Again, looking across all years, the researchers found that a strong, consistent, majority of the American public has supported a woman's right to an abortion under dire circumstances, that is, in cases where the mother's life is in danger (87 percent), when conception occurred during rape (78.3 percent), or if genetic tests confirm fetal abnormality (77.1 percent). That consistently less than a majority supports abortion when the family is too poor (45 percent), when a married woman does not want more children (42.1 percent), when the woman is unmarried and does not want to marry the prospective father (42 percent), and when the woman wants the abortion for "any reason" (38.5 percent) reflects a general but qualified acceptance of abortion rights. Select years and conditions are featured in Table 5.7.

Table 5.7 Support for Abortion under Conditions—Percentage Answering "Yes," Select Years, and Conditions

Abortion Is Okay If	1972	1976	1980	1984	1988	1990	1994	1998	2000	2004	2008	2010	2012
A woman's health is seriously endangered	83.7	89.5	88.5	87.7	85.8	89.9	87.9	83.6	85.2	82.6	85.2	84.2	83.0
There is a strong chance of defect in the baby	74.4	82.1	80.7	77.5	76.2	78.3	79.3	74.1	74.6	68.7	70.1	71.8	70.3
A woman is pregnant as the result of rape	74.5	80.8	80.3	76.2	77.2	81.3	80.8	76.5	75.7	78.2	72.3	77.6	72.0
A woman is low income and can't afford any more children	45.9	50.7	49.6	44.5	40.5	45.0	41.8	41.0	39.4	38.7	41.3	43.7	40.6
A woman wants the abortion for any reason	NA	NA	39.2	36.7	34.9	41.5	44.5	37.8	37.0	37.6	40.0	41.9	41.7
Yes to all items	NA	NA	33.4	32.1	29.9	33.6	39.0	32.8	30.0	31.4	32.8	33.8	33.6

Source: General Social Survey, NORC, Tom W. Smith, and Jaesok Son. General Social Survey 2012 Final Report: Trends in Public Attitudes towards Abortion. May 2013. http://www.norc.org/PDFs/GSS%20Reports/Trends%20in%20Attitudes%20About%20Abortion_Final.pdf.

Underlying these broad historical trends is even more fascinating complexity. Polling data from the Pew Research Center, which is a highly regarded, nonpartisan think tank, illuminates how variables, such as political party affiliation, education, and religion, shape attitudes toward abortion. The gap between the two major political parties is shown in Table 5.8. Democrats are far more likely to be pro-choice, with 91 percent of liberal Democrats expressing the belief that abortion should be legal in all or most cases in contrast to 27 percent of conservative Republicans. Framing abortion as a moral question reveals even more nuances in the ways that religion shapes beliefs. Table 5.9 reveals stark contrasts between the 76 percent of white evangelical Protestants, 51 percent of Catholics, and 46 percent of black Protestants, who say that abortion is morally wrong, compared to the 45 percent of both mainline Protestants and unaffiliated individuals who say that abortion is not a moral issue.

For further exploration, see http://www.pewresearch.org/fact-tank/2016/06/21/where-major-religious-groups-stand-on-abortion/ and http://www.pewforum.org/religious-landscape-study/views-about-abortion/.

Interestingly, gender does not tend to differentiate abortion attitudes; men and women tend to express similar views. For further

Table 5.8   Wide Ideological Gaps in Both Parties in Views of Abortion

	Percentage Who Say Abortion Should Be	
	Illegal in Most Cases	Legal in Most Cases
Total	40	57
Republican	65	34
Conservative	71	27
Moderate/Liberal	45	54
Independent	38	60
Democrat	22	75
Conservative	36	61
Moderate/Liberal	8	91

Source: Pew Research Center Survey conducted June 8–18, 2017. http://www.pewresearch.org/fact-tank/2017/07/07/on-abortion-persistent-divides-between-and-within-the-two-parties-2/.

Table 5.9 Views of Having an Abortion by Religion

Religious Group	Percentage Who Say Abortion Is		
	Morally Wrong	Morally Acceptable	Not a Moral Issue
White evangelical Protestant	76	7	13
Catholic	51	16	31
Black Protestant	46	14	40
White mainline Protestant	33	20	45
Unaffiliated	23	30	45

Source: Survey of U.S. adults conducted, August 16 to September 12, 2016. The Pew Research Center. http://www.pewresearch.org/fact-tank/2017/01/26/5-facts-about-abortion/.

exploration of how race/ethnicity, education, and age shape public opinion about abortion, check out these interactive tables at http://www.pewforum.org/fact-sheet/public-opinion-on-abortion/, or investigate even more types of polling questions that have been asked by Gallup and major news organizations at http://www.pollingreport.com/abortion.htm.

Reference

Downing, Isiah J. " 'No More Baby Parts,' Colorado Planned Parenthood Suspect Said: Reports." November 29, 2015. http://www.newsweek.com/no-more-baby-parts-colorado-planned-parenthood-suspect-399280 (accessed April 26, 2018).

Historical Documents

Comstock Act (1873)

Named for moral crusader and postal inspector, Anthony Comstock, this congressional act banned the distribution of information and materials related to contraception and abortion. Comstock's most publicized arrest took place in 1878 when he posed as a customer seeking help for his wife, entrapping Madame Restell. Viewed as a savior by some and a villain by others, Restell had a flourishing midwifery practice that aided married ladies in the removal of obstructions, as it was euphemistically described in her advertisements. Rather enduring prison, she slit her own throat to which Comstock commented without remorse: "A bloody end to a bloody life" (Stone 2017).

Be it enacted by the Senate and House of Representatives of the United States of America in Congress assembled, That whoever, within the District of Columbia, or any of the Territories of the United Sates, or any other place within the exclusive jurisdiction of the United Sates, shall sell or lend, or give away, or in any manner exhibit, or shall offer to sell, or to lend, or to give away, in any manner to exhibit, or shall otherwise publish or offer to publish in any manner, or shall have in his possession, for any such purpose or purposes, any obscene book, pamphlet, paper, writing, advertisement, circular, print, picture, drawing or other representation, figure, or image on or of paper or other material, or any cast, instrument, or other article of any immoral nature, or any drug or medicine, or any article whatever, for the prevention of conception, or for causing unlawful abortion, or shall advertise the same for sale, or shall write or print, or cause to be written or printed, any card, circular, book, pamphlet, advertisement, or notice of any kind, setting when, where, how, or of whom, or by what means, any of the articles in this section hereinbefore mentioned, can be purchased or obtained, or shall manufacture, draw, or print, or in any wise make any of such articles, shall be deemed guilty of a misdemeanor, and on conviction thereof in any court of the United States . . . shall be imprisoned at hard labor in the penitentiary for not less than six months nor more than five years for each offense, or fined not less than one hundred dollars nor more than two thousand dollars, with costs of the court.

Source: U.S. Statutes. Chapt. CCLVII. March 3, 1873.

Reference

Stone, Geoffrey. "'Sex and the Constitution': Anthony Comstock and the Reign of the Moralists." *The Washington Post*. March 23, 2017. https://www.washingtonpost.

com/news/volokh-conspiracy/wp/2017/03/23/sex-and-
the-constitution-anthony-comstock-and-the-reign-of-
the-moralists/?utm_term=.f632ffff04f3 (accessed April 26,
2018).

American Law Institute Model Penal Code: Abortion (1959)

The American Law Institute (ALI), an influential organization that takes a scholarly approach to improving the law, crafted the first proposal for reform of criminal abortion laws in 1959. The first four of the seven sections of ALI's conditional model are given. It was promoted by many doctors and abortion rights activists, and several states, including Georgia, adopted similar laws. In Doe v. Bolton, *the companion case to* Roe v. Wade, *the Supreme Court ruled that the limitations on what constituted "justifiable abortion" in Georgia's law infringed on a woman's privacy and personal liberty and were thus unconstitutional.*

Section 230.3. Abortion.

(1) Unjustified Abortion. A person who purposely and unjustifiably terminates the pregnancy of another otherwise than by a live birth commits a felony of the third degree or, where the pregnancy has continued beyond the twenty-sixth week, a felony of the second degree.

(2) Justifiable Abortion. A licensed physician is justified in terminating a pregnancy if he believes there is substantial risk that continuance of the pregnancy would gravely impair the physical or mental health of the mother or that the child would be born with grave physical or mental defect, or that the pregnancy resulted from rape, incest, or other felonious intercourse. All illicit intercourse with a girl below the age of 16 shall be deemed felonious for purposes of this subsection. Justifiable abortions shall be performed only in a licensed hospital except in case of emergency when hospital facilities are unavailable. [Additional exceptions from

the requirement of hospitalization may be incorporated here to take account of situations in sparsely settled areas where hospitals are not generally accessible.]

(3) Physicians' Certificates; Presumption from Non-Compliance. No abortion shall be performed unless two physicians, one of whom may be the person performing the abortion, shall have certified in writing the circumstances which they believe to justify the abortion. Such certificate shall be submitted before the abortion to the hospital where it is to be performed and, in the case of abortion following felonious intercourse, to the prosecuting attorney or the police. Failure to comply with any of the requirements of this Subsection gives rise to a presumption that the abortion was unjustified.

(4) Self-Abortion: A woman whose pregnancy has continued beyond the twenty-sixth week commits a felony of the third degree if she purposely terminates her own pregnancy otherwise than by a live birth, or if she uses instruments, drugs or violence upon herself for that purpose.

Source: Model Penal Code copyright © 1980 by The American Law Institute. Reproduced with permission. All rights reserved.

Abortion in Perspective by Robert M. Byrn (1966)

As the American Law Institute's proposal for reform continued to gain traction, it was not without its critics. Among them was Robert M. Byrn, a law professor, who became a strong voice in the emerging pro-life movement. Byrn would later help draft the National Right to Life Committee's Supreme Court brief in Roe v. Wade. *In this excerpt from his 1966 article, which was published in* The Duquesne Law Review, *he calls on the legal profession to maintain reverence for sanctity of innocent human life.*

... The abortion debate is already in vigorous progress in several states, including Pennsylvania and New York, but these states are not unique. Before long, the entire country will be involved.

... if the Bar is to play a meaningful role in the expanding debate, the issues must be reframed within a legal context ...

None of the reasons given by the American Law Institute are sufficient for classifying unborn children as inferior human beings. Quite the contrary, the fallacies inherent in the Institute's position serve to demonstrate the equality of the unborn child with all other human beings ...

As we have seen, there is no qualitative difference, scientifically speaking, between human life in the womb and human life after birth. Hence, legislation, which would remove the life of a person in the womb from the full and equal protection of the law, would be as discriminatory, as "irrational," and as inimical to the equal protection clause as the legislative classification of races. ...

We must ask ourselves, therefore, whether we are prepared to abandon human beings to the moral and social predilections of individual doctors, or whether we shall continue to extend to these persons the equal protection of the law regardless of their socio-economic status. ...

We have a choice in cases of rape-induced pregnancies. We can either kill the child or we can direct all our ingenuity toward smoothing the way for both the mother and the child. The latter is the truly humane choice ...

There is another way to attack the problem of illegal abortion. We, as lawyers, may choose to become the advocates of the cause of the unborn child. In this role, we shall argue to the American people, as we have done before, that differences in size, shape, and color are not valid grounds for taking the life of an innocent human being. We know, of course, how arduous and uphill such a civil rights battle can be, and particularly will it be so here because the minority, whose rights are at stake, is both voiceless and voteless ...

Respect for the sanctity of innocent human life may very well be one of those rules of conduct upon which the survival of mankind depends. And permissive abortion seems to go a long way toward abrogating the rule. Perhaps, when all is said and done, respect for the innocent person's right to life will turn out to be the crucial issue in the abortion controversy, and perhaps, it will be lawyers who have made it so.

Source: *Duquesne Law Review*, vol. 5, no. 2, 1966–1967, pp. 125–141. Used by permission of *Duquesne Law Review*.

Abortion—A Woman's Decision, A Woman's Right (1969)

Legislation and litigation were not the only strategies employed in the fight for and against legalization. Some activists invested their energies in direct service, while others took to the streets with more confrontational tactics. The Chicago Women's Liberation Union established a legendary underground abortion network that came to be known by its nickname "Jane." What began as a referral service eventually grew into a powerful women's health collective with self-taught but skillful volunteers who operated outside the law to assist over 11,000 women in receiving a safe abortion. This excerpt from Jane's original informational pamphlet is striking for its bold defiance, identification of abortion as a social problem linked to socioeconomic and racial disparities, and efforts to demystify a procedure that had been cloaked in shame and secrecy. To learn more, read Laura Kaplan's The Story of Jane: The Legendary Underground Feminist Abortion Service *(1995) or watch the documentary* Jane: An Abortion Service *(1996).*

What is the Abortion Counseling Service [ACS]?

We are women whose ultimate goal is the liberation of women in society. One important way we are working toward that goal is by helping any woman who wants an abortion to get one as safely and cheaply as possible under existing conditions.

Abortion is a safe, simple, relatively painless operation when performed by a trained person in clean conditions. In fact, it's less complicated than a tonsillectomy. People hear about its horrors because desperate women turn to incompetent people or resort to unsafe methods. Much of our time is spent finding reliable and sympathetic doctors who will perform safe abortions for as little money as possible. You will receive the best medical care we know of.

Although abortions are illegal in Illinois, the state has not brought charges against any woman who has had an abortion. Only those who perform abortions have been prosecuted.

Any information you give your counselor is kept confidential. She will not give your name to anyone or discuss anything you tell her without your permission. It is vitally important that you are completely honest about your medical history with your counselor and the doctor.

Loan fund: Because abortions are illegal and in such demand, they are exorbitantly expensive. In fact, an abortion frequently costs as much as the combined doctor and hospital bills for having a baby. The ACS believes that no woman should be denied an abortion because she is unable to pay for it. We have a small and constantly depleted non-interest loan fund for women who would otherwise be unable to have an abortion. It is non-profit and non-discriminatory. . . .

THE OPERATION ITSELF: An abortion is simple and takes only a few minutes. You'll probably be given a local anesthetic. The injections are relatively painless. After the anesthetic has taken effect, the neck of the uterus is opened and the lining of the uterus is scraped out with a loop-shaped instrument called a curette. The operation is called a dilation and curettage, or a D&C. . . . Feel free to ask the doctor or us any question you may have.

AFTERWARD: If the doctor asks you to check back, it is very important that you do so as instructed. Also call us so we know how you are feeling and whether you are perfectly satisfied with the doctor we sent you to. You should be examined by a gynecologist within a few week[s] after your abortion. If you like, we can recommend a gynecologist for the post-operative examination.

You may bleed or cramp mildly for a few days or feel other slight effects for a few weeks. On the other hand; you may have no after-effects except slight bleeding. Physical response varies from woman to woman. If you bleed for longer than three weeks or pass big blood clots, call us or go to a gynecologist. Again, if you have questions or need reassurance, please call us. . . .

You may have some emotional "blues" after your abortion. Partly this is because of the way we're brought up, partly it is because of hormonal changes in your body. If you want to talk this over with someone, call us.

If you have not been using any contraceptive and would like to start now (it beats an abortion), ask the gynecologist about it when you go in for your check-up. . . .

ABORTION AS A SOCIAL PROBLEM: We are giving our time not only because we want to make abortions safer, cheaper and more accessible for the individual women who come to us, but because we see the whole abortion issue as a problem of society. The current abortion laws are a symbol of the sometimes subtle, but often blatant, oppression of women in our society.

Women should have the right to control their own bodies and lives. Only a woman who is pregnant can determine whether she has enough resources—economic, physical and emotional—at a given time to bear and rear a child. Yet at present the decision to bear the child or have an abortion is taken out of her hands by governmental bodies which can have only the slightest notion of the problems involved.

Cultural, moral and religious feelings are largely against abortion, and society does all it can to make a woman feel guilty and degraded if she has one.

The same society that denies a woman the decision not to have a child refuses to provide humane alternatives for women who do have children, such as child care facilities to permit the mother to work, or role flexibility so that men can share in the raising of children. The same society that insists that women should and do find their basic fulfillment in motherhood will condemn the unwed mother and her fatherless child.

The same society that glamorizes women as sex objects and teaches them from early childhood to please and satisfy men views pregnancy and childbirth as punishment for "immoral" or "careless" sexual activity, especially if the woman is uneducated, poor or black. The same morality that says "that's what she gets for fooling around" also fails to recognize society's responsibility to the often unwelcome child that results. Punitive welfare laws reflect this view, and churches reinforce it.

Our society's version of equal opportunity means that lower-class women bear unwanted children or face expensive, illegal and often unsafe abortions, while well-connected middle-class women can frequently get safe and hush-hush "D and Cs" in hospitals.

Only women can bring about their own liberation. It is time for women to get together to change the male-made laws and to aid their sisters caught in the bind of legal restrictions and social stigma. Women must fight together to change the attitudes of society about abortion and to make the state provide free abortions as a human right.

There are currently many groups lobbying for population control, legal abortion and selective sterilization. Some are actually attempting to control some populations, prevent some births—for instance those of black people or poor people. We are opposed to these or any form of genocide. We are for every woman having exactly as many children as she wants, when she wants, if she wants. It's time the Bill of Rights applied to women. Its time women got together and started really fighting for their rights. Governments have to be made to realize that abortions are part of the health care they must provide for the people who support them.

If you are interested in giving your energy and time to help bring about a better life for yourself and your daughters and sons, get in touch with Jane.

Source: CWLU Herstory Website Project, a beautifully curated archive of the Chicago Women's Liberation Union. https://www .cwluherstory.org/jane-documents-articles/abortion-a-womans-decision-a-womans-right. Used by permission of CWLU Herstory Project.

Redstockings Abortion Speakout (March 21, 1969)

Calls for legalization of abortion continued to grow even louder in the late 1960s. In New York, another women's liberation group called the Redstockings garnered media attention with the first-ever public "speak-out" on abortion on March 21, 1969. To a crowd of more than 300, 12 "sisters" gave powerful "testimonies" about their desperate searches for abortion providers. The following excerpts from two women's accounts remind us that while abortion is a heated political debate, it is also a lived experience. The first woman must feign psychiatric illness to obtain a "therapeutic abortion." The second woman must traverse into the clandestine medical underground, assuming unknown risks with a highly questionable practitioner, and she suffers tremendous pain. In 1989, at a time when abortion rights were eroding and clinics were being blockaded, the Redstockings held a 20th-anniversary abortion speak-out. Even today, abortion remains a taboo subject, and telling stories that break the silence is a powerful act.

Opening Remarks: Well, all of us are members of the Women's Liberation Group of New York City. And we discovered that by just talking about our own experience, about our own lives, things that happened to us . . . it was like a technique that I think a lot of people who are involved in trying to struggle for their liberation, a lot of the press people have found that the first thing to talk about is their oppression. The first thing is to talk about themselves. And we discovered that for us and we thought we were gonna talk about abortion here tonight that we would sort of use that same technique. Instead of like just talking about things that were really removed from us, we would talk about our abortion; what happened, what it felt like, what went on. And then from talking about this, then we would learn much more really about abortion. And that was like our plan for this evening. It's very hard for us to start. I know for me it's very hard to start talking about 'cause I never really discussed the fact that I had had an abortion with too many people.

One Woman's Description of the Complex Process of Obtaining a "Therapeutic Abortion"

Look, what I wanna talk about is something that we call a therapeutic abortion. Therapeutic. I don't know. I've been try-ing to think for many years what that meant, but all I know is that . . . I was going in and telling this psychiatrist that was insane because that's what you have to do. You have to tell him that you're going to commit suicide and you can't just say, "Now look, doctor, I'm gonna commit suicide." You have to go and bring a razor or whatever. "You know, if you don't tell me I'm gonna have an abortion right now, I'm gonna go out and jump off the Verrazano Bridge or whatever." But I knew what I was doing then.

But when I had that therapeutic abortion, it cost me more for the therapy after the therapeutic abortion than before. This is a joke. When I got pregnant, I had a sister who is a nurse and I was fortunate because unless you know how to go about doing things, it's very hard. My sister said, "Well, look, go see this obstetrician and talk to him." And I saw him. He said, "Well, you're pregnant. What do you want me to do?" And I said, "Well, look, I don't wanna have the baby." And he said, "Do you have some money?" This is the truth. I'm not making this up. And I said, "Well, I don't have much." I didn't have any, but I was figuring out like what—I wrote on a piece of paper the friends I had. This one can give me $50, 25. And I'd have to sell my body for the rest. You know, that's what happened. I couldn't get pregnant again. So, I told him that I had some money and he gave me the address in his office. He said, "Go see these two psychiatrists." And I won't mention the names here. If you wanna ask me later, I'll tell you. And I went to see them. The first one I saw for approximately 8 to 12 minutes. And he said to me, "Yeah, you're pregnant and you want an abortion. Do you have any history of mental illness? You know, were you ever in a hospital? Are you insane?" He said, "Well, why don't you want this baby?" And I told him why. That I just didn't feel at that time that I could, you know, be a mother. And I couldn't see the carrying the pregnancy and then having to give a child away 'cause there was no need for that. So, he told me—He came out and said, "Well, look, what are you going to do if you don't get an abortion?" And I knew what he wanted me to say and that was "Well, I'm gonna kill myself." And I said, "I'm gonna kill myself." And he wrote it down that I was gonna kill myself. And he said to me, "$60." And I said to him, "I don't have $60." And he told me—This is the truth. He said that if I didn't give him the $60 then or, you know, like come back and give to him, he would not write the report that has to be given for the obstetrician then to present it for the board. That was only 1 minute. Then I saw the other one and it's pretty much the same thing. [Laughter from the crowd]

. . . You know, I feel like I'm telling a joke. But let me tell you something, it's no joke. . . . I called up the obstetrician and I said to him what's happening. He knew I was school. I was going to college and working, supporting myself. Not living at home. And meanwhile, I kept getting bigger and bigger. And he said to me, "Well, look, it has to be brought before the abortion board in the hospital and we'll let you know." Well, one day, I was at school. . . . I was standing outside and my sister came and just saw me there. And she said, "Come on." And

I said, "Where are we going?" She said, "You have to go to the hospital right now." Just like that, I had my book. I went to the hospital. And I was brought up to, you know, labor room.

Meanwhile, I hear these women screaming and yelling. You know, they're going to have their baby. And like I just didn't know what was happening. And a nurse comes in and she shaves you. And she sticks a needle in your arm. . . . I said, "Maybe they're gonna kill me." It's not funny. I honestly thought that maybe this was—they were really gonna kill me. I didn't know what was gonna happen when I got in there and then the doctor came and I was really crying. And he said, "What are you crying about?" I said, "I'm scared." And he said, "You're scared. You're crying. My job is to bring life into this world, not to destroy it." Now, this was a sympathetic obstetrician who was giving me a therapeutic abortion 'cause I was insane. But you know, he handled it very well. Then you have the abortion, which is a very simple procedure. This is something that, you know, should be understood. It's a very simple procedure. Takes about 12 minutes if it's done in a hospital. If it's done in the bathroom of some hotel, it's not such a simple procedure. Well then, you're put up on the maternity board. This is all therapeutic. This is all torture. This is planned. . . . You just had an abortion. You're put on the maternity board. They happen to perform it . . . right next to the nursery and all the little babies crying. And then they bring out the little baby to the mother and you have to see all this shit. Right? And the nurses come in and say, "Oh, you have the abortion." And when you go to the operating room, there's a bulletin board, a blackboard, and it's written therapeutic AB . . . Like you know, the reason we have the law that we have now is because men wanna make women suffer for their sins.

Another Woman's Reflections on Her Experience of Fear and Pain during an Illegal Abortion

He was like giving me pills to take, you know. And I didn't know what they were, but all I knew was it was a strange sort of abortion. I don't know what it's called. They put something inside you and it dilates the uterus and then the child comes down or whatever it is comes out. And that hurts very much and I had to walk around with this thing in me for 24 hours and it had been very painful the first time he put it in. So, I was like really scared for the pain again. So, I just took these pills and I remember thinking to myself I knew the doctor was crazy. I mean, he was crazy with no doubt. He was crazy 'cause we would talk endlessly on and on very weird strange stories and he fell asleep in front of me in the room, you know. And I was with a girlfriend who come with me and he thought it was her that was gonna have the abortion, you know. But I said to myself, "I don't care what these pills are, you know." I thought I didn't know what these pills are and I know this stuff is crazy, but I don't care because I'm not gonna be pregnant and have a kid, you know. So like that suicidal thing was like very real because I thought to myself I could die from these pills, but I don't care.

Source: Redstockings of the Women's Liberation Movement Think Tank and Archive for Action, which carefully catalogues authentic radical feminist source materials to inspire mobilization for change. http://www.redstockings.org/. Used by permission of Redstockings Women's Liberation Archives for Action.

Roe v. Wade (1973)

In 1973, the Supreme Court (7–2) extended the right to privacy to women seeking abortion and refused to declare the fetus a person under the Constitution. This landmark case decriminalized abortion in the United States.

MR. JUSTICE BLACKMUN delivered the opinion of the Court

. . . We forthwith acknowledge our awareness of the sensitive and emotional nature of the abortion controversy, of the vigorous opposing views, even among physicians, and of the deep and seemingly absolute convictions that the subject inspires. One's philosophy, one's experiences, one's exposure to the raw edges of human existence, one's religious training, one's attitudes toward life and family and their values, and the moral standards one establishes and seeks to observe, are all likely to influence and to color one's thinking and conclusions about abortion.

In addition, population growth, pollution, poverty, and racial overtones tend to complicate and not to simplify the problem.

Our task, of course, is to resolve the issue by constitutional measurement, free of emotion and of predilection. We seek earnestly to do this. . .

. . . The principal thrust of appellant's attack on the Texas statutes is that they improperly invade a right, said to be possessed by the pregnant woman, to choose to terminate her pregnancy. Appellant would discover this right in the concept of personal "liberty" embodied in the Fourteenth Amendment's Due Process Clause; or in personal, marital, familial, and sexual privacy said to be protected by the Bill of Rights or its penumbras, see Griswold v. Connecticut, 381 U.S. 479 (1965); Eisenstadt v. Baird, 405 U.S. 438 (1972) . . .

The Constitution does not explicitly mention any right of privacy. In a line of decisions, however, going back perhaps as far as Union Pacific R. Co. v. Botsford, 141 U.S. 250, 251 (1891), the Court has recognized that a right of personal privacy, or a guarantee of certain areas or zones of privacy, does exist under the Constitution. . . .

This right of privacy . . . is broad enough to encompass a woman's decision whether or not to terminate her pregnancy. The detriment that the State would impose upon the pregnant woman by denying this choice altogether is apparent. Specific and direct harm medically diagnosable even in early pregnancy may be involved. Maternity, or additional offspring, may force upon the woman a distressful life and future. Psychological harm may be imminent. Mental and physical health may be taxed by child care. There is also the distress, for all concerned, associated with the unwanted child, and there is the problem of bringing a child into a family already unable, psychologically and otherwise, to care for it. In other cases, as in this one, the additional difficulties and continuing stigma of unwed motherhood may be involved. All these are factors the woman and her responsible physician necessarily will consider in consultation.

On the basis of elements such as these, appellant and some amici argue that the woman's right is absolute and that she is entitled to terminate her pregnancy at whatever time, in whatever way, and for whatever reason she alone chooses. With this we do not agree. Appellant's arguments that Texas either has no valid interest at all in regulating the abortion decision, or no interest strong enough to support any limitation upon the woman's sole determination, are unpersuasive. The Court's decisions recognizing a right of privacy also acknowledge that some state regulation in areas protected by that right is appropriate. As noted above, a State may properly assert important interests in safeguarding health, in maintaining medical standards, and in protecting potential life. At some point in pregnancy, these respective interests become sufficiently compelling to sustain regulation of the factors that govern the abortion decision. The privacy right involved, therefore, cannot be said to be absolute. (p. 24)

. . . We, therefore, conclude that the right of personal privacy includes the abortion decision, but that this right is not unqualified, and must be considered against important state interests in regulation. . . .

The Constitution does not define "person" in so many words . . . throughout the major portion of the 19th century, prevailing legal abortion practices were far freer than they are today, persuades us that the word "person," as used in the Fourteenth Amendment, does not include the unborn. . . .

A state criminal abortion statute of the current Texas type, that excepts from criminality only a lifesaving procedure on behalf of the mother, without regard to pregnancy stage and without recognition of the other interests involved, is violative of the Due Process Clause of the Fourteenth Amendment.

(a) For the stage prior to approximately the end of the first trimester, the abortion decision and its effectuation must be left to the medical judgment of the pregnant woman's attending physician.

(b) For the stage subsequent to approximately the end of the first trimester, the State, in promoting its interest in the health of the mother, may, if it chooses, regulate the abortion procedure in ways that are reasonably related to maternal health.

(c) For the stage subsequent to viability, the State in promoting its interest in the potentiality of human life may, if it chooses, regulate, and even proscribe, abortion except where it is necessary, in appropriate medical judgment, for the preservation of the life or health of the mother. . . .

This holding, we feel, is consistent with the relative weights of the respective interests involved, with the lessons and examples of medical and legal history, with the lenity of the common law, and with the demands of the profound problems of the present day. The decision leaves the State free to place increasing restrictions on abortion as the period of pregnancy lengthens, so long as those restrictions are tailored to the recognized state interests. The decision vindicates the right of the physician to administer medical treatment according to his professional judgment up to the points where important . . . state interests provide compelling justifications for intervention.

Source: *Roe v. Wade*, 410 U.S. 113 (1973).

The Hyde Amendment (1976)

Pro-life activists responded to the Roe *decision with alarm and organized opposition on every front. Their first major victory was the passage of the Hyde Amendment, which eliminated federal subsidies for abortion except in cases where the pregnancy placed the woman's life in danger. Its architect, Henry John Hyde (R-IL), delivered a passionate speech on the House floor on June 24, 1976, excerpted here, that made him a heroic figure to those seeking to defend the lives of the unborn.*

Mr. Chairman, this amendment may stimulate a lot of debate—but it need not—because I believe most Members know how they will vote on this issue.

Nevertheless, there are those of us who believe it is to the everlasting shame of this country that in 1973 approximately 800,000 legal abortions were performed in this country—and so it is fair to assume that this year over a million human lives will be destroyed because they are inconvenient to someone.

The unborn child facing an abortion can best be classified as a member of the innocently inconvenient and since the pernicious doctrine that some lives are more important than others seems to be persuasive with the pro-abortion forces, we who seek to protect that most defenseless and innocent of human lives, the unborn—seek to inhibit the use of Federal funds to pay for and thus encourage abortion as an answer to the human and compelling problem of an unwanted child.

. . . make no mistake, an abortion is violent.

I think in the final analysis, you must determine whether or not the unborn person is human. If you think it is animal or vegetable then of course, it is disposable like an empty beer can to be crushed and thrown out with the rest of the trash.

But medicine, biology, embryology say that growing living organism is not animal or vegetable or mineral—but it is a human life.

And if you believe that human life is deserving of due process of law—of equal protection of the laws, then you cannot in logic and conscience help fund the execution of these innocent defenseless human lives. . . .

Once conception has occurred a new and unique genetic package has been created, not a potential human being but a human being with potential. For nine months the mother provides nourishment and shelter, and birth is no substantial change, it is merely a change of address.

We are told that bringing an unwanted child into the world is an obscene act. Unwanted by whom? Is it too subtle a notion to understand it is more important to be a loving person than to be one who is loved? We need more people who are capable of projecting love.

We hear the claim that the poor are denied a right available to other women if we do not use tax money to fund abortions.

Well make a list of all the things society denies poor women and let them make the choice of what we will give them.

Don't say "poor woman, go destroy your young, and we will pay for it."

An innocent, defenseless human life, in a caring and humane society deserves better than to be flushed down a toilet or burned in an incinerator.

The promise of America is that life is not just for the privileged, the planned, or the perfect.

Source: Congressional Record, House of Representatives, June 24, 1976, page 20410.

Mexico City Policies (1984–2017)

In the 1980s, the abortion debate became fully entrenched in American politics. The polarization between pro-choice Democrats and pro-life Republicans is reflected in their platforms and in the tug-of-war between presidents over the Mexico City Policy. "The Global Gag Rule," as it came to be known, cut off federal funding for international family planning organizations that provide abortion services or even information. As these selected quotes show, the passionate convictions expressed early on seem to dissipate; the later presidential memos appear quite perfunctory.

President Ronald W. Regan: U.S. support for family planning programs is based on respect for human life, enhancement of human dignity, and strengthening of the

family. Attempts to use abortion, involuntary sterilization, or other coercive measures in family planning must
be shunned, whether exercised against families within a
society or against nations within the family of man.

The United Nations Declaration of the Rights of the Child
(1959) calls for legal protection for children before birth
as well as after birth. In keeping with this obligation, the
United States does not consider abortion an acceptable
element of family planning programs and will no longer contribute to those of which it is a part. (U.S. Policy
Statement at the United Nations, August 16–13, 1984)

President William J. Clinton: These excessively broad
anti-abortion conditions are unwarranted. I am informed
that the conditions are not mandated by the Foreign
Assistance Act [of 1961] or any other law. Moreover, they
have undermined efforts to promote safe and efficacious
family planning programs in foreign nations. Accordingly, I hereby direct that AID [Agency for International
Development] remove the conditions not explicitly mandated by the Foreign Assistance Act or any other law from
all current AID grants to NGOs and exclude them from
future grants.

President George W. Bush: It is my conviction that taxpayer
funds should not be used to pay for abortions or advocate
or actively promote abortion, either here or abroad. It is
therefore my belief that the Mexico City Policy should be
restored.

President Barack H. Obama: These excessively broad conditions on grants and assistance awards are unwarranted.
Moreover, they have undermined efforts to promote safe
and effective voluntary family planning programs in foreign nations. Accordingly, I hereby revoke the Presidential memorandum of January 22, 2001. (Memorandum,
January 23, 2009).

President Donald J. Trump: I hereby revoke the Presidential
Memorandum of January 23, 2009. . . and reinstate the

Presidential Memorandum of January 22, 2001. . . . I further direct the Secretary of State to take all necessary actions, to the extent permitted by law, to ensure that U.S. taxpayer dollars do not fund organizations or programs that support or participate in the management of a program of coercive abortion or involuntary sterilization. (Memorandum, January 23, 2017).

Sources: Ronald W. Reagan. "US Policy Statement for the International Conference on Population." The White House Office of Policy Development. *Population and Development Review*, vol. 10, no. 3, September 1984, pp. 574–579; William J. Clinton. "Memorandum on the Mexico City Policy," January 22, 1993. Online by Gerhard Peters and John T. Woolley, *The American Presidency Project*. http://www.presidency.ucsb .edu/ws/?pid=46311; George W. Bush. "Memorandum on Restoration of the Mexico City Policy," January 22, 2001. Online by Gerhard Peters and John T. Woolley, *The American Presidency Project*. http://www.presidency.ucsb.edu/ ws/?pid=29766; Barack Obama. "Memorandum on Mexico City Policy and Assistance for Voluntary Population Planning," January 23, 2009. Online by Gerhard Peters and John T. Woolley, *The American Presidency Project*. http:// www.presidency.ucsb.edu/ws/?pid=85685. Donald J. Trump. "Memorandum on the Mexico City Policy," January 23, 2017. Online by Gerhard Peters and John T. Woolley, *The American Presidency Project*. http://www.presidency.ucsb.edu/ ws/?pid=122515.

Freedom of Access to Clinic Entrances Act (FACE) (1994)

Throughout the 1980s and early 1990s, the pro-life movement, by and large, engaged in peaceful protest. However, an extreme faction escalated to tactics of intimidation and confrontation, including arson, bombings, and murder. Congress found some common ground in passing FACE, a bill to restore law and order, which made forceful obstruction of entrance to women's health facilities a federal offense. The penalties for the first offense were fine and/ or imprisonment of no more than one year and up to three years for subsequent offenses. Aggrieved persons could also pursue civil action seeking injunctive relief as well as compensatory or punitive damages. Although it did not completely stop violence against abortion providers, it did dramatically curtail clinic blockades.

. . .

(a) Prohibited activities.—Whoever—

   (1) by force or threat of force or by physical obstruction, intentionally injures, intimidates or interferes with or attempts to injure, intimidate or interfere with any person because that person is or has been, or in order to intimidate such person or any other person or any class of persons from, obtaining or providing reproductive health services;

   (2) by force or threat of force or by physical obstruction, intentionally injures, intimidates or interferes with or attempts to injure, intimidate or interfere with any person lawfully exercising or seeking to exercise the First Amendment right of religious freedom at a place of religious worship; or

   (3) intentionally damages or destroys the property of a facility, or attempts to do so, because such facility provides reproductive health services, or intentionally damages or destroys the property of a place of religious worship, shall be subject to the penalties provided in subsection (b) and the civil remedies provided in subsection (c), except that a parent or legal guardian of a minor shall not be subject to any penalties or civil remedies under this section for such activities insofar as they are directed exclusively at that minor.

. . .

Source: 18 U.S.C. § 248.

Partial-Birth Abortion Ban Act (2003)

Pro-life activists gained the upper hand in 2003 when President George W. Bush signed the federal ban on partial-birth abortions. It had been vetoed twice by President William Jefferson Clinton, who emphasized the rarity, tragedy, and necessity of the intact dilation and evacuation procedure. The language, displayed in this excerpt, reflected the grisly descriptors that had by that time come to dominate public discourse. A physician who performs this procedure when it has not been deemed necessary to save the life of a mother could face fines and up to a two-year prison sentence. In 2007, the Supreme Court upheld the constitutionality of this law in Gonzales v. Carhart, *550 U.S. 124 (2007)—a decision that departed significantly from past rulings by not insisting an exception to safeguard women's health.*

The Congress finds and declares the following:

(1) A moral, medical, and ethical consensus exists that the practice of performing a partial-birth abortion—an abortion in which a physician deliberately and intentionally vaginally delivers a living, unborn child's body until either the entire baby's head is outside the body of the mother, or any part of the baby's trunk past the navel is outside the body of the mother and only the head remains inside the womb, for the purpose of performing an overt act (usually the puncturing of the back of the child's skull and removing the baby's brains) that the person knows will kill the partially delivered infant, performs this act, and then completes delivery of the dead infant—is a gruesome and inhumane procedure that is never medically necessary and should be prohibited.

(2) Rather than being an abortion procedure that is embraced by the medical community, particularly among physicians who routinely perform other abortion procedures, partial-birth abortion remains a disfavored procedure that is not only unnecessary to preserve the health of the mother, but in fact poses serious risks to the long-term

health of women and in some circumstances, their lives. As a result, at least 27 States banned the procedure as did the United States Congress which voted to ban the procedure during the 104th, 105th, and 106th Congresses.

(3) In Stenberg v. Carhart, 530 U.S. 914, 932 (2000), the United States Supreme Court opined "that significant medical authority supports the proposition that in some circumstances, [partial birth abortion] would be the safest procedure" for pregnant women who wish to undergo an abortion. Thus, the Court struck down the State of Nebraska's ban on partial-birth abortion procedures, concluding that it placed an "undue burden" on women seeking abortions because it failed to include an exception for partial-birth abortions deemed necessary to preserve the "health" of the mother.

. . .

(13) There exists substantial record evidence upon which Congress has reached its conclusion that a ban on partial-birth abortion is not required to contain a "health" exception, because the facts indicate that a partial-birth abortion is never necessary to preserve the health of a woman, poses serious risks to a woman's health, and lies outside the standard of medical care.

. . .

Source: 18 USC 1531; Public Law 108-105, 108th Congress.

Whole Woman's Health v. Hellerstedt **(2016)**

While Roe *has remained the law of the land for more than four decades, access has been slowly and significantly diminished by the imposition of waiting periods, mandated ultrasounds, and onerous licensing requirements for abortion clinics. The pro-choice movement dubbed this strategy as "Targeted Regulation of Abortion Providers" or TRAP laws. In 2017, the Supreme Court struck down (5–3) Texas's House Bill 2, which required hospital admitting privileges for abortion providers and surgical center standards for clinics. These highlights from the majority opinion focus on the "undue burden" that these restrictions impose on women seeking to exercise their constitutional right to an abortion. In the concurring opinion, Justice Ruth Bader Ginsburg harshly rebuked, "It is beyond rational belief that H. B. 2 could genuinely protect the health of women." Pro-life activists must now work to keep the laws that they had helped enact in more than two dozen states from being dismantled.*

. . .

In Planned Parenthood of Southeastern Pa. v. Casey, 505 U.S. 833, 878 (1992), a plurality of the Court concluded that there "exists" an "undue burden" on a woman's right to decide to have an abortion, and consequently a provision of law is constitutionally invalid, if the "purpose or effect" of the provision "is to place a substantial obstacle in the path of a woman seeking an abortion before the fetus attains viability."

. . .

We conclude that neither of these provisions [admitting-privileges and surgical-center requirements] offers medical benefits sufficient to justify the burdens upon access that each imposes. Each places a substantial obstacle in the path of women seeking a previability abortion, each constitutes an undue burden on abortion access, Casey, supra, at 878 (plurality opinion), and each violates the Federal Constitution. Amdt. 14, §1.

. . .

We have found nothing in Texas' record evidence that shows that, compared to prior law (which required a "working arrangement" with a doctor with admitting privileges), the new law [that stipulated the hospital be no more 30 miles away] advanced Texas' legitimate interest in protecting women's health.

We add that, when directly asked at oral argument whether Texas knew of a single instance in which the new requirement would have helped even one woman obtain better treatment, Texas admitted that there was no evidence in the record of such a case. See Tr. of Oral Arg. 47.

. . .

In our view, the record contains sufficient evidence that the admitting-privileges requirement led to the closure of half of Texas' clinics, or thereabouts. Those closures meant fewer doctors, longer waiting times, and increased crowding.

. . .

. . . the dissent suggests that one benefit of H. B. 2's requirements would be that they might "force unsafe facilities to shut down." Post, at 26. To support that assertion, the dissent points to the Kermit Gosnell scandal. Gosnell, a physician in Pennsylvania, was convicted of first-degree murder and manslaughter. . . . Gosnell's behavior was terribly wrong. But there is no reason to believe that an extra layer of regulation would have affected that behavior. Deter-mined wrongdoers, already ignoring existing statutes and safety measures, are unlikely to be convinced to adopt safe practices by a new overlay of regulations.

. . .

The record makes clear that the surgical-center requirement provides no benefit when complications arise in the context of an abortion produced through medication. That is because, in such a case, complications would almost always arise only after the patient has left the facility. . . . The record also contains evidence indicating that abortions taking place in an abortion facility are safe—indeed, safer than numerous procedures that take place outside hospitals and to which Texas does not apply its surgical-center requirements. . . . Nationwide, childbirth is 14 times more likely than abortion to result in death . . . but Texas law allows a midwife to oversee childbirth in the patient's own home.

. . .

Moreover, many surgical-center requirements are inappropriate as applied to surgical abortions. Requiring scrub facilities;

maintaining a one-way traffic pattern through the facility; having ceiling, wall, and floor finishes; separating soiled utility and sterilization rooms; and regulating air pressure, filtration, and humidity control can help reduce infection where doctors conduct procedures that penetrate the skin. App. 304. But abortions typically involve either the administration of medicines or procedures performed through the natural opening of the birth canal, which is itself not sterile.

. . .

Texas suggests that the seven or eight remaining clinics could expand sufficiently to provide abortions for the 60,000 to 72,000 Texas women who sought them each year.

. . .

More fundamentally, in the face of no threat to women's health, Texas seeks to force women to travel long distances to get abortions in crammed-to-capacity superfacilities. Patients seeking these services are less likely to get the kind of individualized attention, serious conversation, and emotional support that doctors at less taxed facilities may have offered. Healthcare facilities and medical professionals are not fungible commodities. Surgical centers attempting to accommodate sudden, vastly increased demand, see 46 F. Supp. 3d, at 682, may find that quality of care declines. Another commonsense inference that the District Court made is that these effects would be harmful to, not supportive of, women's health. See id., at 682–683.

. . .

For these reasons the judgment of the Court of Appeals is reversed, and the case is remanded for further proceedings consistent with this opinion.

It is so ordered.

Source: *Whole Woman's Health v. Hellerstedt,* 579 U.S. ___ (2016).

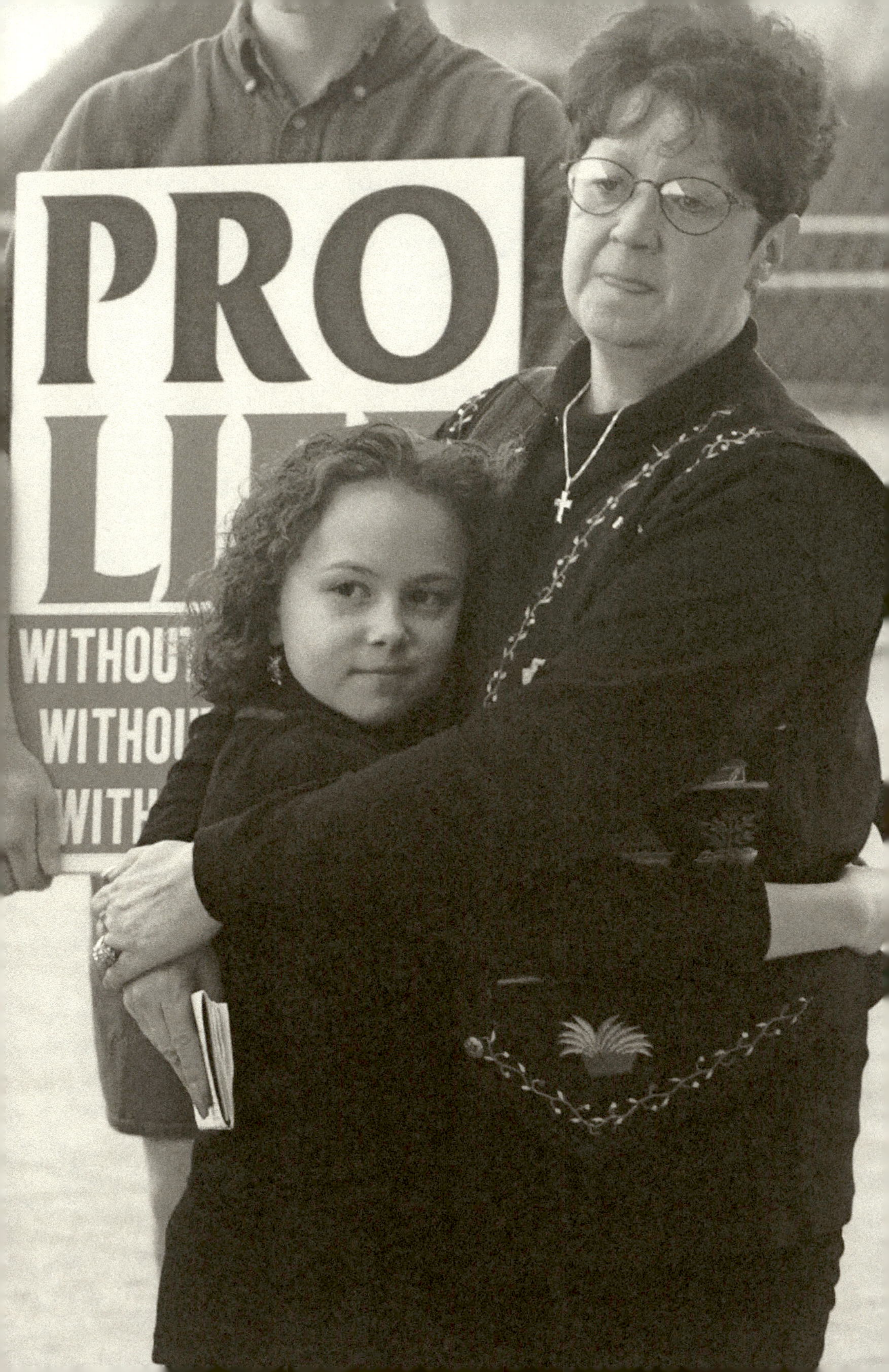
PRO
WITHOU
WITHOU
WITH

Introduction

Because the abortion issue has been on the public agenda for so long, and because it is so contentious, there are more resource materials than it is possible to keep track of, let alone list in one place. This carefully curated list will direct readers to some of the most widely cited scholarship on this topic. It features books rather than academic journal or news articles as these are able to provide a more in-depth discussion of the various points of view in the debate. The nonprint sources spotlight some of the most enlightening documentaries and feature films to watch as well as informative websites to check out.

Norma McCorvey, a historic and controversial figure in the abortion debate, embraces her nine-year-old friend, Meredith Champion, at an Operation Rescue rally in Dallas, Texas, January 22, 1997. It was the 24-year anniversary of the landmark Supreme Court decision legalizing abortion, in which McCorvey served as the anonymous plaintiff, "Jane Roe." She later revealed her identity to the public and was involved in pro-choice activism and abortion clinic work in the 1980s. Her increasingly amicable interactions with the zealous anti-abortion protestor Rev. Flip Benham prompted McCorvey to cross the battle lines. Until her death in 2017, McCorvey devoted herself to the pro-life cause of overturning *Roe*. (AP Photo/Ron Heflin)

Books

Understanding the Abortion Controversy in the United States

Burns, Gene. *The Moral Veto: Framing Contraception, Abortion, and Cultural Pluralism in the United States*. Cambridge, England: Cambridge University Press, 2005.

> For readers interested in an in-depth analysis of the framing processes surrounding abortion debates in the United States, this book is a good choice. It explores frames about abortion and contraception in public debate since the 19th century and examines how these frames developed through the policy debates of the 20th century. The title reflects the author's conceptualization of the significance of framing. The frames of the pro-life movement that express great moral passion make it difficult for the movement actors to obtain their goals. At the same time, these frames prevent—that is, veto—the goals proposed by the pro-choice activists. As a result, policy change is stymied.

Craig, Barbara Hinkson, and David M. O'Brien. *Abortion and American Politics*. Chatham, NJ: Chatham House Publishers, 1993.

> The purpose of Craig and O'Brien's book is to describe and analyze the impact of abortion controversies on American politics. At the same time, the authors review the events in policy making, both at the federal and state levels, from the 1970s to the 1990s. Chapters are devoted to interest groups, state politics, Congress, presidential politics, the courts, and public opinion. Three major cases structure the time frame of the descriptions: *Roe v. Wade* in 1973, *Webster v. Reproductive Services* in 1989, and *Planned Parenthood v. Casey* in 1992.

Critchlow, Donald T. *Intended Consequences: Birth Control, Abortion, and the Federal Government in Modern America*. New York: Oxford University Press, 1999.

Critchlow is the founding editor of the *Journal of Public History* and brings a historian's eye to the changes in public policy affecting contraception and abortion from the 1950s through the 1990s. The goal is to describe the formation of the federal family planning policy and how the legalization of abortion changed the debate over birth control. Key to the change was the growth of the feminist movement, which moved the issue from the purview of population control experts to the combative movements in the abortion debate.

Garrow, David J. *Liberty and Sexuality: The Right to Privacy and the Making of* Roe v. Wade. Berkeley: University of California Press, 1994, 1998.

Here is the definitive legal history of *Roe v. Wade*, the result of meticulous research by Garrow, a professor of law at Emory University. Garrow finds the origins of the decision in the birth control campaigns of Katherine Houghton Hepburn in Connecticut in the early part of the 20th century. These politics eventually led to the ruling that the decision whether or not to have a child was fundamental and within a zone of constitutional privacy. The book goes on to take the reader step by step through the litigation that resulted in the legalization of abortion and the Supreme Court's rejection of conditional abortion laws. This is an essential resource for anyone following the abortion debate.

Ginsburg, Faye. *Contested Lives: The Abortion Debate in an American Community*. Berkeley: University of California Press, 1998.

The abortion clinic in Fargo, North Dakota, is the setting for anthropologist Ginsburg's ethnographic investigation of the abortion debate. The women's health center in that Plains community has been one of the most embattled in the United States. The study here delves into the narratives of the participants on both sides of the divide and places them in historic context. Like Gorney's 1998 book on a clinic in Missouri, it covers the period of the 1980s.

Gorney, Cynthia. *Articles of Faith: A Frontline History of the Abortion Wars*. New York: Simon & Schuster, 1998.
  Gorney tells the tale of the conflict over abortion between 1973 and 1989 from the point of view of impassioned advocates on both sides. The scene is an abortion clinic in Missouri, but she relates the events to the broader picture of abortion politics and policy in the nation. The story ends with the decision in *Webster v. Reproductive Services*.

Hull, N. E. H., Williamjames Hoffer, and Peter Charles Hoffer, eds. *Abortion Rights Controversy in America: A Legal Reader*. Chapel Hill: University of North Carolina Press, 2004.
  Assembled by three law professors, this book collects primary source documents about the abortion debate beginning in the 19th century, including legal briefs, speeches, oral arguments, court opinions, and newspaper articles. Each item has an introduction that places it in a historical context. One item of special interest is an excerpt from a conference among Supreme Court justices in which they discuss their views before deciding the *Roe v. Wade* and *Doe v. Bolton* cases. This book is designed for instructors and students who are exploring the abortion issue.

Levine, Phillip B. *Sex and Consequences: Abortion, Public Policy, and the Economics of Fertility*. Princeton, NJ: Princeton University Press, 2004.
  Levine wants to step away from what he terms the "ideological extremes" provoked by abortion and bring in the cool rationality of economic modeling. His model predicts that when abortion is initially legalized, the rate of abortions will increase, and the rate of both unwanted births and fertility will decline. However, as access expands, the costs of abortion decrease, contraceptive use declines, and

more pregnancies result. Finally, when there are limited restrictions on access to legal abortion, such as administrative hurdles and limits on Medicaid funding, there will be a reduction in abortion demand, thus decreasing the number of abortions without increasing the number of births. People will increase their use of contraceptives when abortion is more costly.

Luker, Kristin. *Abortion and the Politics of Motherhood.* Berkeley: University of California Press, 1984.

By the 1980s, the conflict over the abortion issue had arrived at its fully polarized form between the pro-life and pro-choice movements. Luker's classic study of the abortion issue places this debate in a historical context, following the formation of the issue from the early 19th century to the early 1980s. The descriptions of her interviews with pro-choice and pro-life activists capture the early days of both movements and provide valuable insights into the perspectives, worldviews, and motivations of the people on both sides.

Maxwell, Carol J. *Pro-Life Activists in America: Meaning, Motive, and Direct Action.* Cambridge, England: Cambridge University Press, 2002.

This book is another example of ethnographic studies of abortion activism, in this case the pro-life supporters who engaged in direct action at clinics. Maxwell interviewed many of them to search for the motives for their activism. She found more diversity than might be expected, and the book details the profound impact their activism had on their lives. This study covers the campaigns in the 1990s.

McDonagh, Eileen L. *Breaking the Abortion Deadlock: From Choice to Consent.* Oxford: Oxford University Press, 1996.

In the early 1990s, McDonagh began a campaign to reframe the rationale for legal abortion in a way that would combine the goals of both sides. She argued that advocates for legal abortion should accept the pro-life claim of equal personhood of the fetus. Then, she reasoned that law would support the right of a woman to consent to accept the embryo in her body for gestation and birth and, at the same time, the right to withdraw that consent through terminating the pregnancy. The legal principle is that no person can live off the body of another without her consent. In this book McDonagh elaborates her provocative argument.

Mohr, James C. *Abortion in America: The Origins and Evolution of National Policy, 1800–1900.* Oxford: Oxford University Press, 1978.

Probably the first detailed history of the politics and culture of abortion criminalization in the 19th century, Mohr's book is an essential source used by all who study the abortion issue in the United States. It is a very interesting read, and the book includes some wonderful photographs of abortion ads of the period and newspaper stories of government enforcement of laws.

Morgen, Sandra. *Into Our Own Hands: The Women's Health Movement in the United States, 1969–1990.* New Brunswick, NJ: Rutgers University Press, 2002.

The women's health movement developed at the same time as feminists began demanding legal abortion: both efforts challenged male control over women's health. This book describes the origins of the movement and follows its development, focusing especially on the grassroots efforts through clinics and self-help groups. The movement faced many challenges but can look to the increased funding for women's health initiatives at federal and state levels as real victories.

Olasky, Marvin. *Abortion Rites: A Social History.* Wheaton, IL: Crossway Books, 1992.

Journalism professor Olasky explored documentary sources in the Library of Congress to challenge Mohr's view of 19th-century history in *Abortion in America* (1978). Mohr claimed that the mid-century increase in abortions included many white, middle-class, Protestant women and was the stimulus for the campaign to criminalize the procedure. Olasky begins his book by making the case that three groups of women—prostitutes, those who had been seduced and abandoned, and the followers of free love (in other words, women who were not respectable)—were the main clients for abortionists. Overall, Olasky's book is more agreeable to pro-life advocates than Mohr's book.

Press, Eyal. *Absolute Convictions: My Father, a City, and the Conflict That Divided America*. New York: Henry Holt, 2006.
Press is the son of an abortion doctor who practiced in Buffalo, New York, in the 1970s and 1980s. An anti-abortion activist murdered his father's colleague, Barnett Slepian, in 1998, and Press's father was warned he would be next. The author returned to Buffalo to discover the reasons behind such violence and rage and to try to understand the motives of those who had blockaded his father's office for years. The result combines an interesting case study with research on the rise of the evangelical anti-abortion movement.

Reagan, Leslie J. *When Abortion Was a Crime: Women, Medicine, and Law in the United States, 1867–1973*. Berkeley: University of California Press, 1997.
Historian Reagan combines information about the private life of women with problem pregnancies during the period when criminal abortion laws were in place with descriptions of the public campaigns against abortion and for law reform. An important contribution of this book is to open up the period from the 1900s to the 1960s when most thought the abortion issues were completely

dormant. Her book brings to light evidence that the period was anything but silent as far as abortion politics was concerned.

Riddle, John M. *Eve's Herbs: A History of Contraception and Abortion in the West.* Cambridge, MA: Harvard University Press, 1997.

This history of medicine shows that women have used herbs to regulate fertility ever since ancient times. Riddle has done the research to uncover these practices and name the herbs. This ancient knowledge has been passed down to women through the years. However, the Catholic Church forbid these practices after the 15th century and condemned practitioners of these arts as witches. Regular medicine then criminalized the use of these herbs through law. Nevertheless, Riddle argues, these herbs are still available and are still used today around the world.

Saletan, William. *Bearing Right: How the Conservatives Won the Abortion War.* Berkeley: University of California Press, 2003.

This book delves into the process whereby issues are defined and how these definitions affect outcomes. For his example, Saletan focuses on the alliance between pro-choice activists and antigovernment conservatives in the 1990s. The women's rights frame did nothing but lose support for legal abortion, especially in the South. A particular referendum campaign in Arkansas showed how packaging a pro-choice position in terms of opposition to government interference was successful despite a high percentage of pro-life voters. This led to NARAL's "Who Decides?" campaign, which sought to connect with those who did not want government to interfere in private family decisions. Saletan claims that although the pro-choice movement has saved legal abortion, it has lost the most important power: to define the issue in pro-choice women's rights terms.

Staggenborg, Suzanne. *The Pro-Choice Movement: Organization and Activism in the Abortion Conflict.* New York: Oxford University Press, 1991.

> The author uses social movement theory to study the emergence and activism of the pro-choice movement. The author conducted interviews with many activists in the movement in national organizations as well as with those in state and local activities, mostly in Illinois. The research shows the different ways the movement gained access to policy makers. Staggenborg counters the media claims that the pro-choice movement was dormant during the 1980s, yielding the ground to pro-life activists. What was important, she claims, was that when needed, as in response to the *Webster* decision, movement leaders could rally grassroots activists to wage effective campaigns.

Tribe, Laurence H. *Abortion: The Clash of Absolutes.* New York: W.W. Norton, 1990.

> With his title and his book, legal expert Tribe, professor of law at Harvard Law School, gave a cogent name to the nature of the abortion debate in the United States—that it is a battle between beliefs that defy compromise. The book appeared in the wake of the controversy over the *Webster* decision where some justices invited challenges to legal abortion. Using his knowledge of jurisprudence, Tribe considers this divide, beginning with a historical and world context and then delving into the claims about the law coming from both sides. His discussion of rights to privacy and personhood in constitutional law is especially compelling. He concludes that both sides can find common ground in working toward a world of only wanted pregnancies.

Wilson, Joshua C. *The Street Politics of Abortion: Speech, Violence, and America's Culture Wars.* Redwood City, CA: Stanford University Press, 2013.

Building on Munson's earlier research (2009), Wilson digs deeper into to the "direct-action stream" of the pro-life movement, which has engaged in various on-the-ground tactics, including prayer vigils, sidewalk counseling, and at times physical blockades outside abortion clinics. As discussed in other parts of this book, there was an escalation of more confrontational strategies to shut down abortion clinics in the 1980s and 1990s, which led to the passage of the Freedom of Access to Clinics Act. Wilson asserts that the unintended consequence of this victory for the pro-choice movement was a shifting of pro-life efforts from the street to judicial and legislative arenas. Elite activists received battle training from New Christian Right organizations, such as Pat Robertson's American Center for Law and Justice and Jerry Falwell's Liberty University School of Law. Wilson's detailed descriptions of 3 key court cases and analyses of 50 accompanying interviews offer perceptive insights into the legal consciousness of "street-level activists." Ultimately, the pro-choice movement was unable to effectively frame the victory as it came up hard against free-speech rights, whereas the pro-life picketers could vilify the pro-choice movement for deceiving judges and "rescuers" could appeal to God's higher law to defend their "extralegal" attempts to save unborn babies.

A Global Comparative Examination

Ferree, Myra Marx, William Anthony Gamson, Jürgen Gerhards, and Dieter Rucht. *Shaping Abortion Discourse: Democracy and the Public Sphere in Germany and the United States*. Cambridge, England: Cambridge University Press, 2002.

In the late 1990s, the authors conducted a large and complex study to describe, analyze, and compare the public discourse on abortion in the United States and Germany.

They created a database of newspaper articles from the two countries and used content analysis to uncover the form and substance of the debates. This approach also enabled them to compare constitutional and political patterns. They found, among other things, that abortion has historically been a gendered issue in Germany, while it has more likely been framed in medical terms in the United States.

Githens, Marianne, and Dorothy McBride Stetson, eds. *Abortion Politics: Public Policy in Cross-Cultural Perspective.* New York: Routledge, 1996.

This book brings together distinguished scholars of abortion politics in comparative contexts and yields some interesting studies that remain timely. Examples include the "stability of compromise" in Western Europe, the pressures of European Union membership on restrictions in Ireland, and feminist perspectives on abortion and reproductive technologies.

Haussman, Melissa. *Abortion Politics in North America.* Boulder, CO: Lynne Rienner, 2005.

It is unusual to find a study of policy that compares Mexico with the United States and Canada, but the politics surrounding the North American Free Trade Agreement encouraged Haussman to look beneath the surface to find a common framework from which to analyze the differences. There are two similarities: all have federal constitutions, and all face a paradox between the law on the books and the law in practice. In addition, access to abortion services is increasingly limited in all three countries.

McBride Stetson, Dorothy, ed. and contributing author. *Abortion Politics, Women's Movements and the Democratic State: A Comparative Study of State Feminism.* Oxford: Oxford University Press, 2001.

This book is both a collection of case studies of the development of abortion politics in Western Europe and North America and a comparative research project on the influence of women's movements and women's policy agencies on abortion policies. No other work covers the sweep of movement activism and policy outcomes among the Western democracies. The studies reveal the complex paths policy actors have taken to come to similar outcomes, that is, the legalization of abortion in the first weeks of pregnancy. The exception is Ireland, where the dominant culture makes feminists reluctant to campaign on the issue and instead accept the "escape route" to England.

Tatalovich, Raymond. *The Politics of Abortion in the United States and Canada: A Comparative History*. Armonk, NY: M.E. Sharpe, 1997.

Tatalovich has published widely on moral debates in the United States and Canada, but this is his most in-depth analysis of an issue in the two countries. It places the highly divisive American debate in perspective and shows the effects of institutional similarities—federalism—and differences—parliamentarism versus presidentialism—on the abortion policy and its implementation in the two countries.

Further Insights into the Pro-Choice Perspective

Baer, Judith. *Historical and Multicultural Encyclopedia of Women's Reproductive Rights in the United States*. Westport, CT: Greenwood Press, 2002.

Want a book that will provide not only a definition but also an analysis of just about every legal and political term you can imagine pertaining to reproductive issues? Want it from a feminist perspective? Then this is an excellent reference work. From undue burden standard to fetal protection policies to the squeal rule, you'll find it here. Baer recruited a large number of experts to contribute entries, giving the encyclopedia a solid scholarly foundation.

Baird-Windle, Patricia, and Eleanor J. Bader. *Targets of Hatred: Anti-Abortion Terrorism*. New York: Palgrave, 2001.

The goal of this work is to raise the press and the public's awareness that terrorism in the United States is not limited to Timothy McVeigh and the attacks of September 11, 2001. It reads like a documented diary of the threats and violence abortion providers have experienced since the 1960s. Here is a typical entry: "December 28, 1991: Springfield Missouri: A man in a ski mask walked into the Central Health Center for Women and asked to see a doctor. When he was told that the physician had already gone for the day, the man pulled out a sawed-off shotgun and fired it. He seriously wounded the clinic receptionist and the owner of the building. The gunman was not apprehended, and the clinic closed its doors in early 1992. The pair were the first victims of an abortion-related shooting" (p. 167).

Dombrowski, Daniel A., and Robert Deltete. *A Brief, Liberal, Catholic Defense of Abortion*. Urbana: University of Illinois Press, 2000.

The authors review Catholic thought from the time of Augustine and Thomas Aquinas, showing that the current official Catholic view on abortion does not have an ancient history. In fact, neither of these philosophers considered the embryo to be a person. Today's restrictive Catholic doctrine was established only in the 17th century. The authors go on to show that the Catholic Church's view that moral sexual relations occur only for procreation within marriage is too narrow and has devastating negative consequences for people's lives.

Ehrlich, J. Shoshanna. *Who Decides? The Abortion Rights of Teens*. Westport, CT: Praeger, 2006.

> Ehrlich, a professor of gender and women's studies, examines the Supreme Court's struggle to balance teen protection and autonomy in reproductive health matters and the constitutionality of parental involvement laws. This was one of the first books to explore the development of these rules and their effects on the lives of young women. Ehrlich studied the stories of 26 women to reveal the burdens of these laws on their lives and choices.

Feldt, Gloria. *The War on Choice: The Right-Wing Attack on Women's Rights and How to Fight Back*. New York: Bantam Books, 2004.

> In the introduction to this book, Sally Blackmun, the daughter of Justice Harry Blackmun, recalls what life was like at home when her father was making his historic decision in *Roe v. Wade*. The body of the book is faithful to the promises in the title; each chapter describes the status of an area of reproductive policy, with bullet points to make the message easy to understand. Topics include restrictions on abortion, family planning, sex education and abstinence, fetal personhood, right-wing attacks on science, and the fate of legal abortion.

Hadley, Janet. *Abortion: Between Freedom and Necessity*. Philadelphia, PA: Temple University Press, 1996.

> The goal here is to look beneath the abortion wars to see how women's lives are affected. The first chapters look at countries where the debates over legal abortion remain contentious: the United States, Ireland, and Germany. The author then expands her lens to cover prenatal diagnosis and sex selection in India, China, and Britain and the relation of contraception to abortion in Russia, Holland, and Britain. She answers critics who say abortion is

immoral and makes the case that the right to abortion is really about women's rights to reproductive health.

Joffe, Carol. *Doctors of Conscience: The Struggle to Provide Abortion before and after* Roe v. Wade. Boston: Beacon Press, 1995.

> The motivation for this study was to counter the image of those who practiced abortion before it was legalized as "butchers." Joffe set out to interview doctors and others who helped women get abortions and found that the practitioners were largely motivated by their personal experience with the horrible effects of botched abortions. They tried to help women because they believed it was right, despite the risks of arrest and imprisonment. She also found that the stresses on abortion providers were only slightly lessened after abortion became legal because of the continued portrayal of abortion doctors as "baby killers," even by medical colleagues.

Kaplan, Laura. *The Story of Jane: The Legendary Underground Feminist Abortion Services*. New York: Pantheon Books, 1995.

> From 1969 to 1973, a group of Chicago women developed an informal network to help women in need of abortions. At first they handled referrals to willing doctors, but word soon spread and the demand grew. Eventually, despite the law, they learned to perform the procedure themselves. They also provided counseling to women using the service. This is their story as told by one of the members of the network.

Lader, Lawrence. *Abortion*. Boston: Beacon Press, 1966.

> Like its author, this book played an important part in the abortion reform movement. Through his investigative research, Lader revealed the extent to which women sought abortions and doctors performed them, despite the restrictive criminal laws. Even more important was

the evidence of the large number of illegal abortions that threatened women's health. With the study, Lader provided the evidence of the need to reform these laws.

Lader, Lawrence. *Abortion II: Making the Revolution*. Boston: Beacon Press, 1973.

Abortion II is Lader's story of his experience with the abortion reform/repeal movement. It was written in the wake of the *Roe v. Wade* decision, which he saw as a victory for those demanding a radical rejection of both the Catholic Church and the medical bureaucracies. The book did not foresee the backlash against the movement and the rise of the pro-life forces that stopped Lader's "revolution" in its tracks.

Maguire, Daniel C. *Sacred Choices: The Right to Contraception and Abortion in Ten World Religions*. Minneapolis, MN: Fortress Press, 2001.

Maguire, a professor of religious ethics, finds pro-choice sympathies in all of the world's religions alongside the anti-abortion and anti–family planning beliefs. Pro-life Catholics are especially critical of Maguire's work as it challenges the official doctrine and provides support for groups such as Catholics for Choice. His main point is that beliefs in most religions are pluralistic, not absolute, and one does not have to reject one's faith altogether to support the goals of abortion rights.

Mason, Carol. *Killing for Life: The Apocalyptic Narrative of Pro-Life Politics*. Ithaca, NY: Cornell University Press, 2002.

Mason analyzes narratives that arose from the militants in the pro-life movement in the 1990s and into the anthrax scares of 2001. Rather than the fringe ranting of a few dispossessed criminals, the author makes the case that the narrative is the culmination of a 30-year expansion of right-wing thought that claims American moral society is under threat from forces of evil, in fact, following the steps toward Armageddon as predicted in the Bible. The anti-abortion warrior depicted is male, Christian, and white.

Michelman, Kate. *With Liberty and Justice for All: A Life Spent Protecting the Right to Choose.* New York: Hudson Street Press, 2005.

Michelman combines her personal biography with her political activism as long-time president of NARAL Pro-Choice America. It begins with the story of her own abortion back in the pre-*Roe* days, which required the consent of a hospital board of men as well as the husband who had recently abandoned her and her three daughters. She describes her role and her views of the politics of pro-choice campaigns from 1985 to 2004. The book provides a useful record of NARAL's place in the pro-choice movement.

Nelson, Jennifer. *Women of Color and the Reproductive Rights Movement.* New York: New York University Press, 2003.

Nelson's study of the campaign for legal abortion sheds light on the important roles played by women of color beginning in the 1960s. Nelson documents the success of these activists in expanding the campaign from a narrow idea of abortion rights held by women's liberation and other mainstream feminist groups to addressing a broad spectrum of reproductive rights, including sterilization, child care, health care, and poverty.

Page, Cristina. *How the Pro-Choice Movement Saved America: Freedom, Politics, and the War on Sex.* New York: Basic Books, 2006.

Page, a top official with NARAL Pro-Choice America, claims to uncover a covert war by the pro-life movement against sex education, birth control, and, in fact, sexual freedom itself. The effect of its campaign is to increase, not decrease, the number of abortions by making it impossible for women to prevent unplanned pregnancies. Thus, to Page, the abortion wars are not about women's privacy versus the unborn; the war is on sex itself, that is, any sexual behavior that is not within heterosexual marriage and for the purposes of procreation. Her conclusion is that the pro-choice movement is doing the most to reduce abortions.

Petchesky, Rosalind Pollack. *Abortion and Woman's Choice: The State, Sexuality, and Reproductive Freedom*. Boston: Northeastern University Press, 1984.

Socialist feminism was not popular among feminist writers in the 2000s, so Petchesky's analysis of the abortion issue in the early 1980s using a socialist feminist perspective is especially interesting. The success of the pro-life attack on abortion rights prompted her to write the book, in which she defends women's need for safe, legal abortion and develops a theory of social relations and reproduction. Her approach is based on the assumption that historical and cultural conditions shape ideas; the book traces the abortion debate from the 19th century to the 1980s. Her arguments presage subsequent arguments that feminists must claim the moral argument for women's rights.

Schrage, Laurie. *Abortion and Social Responsibility: Depolarizing the Debate*. Oxford: Oxford University Press, 2003.

The solution to the polarization of the abortion debates, according to philosophy professor Schrage, is to reframe the debate to bring in the moral issues and the social conditions that influence women's lives. She lays blame on the frame of debate left by the *Roe v. Wade* court—abortion on demand for the first six months of pregnancy—which inflamed divisions on the issue rather than healed them.

The pro-life side has dominated not only the debate but also the images of the debate, and the author suggests that it is time for feminists to retake this territory. The author includes many illustrations of feminist artwork and makes concrete suggestions, such as limiting the time for non-therapeutic abortions along with removing administrative and funding hurdles.

Silliman, Jael, Marlene Gerber Fried, Loretta Ross, and Elena R. Gutiérrez. *Undivided Rights: Women of Color Organize for Reproductive Justice*. Cambridge, MA: Southend Press, 2004.

Like Nelson's 2003 book, *Undivided Rights* documents the role of women of color in developing what the authors call "reproductive justice." The material is organized according to organizations and their activities, such as the National Black Women's Health Project, and the health organizations for Asian, Native American, and Latina women.

Solinger, Rickie, ed. *Abortion Wars: A Half Century of Struggle, 1950–2000*. Berkeley: University of California Press, 1998.

Solinger has brought together 18 articles that look at parts of the abortion debate. Many of these are written by those who participated in the events, such as the description of *Jane*, the feminist clandestine abortion network, while others are more scholarly works. All examine abortion politics from a feminist perspective.

Further Insights into the Pro-Life Perspective

Baird, Robert M., and Stuart E. Rosenbaum, eds. *The Ethics of Abortion: Pro-Life vs. Pro-Choice*, 3rd ed. Amherst, NY: Prometheus Books, 2001.

Although the title suggests a balanced presentation of views on the abortion debate, the articles in this book are overwhelmingly in support of the pro-life position.

Even the articles by feminists are pro-life. Designed as a textbook, the articles are all reprinted from journals and newspapers. The authors are professors of philosophy at Baylor University, a department that focuses on a pro-life moral philosophy.

Beckwith, F. J. *Defending Life: A Moral and Legal Case against Abortion Choice*. Cambridge, England: Cambridge University Press, 2007.

Beckwith, a professor of law and philosophy, provides pro-life activists with an extensive set of arguments to debunk pro-choice claims that are carefully constructed and nonreligious. He asserts that from the moment of conception that the unborn entity is fully human and that it is prima facie wrong to kill any member of our human community. Divided into three main sections, the book tackles the morality, legality, and politics of abortion, which is followed by a scientific embryological approach and ends in a discussion of the bioethics of cloning and stem cell research.

Dyer, Frederick. *Physicians' Crusade against Abortion*. Sagamore Beach, MA: Science History Publishers, 2005.

In 1996, Dyer published a detailed biography of the life and work of Dr. Horatio Robinson Storer. In this 2005 book he focuses more directly on Storer's role as lead advocate for criminalizing abortion in the 19th century. The book is presented as a challenge to assumptions that the people in the 19th century wanted abortions to be illegal because they were dangerous to women or because doctors wanted to drive "irregulars" who performed them out of business. This book makes the case that the primary reason was the protection and defense of the unborn children. Thus, pro-life advocates today can show that their crusade has strong roots in American history.

Nathanson, Bernard. *Aborting America*. New York: Doubleday, 1979.

In this book, Nathanson, the former clinic director and founder of NARAL, described his rebirth as a Christian and pro-life advocate. He also told his story about his life as an advocate for legal abortion in the 1960s. This book is oft quoted by pro-life activists, especially the author's confession that pro-choice people made up statistics to make their case, in particular claiming that thousands of women died because of backstreet illegal abortions. The danger to women's health of illegal abortion was fundamental to the pro-choice case and, according to this author, it was all based on a lie. Nathanson went on to produce the film *Silent Scream* and to write another book in 1996 on the same theme of his remarkable conversion, *The Hand of God: A Journey from Death to Life by the Abortion Doctor Who Changed His Mind.*

Ramesh, Ponnuru. *The Party of Death: The Democrats, the Media, the Courts, and the Disregard for Human Life*. Washington, DC: Regnery Publishing, 2006.

Ramesh, senior editor of the conservative *National Review* magazine, selected a provocative title for his book describing how the Democratic Party went from being primarily a pro-life party to being a pro-choice party. He warns that abortion was the means by which left-wing radicals took over the party, and now they want to add euthanasia and embryo destruction to their agenda. As a result, rights of humans will apply to a smaller and smaller group, while many of these radicals support animal rights. He names Hillary Rodham Clinton as the most dangerous Democrat in her campaign to bring the "party of death" to the White House.

Reagan, Ronald. *Abortion and the Conscience of the Nation*. Sacramento, CA: New Regency Publishing, 2000.

In this essay, originally published in 1983 to mark the 10th anniversary of *Roe v. Wade*, President Reagan uses this medium to denounce the decision to allow "abortion on demand through nine months of pregnancy" (p. 37) and to call the pro-life faithful to action. He states that the question is not when human life begins but "what is the value of human life?" He uses the language of equality to argue for the rights of the unborn and endorses the human life amendment and human life bill then under discussion in Congress. The introduction is written by Wanda Franz, president of the National Right to Life Committee.

Scheidler, Joseph M. *Closed: 99 Ways to Stop Abortion*, rev. ed. Rockford, IL: Tan Books and Publishers, 1993.
This book is a guide to tactics for the pro-life true believer, that is, the ordinary individual who, convinced that abortion is the same as murder, wants to act to stop every single such "murder." Scheidler, the founder of the Pro-Life Action League, describes 99 nonviolent actions. The first is sidewalk counseling—"a method of saving babies by talking to their parents in front of the abortion clinic" (p. 19). The book describes each action, such as leafleting, getting the story to the press, getting on talk shows, exposing abortionist lies, and filing countercharges for false arrest, along with organization contacts and other resources.

Wagner, Teresa, ed. *Back to the Drawing Board: The Future of the Pro-Life Movement*. South Bend, IN: St. Augustine Press, 2003.
The editor of this book served for years as a lobbyist for the National Right to Life Committee, so she was in a central place to collect a series of essays from pro-life leaders for this book. The purpose is to assess the status of the movement 30 years after *Roe v. Wade*. Included are writings by James Dobson, Congressman Chris Smith

(R-NJ), Phyllis Schlafly, and Paul Weyrich. They and others provide food for thought for the next generation of pro-life leaders.

Nonprint Sources

Documentary

Abort73.com. Laxafamosity Ministries, 2003. www.abort73.com.
   Mike Spielman and his group have established the website and the video that is available there to make a case against abortion. Although they have fundamentalist principles, they base their case on secular evidence, not religious belief. That evidence consists of graphic photos of aborted fetuses from 7 to 24 weeks. Spielman and his group say that millions of children are dying by a brutal act of violence and invite viewers to look at the video. They also warn of the graphic nature of the pictures.

Abortion: Stories Women Tell. HBO Documentary Films, 2016. www.storieswomentell.com.
   At the one remaining abortion clinic in Missouri, women seeking abortion must wait 72 hours. Many drive across the border to Illinois to the Hope Clinic, where they may encounter compassionate pro-life activists or protestors who hurl insults like "You have blood on your hands, you will answer to almighty God." Deeply personal accounts from women demonstrate the complexity of circumstances—poverty, domestic violence, fetal abnormalities—that informed the careful decision to terminate, but it is often not without a mix of emotions, like shame and heartbreak. The overarching message is that both sides are doing what they believe is right. A short list of post-viewing questions can be found in the screening guide.

Abortion Denied: Shattering Young Women's Lives. Feminist Majority Foundation, 1990. www.feminist.org.

> Feminist Majority founder Eleanor Smeal cowrote this video, which aims to show that parental consent and notification laws discourage teens from getting help when they are pregnant. It tells the story of Becky Bell and her parents; Bell had been so reluctant to tell her parents she was pregnant that she fled to another state for an illegal abortion and died as a result. This video was shown on TV in 1990 and is available today primarily in libraries.

After Tiller. PBS, 2013. www.aftertillermovie.com/.

> After the assignation of Dr. George Tiller in Kansas in 2009, there were only four known providers of third-trimester abortions in the United States. This Emmy-winning documentary introduces us to the external and internal struggles of Dr. LeRoy Carhart, Dr. Warren Hern, Dr. Susan Robinson, and Dr. Shelley Sella, who put their lives on the line every day. Tiller was their friend and mentor, and his absence is profound. Intimate scenes with patients are as somber as they are complex. We see a caring medical professional sitting with parents as unseen faces, while they make a gut-wrenching decision to end a wanted pregnancy that will result in, at best, a brief, painful life for their baby. An excellent 24-page viewing guide is explicit about the filmmakers' goals which are more humanistic than political, and it promotes even deeper empathy through nonjudgmental perspective taking.

Birthright: A War Story. Abramaorama, 2017. www.birthright film.com/.

> This gripping documentary calls attention to the women who have become "collateral damage" in the abortion war. State control, surveillance, and punishment of pregnant women is identified by experts and poignantly described by six women who suffered nightmarish experiences.

Danielle Deaver, for example, was forced to continue a nonviable pregnancy as a consequence of Nebraska's 20-week ban on abortion. In many states, drug-addicted pregnant women are being jailed for "child abuse." Brief interviews with pro-life movement leaders, who, at times, make dubious claims, are interspersed to show the conviction and strategic agility. On the street, interviews with young people who appear to not be fully informed are intended to convey the urgency of opening the public's eyes to the assaults on women's bodily integrity. Some have critiqued the film for its emphasis on shocking cases over the thousands of stories of diverse women who face restricted access to abortion every day.

Lake of Fire. ThinkFilm, 2006. www.vimeo.com/15753150.
This sweeping two-and-a-half-hour exposé took 17 years to complete. The film is strikingly shot in black and white, meant to evoke the shades of gray that belie the deep divide over abortion, and it is accompanied by a sometimes-chilling musical score. The panoply of activists is painstakingly balanced. We hear from Randall Terry and Flip Benham from the pro-life camp and learn more about what drove Michael F. Griffin and Paul Hill to murder abortion providers. The title references what one fervent pro-life activist believes is awaiting those who murder babies in hell. On the pro-choice side, there are interviews with Kate Michelman and Frances Kissling. Sociologist Dallas Blanchard and philosopher Peter Singer add additional nuances to our understanding of the debate. Not for the faint at heart, as the documentary includes graphic still images of Gerri Santoro, whose lifeless body is splayed on a motel room floor after a botched illegal abortion in 1964, and moving footage of a postabortion cataloguing of easily recognizable fetal parts.

The Last Abortion Clinic. Public Broadcasting System, 2005. www.pbs.org.

In the summer of 2005, documentary filmmakers spent several months in southern states examining the pro-life/pro-choice debate. They found that since the ruling in *Planned Parenthood v. Casey* (505 U.S. 833), pro-life activists have taken advantage of the "undue burden" standard to press state legislatures to pass restrictions. They have been quite successful in the South, especially in Mississippi, which has enacted 10 laws since 1992: fetal homicide prosecution, new clinic regulations, requirements to report abortion complications, rights of conscience, and a law that would prohibit the state's last abortion clinic from offering abortions beyond the first trimester. The effect is that abortion is legal but very difficult and expensive to get. This video is available for viewing on the PBS website.

The Silent Scream. American Portrait Films, 1984. www.silent scream.org/.

This controversial video has been very important for the pro-life movement. In it, Dr. Bernard Nathanson narrates scenes portraying an abortion on an 11-week-old fetus, as seen on an ultrasound screen. The makers of the film claim that it demonstrates, unequivocally, the humanity of the fetus. Pro-choice activists charge that it is the Nathanson pro-life narration, not the images, that persuades the viewers they have witnessed an abortion where the fetus fights back. Available at www.silentscream.org/.

Trapped. PBS, 2016. www.trappeddocumentary.com/.

"This Clinic Stays Open" has become a powerful rallying cry in response to the dramatic increase in Targeted Regulations of Abortion Providers. The film forcefully contends that the purpose of TRAP laws is not truly aimed at improving women's health, but it is a stealthy campaign to chip away at women's constitutional right to abortion. Flurries of news headlines, including Wendy Davis's courageous stand, heighten the viewer's awareness of the contentious political climate, while clinic workers' front-line accounts testify to frightening implications. The prospect of returning to the days of dangerous self-induced abortions is very real when a caller asks, "What if I tell you what I have in my kitchen cabinet and you tell me what I can do?"

Unborn in the U.S.A.: Inside the War on Abortion. First Run Features, 2007. www.firstrunfeatures.com/unbornintheusadvd.html.

Emerging from a student film project, this documentary offers a fascinating and expansive look inside the pro-life movement. While some extremists who advocate violence against abortion providers are included, most of the 70 activists interviewed are depicted as committed, rational, and effective strategists. Their tools for social change range from folk art sculptures of fetal development to the use of sonograms at crisis pregnancy clinics to postabortive women sharing their stories of pain and regret. In a behind-the-scenes look at Justice for All's training sessions, we see young activists thoughtfully weighing the morality and impact of using pictures of aborted fetuses. Viewers may be particularly disturbed by the discussion of Monica Miller, who, in the mid-1980s, retrieved aborted fetuses discarded in a dumpster at a Chicago abortion clinic.

Vessel. Sovereignty Productions, 2014. www.vesselthefilm.com/.

Every 10 minutes a woman dies as a consequence of restrictive abortion laws. This alarming crisis inspired Dutch physician Dr. Rebecca Gompers to found *Women on Waves*. She sets sail to provide medical abortions off-shore from countries where women do not have access to safe, legal abortion. With dramatic footage, this documentary chronicles and celebrates her journey, which includes facing protestors in Morocco and a naval blockade by the Portuguese government.

When Abortion Was Illegal: Untold Stories. Concentric Media, 1992. www.concentric.org/projects/when.html.

> Before *Roe v. Wade* legalized abortion, there was an aura of shame around anyone having anything to do with the procedure. Women, especially, were afraid to speak about their experiences and their hardships. This award-winning documentary provides an oral history of an unknown era. Women, many for the first time, talk about their experiences. There is also testimony from doctors, heath care workers, family, and friends.

Feature Films

Can I Live? Cannon, Nick, 2005. www.nickcannon.com.

> In this music video, rap singer Nick Cannon's song tells the story of his mother's decision not to have an abortion when she was pregnant with him, at age 17. The music video portrays Cannon trying to persuade his mother not to have the abortion, as she comes to an abortion clinic in 1979. After the ultrasound shows her unborn child, Cannon's mother leaves the clinic and decides to have her baby. At the end of the song, Cannon thanks his mother for letting him live.

Cider House Rules. Miramax Home Entertainment, 1999.

> This movie is based on the novel by John Irving. It tells the story of a young man raised in an orphanage in the backwoods of Maine. His surrogate father is the chief doctor who performs abortions illegally on pregnant women in distress and passes on his knowledge to his protégé. He believes he is doing the Lord's work by helping desperate young women. However, his "son" believes it is immoral. When he glimpses another, more prosperous life, he leaves the orphanage but is called upon to perform an abortion himself. Eventually he returns to the orphanage as director.

If These Walls Could Talk. Home Box Office, 1996. www
.youtube.com/watch?v=PzfHXyk9TT0

Using the stories of three women—in 1952, 1974, and
1996—this film strongly portrays the complex interplay
between the realities of women with unintended pregnancies and the social and legal environments that constrain
them. The first episode shows the frustration and moral
condemnation of a widow and the danger of clandestine
abortion. In the third story, the woman's confusion grows
in the context of threatening pro-life blockades at legal
clinics. Only in the second does the woman face a choice
that she could exercise without violence, although the
effects of that choice on her family and her own life are
very serious. The video is streamable on YouTube.

A Private Matter. HBO Productions, 1992. www.youtube
.com/watch?v=OHDqCRzGqg4

Based on the true story of Sherri Finkbine, this film portrays the media frenzy that followed the Romper Room
host as she sought an abortion in 1962. Sissy Spacek stars
as Sherri with Aidan Quinn as her husband. The two
face the uproar that followed their realization that their
fourth child would likely be horribly deformed by thalidomide. The story traces the Finkbines' ordeal all the
way to Sweden where the abortion was finally performed
after being denied in U.S. hospitals. The video is streamable on YouTube.

Vera Drake. New Homeline Video, 2005.

British actress Imelda Staunton was nominated for an
Academy Award for her role in this film by Mike Leigh.
Vera Drake is a middle-aged cleaning lady in 1950s' London. She devotes herself to her family and visits shut-ins
and invalids. She also readily helps young women with
unwanted pregnancies by performing abortions despite
strict criminal laws. The film evokes a way of life, a wife

and mother, a family, and the destruction that ensues when the police show up.

Internet Sources

Centers for Disease Control and Prevention. Abortion Surveillance Report. www.cdc.gov/mmwr/.
> This federal agency collects data on abortion rates and characteristics of women who get abortions from health departments in the states. It publishes a surveillance report on the website of the *Morbidity and Mortality Weekly Report.* Because some states do not report and others may not have accurate data, the Centers for Disease Control and Prevention data should be compared with Guttmacher reports.

Findlaw for Legal Professionals. www.findlaw.com/casecode/.com.
> Although it takes a little practice, most readers will be able to use this website to find and download cases decided by the Supreme Court as well as the circuit courts. There are also links to the U.S. Code, the Code of Federal Regulations, and laws for every state.

Guttmacher Institute. www.guttmacher.org.
> This is the premier source for data on practices relating to sexual and reproductive health matters, including abortion, birth control, HIV/AIDS, and pregnancy in the United States and internationally. The institute staff collects and makes available to the public statistics as well as information on laws in all the states and in other countries. The data center allows users to make tables from Guttmacher Institute data. In addition, articles from the institute's two peer-reviewed journals, *Perspectives on Sexual and Reproductive Health* and *International Perspectives on Sexual and Reproductive Health*, can be downloaded.

Human Life Review. www.humanlifereview.com/.
> For those interested in scholarly writing from a pro-life perspective, this journal makes its articles available online.

The journal's primary concern is abortion, but it also publishes articles dealing with family, moral relativism and its effects, and "what the 'abortion mentality' has done to our culture."

Kaiser Family Foundation. www.kff.org.

Kaiser Family Foundation provides up-to-date information on health policy and politics. One of the topics it monitors is women's health policy, where there are news stories on such matters as abortion rights, pregnancy, and child birth in the states, nationally, and in other countries. This is a very useful source for keeping up with the latest information on the topic of reproductive health.

Sex Respect. www.sexrespect.com/.

This website offers materials and advice written from a Catholic perspective to help parents and teachers offer abstinence-only sex education for teens. An entire curriculum and videos and other materials are available. Guidebooks and manuals are available for teachers, parents, and students as well as "I'm worth waiting for" stickers. The program was developed by author, speaker, and radio personality Coleen Kelly Mast. According to the website, "The curriculum defines what is human about 'human' sexuality, recognizes influences on sexual decision making, identifies emotional, psychological, and physical consequences of teenage sexual activity."

The events in this chronology impart an impression of the origins, development, and outcomes of policy debates in three eras: the 19th century, which led to criminalization of abortion in the United States and other countries; the movement for reform of those criminal abortion policies in the first 70 years of the 20th century; and the contemporary pro-choice versus pro-life standoff since 1973.

1821   The Connecticut legislature passes the first abortion statute in the United States, which makes performing abortion by poison after quickening (first fetal movement) a crime. Missouri (1825) and Illinois (1827) pass similar statutes, beginning the process of criminalization.

1828   The New York State legislature passes a law that makes performing abortion by any means after quickening a crime.

1830   The decade that follows shows a noticeable increase in the number and rate of abortions, especially among middle-class married women.

Clinic escorts stand guard against the anticipated onslaught of pro-life protestors outside the EMW Women's Surgical Center in Louisville, Kentucky, on July 17, 2017. To protect women's access to the state's last remaining abortion clinic, which had been aggressively blockaded in May, U.S. district court judge David Hale declared a protective "buffer zone." Though Operation Save America, led by Director Rusty Thomas, challenged the restraining order in court as an infringement on the group's free speech rights, pro-life activists agreed to abide by it. (AP Photo/Dylan Lovan)

1840   New abortion statutes spread among the states until by this date 10 of the 26 states have some restrictions.

1845   J. Marion Sims, a gynecologist in New York, develops the modern speculum for vaginal medical examinations. His medical accomplishments are later marred by revelations that he experimented on slave women without anesthesia.

1847   The American Medical Association (AMA) forms and, from the outset, stands in opposition to abortion, thereby establishing professional distance from the competitor midwives it characterized as dangerous and immoral.

1857   Dr. Horatio Storer, an obstetrician/gynecologist, urges medical doctors to establish a committee to investigate abortion practices and use their connections with politicians to make abortion illegal.

1859   The AMA declares that abortion at any stage of pregnancy kills a human being and resolves to campaign to criminalize abortion in all states.

1869   Pope Pius IX officially puts the Roman Catholic Church in opposition to contraception and abortion in the papal bull (constitutional proclamation) *Apostolicae Sedis Moderationi*.

1870s   Dilation and curettage, or D&C, is developed as a method of early abortions, first in Germany and later in the United States.

1873   Congress enacts the Comstock Act, which makes it a federal crime to import or sell obscene materials, including information about and devices for contraception and abortion, through interstate commerce.

1884   Pope Pius IX declares that an embryo has a soul from conception and that abortion for any reason, even to save the mother's life, is against Roman Catholic Church doctrine.

1900   At this time all states have criminalized abortion throughout pregnancy; some statutes permit exceptions only to save the life of the mother, and some hold the woman as well as the abortionist liable for prosecution.

1915 The surgical procedures Joseph Lister developed in the 1860s finally come into common practice in both the operating room and the delivery room, reducing mortality in both abortion and childbirth.

1916 Margaret Sanger opens the first birth control clinic in the United States. Within a few years she is jailed for violating the Comstock Act.

1921 The American Birth Control League (ABCL) forms after the reorganization of its parent organization, the National Birth Control League, which had been established in 1916. The ambitious agenda of founder and president Margaret Sanger included dissemination of birth control information, lobbying for legislative reform, and research.

1928 Sanger resigns from the ABCL and shifts her energies to the Clinical Research Bureau, the first legal birth control clinic in the United States, which had opened in 1923.

1931 The economic hardships of the Great Depression coincide with an upsurge in abortions. A study shows that 14 percent of maternal deaths are caused by unsafe illegal abortion procedures.

1936 A study by Frederick J. Taussig shows that the illegal abortion rate in the United States has skyrocketed to 500,000 per year.

A federal circuit court's decision in *U.S. v. One Package of Japanese Pessaries* (86 F.2d) rules that the Comstock Act does not prevent the import and distribution of contraceptives and abortion devices for physicians to use in their medical practice. Unless state laws prevent it, contraceptives such as diaphragms are now available with doctors.

1937 The AMA recognizes birth control as integral to medical practice.

1939 The renamed Birth Control Clinical Research Bureau merges with ABCL to form the Birth Control Federation of America.

1942   Dr. Alan Guttmacher calls for extensive liberalization of criminal abortion laws at the New York meeting of the Birth Control Federation of America. At the same meeting, the members vote to change the organization's name to Planned Parenthood Federation of America.

1944   American Society for Reproductive Medicine is founded to advance the science and practice of reproductive medicine.

1950s   To better regulate the practice of legal abortions in response to policy crackdowns and publicity, many hospitals create "therapeutic abortion" committees that must approve the procedures before doctors can perform them.

1953   Alfred Kinsey's controversial *Sexual Behavior in the Human Female* appears. He reports that 22 percent of married women have had an abortion and that 90 percent of pregnancies outside marriage end in abortion.

1955   Planned Parenthood sponsors the first high-profile national conference, "Abortion in America," led by its medical director Mary Calderone. The conference report, published in 1958, includes estimates that somewhere between 200,000 and 1,200,000 illegal abortions were being performed each year.

1956   The Motion Picture Production Code dictated that abortions be discouraged, be condemned, and never be shown explicitly or treated lightly, and that the word "abortion" should not be used.

1957   British physician Dr. Ian Donald develops technological applications for using ultrasound to view a developing fetus during pregnancy. It becomes widely available during the 1970s.

1959   The American Law Institute (ALI) drafts a model abortion reform statute that would allow doctors to perform abortions for "indications" such as the physical or mental health of the mother, if the fetus is deformed, or if the pregnancy was the result of rape or incest.

In his book *Babies by Choice or Chance*, Dr. Alan Guttmacher calls for more liberal abortion laws across the country.

1960   The U.S. Food and Drug Administration (FDA) approves the use of the hormone pill to prevent conception.

Dr. Alan Guttmacher and other physicians in New York form the Association for the Study of Abortion, one of the first organizations promoting reform of criminal abortion laws.

1962   Pat Maginnis of California forms the feminist Citizens' Committee for Humane Abortion Laws, which seeks to repeal criminal abortion laws.

Sherri Finkbine takes prescribed thalidomide during her pregnancy. On learning of the eminent risks, she fears serious birth defects. After going public about her situation to warn others, her previously arranged abortion was denied, and so Finkbine travels to Sweden to obtain a legal abortion. This marks the beginning of major public debate on abortion law reform.

1963   The U.S. government establishes the National Institute of Child Health and Human Development. Part of its mandate is to support and oversee research in reproductive science and contraceptive development.

1964   A rubella epidemic breaks out in the United States. Women without means are prevented by restrictive laws from securing abortions, and thousands of children are born with birth defects, intensifying the calls for legalization.

Bill Baird opens a birth control clinic on Long Island and becomes one of the first abortion referral services in the country.

1965   The Supreme Court issues its (7–2) ruling in *Griswold v. Connecticut* (381 U.S. 479) that the Constitution creates a zone of privacy where government may not intrude that includes decisions by married couples about whether and when to have a child. Therefore, states may not prohibit married couples from access to contraceptive information and services.

CBS Reports broadcasts "Turning Points in the Debate on Abortion and Birth Control," which includes interviews with clergy, doctors, lawyers, and population control advocates.

The New York Times endorses abortion law reform in an editorial.

1966 The National Organization for Women (NOW) forms as the first civil rights organization for women. Although its Statement of Purpose does not explicitly mention abortion rights, it calls for action to address the conditions that "prevent women from enjoying the equality of opportunity and freedom of choice which is their right."

Lawrence Lader's book *Abortion* is published; it details the extent of both legal and illegal abortion in the United States and the effects on women.

1967 The vacuum aspiration technique for performing abortions in the first weeks of pregnancy, first used in China in 1958, is presented to U.S. physicians in the journal *Obstetrics and Gynecology*. It quickly becomes the preferred method for first-trimester abortions, replacing the D&C.

At its second annual convention, NOW calls for the repeal of criminal abortion laws.

The AMA endorses the ALI model reform statute.

Colorado becomes the first state to pass the ALI model reform statute, followed by North Carolina and California.

The Virginia Society for Human Life forms, becoming the first state pro-life organization; others are subsequently formed in Minnesota, Colorado, and Illinois.

National Conference of Catholic Bishops selects James McHugh, then a priest, later a bishop, to guide the National Right to Life Committee (NRLC), which becomes a national coordinating organization in 1971.

1968 The American College of Obstetricians and Gynecologists endorses the ALI model reform statute.

The American Public Health Association becomes the first professional organization to support repeal of criminal abortion laws.

Pope Paul VI issues *Humanae Vitae* (Human Life), a papal encyclical that reaffirms the opposition of the Roman Catholic Church to contraception and abortion.

The American Civil Liberties Union calls for repeal of all criminal abortion laws, saying they obstruct women's reproductive rights and freedoms.

The Alan Guttmacher Institute is founded to conduct research and develop policies that advance sexual and reproductive health.

1969 The First National Conference on Abortion Laws convenes in Chicago. Lawrence Lader and Lonny Myers take this opportunity to form the National Association for the Repeal of Abortion Laws (NARAL).

Jane, the abortion counseling service of women's liberation, provides abortions outside the law and does so safely for 12,000 women in Chicago.

Redstockings holds an Abortion Speakout with the first public testimonies about women's experiences with dangerous back-alley abortions and forced adoptions.

Attorneys Sarah Weddington and Linda Coffee ask Norma McCorvey to be the plaintiff Jane Roe in a case challenging the constitutionality of the 19th-century criminal abortion statute in Texas.

The Centers for Disease Control and Prevention begins its annual Abortion Surveillance report of the number of legal abortions and the characteristics of the women who obtain them.

1970 The Hawaiian legislature repeals its criminal abortion statute, becoming the first state to legalize all abortions in the first 20 weeks of pregnancy. New York repeals its abortion law and permits abortion up to 24 weeks of pregnancy, followed by Alaska. The state of Washington repeals its law through a referendum.

Congress enacts the Family Planning Services and Population Research Act, which authorizes grants to organizations and public clinics for family planning.

The AMA extends support to doctors who perform abortions for social and economic conditions of women with problem pregnancies.

Americans United for Life is founded to pursue laws and litigation that would advance pro-life goals.

1971   A national poll shows that a majority of Americans support liberalization of abortion laws.

Congress repeals most of the provisions of the 1873 Comstock Act.

Dr. Jane Hodgson, OB/GYN and abortion rights advocate, performs an in-hospital abortion as a test case to challenge the Minnesota law. Her conviction and 30-day jail sentence is suspended on appeal and overturned after *Roe v. Wade*.

1972   By this year, 14 states have passed abortion reform statutes modeled after the ALI conditional reform.

The American Bar Association goes on record in favor of legal abortion through the 20th week of pregnancy.

Governor Nelson Rockefeller of New York vetoes the state legislature's effort to rescind the 1970 abortion law that repealed criminal abortion.

The Report of the Commission on Population Growth and the American Future calls for liberalizing abortion laws and providing federal support for family planning.

In *Eisenstadt v. Baird* (405 U.S. 438), the Supreme Court rules (6–1) that individuals have a right to privacy in contraception regardless of marital status, which legalizes contraception completely.

On CBS's *Maude*, the title character wrestles with her decision and ultimately terminates her unexpected pregnancy.

Such frank, realistic depictions continue to be rare on television and film.

1973   On its now-historic anniversary date, January 22, The Supreme Court rules (7–2) that states may not prohibit abortion before the third trimester in *Roe v. Wade* (410 U.S. 959). The decision between a woman and her doctor regarding abortion is determined to be in the zone of privacy.

In a significant but overshadowed ruling, *Doe v. Bolton* (410 U.S. 179), the Court determined that cumbersome restrictions on abortion access violate the rights of women to health care and of physicians to practice.

Senator James Buckley (R-NY) and six senators introduce the first constitutional amendment to supersede *Roe v. Wade*.

Referendums to permit abortion without condition up to 20 weeks of pregnancy fail by large margins in Michigan and South Dakota, a setback for the repeal advocates.

The NRLC is formally incorporated with the express purpose of overturning the *Roe v. Wade* decision. The NRLC holds the first national right-to-life convention.

The Religious Coalition for Abortion Rights and Catholics for a Free Choice are founded to support the right to family planning and abortion.

In response to fierce *Roe* opposition, NARAL reorganizes with a new name, The National Abortion Rights Action League.

1974   The ACLU launches its Reproductive Freedom Project.

Pro-life activists organize the March for Life in Washington, D.C., on the anniversary of *Roe v. Wade*, which becomes an annual event.

Senator Bob Dole (R-KS) wins reelection against opponent William Roy, a congressional representative and a doctor who performed abortions. This tight and acrimonious race is notable for how the abortion issue became pivotal and for how it demonstrated the pro-life movement's political force.

1975   The Subcommittee on Constitutional Amendments of the Senate Judiciary Committee holds extensive hearings on human life amendments that would reverse *Roe v. Wade*. The committee votes not to report any of the amendments to the full committee.

The National Women's Health Network forms to promote empowerment of women in relation to reproductive health.

Lawrence Lader leaves NARAL and forms the more radical Abortion Rights Mobilization.

1976   The Republican Party platform recognizes that there is an ongoing debate on abortion but supports a Human Life Amendment.

The Supreme Court rules (6–3) that administrative regulations, including a requirement for spousal consent, unconstitutionally limit women's privacy in making decisions about abortion in *Planned Parenthood of Central Missouri v. Danforth* (428 U.S. 552).

Congress attaches the Hyde Amendment to a health appropriations bill; this outlaws Medicaid funding for abortions except in cases of rape, incest, or endangerment of the woman's life. It has been renewed annually by Congress for over 40 years.

1977   The Supreme Court rules that the state governments' denial of Medicaid funds for abortions is legal and constitutional in *Beal v. Doe* (432 U.S. 454) and *Maher v. Roe* (432 U.S. 464).

In *Carey v. Population Services International* (431 U.S. 678), the Supreme Court holds (7–2) that prohibitions on contraceptive advertisements and sales for minors are unconstitutional.

The National Abortion Federation is established as a professional organization to set standards, increase access, and provide support to abortion providers.

1979   In *Bellotti v. Baird* (433 U.S. 622), the Supreme Court rules (8–1) that states may require minors to obtain parental consent to get an abortion as long as there is an alternative judicial procedure if consent is denied or the minor does not want to seek parental consent.

The Supreme Court rules (6–3) that states must set precise standards for determining the viability of fetuses for statutes prohibiting third-trimester abortions in *Colautti v. Franklin* (439 U.S. 379).

The American Life League is founded with an uncompromising belief that human life is sacred from conception to natural death without exception.

1980 The Republican Party platform once again endorses a Human Life Amendment and advocates that anti-abortion justices be appointed at all levels.

The Supreme Court rules (5–4) that the federal government may deny Medicaid funds for abortions in *Harris v. McRae* (448 U.S. 297).

Joe Scheidler forms the Pro-Life Action League, an organization devoted to direct action against abortion clinics and other providers. In 1985 he writes a manual for activists: *Closed: 99 Ways to Stop Abortion*.

1981 Ronald Reagan, the first president to adopt the pro-life position on abortion, takes office. His right-to-life essay "Abortion and the Conscience of the Nation" appears in 1983.

The Adolescent Family Life Act (AFLA) requires active involvement of religious groups in family planning and mandates adoption over abortion and abstinence over contraceptive education.

The U.S. Department of Health and Human Services issues regulations prohibiting family planning clinics supported by federal Title X funds from providing any information about abortion.

The Senate Judiciary Committee holds hearings on the Helms Bill to prohibit abortion and on a Human Life Amendment. Although the committee recommends both be enacted, Senator Robert Packwood (R-OR) successfully filibusters until they are withdrawn.

1983 The Human Life Amendment, which becomes the standard term for hundreds of proposals that would have the effect of overturning *Roe v. Wade*, reaches a formal vote in the Senate. This "Hatch-Eagleton" version of the amendment receives 49 supporting votes, falling 18 short of the 67 required for passage. Most of the subsequent proposals die in committee.

In *City of Akron v. Akron Center for Reproductive Health* (462 U.S. 416), the Supreme Court invalidates (6–3) a city ordinance requiring that abortions be performed in hospitals, with parental and/or informed consent, and after a 24-hour waiting period. The Court rules that these administrative hurdles unduly interfere with women's rights to obtain abortions.

The National Black Women's Health Project, dedicated to informing African American women about all health matters including reproductive health, is founded. It later changes its name to the Black Women's Health Imperative.

1984 Dr. Bernard Nathanson narrates a 30-minute film entitled *The Silent Scream*, purporting to show an ultrasound of a fetus crying out during an abortion. The film is shown around the country by pro-life activists. To debunk their claims, NARAL launches "Abortion Rights, Silent No More" (1985).

At the United Nations (UN) Conference on Population held in Mexico City, the Reagan administration announces that no foreign aid funds will be given to organizations or individuals that provide abortions, counsel abortions, or promote legalization of abortion anywhere in the world. This becomes known as the Mexico City policy or the "Global Gag Rule." In what becomes a ritual, every Democratic president who follows rescinds it and every Republican president reinstates it.

1985 The Reagan administration presents a brief in *Thornburgh v. American College of Obstetricians & Gynecologists* (476

U.S. 747), asking the Supreme Court to overturn *Roe v. Wade*. The Court holds (5–4) that the Pennsylvania "informed consent" requirements "wholly subordinate constitutional privacy interests and concerns with maternal health."

The ban on Department of Defense (DOD) funds to perform abortions, except in cases of life endangerment, is made permanent in FY 1985 DOD authorization bill.

1986   The Supreme Court (5–4) invalidates a Pennsylvania law with administrative regulations in *Thornburgh v. American College of Obstetricians & Gynecologists* (476 U.S. 747); it rejects the request by the Reagan administration to overturn *Roe v. Wade*.

NOW and other feminist organizations organize the first national March for Women's Lives, bringing more than 100,000 advocates of the right to choose to Washington, D.C.

1987   The Senate holds hearings on President Reagan's nomination of Robert Bork to the Supreme Court. Bork is an outspoken critic of the constitutional right to privacy for contraception and abortion. The Senate votes not to confirm the nomination. President Reagan then nominates Anthony Kennedy, who wins confirmation easily.

1988   Operation Rescue, organized by Randall Terry, comes to prominence at the Democratic Convention in Atlanta. In 1991, the group stages weeks-long protests at an abortion clinic in Wichita, Kansas, an event that becomes a template for pro-life direct action against abortion practice.

The Elliot Institute is founded to advance the research of Dr. David Reardon, who claims that abortion harms women physically and psychologically.

In *Bowen v. Kendrick* (487 U.S. 589), the Supreme Court reviews and upholds the AFLA (1981) and its denial of funding to programs that "advocate, promote, or encourage abortion."

U.S. activists seek to bring RU-486, now known as mifepristone, to the United States. It had been approved in France as a nonsurgical alternative to early abortion.

Becky Bell, age 17, dies after obtaining an illegal abortion to evade the parental notification statute. Her case becomes a rallying point for pro-choice activists seeking to limit parental involvement laws.

1989   In a splintered decision, *Webster v. Reproductive Health Services* (492 U.S. 490), the Supreme Court holds (5–4) that none of the challenged provisions of the Missouri legislation—the preamble stating "human life begins at conception," restrictions on state aid and public facilities, and the requirement of fetal viability tests prior to abortion—were unconstitutional. While the Court did not grant the George H. W. Bush administration's request to overturn *Roe v. Wade*, this decision inspired hundreds of restrictive bills across the country.

Republicans for Choice Political Action Committee is founded to fund Republican candidates who support legal abortion and women's privacy.

1990   The Supreme Court rules (6–3) in *Ohio v. Akron Center for Reproductive Health* (497 U.S. 502) and (5–4) in *Hodgson v. State of Minnesota* (497 U.S. 417) that states may require notification of one or both parents before a teenager may have an abortion, as long as she has the option of a judicial bypass.

The Center for Bio-Ethical Reform is founded to "seek prenatal justice" and "awaken the nation to the horrible injustice of abortion."

1991   In *Rust v. Sullivan* (500 U.S. 173), the Supreme Court (5–4) concludes that President George H. W. Bush's "Gag Rule" does not violate the free-speech rights. The result is that the government can prohibit federal funds going to family planning programs from being used to discuss, counsel, give information about, or perform abortions.

1992   In *Planned Parenthood of Southeastern Pennsylvania v. Casey* (505 U.S. 833), the Supreme Court upholds (5–4) the central holding in *Roe v. Wade* that a woman has liberty to choose abortion before the fetus is viable and the state can regulate from conception. The case establishes the undue burden standard that state regulations are acceptable unless, like spousal notification, they constitute an obstacle to woman's exercise of her liberty. The decision allows 24-hour waiting periods, parental notification, and mandated information about gestational age.

Mississippi is the first state to impose a mandatory delay and biased-information requirement.

The Center for Reproductive Rights is founded and later becomes the Center for Reproductive Law and Policy. It focuses on using the law to secure reproductive rights, with particular attention to supporting the rights of adolescents and low-income women.

1993 Immediately after taking office, President Bill Clinton rescinds and reinstates abortions for military personnel in military hospitals.

Congress permits the use of fetal tissue from abortions in National Institutes of Health–funded research under strict regulations.

Dr. David Gunn, a physician who provides abortion in Georgia, Alabama, and Florida, is shot three times when entering a clinic in Pensacola, Florida. The shooter, Michael Griffin, serves a life sentence for the murder.

NARAL changes its name to National Abortion and Reproductive Rights Action League and pledges to work to guarantee all women full reproductive choices, not limited to abortion.

Medical Students for Choice is founded.

National Network of Abortion Funds is founded to remove financial and logistical barriers to abortion access and work toward reproductive justice.

Dr. Abu Hayat is convicted of performing an illegal third-trimester abortion, resulting in the birth of Ana Rosa Rodriguez, and of assault for severing her arm. The pro-life movement identifies Ana and others as "survivors of the abortion war."

1994   In *NOW v. Scheidler* (510 U.S. 249), the Supreme Court unanimously rules that violations do not have to have an economic component to be covered under the federal RICO statute. There are many twists in the case, as noted in entries 1998 and 2006.

Congress enacts the Freedom of Access to Clinic Entrances (FACE) Act, which makes it a federal crime to use physical force to disrupt the business of abortion clinics.

In *Madsen v. Women's Health Center* (512 U.S. 753), an appeal by anti-abortion protesters in Florida, the U.S. Supreme Court upholds as constitutional a buffer zone around health care clinics that is intended to protect access to the clinic.

Dr. John Britton and Lt. Col. Jim Barrett are killed in front of a Pensacola clinic. Two abortion clinic workers, Shannon Lowney and Leanne Nichols, are murdered in Brookline, Massachusetts.

1995   Congress reinstates the ban on abortions in military hospitals.

Norma McCorvey, the anonymous plaintiff in the historic *Roe v. Wade* case, announces her conversion to the pro-life position to a nationwide audience on *Nightline*. She quits her job at an abortion clinic and starts working with Operation Rescue.

1996   President Clinton vetoes the Partial Birth Abortion Ban Act passed by Congress because it fails to include an exception for the mother's health.

The FDA's Reproductive Health Advisory Committee recommends approval of RU-486, mifepristone, for use in nonsurgical abortions in the United States. However, final approval does not happen for four years.

1997   Congress again passes the Partial Birth Abortion Ban Act, and President Clinton vetoes it a second time.

The American Medical Association goes on record as opposing partial-birth abortions.

The Center for Bio-Ethical Reform's Genocide Awareness Project, a gigantic anti-abortion display, is erected on college campuses, with graphic images of aborted fetus juxtaposed with pictures of genocide victims.

1998   In upstate New York, an anti-abortion extremist assassinates abortion doctor Barnett Slepian, who is standing at a window in his house with his family around him. His killer, James Kopp, receives a sentence of 25 years to life in 2003.

The FDA approves the first dedicated product for emergency contraception for use in the United States.

The Department of Defense prohibits service women from using their own money to obtain an abortion at military facilities overseas.

A jury sides with NOW against Operation Rescue, Joe Scheidler, and PLAN, using RICO to award triple damages for the harm their violent acts had done to women's health clinics.

1999   Democrats for Life forms; the mainstream Democratic Party refuses affiliation.

In *Planned Parenthood v. ACLA* (41 F. Supp. 2d 1130), an Oregon circuit court issues a permanent injunction against American Coalition of Life Activists, concluding that the wanted style posters and the Nuremberg Files, which listed the names of abortion providers, called "baby butchers," constituted intentional threats and intimidation under FACE.

2000   The FDA approves the use of mifepristone, the abortion pill.

The Supreme Court invalidates state bans on partial-birth abortions in *Stenberg v. Carhart* (530 U.S. 914) because the statutes are unconstitutionally vague and do not include an exception for a woman's health.

There is no identifiable abortion provider in 87 percent of U.S. counties nor in 97 percent of counties in nonmetropolitan areas.

"Choose Life" license plates appear first in Florida, with funding going to pro-life pregnancy help centers, and are eventually available in 33 states.

2001   Center for Bio-Ethical Reform debuts its "truth trucks," displaying color photographs of aborted fetuses.

More than 250 abortion clinics receive letters containing a powdery substance and the words "You have been exposed to anthrax."

2002   Secretary of Health and Human Services Tommy Thompson issues a regulation making fetuses eligible for health care under the Children's Health Insurance Program. Pro-choice activists claim the action is a way to establish legal personhood for the fetus.

Congress passes and President George W. Bush signs the Born Alive Infants Protection Act (HR-2175), which requires doctors to take all possible steps to save the lives of fetuses that survive abortions.

2003   NARAL becomes NARAL Pro-choice America and pledges to educate citizens and politicians about reproductive rights and to work to elect pro-choice candidates to office.

The state of Florida executes Paul Hill for the 1994 murders of Dr. John Britton and his escort James Barrett outside an abortion clinic in Pensacola, Florida. Connected to the Army of God, Hill claims before his death that he has no remorse for his actions and will meet his reward in heaven.

President George W. Bush signs the federal Partial Birth Abortion Ban Act, which places an absolute prohibition on the intact dilation and extraction procedure with no exceptions. Congress reports its finding that the procedure is never necessary to protect a woman's health. Similar bills were passed in 1996 and 1998 and vetoed by President Clinton.

2004   An estimated 800,000 pro-choice activists organize the March for Women's Lives in Washington, D.C., one of the largest demonstrations in U.S. history.

President George W. Bush signs the Unborn Victims of Violence Act, also called "Laci and Connor's Law," which makes injury to a fetus by an attack on a pregnant woman a separate crime in federal jurisdictions.

2005   The Republican governor of South Dakota, Mike Rounds, signs the Women's Health and Human Life Protection Act, which prohibits abortions except to save the life of the mother. Some pro-life activists hope this will be the challenge that overturns *Roe v. Wade*. Pro-choice activists begin campaigning to rescind the law.

Susan Wood, director of the Office of Women's Health in the FDA, resigns over the FDA's failure to approve over-the-counter sales of emergency contraception. She claims the agency head is motivated by ideology and ignores advice by science committees.

Representative Louise Slaughter (D-NY) and Senator Harry Reid (D-NE) introduce the Prevention First Act in Congress. The act, which was introduced multiple times, dies in 2010; it was intended to promote the use of contraception, reduce the incidence of unintended pregnancies, and improve access to women's health care.

The Supreme Court declines to hear the appeal submitted by one of the original litigants of *Roe v. Wade*, Norma McCorvey, who had hoped to present evidence that abortion harms women.

2006   Voters approve a referendum to rescind the restrictive criminal abortion law in South Dakota.

Congress rejects the Child Custody Protection Act, which would make it a federal crime to accompany a minor across state lines to avoid parental notification requirements.

After news of fatal infections among women taking the abortion pill, pro-life activists promote "Holly's Law," which would suspend the approval. They claim that the FDA approval process was too hasty, and the drug is dangerous to women.

The FDA approves the sale of emergency contraception over the counter (without prescription) to women over 17.

The Supreme Court rules (8–0) again in *Scheidler v. NOW* (547 U.S. 9) that "physical violence unrelated to robbery or extortion falls outside the scope of the Hobbs Act." This overturns the 1994 decision that the NOW could sue for damages under the RICO Act.

In *Ayotte v. Planned Parenthood of Northern New England* (546 U.S. 320), the Supreme Court unanimously rules that New Hampshire's Parental Notification Prior to Abortion Act violates the undue burden test. The Court sustains its precedent that abortion laws must protect a woman's health and safety.

In *Arpaio v. Doe* (07-839), the Supreme Court, without comment, lets the lower court's ruling stand that female inmates have a constitutional right to abortions off jail grounds. The case, supported by the ACLU, involved an Arizona inmate, who was refused transportation to obtain an abortion, as it was not deemed "medically necessary."

President George W. Bush vetoes an act to fund embryonic stem cell research, based on his view that such research kills human beings. On the same day he signs the Fetal Farming Prohibition Act (S.3504), which prohibits use of human fetal tissue from pregnancies deliberately initiated to provide such tissue.

2007 The Democratic Party regains the majority in the House of Representatives and the Senate.

The Supreme Court rules (5–4) that the federal Partial Birth Abortion Ban Act is constitutional in *Gonzales v. Carhart* (550 U.S. 124). This is the first time that the Court has approved abortion restrictions that do not include exceptions for women's health.

2008 Prenatally and Postnatally Diagnosed Conditions Awareness Act (S. 1810) is enacted to increase the provision of scientifically sound information and support services to patients receiving a positive test diagnosis.

Planned Parenthood of Iowa makes it possible for women in rural areas to consult with a doctor who can remotely unlock a container holding the abortion pills. In 2013 the Iowa Board of Medicine votes to eliminate this telemedicine program despite being deemed safe in an independent review. In 2015 the Iowa Supreme Court (6–0) overrules, and the program is reinstated.

2009   After being targeted by anti-abortion extremists for two decades, Dr. George Tiller, one of the few remaining doctors to provide late-term abortions, is shot for the second time and killed at his church in Wichita, Kansas.

More Americans identify as pro-life (51 percent) than pro-choice (42 percent) for the first time, according to a Gallup Poll conducted in May.

2010   President Barack Obama's administration eliminates what had been robust funding streams for abstinence-only-until-marriage programs, including AFLA (1981), but it reappears as part of health care reform, with $50 million mandated to be allocated annually through Title V.

A disturbing claim appears on anti-abortion billboards: "Black children are an endangered species," drawing sharp criticism from reproductive justice organizations like SisterSong.

2011   Voters in Mississippi reject the "personhood amendment," which would have criminalized all forms of abortions without exception.

According to the Alan Guttmacher Institute, the abortion rate drops significantly to pre-*Roe* levels.

On ABC's *Grey's Anatomy*, the ambitious Dr. Christina Yang opts to terminate her pregnancy with a surprising lack of shame for a prime-time television character.

2012   As the battle ensues over the funding of Planned Parenthood, Susan G. Komen for the Cure announces it will cut off funding, only to retract three days later due to public uproar.

A study finds that a woman who carries a baby to term is 14 times more likely to die than a woman who chooses to have a legal abortion.

The Family Research Council urges its members to boycott Girl Scouts cookies due to the organizations' alleged ties with Planned Parenthood.

2013   More than half of the states have instituted Targeted Regulation of Abortion Providers (TRAP). TRAP laws reflect a new and highly effective pro-life strategy; thwarted in their attempts to make abortion illegal, the movement concentrates its efforts on restricting access with waiting periods, mandated ultrasounds, and onerous licensing requirements.

With a historic 11-hour filibuster, Senator Wendy Davis stands up against a bill that would shut down all but five abortion clinics in Texas that could meet the ambulatory surgical center requirements. #StandWithWendy trends worldwide on twitter.

Emergency contraception (a.k.a. the morning after pill, Plan B) is made available over the counter.

The Shaheen Amendment provides servicewomen coverage for abortions if they are victims of sexual assault.

Disreputable abortion provider Dr. Kermit Gosnell is sentenced to life in prison for cutting the spinal cords of babies born alive and involuntary manslaughter for oversedation of Karnamaya Mongar, a refugee. Investigations revealed appalling conditions, improperly trained staff, and botched procedures.

2014   *Obvious Child* becomes a feature film, noted for its matter of fact rather than the typically tragic take on abortion.

Nine states—Alabama, Arizona, Georgia, Idaho, Indiana, Kansas, Louisiana, Nebraska, and North Carolina—have enacted "fetal pain" laws that prohibit abortions at 20 weeks or earlier based on the scientifically contested claim that the fetus has developed pain sensors.

2015   The abortion rate decreases by 12 percent since 2010 according to the Associated Press.

700,000 Google searches reveal a hidden and increased demand for self-induced abortion amid tighter restrictions according to a study by the Guttmacher Institute.

California's Reproductive Freedom, Accountability, Comprehensive Care, and Transparency (FACT) Act requires pregnancy-related centers in the state to be transparent about their services.

The Center for Medical Progress posted an edited, undercover video that purports to show a Planned Parenthood doctor selling organs from aborted fetuses, subjecting the organization to vilification and threats. None of the ensuing investigations find any evidence of wrongdoing. The self-dubbed "citizen journalists" who released the video were charged in 2017 with 15 felony counts of invasion of privacy.

2016   A Zika outbreak is linked with birth defects such as microcephaly, leading some to wonder whether it will, like rubella in the 1960s, lead to an easing of abortion restrictions in southern states and Latin American Catholic countries.

Texas governor Greg Abbott institutes new regulations requiring all fetal remains to be cremated or buried as if they were expired human beings with the costs covered by the medical facilities.

In *Whole Woman's Health v. Hellerstedt* (5–3), the Supreme Court ruled that the provisions of Texas's House Bill 2—hospital admitting privileges and ambulatory surgical center requirements—do not confer medical benefits sufficient to justify the burdens on women exercising their constitutional right to an abortion.

The Obama administration's Department of Health and Human Services issues a final rule to prevent state lawmakers from cutting funding for Planned Parenthood by clarifying that providing abortion services cannot disqualify an organization from receiving funding.

Presidential candidate Donald Trump, formerly a supporter of abortion rights, is harshly rebuked by both sides of the abortion debate for his quickly retracted statement that there would need to be "some form of punishment" for women who have abortions if the procedure were to be criminalized.

Utah passes a "fetal pain" abortion law, requiring that anesthesia, which is more costly and medically risky, be administered to women seeking abortion after 20 weeks.

2017 Five-time Olympic gold medal sprinter Sonya Richards-Ross reveals in her memoir her difficult decision to have an abortion prior to competing in the 2008 Olympics.

Conservative policy makers seek to dismantle Medicaid, which provides 13 million low-income women of reproductive age with coverage for family planning and other reproductive health services.

Vice President Mike Pence casts the tie-breaking vote in the Senate that allows states to deny federal grants to Planned Parenthood.

When asked what would happen if *Roe v. Wade* were ever overturned, President Donald J. Trump said women could "go to another state." West Virginia, Mississippi, North Dakota, South Dakota, and Kentucky have just one remaining abortion provider.

There is tremendous speculation about the current Supreme Court. In their confirmation hearings, the "liberal" justices—Stephen Breyer (1994), Ruth Bader Ginsburg (1993), Sonia Sotomayor (2009), and Elena Kagan (2010)—responded that there is indeed a constitutional right to abortion, whereas the "conservative" justices—Antonin Scalia (1986), Anthony Kennedy (1987), Clarence Thomas (1991), Chief Justice John Roberts (2005), and Samuel Alito (2006)—all professed impartiality or stare decisis, deep respect for the Court's prior decisions. It is too soon to tell whether the appointment of Justice Neil Gorsuch (2017) will deliver on President Donald J. Trump's promises to his conservative base.

Glossary

abortifacient   Any drug or practice that terminates a pregnancy.

abortion reform   A process to make small changes in existing laws, such as expanding the conditions for legal abortions.

abortion repeal   The removal of all government policies regulating abortion; treating abortion like any medical procedure.

case law   All the judicial decisions pertaining to a particular issue under litigation, such as states' power to regulate abortion or birth control.

common law   Also called "judge-made law"; it is the legal system found in England and many of its former colonies, including the United States.

compulsory pregnancy   A term used by feminists to characterize the effect of criminal abortion laws on women's lives.

Comstock Act   The 1873 federal law that outlawed the provision of information about contraception and abortion.

conditional abortion law   A policy that regulates abortion according to the circumstances of pregnancy, such as threats to the life and health of the mother, fetal deformity, or pregnancies resulting from rape or incest; also called an *indications law*.

constitutional law   The provisions of the U.S. Constitution and all judicial interpretations, especially those of the Supreme Court.

diagnosis   That portion of a pro-choice or pro-life collective action frame that defines the reasons a particular situation is a public problem.

frames   Ways of giving meaning to a particular condition, question, or problem; social movements use frames to mobilize followers and achieve public policy goals.

"irregular" physicians   A term used in the 19th century to refer to people who practiced medicine but who had no formal training.

issue frame   The terms of the debate on a public problem used by policy makers in government institutions.

judicial bypass   The provisions in parental involvement laws that allow a judge to grant permission for an abortion to be performed on a minor if informing the parents would cause hardship to the young woman.

litigation strategy   A plan to change policy by bringing challenges to existing laws to courts, urging them to declare the laws unconstitutional or interpret the laws is a particular way.

Medicaid   The government health program for poor families and the destitute that is funded by both the federal and state governments.

menstrual regulation treatments   Seen as an alternative to abortion, this procedure extracts the contents of the uterus before results of pregnancy tests are known.

mifepristone   The drug used in the so-called abortion pill or medical abortion. It involves two doses, one of mifepristone and the other of misoprostol, which bring about miscarriage. In the 1980s, it was called RU-486.

nontherapeutic abortion   Terminating a pregnancy for other than health reasons, such as economic or personal reasons or inability to care for a child.

parental involvement laws   Regulations in states requiring the notification or permission of parents before physicians can perform abortions on minors (usually defined as a girl younger than 18 years).

personhood   The status of individuals under the U.S. Constitution, especially in reference to the rights to due process and equal protection under the Fourteenth Amendment.

policy debate A structured discussion about a public problem that takes place in a public arena, usually centered on a government institution.

postabortion syndrome The pro-life claim that women who have abortions suffer psychological trauma. There is little scientific evidence that this syndrome exists.

precedent Also called stare decisis, it is the practice in U.S. courts to decide current cases the same way previous cases were decided.

privacy, right to The constitutional limit on the government's power to make laws that interfere with an individual's decisions in a particular area of life; has been applied to the individual's decision whether to bear or beget a child.

prognosis That portion of a pro-life or pro-choice movement's collective action frame that sets forth the solution to a problem; in most cases, it refers to what they want government to do about a problem they have described.

quickening The point in a pregnancy where the mother can feel the fetus move; also called *animation*.

"regular" physicians A term used in the 19th century to refer to those practicing medicine who had received some formal training.

strategic frames The definition or diagnosis of a problem and the policy solution or prognosis offered by movement actors in particular policy debates.

therapeutic abortion Terminating a pregnancy for reasons of health of the mother or the fetus.

triad The pattern of relationships among the government, doctors, and women that results from any abortion policy.

undue burden standard States may limit abortion practice up to the point where the regulations constitute an insurmountable obstacle to a woman's liberty to exercise her right to seek abortion.

unintended pregnancy When a woman is pregnant but does not want to be pregnant at that time. It does not imply whether or not the woman wants the baby that results.

vacuum aspiration The preferred technique for surgical abortion in the early stages of pregnancy.

viability The state in the gestation of a fetus when it is able to live outside the mother's uterus either naturally or with artificial assistance.

Index

Note: page numbers followed by the letters "t" and "f" in italics indicate tables and figures, respectively.

Abbott, Greg, 339
ABCL (American Birth Control League), 12, 177, 182, 319. *See also* Planned Parenthood Federation of America (PPFA)
Aborted Women: Silent No More (Reardon), 208
abortifacients, 84, 108, 239, 365
Aborting America (Nathanson), 305
abortion
  access to, 67, 80–81, 90–93
  alternatives to, 208
  commercialization of, 5
  conditional, 19
  constitutional legality of, 41–52
  on demand, 19

  and disability rights, 163–166
  for female inmates, 60, 91, 336
  government support of, 58–65
  as harmful to women, 85
  illegal, 10, 12, 269–270, 319
  as infanticide, 68, 70, 194
  justifiable/unjustifiable, 259–260
  late-term, 22–23, 38, 68, 70–74, 105, 184, 337
  linked to breast cancer, 85, 101, 200, 207, 242–245t, 246
  linked to negative psychological outcomes, 85, 86, 208–209, 242–245t, 246–247, 329

medical vs. surgical,
128–129
medication (medical), 56,
67, 81–83
in military hospitals, 331,
332, 333
for minors, 53–55
moral implications of, 5,
9–10
normalizing, 130–131
partial-birth, 38, 50,
59–60, 68–72, 105,
180, 279–280, 332
and party affiliation, 60
post-abortion experience,
263–264
procedure described, 263
proposed conditions for
legalizing, 14–15
psychological justifications
for, 14, 16
and race, 94, 218–219,
337
re-framing of, 98–99
as right, 262–263
to save the life of the
mother, 6–7, 11, 14, 21,
23, 51, 62, 72, 73, 197,
272–273, 318, 326,
335
self-induced, 4, 10, 13, 54,
92–93, 138, 223–224,
260, 338
sex-selective, 67
as social problem,
264–266

state regulation of,
238–240*t*
on television programs,
325, 337
therapeutic, 13, 13–14,
180, 267–269, 320
before the third trimester,
22–23
the third trimester, 327,
331–332
See also abortion funding;
abortion law; abortion
statistics; abortion
techniques; pregnancy
Abortion (Lader), 178,
299–300
*Abortion: Between Freedom
and Necessity* (Hadley),
298–299
Abortion: Stories Women Tell
(documentary), 307
*Abortion: The Clash of
Absolutes* (Tribe), 293
*Abortion and American
Politics* (Craig and
O'Brien), 286
*Abortion and Social
Responsibility:
Depolarizing the Debate*
(Schrage), 302–303
*Abortion and the Conscience
of the Nation* (Reagan),
190, 305–306
*Abortion and the Politics of
Motherhood* (Luker),
289

Abortion and Women's Choice: The State, Sexuality, and Reproductive Freedom (Petchesky), 302
Abortion Care Network (ACN), 184, 220
abortion clinics, 38, 52
  environmental safety at, 80, 88–90
  regulation of, 48, 57–58, 151
  requirements for, 38, 52, 57–58, 282–283
  violence at, 88–90, 184, 190–191, 205, 210–211, 252–254, 253*t*, 278, 331, 332, 334, 337
  See also abortion providers; Planned Parenthood Federation of America (PPFA)
Abortion Conversation Project (ACP), 220
abortion counseling. *See* counseling
Abortion Counseling Service (Chicago Women's Liberation Union), 137, 262–266
abortion debates, 119–120
  areas of consensus, 103–105
  frames and framing, 30–33, 44

toning down rhetoric, 100–103
Abortion Denied: Shattering Young Women's Lives (documentary), 183, 308
The Abortion Diary (TAD), 134–140, 201, 220
Abortion for Survival (documentary), 183
abortion funding
  for global organizations, 63–64
  private, 340
  public (Medicaid), 59, 60–62, 91, 238–241, 273–277, 326, 327
  restrictions on, 62–65
  state regulation of, 238–240*t*
Abortion in America: The Origins and Evolution of National Policy, 1800–1900 (Mohr), 4, 290
abortion law
  based on quickening, 2–3, 9, 10
  common law, 2–3
  conditional, 3–4, 19, 21
  constitutional, 1–2
  criminalization, 3–11, 51, 259–260, 197, 317, 318, 339
  debate over, 222
  decriminalization, 11–21, 65, 323–324

First National Conference
on Abortion Laws, 16,
323
prenatal drug laws, 74–76
state, 23, 47, 51, 52–58,
72, 237–247, 317–318,
323–324
support for liberalization
of, 324
abortion pill, 38, 80, 81–83,
179, 184, 221, 329,
332, 333, 337
*Abortion Politics: Public
Policy in Cross-Cultural
Perspective* (Githens and
McBride), 295
*Abortion Politics, Mass Media,
and Social Movements in
America* (Rohlinger), 84
*Abortion Politics, Women's
Movements and the
Democratic State:
A Comparative Study
of State Feminism*
(McBride Stetson),
295–296
*Abortion Politics in North
America* (Haussman),
295
abortion providers
hospital admitting
privileges for, 52, 57,
58, 281
interview with, 126–134
licensing requirements
for, 57

negative portrayal of, 203,
299, 333
professional association of,
226, 326
regulation of, 58, 151, 246
shortage of, 90, 225, 333,
340
violence against, 38, 80,
89, 126, 146, 186, 191,
195, 211, 248,
252–254, 278, 297,
309, 311
See also abortion clinics;
Planned Parenthood
Federation of America
(PPFA)
abortion reform, 10, 15, 20,
179, 221, 222, 299,
300, 320, 324
*Abortion Rights Controversy in
America: A Legal Reader*
(Hull, Hoffer, and
Hoffer), 288
Abortion Rights Mobilization
(ARM), 81, 179, 221,
326
*Abortion Rites: A Social
History* (Olasky),
290–291
abortion services
characteristics of women
having abortions,
249–252
prevalence of, 247–249
See also abortion clinics;
abortion providers

Abortion Speakout, 17,
266–270, 323
abortion statistics
abortion clinic violence,
253*t*
areas of conflict between
pro-choice and pro-life
arguments, 104*t*
areas of consensus between
pro-choice and pro-life
arguments, 104*t*
characteristics of women
having abortions,
249–250*t*, 251*t*, 323
ideological gaps in both
parties, 256*t*
number, rate, and ratio
of reported abortions,
1970–2013, 248*t*
public opinion on issues,
255*t*
state mandates, 242–245*t*
state regulations of
abortion practice and
funding, 238–240*t*
views on abortion by
religion, 256*t*
Abortion Surveillance report,
323
abortion techniques
dilation and curettage
(D&C), 318
dilation and extraction, 68
intact dilation and
evacuation (intact
D&E), 69
vacuum aspiration, 322
abortion triad, 10
*Abortion II: Making the
Revolution* (Lader), 179,
300
*Abortion Wars: A Half
Century of Struggle,
1950–2000* (Solinger
et al.), 13, 303
AbortionNO Campaign, 205
Abort73.com (documentary),
307
*Absolute Convictions: My
Father, a City, and the
Conflict That Divided
America* (Press), 291
abstinence, 8, 207, 219
in sex education, 39, 209,
327, 337
Access Initiative Project, 226
ACLA (American Coalition
of Life Activists),
203–204, 333
ACLJ (American Center for
Law and Justice), 203
ACLU. *See* American Civil
Liberties Union
ACN (Abortion Care
Network), 184, 220
ACP (Abortion Conversation
Project), 220
activism
pro-choice, 37, 98
pro-life, 36*f*, 37, 67
Adolescent Family Life Act
(AFLA), 327, 329, 337

adoption, 155, 222, 327
Advancing New Standards
    in Reproductive Health
    (ANSIRH), 56, 93, 221
Advocates for Youth, 231
Affordable Care Act
    (Obamacare), 40, 208,
    218
AFLA (Adolescent Family
    Life Act), 327, 329, 337
After Tiller (documentary),
    184, 308
AG (Army of God), 89, 190,
    201, 205, 253, 334
Agency for International
    Development (AID),
    276
Akin, Todd, 62
Alabama
    fetal pain law, 338
    state mandates, 242*t*
    state regulations of
        abortion practices and
        funding, 238*t*
Alan Guttmacher Institute
    (GI), 102, 134, 155,
    177, 201, 224–225,
    323, 337, 338
Alaska
    abortion and the guarantee
        of privacy, 47
    legalization of abortion,
        324
    repeal of abortion laws, 19
    state mandates, 242*t*
    state regulations of

abortion practices and
    funding, 238*t*
ALI. *See* American Law
    Institute
Alito, Samuel, 50, 52, 69,
    340
ALL (American Life League),
    187, 204, 327
AMA. *See* American Medical
    Association
American Association of Pro-
    Life Obstetricians and
    Gynecologists, 82
American Birth Control
    League (ABCL), 12,
    177, 182, 319. *See also*
    Planned Parenthood
    Federation of America
    (PPFA)
American Cancer Society, 85
American Center for Law
    and Justice (ACLJ), 203
American Civil Liberties
    Union (ACLU), 92,
    189, 323, 325, 336
    Reproductive Freedom
        Project, 221–222
American Coalition of Life
    Activists (ACLA),
    203–204, 333
American College of
    Obstetricians and
    Gynecologists, 73,
    85–86, 322
American Collegians for Life,
    218

American Law Institute
(ALI), 14, 15, 16, 19,
222, 320
Model Penal Code:
Abortion (1959),
259–260
American Life League (ALL),
187, 204, 327
American Medical
Association (AMA),
6–7, 197, 318, 319,
322, 324, 333
endorsing ALI model
reform statute, 322
opposition to abortion by,
318
opposition to partial-birth
abortion, 333
resolution against
abortion, 6–7
supporting doctors who
perform abortions, 324
American Psychological
Association, 86, 209
American Public Health
Association, 323
American Society for
Reproductive Medicine,
320
American Values, 199
Americans United for Life
(UAL), 57, 76, 199,
204, 324
amniocentesis, 74
Anand, Kanwaljeet
"Sunny," 72

Annenberg Public Policy
Center (University of
Pennsylvania), 103
ANSIRH (Advancing
New Standards in
Reproductive Health),
56, 93, 221
Anthony, Susan B., 8,
210
anti-torture, 142, 213
antiwar, 142, 213
Arcana, Judith, 137
Arizona
fetal pain law, 338
state mandates, 242*t*
state regulations of
abortion practices and
funding, 238*t*
Arkansas
ban on sex-selective
abortion, 67
conditional abortion
laws, 19
state mandates, 242*t*
state regulations of
abortion practices and
funding, 238*t*
Unborn Child Protection
from Dismemberment
Abortion Act, 53
ARM (Abortion Rights
Mobilization), 81, 179,
221, 326
Army of God (AG), 89, 190,
201, 205, 253, 334
Arpaio v. Doe, 336

Articles of Faith: A Frontline History of the Abortion Wars (Gorney), 288

Association for the Study of Abortion, 15, 177, 321

Atwood, Margaret, 76, 236f, 237

Augustine of Hippo (saint), 9

Avery, Byllye Y., 222

Ayotte v. Planned Parenthood of Northern New England, 336

Babies by Choice or Chance (Guttmacher), 177

Back Rooms: Voices from the Illegal Abortion Era (Messer and May), 13

Back to the Drawing Board: The Future of the Pro-Life Movement (Wagner), 306–307

Bader, Eleanor J., 297

Baer, Judith, 296–297

Baird, Bill, 172–173, 321

Baird, Robert M., 303–304

Baird-Windle, Patricia, 297

Baker, Aspen, 203

Barrett, James, 89, 191, 332

Bauer, Gary, 209

Baumgardner, Jennifer, 173

Beal v. Doe, 61, 326

Beckwith, F. J., 304

Bearing Right: How the Conservatives Won the Abortion War (Saletan), 292

Behind Every Choice Is a Story (Feldt), 175

Bell, Becky, 54, 330

Bellotti v. Baird, 54, 172, 326

Benham, Philip "Flip," 185–186, 193, 214

Beninato, Patricia, 95

Bensing, Sandra, 21

Beyond the Abortion Wars: A Way Forward for a New Generation (Camosy), 99–100

Bipartisan Pro-Life Congressional Caucus, 82, 188, 196, 232

birth control. *See* contraception; contraceptives

Birth Control Clinical Research Bureau, 319

birth control clinics, 319, 321

Birth Control Federation of America, 319–320

Birthright: A War Story (documentary), 308–309

Birthright International, 87

Bixby Center for Global Reproductive Health, 221

Black, Hugo, 125

Black Lives Matter Movement, 94, 232

Black Women's Health
Imperative (BWHI),
222, 328
Blackmun, Harry, 21, 47,
121, 122, 125, 179
Roe v. Wade opinion,
270–273
Boehner, John, 89–90
Bomberger, Ryan, 94,
218–219
Bonow, Amelia, 95, 231
books
on the abortion
controversy in the US,
286–294
global comparative
examinations, 294–296
pro-choice perspective,
296–303
pro-life perspective,
303–307
Bork, Robert, 46, 59, 179,
329
Born-Alive Abortion
Survivors Protection
Act, 71
Born-Alive Infants Protection
Acts, 59, 70, 334
Bowen v. Kendrick, 329
*Breaking the Abortion
Deadlock: From Choice
to Consent* (McDonagh),
289–290
breast cancer, 85, 101, 200,
207, 242–245t, 246
Brennan, William, 121

Breyer, Stephen, 50, 52, 340
*A Brief, Liberal, Catholic
Defense of Abortion*
(Dombrowski and
Deltete), 297
Britton, John, 89, 190–191,
332
Brown, Judie, 186–187, 204
Brown, Paul, 186, 204
Buchanan, Patrick, 195–196
Buckley, James, 325
Burkhart, Julie, 118f, 119
Burns, Gene, 286
*Burwell v. Hobby Lobby
Stores, Inc.*, 39, 48
Bush, George H. W., 46, 48,
49, 58, 59, 190, 330
Bush, George W., 50, 51, 69,
70, 77, 84, 192, 334,
335, 336
Mexico City policy, 276
Partial Birth Abortion Ban
Act, 279–280
Bush, Jeb, 152
BWHI (Black Women's
Health Imperative),
222, 328
Byrn, Robert M., abortion in
perspective, 260–262

Calderone, Mary Steichen,
173–174, 320
California
abortion activism in, 16
abortion and the guarantee
of privacy, 47

conditional abortion laws, 19
Reproductive Freedom, Accountability, Comprehensive Care, and Transparency (FACT) Act, 339
state mandates, 242t
state regulations of abortion practices and funding, 238t
Camosy, Charles, 99–100
C.Am.P.U.S., 218
Can I Live? (film), 312
Cannon, Nick, 312
capital punishment, 208, 213
care centers, 207
Care Net, 87, 207
Carey v. Population Services International, 326
Carhart, Le Roy, 195
Carter, James Earl "Jimmy," 58–59, 185
case law, 2, 4. *See also* abortion law
Casey, Robert, 47
Catholics for a Free Choice (CFFC), 25, 178, 201, 222–223, 227, 325
CCA (Christian Coalition of America), 206
Center for Bio-Ethical Reform (CBR), 205, 330, 333, 334

Center for Family Planning Program Development, 224
Center for Medical Progress (CMP), 64, 89, 182, 195, 205–206, 339
Center for Reproductive Law and Policy, 331
Center for Reproductive Rights (CRR), 51, 223, 331
Center on Reproductive Rights and Justice (CRRJ), 201, 223–224
Centers for Disease Control and Prevention, 201, 232, 323
Centers for Disease Control and Prevention: Abortion Surveillance Report, 314
CFFC (Catholics for a Free Choice), 25, 178, 201, 222–223, 227, 325
Chaffetz, Jason, 65
Charity Watchlist, 204
Chicago Women's Liberation Union, 17, 18, 137
Abortion Counseling Service, 262–266
Child Custody Protection Act, 54, 335
child support, 100, 160
Children's Health Insurance Program, 334

Choices Campus Leadership Program, 184

Christian Coalition of America (CCA), 206

Christian Right, 58

Christianity, 58, 206
    evangelical, 8, 27, 59, 65, 87, 155, 198, 212, 256, 291
    Protestant, 5, 155, 256, 291
    See also Roman Catholic Church

Cider House Rules (film), 312

Citizens' Committee for Humane Abortion Laws, 16, 321

Citizens for a Pro-Life Society, 217

City of Akron v. Akron Center for Reproductive Health, 45, 328

Clinic Access project, 183

Clinical Research Bureau, 319

Clinton, Hillary Rodham, 59–60, 62, 83–84, 98, 181, 188

Clinton, William J. "Bill," 48, 50, 51, 59, 68, 97, 180, 331
    Mexico City policy, 276
    and the Partial Birth Abortion Ban Act, 279–280

cloning, 304

Closed: 99 Ways to Stop Abortion (Scheidler), 306

CMP (Center for Medical Progress), 64, 89, 182, 195, 205–206, 339

Coffee, Linda, 21, 185, 193, 323

Colautti v. Franklin, 327

Colorado
    conditional abortion laws, 19
    pro-life organization in, 322
    state mandates, 242*t*
    state regulations of abortion practices and funding, 238*t*

Commission on Population Growth, 324

Committee for the Suppression of Vice, 8

Common Ground Network for Life and Choice, 202

Comstock, Anthony, 7–8

Comstock Act/Laws, 1, 8, 12, 147, 182, 257–258, 318, 319, 324

Concentric Media, 312

Concerned Women for America (CWFA), 199, 206–207

conditional laws, 3–4, 19, 21

Congress, powers of, 2

Congressional Pro-Choice
    Caucus, 232
Congressional Pro-Life
    Caucus, 82, 188, 196,
    232
Connecticut
    abortion laws in, 5
    first abortion statute
        (1821), 317
    state mandates, 242*t*
    state regulations of
        abortion practices and
        funding, 238*t*
    See also *Griswold v.
        Connecticut*
Connor, Ken, 80
consciousness-raising, 17
Consistent Life Ethic, 142
constitutional law, 1–2
*Contested Lives: The Abortion
    Debate in an American
    Community* (Ginsburg),
    287–288
contraception, 8, 12, 38,
    120–121, 147, 149,
    182–183, 192, 200,
    210, 319
    information about, 8
    insurance coverage for,
        147
    legalizing, 172
    promotion of use of, 335
    See also contraceptives;
        emergency
        contraception (EC);
        family planning

contraceptives, 12, 16, 29,
    30, 40, 321
    access to, 39–40
    legalization of, 324
    reversible, 39
    See also contraception
Coombs, Roberta, 206
counseling, 55–56, 63, 172,
    323
    mandatory, 4, 421–427,
        242–245*t*
    post-abortion, 207
    by video, 83
CPC (Crisis Pregnancy
    Centers), 86–87,
    207–208
"crack babies," 74
Craig, Barbara Hinkson, 286
Crawford, Lester, 83, 84
Created Equal, 217
criminalization, 3–11, 51,
    197, 259–260, 317,
    318, 339
Crisis Pregnancy Centers
    (CPC), 86–87,
    207–208
Critchlow, Donald T.,
    286–287
Crouse, Janice Shaw, 199
CRR (Center for
    Reproductive Rights),
    51, 223, 331
CRRJ (Center on
    Reproductive Rights
    and Justice), 201,
    223–224

Cruz, Ted, 151–152
Culture of Life Family
    Services, 87
CWFA (Concerned Women
    for America), 199,
    206–207

Daleiden, David, 206
Daly, Jim, 210
Dannenfelser, Marjorie, 64,
    187–188, 199,
    218
Dannenfelser, Marty, 188
Davis, Wendy, 57, 78–79,
    338
deaf community, 166
death penalty, 208, 213
*Defenders of the Unborn:
    The Pro-Life Movement
    before Roe v. Wade*
    (Williams), 66
*Defending Life: A Moral
    and Legal Case against
    Abortion Choice*
    (Beckwith), 304
Defensive Action, 190
Delaware
    conditional abortion
        laws, 19
    state mandates, 242*t*
    state regulations of
        abortion practices and
        funding, 238*t*
Delgado, George, 87
Deltete, Robert, 297
Democrat Party

as "pro-choice party,"
    58–59
pro-life factions, 60, 208,
    333
Democrats for Life, 333
Democrats for Life of
    America (DLA), 60,
    208
Department of Health and
    Human Services, 327,
    339
Department of Justice, 46
designer babies, 163–166
dilation and curettage
    (D&C), 318
dilation and extraction, 68
disability rights, 228
    and abortion, 163–166
DLA (Democrats for Life of
    America), 60, 208
Do No Harm, 127
Dobson, James, 210
doctors. *See* American
    Medical Association
    (AMA); physicians
*Doctors of Conscience: The
    Struggle to Provide
    Abortion before and after*
    Roe v. Wade (Joffe), 299
documentaries, 307–312
Doe v. Bolton, 20–24, 325
Dole, Bob, 325
Dombrowski, Daniel A., 297
domestic violence, 21, 100,
    176, 307
Donald, Ian, 320

Douglas, William O., 121
drug use, prenatal, 38,
    68, 74–76. *See also*
    thalidomide
Dubay, Matthew, 160
Dyer, Frederick, 304

economic justice, 228
The Edge of Reason
    (documentary), 194
Ehrlich, J. Shoshanna, 298
Eisenstadt v. Baird, 121, 123,
    172, 271, 324
Elliot Institute (EI), 85,
    208–209
embryo
    advocacy for, 305
    development of, 44
    editing genetic code of,
        165
    implantation of, 84
    laws protecting, 76
    legal rights of, 200
    mother's consent to, 29,
        122, 290
    personhood of, 3, 6, 9, 26,
        28, 29, 66, 297, 318
embryonic stem cell research,
    212, 304, 336
embryonic tissue research,
    206–207
emergency contraception
    (EC), 38, 39, 80,
    83–84, 147, 148, 227,
    333, 335, 336, 338

EMW Women's Surgical
    Center (Louisville, KY),
    316–317
English common law, 2–3
environmental safety, 80,
    88–90
The Ethics of Abortion:
    Pro-Life vs. Pro-Choice
    (Baird and Rosenbaum),
    303–304
euthanasia, 206, 208, 212,
    215
Eve's Herbs: A History of
    Contraception and
    Abortion in the West
    (Riddle), 292
Exhale, 202–203

FACE (Freedom of Access to
    Clinic Entrances Act),
    88, 147, 176, 183, 196,
    252, 277–278, 332
"Face the Truth" tours, 196,
    216
facilities. *See* abortion
    clinics
Factcheck.org, 103
Faithful for Life (Marx), 192
Falwall, Jerry, 212
family planning, 19,
    120–121, 209, 325
    federal support for, 324
    natural, 192
    See also contraception;
        contraceptives

Family Planning Services and
Population Research
Act, 324
Family Research Council
(FRC), 80, 209, 338
fathers
counseling and support
for, 158, 216
mental health of, 158
perspectives of, 157–162
rights of, 53
FDA. *See* Food and Drug
Administration
Feldt, Gloria, 174–175, 298
feminism, 18
first-wave, 8
New Wave, 141, 213
pro-choice, 97
pro-life, 141–145,
188–189
second-wave, 19, 22
third-wave, 173
Feminist Majority (FM), 224
Feminist Majority
Foundation (FMF), 81,
179, 183–184, 224
*Abortion Denied: Shattering
Young Women's Lives*,
308
Feminists for Life of America
(FFL), 188, 201,
209–210
Ferree, Myra Marx, 294–295
Fessler, Ann, 13
fetal anesthesia bill, 4, 340

fetal deformity/abnormality,
3, 14, 15, 16, 21, 60,
103, 157, 321, 339
and disability rights,
163–166
rubella, 15, 321
thalidomide, 15, 175, 313,
321
Zica, 339
Fetal Farming Prohibition
Act, 336
fetal homicide, 68, 76–78,
77–78, 204
fetal pain, 55, 72–73, 246
laws addressing, 3,
242–245*t*, 338, 340
fetal tissue research,
206–207, 331, 336
fetal-harm statutes, 71,
76–78
fetus
definition of, 77
development of, 43
heartbeat of, 67
personhood of, 24, 65, 66,
68, 77–78, 97,
195–196, 224, 272,
334, 337
pro-choice view of, 66
pro-life view of, 66
remains of, 339
rights of, 38, 98–99, 122
viability of, 2–3, 124, 327,
331
See also unborn rights

FFL (Feminists for Life of
America), 188, 201,
209–210
films, 312–314
*Findlaw for Legal
Professionals*, 314
Finkbine, Sherri Chessen, 15,
175–176, 321
First National Conference on
Abortion Laws, 16, 323
Flavin, Jeanne, 75
Florida
abortion and the guarantee
of privacy, 47
"Choose Life" license
plates, 334
state mandates, 242*t*
state regulations of
abortion practices and
funding, 239*t*
FM (Feminist Majority),
179, 224
FMF (Feminist Majority
Foundation), 81,
183–184, 224, 252
*Abortion Denied: Shattering
Young Women's Lives*,
308
FOCA (Freedom of Choice
Act), 48, 49, 226
Focus on the Family (FOF),
200, 210
Food and Drug
Administration (FDA),
221, 232, 321
approval of emergency

contraception, 336
Office of Women's Health
(FDA), 84, 232, 335
Reproductive Health
Advisory Committee
(FDA), 332
Foreign Assistance Act
(1961), 276
Forsythe, Clarke, 57
Foster, Serrin, 188–189
framing
diagnosis, 32
pro-choice, 78–81,
96–100
prognosis, 32
pro-life, 65–68, 75, 77,
96–100
Franz, Wanda, 189–190
FRC (Family Research
Council), 80, 209, 338
Freedom of Access to Clinic
Entrances Act (FACE),
88, 147, 176, 183, 196,
252, 277–278, 332
Freedom of Choice Act
(FOCA), 48, 49, 226
Fried, Marlene Gerber, 303
Friedan, Betty, 179, 194, 228

Gag Rule, 330. *See also*
Global Gag Rule
Gamson, William Anthony,
294–295
Gandy, Kim, 176
Garrow, David J., 287
Gays against Abortion, 217

Genocide Awareness Project, 205, 333

George Tiller Memorial Fund, 91

Georgia
conditional abortion laws, 19
criminalization of abortion, 21
Doe v. Bolton case, 21
fetal pain law, 338
state mandates, 242*t*
state regulations of abortion practices and funding, 239*t*

Gerhards, Jürgen, 294–295

GI. *See* Guttmacher Institute

Ginsburg, Faye, 287–288

Ginsburg, Ruth Bader, 50, 51, 52, 69, 340
Supreme Court opinion on *Whole Woman's Health v. Hellerstedt*, 281–283

Giric, Stefanija, 163–166

The Girls Who Went Away: The Hidden History of Women Who Surrendered Children for Adoption in the Decades before Roe v. Wade (Fessler), 13

Githens, Marianne, 295

Global Gag Rule, 63, 275–277, 328

Gonzales v. Carhart, 51, 69, 203, 279, 336

Gorney, Cynthia, 288

Gorsuch, Neil, 52, 213, 340

Gosnell, Kermit, 70–71, 338

government agencies, 232

Great Depression, 11–12, 319

Griffin, Michael, 190, 331

Griswold, Estelle, 149

Griswold v. Connecticut, 16, 20, 22, 46, 120, 123, 149, 152, 179, 271, 321

Gunn, David, 146, 190, 331

Gutiérrez, Elena R., 303

Guttmacher, Alan, 12, 15, 176–177, 224, 320, 321

Guttmacher Institute (GI), 102, 134, 155, 177, 201, 224–225, 314, 323, 337, 338

Hadley, Janet, 298–299

Hale, David, 317

Hales, Steven, 160

Hames, Margie, 21

Hand of God: A Journey from Death to Life by the Abortion Doctor Who Changed His Mind (Nathanson), 194

The Handmaid's Tale, 76, 236*f*, 237

Harlan, John Marshall II, 125

Harris v. McRae, 62, 90, 327

Hatch, Orrin, 43, 44

hate speech, 89

Haussman, Melissa, 84, 295

Hawaii
  legalization of abortion,
    323
  repeal of abortion laws, 19
  state mandates, 242t
  state regulations of
    abortion practices and
    funding, 239t
Hawkins, Kristan, 218
Hayat, Abu, 331
health care
  access to, 151
  for fetuses, 334
  See also reproductive health
    care
health insurance coverage
  for birth control, 40
  for fetuses, 334
  for military personnel, 92
  restrictions on, 229
  for students, 189
  See also Medicaid funding
Heartbeat International, 87,
    201, 207
Helms, Jesse, 42, 44, 191
Helms Bill, 327
Hembree, Greg, 74
Hendershott, Anne, 97
Herbert, Gary, 4
Herndon de La Rosa,
    Destiny, 141–145, 213
Hickman, Harrison, 98
Hill, Paul T., 89, 190–191,
    334
Historical and Multicultural
    Encyclopedia of Women's

Reproductive Rights in
    the United States (Baer),
    296–297
HIV/AIDS, 63–64
Hobbs, Jay, 153–156
Hobbs Act, 336
Hodgson, Jane, 324
Hodgson v. State of Minnesota,
    330
Hoffer, Peter Charles, 288
Hoffer, Williamjames, 288
"Holly's Law," 82, 335
homosexuality, 216–217
  criminalization of, 123
  opposition to, 214
  See also LGBT community
How the Pro-Choice
    Movement Saved
    America: Freedom,
    Politics, and the War on
    Sex (Page), 301–302
Hull, N. E. H., 288
Human Capital Project,
    206
Human Life Amendment,
    42, 44, 58, 211, 326,
    327, 328
Human Life Bill, 191
Human Life International,
    192, 232
Human Life Review, 314–315
Humanae Vitae (Human
    Life), 25, 192
Hutchinson, Asa, 53
Hyde, Henry J., 61,
    191–192, 212

Hyde Amendment, 38,
60–62, 90, 191, 204,
273–275, 326

I Am Roe (McCorvey), 193
Idaho
fetal pain law, 338
restrictions on
abortion, 47
state mandates, 242*t*
state regulations of
abortion practices and
funding, 239*t*
If These Walls Could Talk
(film), 313
If/When/How: Lawyering
for Reproductive Justice
(IWH), 91, 225
IHS (Indian Health Service),
60–62
Illinois
abortion statute (1821),
317
pro-life organization in,
322
state mandates, 242*t*
state regulations of
abortion practices and
funding, 239*t*
Indian Health Service (IHS),
60–62
Indiana
fetal pain law, 338
state mandates, 242*t*
state regulations of
abortion practices and

funding, 239*t*
*Indivisible: A Practical Guide
for Resisting the Trump
Agenda*, 227
infanticide, 38, 68, 70, 194,
212
abortion as, 68, 70, 194
and partial-birth abortion,
50, 68–72
infertility, 76, 207
information
about fetal pain, 72–73
about gestational age, 331
accuracy of, 84–87, 147,
241–247
provision of, 72–73
informed consent, 46, 52,
55, 103, 105
intact dilation and evacuation
(intact D&E), 69
*Intended Consequences: Birth
Control, Abortion, and
the Federal Government
in Modern America*
(Critchlow), 286–287
International Planned
Parenthood Council, 99
International Right to Life
Federation, 232
International Women's
Health Coalition, 232
Internet sources, 314–315
interviews
with an abortion provider,
126–134
with women about their

abortion experiences,
134–140
*Into Our Own Hands:
The Women's Health
Movement in the United
States, 1969–1990*
(Morgen), 290
Iowa
access to abortion pills,
337
state mandates, 242*t*
state regulations of
abortion practices and
funding, 239*t*
Ipas, 232
issue frames, 32. *See also*
framing
#istandwithpp, 65, 229
IWH (If/When/How:
Lawyering for
Reproductive Justice),
91, 225

Jacksteit, Mary, 202
Jane (abortion counseling
service), 18, 323
Jane's Due Process, 55
Joffe, Carol, 299
John Merck Foundation,
221
judicial bypass, 47, 54, 55,
138, 247, 330

Kagan, Elena, 52, 340
Kaiser Family Foundation,
315

Kansas
conditional abortion
laws, 19
fetal pain law, 338
state mandates, 243*t*
state regulations of
abortion practices and
funding, 239*t*
Kaplan, Laura, 299
Kaufmann, Adrienne, 202
Kennedy, Anthony, 46, 52,
340
Kentucky
limited abortion access in,
340
state mandates, 243*t*
state regulations of
abortion practices and
funding, 239*t*
Kerber, Linda, 138
Keys, Jennifer, 125–134
*Killing for Life: The
Apocalyptic Narrative
of Pro-Life Politics*
(Mason), 300–301
Kinsey, Alfred, 14, 320
Kissling, Frances, 177–178,
222–223
Kopp, James, 186, 198, 211,
333

"Laci and Connor's Law," 77,
189, 335
Lader, Lawrence, 81,
178–179, 194, 221,
299–300, 322, 323, 326

Lafferty, Andrea, 219
LaHaye, Beverly, 206
Lake of Fire (documentary),
    309
Lambs of Christ (LC), 89,
    210–211
The Last Abortion Clinic
    (documentary), 180,
    309–310
Law Students for
    Reproductive Justice,
    225
Lawrence v. Texas, 123
Leahy, Brigid, 146–153
Leavitt, Michael, 84
Lejeune, Jérôme, 43–44
Levine, Phillip B., 288–289
LGBT community, 216–217,
    225
    LGBT issues, 186, 214
    LGBT rights, 228
*Liberty and Justice for All:
    A Life Spent Protecting
    the Right to Choose*
    (Michelman), 180
*Liberty and Sexuality: The
    Right to Privacy and the
    Making of* Roe v. Wade
    (Garrow), 287
licensing requirements, 38,
    52, 57–58
*Life's Work: A Moral Argument
    for Choice* (Parker), 180
Lister, Joseph, 319
Live Action (LA), 211
Live Action News, 70, 181

Louisiana
    compulsory ultrasound, 56
    fetal pain law, 338
    Judicial Bypass Project, 55
    restrictions on abortion, 47
    state mandates, 243*t*
    state regulations of
        abortion practices and
        funding, 239*t*
Lowney, Shannon, 332
Lucio, Eddie, 142
Luker, Kristin, 11, 26–27,
    29, 38, 289

Madera, Melissa, 134–140,
    220
*Madsen v. Women's Health
    Center*, 332
Maginnis, Patricia, 16, 321
Maguire, Daniel C., 300
Maher v. Roe, 62, 326
Maine
    state mandates, 243*t*
    state regulations of
        abortion practices and
        funding, 239*t*
*The Making of Pro-Life
    Activists: How Social
    Movement Mobilization
    Works* (Munson), 26, 67
Manninen, Bertha Alvarez,
    157–162
March for Life (ML), 25, 42,
    186, 211, 217, 325
    Education and Defense
        Fund (ML), 211–212

March for Women's Lives, 175, 176, 183, 329, 334

Marie Stopes International, 232

Markovsky, Jennifer, 152

Marshall, Thurgood, 48, 90

Marx, Paul, 192

Maryland
  conditional abortion laws, 19
  state mandates, 243*t*
  state regulations of abortion practices and funding, 239*t*

Mason, Carol, 300–301

Massachusetts
  state mandates, 243*t*
  state regulations of abortion practices and funding, 239*t*

maternal health, 3, 23
  abortion to preserve, 6–7, 11, 14, 21, 23, 51, 62, 72, 73, 197, 272–273, 318, 326, 335

Maxwell, Carol J., 289

May, E. Kathryn, 13

McBride Stetson, Dorothy, 295–296

McCain, John, 59

McConnell, Mitch, 79

McCorvey, Norma, 21, 42, 171, 185, 186, 192–193, 284*f*, 285, 323, 332, 335

McDonagh, Eileen, 98–99, 289–290

McDonnell, Kathleen, 161–162

McHugh, James, 322

McNight, Regina, 74–75

Medicaid funding, 59, 61–62, 91, 238–241, 273–275, 326, 327, 340

Medical Students for Choice (MSFC), 126, 127, 201, 225, 331

men. *See* fathers

mental health, 14–16
  and abortion, 85, 86, 208–209, 242–245*t*, 246–247, 329
  of men, 158

Merritt, Sandra, 206

Messer, Ellen, 13

methotrexate, 82. *See also* abortion pill

Mexico City policies, 63, 180, 275–277, 328

Michelman, Kate, 79–80, 98, 179–180, 301

Michigan
  failure of abortion referendum, 19, 325
  state mandates, 243*t*
  state regulations of abortion practices and funding, 239*t*

mifepristone, 333. *See also* RU-486

military, access to abortion
in, 60, 92, 332, 333
Minnesota
pro-life organization in,
322
state mandates, 243*t*
state regulations of
abortion practices and
funding, 239*t*
minors
abortion procedures for,
39, 53–55, 330, 331
teen pregnancy, 38–39,
231, 249
misoprostol, 82. *See also*
abortion pill
Mississippi
clinician requirements, 58
limited abortion access in,
92, 340
rejection of "personhood
amendment," 337
requirement for mandatory
delay and biased
information, 331
restrictions on abortion,
331
state mandates, 243*t*
state regulations of
abortion practices and
funding, 239*t*
Missouri
abortion statute (1821),
317
state mandates, 243*t*
state regulations of

abortion practices and
funding, 239*t*
ML. *See* March for Life
MMC (Moral Majority
Coalition), 212
Mohr, James, 4–5, 7, 290
Mongar, Karnamaya, 70–71,
338
Montana
abortion and the guarantee
of privacy, 47
state mandates, 243*t*
state regulations of
abortion practices and
funding, 239*t*
Moore, Roy, 186, 187
Moral Majority Coalition
(MMC), 212
*The Moral Veto: Framing
Contraception, Abortion,
and Cultural Pluralism
in the United States*
(Burns), 286
Morgen, Sandra, 290
morning after pill, 83–84,
338. *See also* emergency
contraception (EC)
Mother and Prenatal Child
Protection Act, 100
*Mother in the Middle:
Searching for Peace in the
Mommy Wars* (Yoest),
199
motherhood
and abortion decisions, 93
demands of, 93

meaning of, 26–27
plan for, 39
pro-choice view of, 29
societal view of, 265, 272
voluntary, 8
Motion Picture Production
    Code, 320
MSFC (Medical Students for
    Choice), 126, 127, 201,
    225, 331
Muñoz, Marlise, 71
Munson, Ziad, 26, 67
Murray, Patty, 83–84
Mutcherson, Kimberley, 124
My Fight for Birth Control
    (Sanger), 183
Myers, Lonny, 323

NAF (National Abortion
    Federation), 71, 82, 89,
    125, 178, 226, 326
Nance, Penny Young, 207
NAPW (National Advocates
    for Pregnant Women),
    72, 226–227
NARAL. *See* National
    Abortion Rights Action
    League (NARAL);
    National Association for
    the Repeal of Abortion
    Laws (NARAL)
NARAL Pro-Choice
    America, 226, 334
Nathanson, Bernard, 42,
    179, 193–194, 305,
    328

National Abortion and
    Reproductive Rights
    Action League (NARAL
    PCA), 79, 226, 331
National Abortion Federation
    (NAF), 71, 82, 89, 125,
    178, 226, 326
National Abortion Rights
    Action League
    (NARAL), 28, 31, 79,
    98, 194, 200, 325, 331,
    334
National Advocates for
    Pregnant Women
    (NAPW), 72, 226–227
National Association for
    the Repeal of Abortion
    Laws (NARAL), 16, 79,
    179, 226, 323
National Birth Control
    League, 319
National Black Women's
    Health Project, 222,
    328
National Clinic Access
    Project, 224
National Clinic Violence
    Survey, 252
National Coalition of
    Abortion Providers, 220
National Conference of
    Catholic Bishops
    (USCCB), 82, 219, 322
National Institute of Child
    Health and Human
    Development, 321

National Institute of Family and Life Advocates v. Becerra, 87, 208

National Institutes of Health (NIH), 331

National Latina Institute for Reproductive Health (NLIRH), 227

National Network of Abortion Funds (NNAF), 91, 201, 227, 331

National Network to End Domestic Violence, 176

National Organization for Women (NOW), 16–17, 88, 176, 183, 196, 200, 228, 322, 329, 333
    Political Action Committee, 176

National Right to Life (NRL), 212–213

National Right to Life Committee (NRLC), 25, 31, 42, 67, 76, 186–187, 189–190, 197, 200, 322, 325

National Women's Health Network, 326

National Women's Law Center (NWLC), 228

Native American Women's Health Education Resource Center, 91

natural family planning, 192

Nebraska, fetal pain law, 338

Nelson, Jennifer, 301

Nevada
    state mandates, 243*t*
    state regulations of abortion practices and funding, 239*t*

New Hampshire, Parental Notification Prior to Abortion Act, 336
    state mandates, 243*t*
    state regulations of abortion practices and funding, 239*t*

New Homeline Video, 313–314

New Jersey Right to Life Committee, 196
    state mandates, 243*t*
    state regulations of abortion practices and funding, 239*t*

New Mexico
    conditional abortion laws, 19
    state mandates, 243*t*
    state regulations of abortion practices and funding, 239*t*

New Right, 27

New Wave Feminists (NWF), 141, 213

New York
    abortion statute (1828), 317

legalization of abortion, 323
repeal of abortion laws, 19
Rockefeller's veto of bill to recriminalize abortion, 20
state mandates, 243*t*
state regulations of abortion practices and funding, 239*t*
New York City Redstockings, 17, 266–270, 323
Newman, Troy, 194–195, 210, 213–214
Nichols, Leanne, 332
NLIRH (National Latina Institute for Reproductive Health), 227
NNAF (National Network of Abortion Funds), 91, 201, 227, 331
North Carolina
conditional abortion laws, 19
fetal pain law, 338
state mandates, 243*t*
state regulations of abortion practices and funding, 240*t*
North Dakota
failure of abortion referendum, 19
limited abortion access in, 340
state mandates, 243*t*

state regulations of abortion practices and funding, 240*t*
Not Equal: Civil Rights Gone Wrong (Bomberger), 219
NOW. *See* National Organization for Women (NOW)
NOW Political Action Committee, 176
NOW v. Scheidler, 176, 198, 332
NRL (National Right to Life), 212–213
NRLC (National Right to Life Committee), 25, 31, 42, 67, 76, 186–187, 189–190, 197, 200, 322, 325
NWLC (National Women's Law Center), 228

Obama, Barack, 39–40, 52, 59, 65, 92, 337, 339
Mexico City policy, 276
O'Brien, David M., 286
O'Connor, Sandra Day, 45, 46, 47, 49, 50
Office of Adolescent Health Teen Pregnancy Prevention Program (TPP), 39
Office of Women's Health (FDA), 84, 232, 335
#OHHandmaids, 76

Ohio
  state mandates, 244*t*
  state regulations of
    abortion practices and
    funding, 240*t*
*Ohio v. Akron Center for
  Reproductive Health*, 330
Oklahoma
  state mandates, 244*t*
  state regulations of
    abortion practices and
    funding, 240*t*
Olasky, Marvin, 290–291
1 in 3 Campaign, 231
Operation Rescue (OR), 88,
    183, 194–195, 198,
    210, 213–214, 284*f*,
    285, 329, 332, 333
Operation Rescue National,
    185
Operation Rescue West
    (ORW), 195, 213
Operation Save America
    (OSA), 185, 195, 213,
    214, 317
opt-out provisions, 40
  for pharmacists, 84, 103
OR. *See* Operation Rescue
Oregon
  conditional abortion
    laws, 19
  state mandates, 244*t*
  state regulations of
    abortion practices and
    funding, 240*t*
O'Reilly, Bill, 184

organizations
  common ground, 202–203
  government agencies, 232
  international, 232
  pro-choice, 220–232
  pro-life, 203–219
  *See also specific
    organizations by name*
OSA (Operation Save
    America), 185, 195,
    213, 214, 317
*Our Bodies, Our Crimes:
  The Policing of Women's
  Reproduction in America*
  (Flavin), 75

Packwood, Robert, 44, 328
Page, Cristina, 301–302
Pain-Capable Unborn Child
    Protection Act, 73
Palin, Sarah, 59
Paltrow, Lynn, 71–72
papal decrees, 9, 19, 25, 66,
    187, 192, 318, 323.
    See also Roman Catholic
    Church
Parens, Erik, 164
parental consent, 47, 52,
    53–54, 242–245*t*, 247,
    327
parental involvement,
    242–245*t*
parental leave, 100
parental notification,
    242–245*t*, 247, 330,
    331, 335, 336

Parental Notification Prior
to Abortion Act (New
Hampshire), 336
parental rights, 53–54
Parker, Willie, 180–181
Partial Birth Abortion Ban
Act, 51, 279–280, 332,
334, 336
*The Party of Death: The
Democrats, the Media,
the Courts, and the
Disregard for Human
Life* (Ramesh), 305
Patel, Purvi, 223–224
Pathfinder International, 232
Patterson, Holly, 82
Paul, John II (pope), 187,
192
Paul VI (pope), 19, 192, 323
Pavone, Frank, 90, 193,
215–216
Pelosi, Nancy, 181
Pence, Mike, 65, 150, 340
Pennsylvania
restrictions on
abortion, 47
state mandates, 244*t*
state regulations of
abortion practices and
funding, 240*t*
See also *Planned
Parenthood of
Southeastern
Pennsylvania v. Casey*
perinatology, 65–66
Perkins, Tony, 209

personhood
of the embryo, 3, 6, 9, 26,
28, 29, 66, 297, 318
for fertilized eggs, 40
of the fetus, 24, 65, 68,
77–78, 97, 195–196,
224, 272, 334, 337
Petchesky, Rosalind Pollack,
302
Peterson, Connor, 77
Peterson, Laci, 77
Peterson, Scott, 77
PFLI (Pharmacists for Life
International), 214–215
pharmacists
opt-out provisions for, 84,
103
pro-life, 201, 214–215
Pharmacists for Life, 201
Pharmacists for Life
International (PFLI),
214–215
physicians
control of abortion by,
6–7, 11
pro-choice, 73, 191,
228–229
pro-life, 215
*Physicians' Crusade against
Abortion* (Dyer), 304
Physicians for Life (PL), 215
Physicians for Reproductive
Choice and Health
(PRH), 73, 181,
228–229
Pius IX (pope), 9, 318

Pius XII (pope), 66
PL (Physicians for Life), 215
PLAGAL (Pro-Life Alliance
of Gays and Lesbians),
216–217
PLAL (Pro-Life Action
League), 67, 88, 195,
216, 217, 327
PLAN, 333
Plan B, 83, 91, 338
Planned Parenthood Action
Fund (PPAF), 79
Planned Parenthood
Federation of America
(PPFA), 12, 14, 39, 48,
51, 71, 74, 79, 94, 174,
177, 181, 224, 229,
320
abortions performed by,
128–129
accused of selling fetuses,
89–90, 182, 195, 252,
339
activism against, 217
bill to defund, 150–151
defunding of, 197, 207,
339, 340
government support of,
64–65
as service provider, 148
working for, 146–153
Planned Parenthood League
of Connecticut, 149
*Planned Parenthood of Central
Missouri v. Danforth*,
326

*Planned Parenthood
of Southeastern
Pennsylvania v. Casey*,
4, 48–49, 52–53, 229,
330–331
Planned Parenthood Political
Action Committee, 174
Planned Parenthood v. ACLA,
333
podcasts, 135–140, 220
policy debates, 30–33
*The Politics of Abortion in
the United States and
Canada: A Comparative
History* (Tatalovich),
296
Population Council (PC), 81,
232
Population Institute, 39, 48
Population Research
Institute, 192
postabortion counseling,
207. *See also* counseling
postabortion rituals, 136
postabortion support, 189,
201, 202–203, 215–216
postabortion syndrome,
85, 86
Powell, Lewis, 46, 125
PPFA. *See* Planned
Parenthood Federation
of America (PPFA)
Prayer and Fasting, 204
pre-abortion counseling, 55,
56, 63, 172, 323.
See also counseling

pregnancy
  compulsory, 16
  pre- vs. post-viability, 2
  and race, 13, 30
  resulting from rape or
    incest, 3, 14–15, 16,
    21, 53, 62, 73, 92, 148,
    247, 326, 338
  stages of, 2
  substance use during, 38,
    68, 74–76
  trimester framework,
    22–23, 47, 49,
    122
  unwanted, 83
pregnancy discrimination,
  100
Pregnancy Resource Centers,
  153–156, 207
prenatal genetic testing, 163–
  166, 336
prenatal justice, 330
Prenatal Testing and Disability
  Rights (ed. Parens and
  Asch), 164
Prenatally and Postnatally
  Diagnosed Conditions
  Awareness Act, 336
Press, Eyal, 291
Prevention First Act, 335
PRH (Physicians for
  Reproductive Choice
  and Health), 73, 181,
  228–229
Priests for Life (PFL), 90,
  215–216

privacy
  and abortion, 61
  right to, 22, 32, 46, 78,
    120–124, 150,
    271–272, 321, 324
  zones of, 22, 121, 321
  See also Roe v. Wade
A Private Matter (film), 176,
  313
Pro-Choice America
  (PCA), 80
Pro-Choice League,
  172
pro-choice movement,
  28–30
  areas of conflict with pro-
    life, 104t
  areas of consensus with
    pro-life, 104t
  framing, 78–81, 96–100
  organizations representing,
    220–232
  profiles of people involved
    in, 172–185
  and the Supreme Court,
    46, 47
The Pro-Choice Movement:
  Organization and
  Activism in the Abortion
  Conflict (Staggenborg),
  293
Project Life, 198
Project Rachel, 189, 201
Pro-Life Action League
  (PLAL), 67, 88, 195,
  216, 217, 327

Pro-Life Activists in America: Meaning, Motive, and Direct Action (Maxwell), 289
Pro-Life Alliance of Gays and Lesbians (PLAGAL), 216–217
Pro-Life Caucus, 82, 188, 196, 232
pro-life movement, 25–28, 43–44
  areas of conflict with pro-choice, 104*t*
  areas of consensus with pro-choice, 104*t*
  and feminism, 141–145, 188–189
  framing, 65–68, 75, 77, 96–100
  organizations representing, 203–219
  profiles of people involved in, 185–200
  and the Supreme Court, 47
pro-life terrorism, 89.
  See also abortion clinics: violence at
promiscuity, 38, 84, 192
#ProtestPP (#PPP), 65, 196, 217
public opinion polling, 254–257*t*
  by political party, 256*t*
  by religion, 256*t*

support for abortion under conditions, 255*t*

quickening, 2–3, 9, 10

race
  and abortion, 94, 218–219, 337
  and access to abortion, 91
  and pregnancy, 13, 30
  See also women: African American
Rachel's Vineyard, 215
racial justice, 228
Racketeer for Life: Fighting the Culture of Death from the Sidewalk to the Supreme Court (Scheidler), 196
Radiance Foundation, 94, 219
Ramesh, Ponnuru, 305
RCRC (Religious Coalition for Reproductive Choice), 201, 229
Reagan, Leslie J., 291
Reagan, Ronald, 45, 46, 58, 63, 190, 199, 212, 327, 329
  Abortion and the Conscience of the Nation, 190, 305–306
  Mexico City policy, 275–276
Reardon, David, 85, 208–209, 329

Redstockings, 17, 266–270, 323
Reed, Ralph, 206
Rehnquist, William, 45, 46, 50, 125
Reid, Harry, 335
Religious Coalition for Abortion Rights, 325
Religious Coalition for Reproductive Choice (RCRC), 201, 229
reproductive choice, 165, 201, 228–331
Reproductive FACT Act, 208
reproductive freedom, 30, 80, 99, 164, 172, 221–222, 223, 230, 325
Reproductive Freedom, Accountability, Comprehensive Care, and Transparency (FACT) Act, 339
Reproductive Freedom Project (ACLU), 221–222, 325
reproductive health
    adolescent, 225, 231, 298
    advocates for, 57, 84, 150, 224, 228, 229, 231, 241, 247, 249, 252
    for African American women, 328
    curricula for, 225
    equity in, 227
    health coverage for, 181
    information on, 314, 315, 323
    legislation related to, 67, 79
    men's, 225
    promotion of, 148
    scientific consensus on, 101, 221, 230
    support for, 230
    women's decisions regarding, 25, 254, 223
    women's rights to, 299, 326
    See also reproductive health care
Reproductive Health Advisory Committee (FDA), 332
reproductive health care,
    access to, 139, 150, 151, 152, 176, 181, 222, 340
    providers of, 65, 77, 125–134, 151, 180, 184, 226, 278
    regulation of, 71
    training in, 225, 226
Reproductive Health Technologies Project (RHTP), 230
reproductive justice, 30, 38, 79–80, 90
Reproductive Justice (Ross and Solinger), 80
reproductive rights, 69, 79–80, 331

and disability rights,
163–166

*Reproductive Rights and the
State: Getting Birth
Control, RU-486, and
Morning-After Pills and
the Gardasil Vaccine
to the U.S. Market*
(Haussman), 84

Republican Majority for
Choice (RMC), 60, 230

Republican National
Coalition for Life
(RNCL), 217

Republican Party, 27, 188,
326, 327
pro-choice contingent, 60,
230, 330
as "pro-life party," 58, 217

Republicans for Choice
Political Action
Committee, 330

rhetoric, toning down,
100–103

Rhode Island
state mandates, 244*t*
state regulations of
abortion practices and
funding, 240*t*

RHTP (Reproductive Health
Technology Project),
230

Richard, Amy, 173

Richards, Ann, 181

Richards, Cecile, 39, 65, 170,
170*f*, 171, 181–182

Richards-Ross, Sonya, 340

RICO statute, 332, 333, 336

Riddle, John M., 292

right of refusal, 160, 215,
241
by pharmacists, 84, 103
by providers or
institutions, 242–245*t*

RMC (Republican Majority
for Choice), 60, 230

RNCL (Republican National
Coalition for Life), 217

Roberts, John, 50, 52, 69,
340

Robertson, Pat, 89, 206

Rockefeller, Nelson, 20, 324

Rodriguez, Ana Rosa,
331–332

Roe No More Ministry, 193

Roe v. Wade, 4, 20–24, 65,
138, 179, 185, 204,
324
congressional response
to, 42
efforts to overturn, 25,
44–59, 66, 102, 120,
142, 193, 208, 285,
325, 326, 328–329,
330, 335, 340
as issue frame, 32
and the pro-choice
movement, 28–30
and the pro-life
movement, 25–28
and the right to privacy,
120–124, 150

and the Supreme
    Court, 47
Supreme Court opinion,
    270–273
two arguments, 125
Roeder, Scott, 89, 184, 195,
    205
Rohlinger, Deana, 84
Roman Catholic Church,
    8, 18, 19–20, 48, 177,
    179, 188, 219, 221
    on birth control, 40
    papal decrees, 9, 19, 25,
    66, 187, 192, 318,
    323
Romney, Mitt, 151
Rose, Lila, 211
Rosenbaum, Stuart E.,
    303–304
Rosenberg, Leon E., 44
Ross, Loretta, 30, 80,
    303
Rounds, Mike, 335
Roussel-Uclaf, 81
Roy, William, 325–326
rubella, 15, 321
Rucht, Dieter, 294–295
Rue, Vincent, 85
RU-486, 81–83, 179, 184,
    221, 230, 329, 332,
    333. *See also* abortion
    pill
Rust v. Sullivan, 63,
    330
Ryan, Paul, 79, 212

*Sacred Choices: The Right
    to Contraception and
    Abortion in Ten World
    Religions* (Maguire),
    300
safe sex, 39
Saletan, William, 98, 292
Sanger, Alexander, 99
Sanger, Margaret, 1, 12, 147,
    182–183, 229, 319
Santorum, Rick, 40, 48
Saxton, Marsha, 163–164
SBAL (Susan B. Anthony
    List), 64, 181, 187, 201,
    218
Scalia, Antonin, 45, 46, 47,
    50, 340
Scheidler, Eric, 196
Scheidler, Joseph M., 88, 89,
    195–196, 216, 327, 333
    *Closed: 99 Ways to Stop
    Abortion*, 306
Scheidler v. NOW, 336
Schlafly, Phyllis, 217
Schrage, Laurie, 302–303
Schroedel, Ruth, 76
Search for Common Ground,
    202
Sekulow, Jay, 203
self-help clinics, 18
*Sex and Consequences:
    Abortion, Public Policy,
    and the Economics
    of Fertility* (Levine),
    288–289

sex education, 38–39, 147
    abstinence-only, 39, 209, 327, 337
Sex Respect, 315
Sexual Behavior in the Human Female (Kinsey), 14, 320
sexual health, 39. *See also* reproductive health
sexuality, 75, 123, 173, 174, 183, 216, 223, 228, 230, 231, 315
Sexuality Information and Education Council of the United States (SIECUS), 174, 230–231
Shaheen Amendment, 92, 338
Shaping Abortion Discourse: Democracy and the Public Sphere in Germany and the United States (Ferree, Gamson, Gerhards, and Rucht), 294–295
Sheldon, Louis P., 219
Shostak, Arthur, 157
#ShoutYourAbortion (SYA), 95, 231
Shuai, Bei Bei, 71
Shvarts, Aliza, 189
SIECUS (Sexuality Information and Education Council of the United States), 174, 230–231
Silent No More Awareness Campaign, 211, 215–216
The Silent Scream (documentary), 194, 310
Silliman, Jael, 303
Sims, Marion, 318
SisterSong Women of Color Reproductive Justice Collective (SS), 30, 95, 231–232, 337
16 and Pregnant (MTV television show), 39
SL (Students for Life), 201, 218
Slaughter, Louise, 335
Slepian, Barnett, 186, 198, 211, 291, 333
slut shaming, 94
Smeal, Eleanor, 183–184
Smith, Christopher, 62, 82, 188, 196–197
social purity movement, 8
Society for the Protection of Unborn Children, 232
Soldiers in the Army of God (documentary), 205
Solinger, Rickie, 13, 80, 102, 303
Sotomayor, Sonia, 52, 340
Souter, David, 49

South Carolina
  case of Regina McNight,
    74–75
  conditional abortion
    laws, 19
  state mandates, 244t
  state regulations of
    abortion practices and
    funding, 240t
South Dakota
  abortion ban, 176
  criminalization of
    abortion, 51
  failure of abortion
    referendum, 325
  limited abortion access in,
    340
  repeal of restrictions on
    abortion, 335
  state mandates, 244t
  state regulations of
    abortion practices and
    funding, 240t
  waiting period, 55
  Women's Health and
    Human Life Protection
    Act, 335
Southern Poverty Law
  Center, 219
Sovereignty Productions, 311
speak-outs, 17–18, 95,
  266–270, 323
Spitz, Donald, 205
spousal consent, 52–53
spousal notification, 4, 38,
  47, 49, 52, 53

SS (SisterSong Women of
  Color Reproductive
  Justice Collective), 30,
  95, 231–232, 337
Staggenborg, Suzanne, 293
Stand Up for Women's
  Health Rally, 170f, 171
Stanek, Jill, 70
Stanton, Elizabeth Cady, 8,
  210
stem cell research, 212, 304,
  336
Stenberg v. Carhart, 50, 69,
  223, 280, 333
sterilization, 17, 19, 30, 147,
  228, 265, 276, 277, 301
Sterling, Alton, 94
Stewart, Ke'Arre M., 152
stigma, 94–96
Stone, Ann E. W., 230
Storer, Horatio Robinson,
  197–198, 318
The Story of Jane: The
  Legendary Underground
  Feminist Abortion
  Services (Kaplan), 299
strategic frames. See framing
The Street Politics of Abortion:
  Speech, Violence, and
  America's Culture Wars
  (Wilson), 293–294
Students for Life (SL), 201,
  218
Subcommittee on
  Constitutional
  Amendments of

the Senate Judiciary
Committee, 326
Summer of Mercy, 213, 214
Supreme Court, 1, 4, 20–21,
39, 41
makeup of, 44–52, 340
Supreme Court decisions
Arpaio v. Doe, 336
*Ayotte v. Planned
Parenthood of Northern
New England*, 336
Beal v. Doe, 61, 326
Bellotti v. Baird, 54, 172,
326
Bowen v. Kendrick, 329
*Burwell v. Hobby Lobby
Stores, Inc.*, 40, 48
*Carey v. Population Services
International*, 326
*City of Akron v. Akron
Center for Reproductive
Health*, 45, 328
Colautti v. Franklin, 327
Doe v. Bolton, 20–24, 325
Eisenstadt v. Baird, 121,
123, 172, 271, 324
Gonzales v. Carhart, 51,
69, 203, 279, 336
Griswold v. Connecticut,
20, 22, 46, 120, 123,
149, 152, 179, 271, 321
Harris v. McRae, 62, 90,
327
*Hodgson v. State of
Minnesota*, 330
Lawrence v. Texas, 123

*Madsen v. Women's Health
Center*, 332
Maher v. Roe, 62, 326
NOW v. Scheidler, 176,
198, 332
*Ohio v. Akron Center for
Reproductive Health*, 330
*Planned Parenthood of
Central Missouri v.
Danforth*, 326
*Planned Parenthood
of Southeastern
Pennsylvania v. Casey*,
4, 48–49, 52–53, 229,
330–331
Roe v. Wade, 20–24, 25,
26, 32, 42, 44–46, 47,
48, 65, 66, 120–124,
125, 138, 179, 185,
193, 204, 324, 325, 329
Rust v. Sullivan, 63, 330
Scheidler v. NOW, 336
Stenberg v. Carhart, 50, 69,
223, 280, 333
*Thornburgh v.
American College
of Obstetricians &
Gynecologists*, 45, 46,
328–329
*Union Pacific Railroad Co.
v. Botsford*, 271
*Webster v. Reproductive
Health Services*, 46–47,
59, 96, 330
*Whole Woman's Health v.
Hellerstedt*, 37, 52, 57,

151, 223, 229,
280–283, 339
Susan B. Anthony List
(SBAL), 64, 181, 187,
201, 218
Susan G. Komen
Foundation, 182,
337
Sutherland, Pam, 146
Swasey, Garrett, 152
sympathetic bystander
publics, 27

TAD (The Abortion Diary),
134–140, 201, 220
Take the Lead, 175
Targeted Regulation of
Abortion Providers
(TRAP) laws, 57, 207,
280–283, 338
*Targets of Hatred: Anti-
Abortion Terrorism*
(Baird-Windle and
Bader), 297
Tatalovich, Raymond, 296
Taussig, Frederick, 319
TBW (Trust Black Women),
201, 231–232
teen pregnancy, 38–39, 231,
249
telemedicine, 83, 221
Tennessee
state mandates, 244*t*
state regulations of
abortion practices and
funding, 240*t*

Terry, Randall, 88, 195, 197,
198–199, 213, 214,
329
Texas, 237
anti-abortion bill protest,
236*f*
compulsory ultrasound, 56
Jane's Due Process, 55
restrictions on abortion,
52, 339
Senator Davis's filibuster,
57, 78–79, 338
state mandates, 244*t*
state regulations of
abortion practices and
funding, 240*t*
See also *Roe v. Wade*
thalidomide, 15, 175, 321
Their Blood Cries Out
(Newman), 195
ThinkFilm, 309
Thomas, Clarence, 48, 52
Thomas, Rusty, 214, 317,
340
Thompson, Tommy, 334
Thomson, Judith Jarvis,
159
*Thornburgh v. American
College of
Obstetricians &
Gynecologists*, 45–46,
328–329
Tiebow, Tim, 212
Tiller, George, 89, 184, 195,
205, 214, 337
Tiller Fund, 91

Title X Family Planning,
64–65, 327, 232
Tobias, Carol, 213
TooManyAborted.com
(TMA), 218–219
TPP (Office of Adolescent
Health Teen Pregnancy
Prevention
Program), 39
Traditional Values Coalition
(TVC), 219
transparency, 339
TRAP (Targeted Regulation
of Abortion Providers)
laws, 57, 207, 280–283,
338
Trapped (documentary), 180,
310–311
Travis, Trysh, 120–124
Tribe, Laurence, 96–97,
293
Trump, Donald J., 39–40,
52, 59, 62, 63–64, 67,
74, 119, 152, 187, 199,
203, 211, 213, 214,
276–277, 339, 340
on the March for Life, 42
Trust Black Women (TBW),
201, 231–232
Trust Women South Wind
Women's Center, 118*f*,
119
Truth Trucks, 194, 214, 334
Tucci, Keith, 214
TVC (Traditional Values
Coalition), 219

Twelfth and Delaware
(documentary), 87

UAL (Americans United for
Life), 57, 76, 199, 204,
324
ultrasound viewing, 66, 74,
83, 103, 132, 221, 320
compulsory, 56–57
UN Women, 232
Unborn Child Pain
Awareness Act, 72
Unborn Child Protection
from Dismemberment
Abortion Act, 53
*Unborn in the U.S.A.: Inside
the War on Abortion*
(documentary), 311
unborn rights, 20, 23–24,
28, 32, 46, 51,
260–262
Unborn Victims of Violence
Act (UVVA), 77,
188–189, 335
#UnbornLivesMatter, 94
and late-term abortion,
72–74
and partial-birth abortion,
68–72
and prenatal drug use,
74–76
pro-life framing, 65–78
and third-party fetal
killing, 76–78
See also embryo; fetus
UnChoice campaign, 208

Undivided Rights: Women of Color Organize for Reproductive Justice (Silliman, Fried, Ross, and Gutiérrez), 303
undue burden test, 4, 56, 281–282, 336
Union Pacific Railroad Co. v. Botsford, 271
United Nations
    Conference on Population (1984), 328
    Declaration of the Rights of the Child, 276
    1994 Population and Development Conference, 175, 190
    Population Division, 232
    Universal Declaration of Human Rights, 223
United States Conference of Catholic Bishops (USCCB), 82, 219, 322
Uniting Our Voices program, 220
Universal Declaration of Human Rights, 223
unwed mothers, 13, 265, 272
U.S. Agency for International Development, 232
U.S. Constitution
    Article 1, 1–2
    First Amendment, 121, 186, 204, 208, 241
    Fourteenth Amendment, 24, 50, 65, 123, 271, 272, 273
    Fourth Amendment, 121
    proposals to amend, 42–44
U.S. v. One Package of Japanese Pessaries, 12, 182, 319
Utah
    abortion restrictions, 47
    fetal anesthesia bill, 4
    fetal pain law, 4, 340
    state mandates, 244*t*
    state regulations of abortion practices and funding, 240*t*
UVVA (Unborn Victims of Violence Act), 77, 188–189, 335

vacuum aspiration technique, 322
Vera Drake (film), 313–314
Vermont
    state mandates, 244*t*
    state regulations of abortion practices and funding, 240*t*
Vessel (documentary), 311
viability, 2–3, 124, 327, 331
Virginia
    conditional abortion laws, 19
    pro-life organization in, 322
    state mandates, 244*t*
    state regulations of

abortion practices and
funding, 240*t*
Virginia Society for Human
Life, 322
Voice of Resistance, 199
voluntary motherhood, 8. *See
also* motherhood
Von Eschebach, Andrew, 84

Wagner, Teresa, 306–307
waiting periods, 4, 38, 45,
52, 55, 56, 180,
241–247, 242–245*t*,
331
*Wake Up Little Susie: Single
Pregnancy and Race
before Roe v. Wade*
(Solinger), 13
War on Birth Control, 48
*The War on Choice: The Right-
Wing Attack on Women's
Rights and How to Fight
Back* (Feldt), 175, 298
Warren, Elizabeth, 64
Washington, D.C.
state mandates, 242*t*
state regulations of
abortion practices and
funding, 239*t*
Washington (state)
repeal of abortion laws, 19,
324
state mandates, 244*t*
state regulations of
abortion practices and
funding, 240*t*

Wattleton, Faye, 198
*Webster v. Reproductive
Health Services*, 46–47,
59, 96, 330
Weddington, Sarah, 21,
123–124, 185, 193, 323
Weddington Center, 185
West, Lindy, 95–96
West Virginia
limited abortion access in,
340
state mandates, 244*t*
state regulations of
abortion practices and
funding, 240*t*
West Virginia Right to Life
Committee, 190
Weston, Norman, 210
Whalen, Jennifer, 93
*What Every Mother Should
Know* (Sanger), 183
*When Abortion Was a Crime:
Women, Medicine, and
Law in the United States*
(Reagan), 291–292
*When Abortion Was
Illegal: Untold Stories*
(documentary), 312
When Sex Goes to School
(Luker), 38
White, Byron, 46
*Who Decides? The Abortion
Rights of Teens* (Ehrlich),
298
*Whole Woman's Health v.
Hellerstedt*, 37, 52, 57,

151, 223, 229,
280–283, 339
*Why and How Women Will
Elect the Next President*
(Smeal), 183
*The Wichita Divide: The
Murder of Dr. George
Tiller and the Battle over
Abortion* (Singular), 184
Williams, Daniel K., 66
Wilson, Joshua C., 293–294
Wisconsin
compulsory ultrasound, 56
state mandates, 245*t*
state regulations of
abortion practices and
funding, 240*t*
*With Liberty and Justice
for All: A Life Spent
Protecting the Right to
Choose* (Michelman),
301
Wolf, Naomi, 97–98
women
adolescent, 39, 53–55,
330, 331
African American, 17,
94–95, 218–219, 222,
231–232, 328, 337
Asian American, 231
characteristics of women
having abortions, 5,
249–250*t*, 251*t*
with disabilities, 91
disempowerment of, 11
drug addicted, 74–75

in immigrant detention
centers, 92
inmates, 60, 91, 336
Latina, 227, 231, 303
marginalized, 91
military personnel, 60, 92,
332, 333
Native American, 60, 91,
231, 303
Peace Corps volunteers, 60
poor and low-income,
60–61, 90–91, 182,
331
and the right to vote, 8
in rural areas, 90–91,
337
Women Deserve Better
campaign, 189
*Women of Color and the
Reproductive Rights
Movement* (Nelson), 301
Women on Waves, 232
Women on Web, 92
Women's Global Network for
Reproductive Rights,
232
Women's Health and Human
Life Protection Act, 51,
335
women's health movement,
18, 78–79
Women's Liberation Group
(New York), 266–270
Women's Liberation
Movement, 17–18, 28,
39, 137, 266, 301, 323

Women's Marches, 62, 119.
   See also March for Life;
   March for Women's
   Lives; Women's
   March on Washington
   (WMoW)
Women's March on
   Washington (WMoW),
   141, 144, 213
Women's Reproductive
   Rights Assistance
   Project, 227
women's rights
   and the abortion pill,
      81–83
   and accurate information,
      84–87
   and emergency
      contraception, 83–84
   and environmental safety,
      88–90
   and issues of access, 90–93

and issues of stigma,
   94–96
pro-choice framing, 78–81
Wood, Susan, 84, 335
World Health Organization
   (WHO), 82
World Population Fund, 232
Worldwide Directory of
   Pregnancy Help, 155
Wyoming
   fetal heartbeat law, 67
   state mandates, 245*t*
   state regulations of
      abortion practices and
      funding, 240*t*

Yoest, Charmaine, 199–200,
   204

Zika, 339
zones of privacy, 22, 121,
   321. *See also* privacy

About the Authors

Dorothy E. McBride, PhD, is professor emeritus of political science at Florida Atlantic University, Boca Raton, Florida. She currently resides in western Washington State, where she continues to write about women and public policy. She is editor and contributing author of *Abortion Politics, Women's Movements, and the Democratic State: A Comparative Study of State Feminism* and author of *Women's Rights in the U.S.A.: Policy Debates and Gender Roles*.

Jennifer L. Keys, PhD, is professor of sociology and director of the Center for the Advancement of Faculty Excellence at North Central College, Naperville, Illinois. Her specializations in gender and social movements sparked her ongoing fascination with the intense controversy surrounding abortion. Her published articles include "Running the Gauntlet: Women's Use of Emotion Management Techniques in the Abortion Experience" (*Symbolic Interaction*, 2010), which explores how women's feelings get caught in the cross fire of competing ideologies. She is also coauthor of "Reflections on Two Studies of Emotionally Sensitive Topics: Bereavement from Murder and Abortion" with Sarah Goodrum, PhD (*International Journal of Social Research Methodology*, 2007), and "Competitive Framing Processes in the Abortion Debate: Polarization-Vilification, Frame Saving, and Frame Debunking" with Dawn McCaffrey (*The Sociological Quarterly*, 2000). Keys infuses her scholarly interests into her teaching in courses like Protest and Change and Perspectives of Abortion: From the Personal to the Political.